Strategic Marketing

Fully updated and revised to include the latest case studies and examples from a broad range of industry sectors, this second edition of *Strategic Marketing: An Introduction* is a concise, thorough and enlightening textbook that demonstrates how organizations can cope with a myriad of demands by better understanding themselves, their products or services and the world around them.

From assessing internal relationships to planning and implementing marketing strategies, and featuring analysis of relationship marketing and strategic alliances, Proctor uses insights from a range of key models and theoretical frameworks to illustrate how an organization can successfully take advantage of 'strategic windows' to improve its position. Core issues covered include:

- marketing strategy
- analysing the business environment
- the customer in the market place
- targeting and positioning
- marketing mix strategy.

This textbook is the complete guide to assessing and imposing a realistic and successful marketing strategy to fit an organization, its resources and objectives, and the environment in which it operates. Accessibly written and supported by a user-friendly companion website, this new edition of *Strategic Marketing: An Introduction* is an essential resource for all students of marketing and business and management.

Tony Proctor is Professor in Marketing at the University of Chester, UK. He has written extensively on marketing and related issues, including *Creative Problem Solving for Managers, Second Edition* (Routledge, 2005).

Strategic Marketing

An introduction

Second edition

Tony Proctor

Routledge
Taylor & Francis Group

LONDON AND NEW YORK

First published 2000 by Routledge
2 Park Square, Milton Park, Abingdon, Oxon, OX14 4RN

Simultaneously published in the USA and Canada
by Routledge
270 Madison Avenue, New York, NY 10016

Second edition 2008

Routledge is an imprint of the Taylor & Francis Group, an informa business

© 2008 Tony Proctor

Typeset in Perpetua and Bell Gothic by
Keystroke, 28 High Street, Tettenhall, Wolverhampton
Printed and bound by
TJ International Ltd, Padstow, Cornwall

British Library Cataloguing in Publication Data
A catalogue record for this book is available from the British Library

Library of Congress Cataloging in Publication Data
Proctor, Tony.
    Strategic marketing: an introduction / Tony Proctor. — 2nd ed.
        p. cm.
    1. Marketing—Decision making.   2. Marketing—Management.   I. Title.
    HF5415.135.P76 2008
    658.8′02—dc22   2007050239

ISBN10: 0–415–45816–1 (hbk)
ISBN10: 0–415–45817–X (pbk)

ISBN13: 978–0–415–45816–0 (hbk)
ISBN13: 978–0–415–45817–7 (pbk)

Every effort has been made to contact copyright holders for their permission to reprint material in this book. The
publishers would be grateful to hear from any copyright holder who is not here acknowledged and will undertake to
rectify any errors or omissions in future editions of this book.

Contents

Illustrations

FIGURES

TABLES

EXHIBITS

Preface

The second edition of this book features additional material to what was in the first volume. Many new tools and techniques are visited and illustrations of how these can be used in conjunction with a spreadsheet are highlighted. The accompanying website and instructor manual provide computer file download files which can be used to employ the illustrated models and techniques. The spreadsheet models incorporate graphical material so that the models can be viewed in spatial terms and not just numerical outputs.

Additional case studies and accompanying questions have been incorporated into the text which provide material for reflection and study. I am particularly grateful to two of my colleagues, Ioanna C. Papasolomou in Cyprus and Rosmimah Mohd Roslin in Malaysia, for their additional case study material and continued interest in the book. The case studies they have provided add an international flavour to the book. I have also included material in the text which relates aspects of international marketing and which will provide some underpinning for the cases written by my two colleagues.

I was originally spurred on to write a book about strategic marketing in the belief that it was somehow a different subject to that one normally reads about in most textbooks on marketing management. I was fascinated by such metaphors as the strategic window, the boiled frog company and future shock. I thought that it represented a new dimension to marketing. I have not been too disappointed by my endeavours. The book contains a lot of material that one does not usually find in a volume on marketing management but at the same time some of the old familiar terms still appear.

There are many definitions of strategy, but in business it refers to how a firm approaches both setting and achieving organizational objectives. In this book we look specifically at marketing strategy and in particular the strategy concerning the formulation and implementation of the marketing mix. The successful implementation of the marketing mix leads to satisfaction of customer wants and needs and increases the likelihood of achieving an organization's objectives in the market place. In recent years, relationship marketing has come to the fore as strategic alliances and networks involving firms working together towards shared goals has become more fashionable. The strategic management of such relationships is at the core of relationship marketing. The argument put forward in this book is that when changes in the market and the marketing environment are incremental in nature, firms can successfully adapt themselves to the new situation by modifying current marketing and other functional programmes.

Such changes can be introduced through technological innovations, changes in customer tastes, changes in legal regulations, economic and financial constraints or any changes in environmental conditions. The nature of competition may also change and in particular the elements which make up the five forces of Porter's competition model. New entrants to the industry may appear; substitute products may become more attractive propositions to customers; both suppliers and customers may find their bargaining powers strengthened; and the balance of competition power between the incumbent firms in the industry may change as one firm develops a competitive advantage. However, if the cumulative changes in the economic, technological, social, political and cultural environments remain unnoticed by a company's managers until it is too late to respond, the problems which they create for the firm may be overwhelmingly difficult to overcome. Similarly, when the degree of market change is of such magnitude that the competence of a firm to continue to compete effectively is questioned, then the firm may be experiencing the closure of an important *strategic window*. Where change, leading eventually to the closure of a strategic window, is either very rapid or very slow the consequences may well be disastrous. In the first case, the window closes before an organization can respond and, in the second instance, it does not even notice that the window is about to close until it is too late to respond.

It is important to examine not only where the firm is today, but how well equipped it is to deal with tomorrow. In particular, the task of predicting non-incremental changes in the market is of critical importance. Existing firms and their competitors can sometimes be replaced in a comparatively short space of time by a whole new range of competitors. Firms which are oblivious to the opening and closing of strategic window or firms which fail to utilize overlapping strategic windows to best advantage, or firms which are unable to divest when a window closes, risk disaster.

Organizations need to:

1 Identify the opportunities and threats posed by the opening and closing of strategic windows.
2 Analyse all the relevant internal and external environmental factors acting upon the firm in the context of the strategic windows.
3 Determine the best strategy or set of strategies that are likely to enable the firm to take best advantage of the strategic window while it is open.
4 Ensure that adequate resources are available to implement the chosen strategies.
5 Implement the chosen strategy to take best advantage of the opportunities presented by the strategic window and to minimize the risks posed by the threats.

In this book we will be systematically working through the process. It is the opening and shutting of strategic windows and how the firm might react to this that is the topic of interest. We discuss the nature and formulation of business and marketing strategy and point to the need for strategic marketing management in order to carry it out. We also outline the nature of the marketing management process that is involved.

The organization has to keep abreast of developments in its external and internal environments. It also has to ensure that a matching process between skills and resources is available to take best advantage of developments and opportunities in the environment and to avoid any threats that are posed. We look at the resources that the firm has available and at the developments in the environment that can take place that lead to opportunities and threats with which the firm has to get to grips. An analysis of the relevant factors which impinge on the opening and shutting of strategic windows needs to be undertaken by an organization prior to making strategic decisions.

Tony Proctor, 2008

Chapter 1

Marketing strategy

Introduction and overview

INTRODUCTION

A strategy is a plan that integrates an organization's major goals, policies, decisions and sequences of action into a cohesive whole. It can apply at all levels in an organization and pertain to any of the functional areas of management. Thus there may be production, financial, marketing, personnel and corporate strategies, just to name a few. If we look specifically at marketing then there may be pricing, product, promotion, distribution, marketing research, sales, advertising, merchandising, etc. strategies. Strategy is concerned with effectiveness rather than efficiency and is the process of analysing the environment and designing the fit between the organization, its resources and objectives and the environment.

The strategic process refers to the manner in which strategy is formulated. There are several approaches:

- the rational approach, making use of tools such as SWOT analysis and portfolio models
- the flexible approach, which employs multiple scenario planning
- the creative approach reflects the use of imagination in planning
- the behavioural approach reflects the influence of power, politics and personalities; and finally,
- the incremental approach is based on small adjustments or changes to previously successful strategies.

Nohria *et al.* (2003) put forward an analysis of 160 successful USA companies in the period 1986 to 1996. They all outperformed their competitors in terms of strategy their implementation. This supremacy was founded on:

- clarity
- consistent communication to customers, employees and shareholders
- a value proposition relevant to targeted customers; and
- a realistic appreciation of the company capabilities.

Marketing is about satisfying customer wants and needs and in the course of doing so facilitating the achievement of an organization's objectives. By paying attention to customer wants and needs, organizations are more likely to achieve their objectives in the market place. Of course, organizations have to compete with each other and so also have to satisfy customers' wants and needs at least as well as their competitors. Fortunately, organizations can do this in different ways. Competition involves finding a different way to satisfy customers from other organizations in the market place. In the pursuit of this end, products and services need to be seen as more than physical entities – it is the benefits they offer customers that are being purchased.

Competition involves positioning products and services in the minds of customers in such a way that the products and services are perceived to be different from one another. Marketing is about the competitive positioning of products and services in the minds of customers. It is also about the communication of messages and images (reflecting product and service positioning) and the means which are used to convey these messages and images to the customers (see Figure 1.1).

Marketing is also about managing relationships. In order to persuade the ultimate consumers of the products to buy, others concerned with the product have to be persuaded that what is on offer will satisfy customers' wants and needs. The chain of persuasion can stretch right back into the organization itself and involve employees of the company. This is the area where *internal marketing* has come to the fore in recent years. Building relationships with other organizations is also important. In fact this extends to anyone who has an interest or stake in the organization. Stakeholders are held to be those individuals or groups that have a 'stake' in the organization (see Carroll, 1993, p. 22). Stakeholders include customers, employees, management, stockholders, creditors, suppliers, community, and sometimes even competitors.

Shareholders are only one set of stakeholders in a business for customers, employees, suppliers and many others also have a vested interest in how the organization fares. The objective for a profit making organization might be to create value for its stakeholders in order to retain their interest and commitment of time and investment, financial or otherwise, to the organization.

During the 1980s and 1990s academics and practitioners in the field of strategic management began to focus on creating 'shareholder value' as the overall purpose of any commercial enterprise

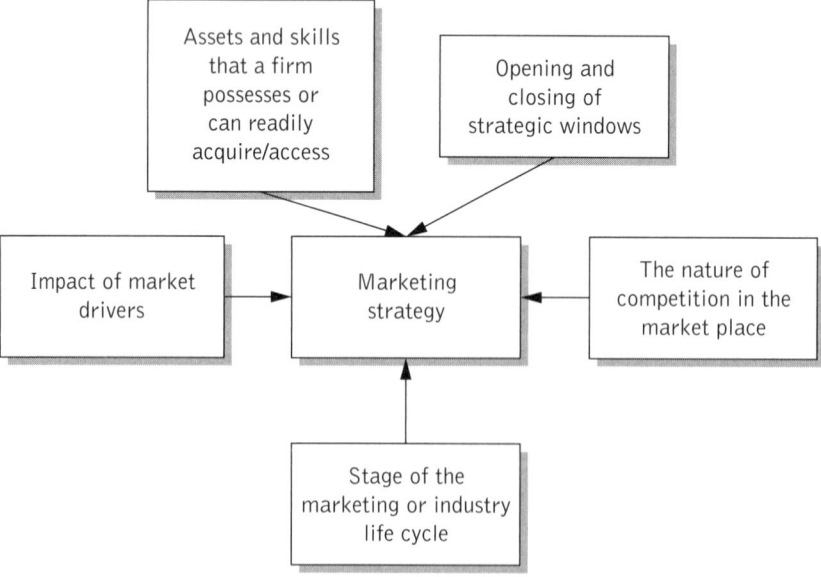

Figure 1.1 Factors impacting on marketing strategy

(Rappaport, 1986). The benefits suggested for this approach to strategic management were considered twofold: first, it put the interests of the owners of the business at the heart of strategy and, second, it engendered a more long-term approach to business decision-making than an emphasis upon profitability. Doyle (2000) argued that the creation of shareholder value should be used as the yardstick against which to measure marketing strategies. We might consider replacing the term "customers" with stakeholders in any definition of the role and scope of marketing since these include customers as well as the many other individuals, groups and organizations that deal with or are even employed by an organization. This could lead to defining marketing as:

Marketing is the management process responsible for identifying, anticipating and satisfying stakeholder requirements and in so doing serves to facilitate the achievement of the organization's objectives.

The twenty-first century is seeing the development of strategic alliances and networks where firms work together towards shared goals and collaborate in their operations. Managing such relationships productively is almost certainly the key to success or failure.

The foregoing is at the heart of marketing strategy, which has to take into account the following factors:

1 the opening and closing of strategic windows
2 the impact of market drivers
3 the nature of competition in the market place
4 the stage of the market or industry life cycle
5 the assets and skills that a firm possesses or can readily acquire/access
6 stakeholder interests.

Cognizance of all of these factors is essential if effective long-term marketing strategies are to be evolved which will lead to a firm securing a strategic competitive advantage in industries or product markets. We will introduce these various ideas below.

Stakeholder interests and values

Stakeholder interests and values are important factors when considering strategic decisions (viz. Jensen, 2001). Stakeholder interests and values vary from firm to firm according to the industry and the markets that are served by the firm. Hence, there is no universal model which can be applied to every situation. However, to give some idea of the nature of these interests and the demands they place on a firm or other form organization consider the examples (Exhibits 1.1 and 1.2).

In undertaking an analysis of stakeholder interests, marketers should make sure the analysis considers how factors such as, product/service development and delivery, promotional mix, support services, manufacturing and production processes, R&D, and material purchasing affect the stakeholders' interested in healthcare in both the public and private sectors. The influence exerted by stakeholders over decisions related to these factors will depend on the power they wield and the attitude they have. In a private-sector organization management may have the most influence unless there is a single major shareholder with a very active interest in the business. Management's attitude towards decisions may therefore be the key determining factor in influencing what actions transpire.

EXHIBIT 1.1   SELECTED STAKEHOLDERS' INTERESTS FOR AN NHS ORGANIZATION

Stakeholder	Interests
Staff	■ Provision of quality healthcare ■ Self-development and promotion prospects ■ Job satisfaction ■ Work in a safe and good quality environment
Current patients	■ Receive excellent care and attention ■ Enhance health prospects and life expectancy ■ Advice on how best to recover from treatment and avoid future health problems ■ Access to information ■ Support from medical staff
Unions	■ Responsibility to members to ensure fair working practices, safe environment ■ Support and advise members in all areas of employment rights, e.g. equal opportunities, discrimination, racial incidents ■ Recruitment of new members
Government	■ Quality standards ■ Legal requirements/health and safety/equal opportunities/pay and conditions ■ Financial management, ensure resources being used and managed effectively
Press	■ Praise and publicity for high achievement ■ Adverse publicity – making the facts known ■ Challenging use of finances
Prospective patients	■ Excellent treatment in a caring and pleasant environment ■ Access to information ■ Choices ■ Achievement of a full recovery after treatment

MARKET DRIVERS: POLITICAL, ECONOMIC, SOCIO-CULTURAL AND TECHNOLOGICAL (PEST) FORCES

Markets or customers are driven towards wanting certain products and services. Political, economic, socio-cultural and technological (PEST) influences all impact upon the nature of customer wants and needs.

EXHIBIT 1.2 STAKEHOLDERS FOR A PHARMACEUTICAL COMPANY

Stakeholders	Interests
General public	Safe, reliable, tested drugs
Legal/courts	Tested drugs which do not result in serious side effects for the users
Government	Reasonably priced drugs which have been shown to be effective in use
Media	Stories showing either the benefits of drugs or very harmful side-effects of drugs which have not been properly tested
Scientific community	Details of development and testing of new drugs
Shareholders	Return on investment and shareholder value created
Suppliers	Steady and secure demand for the products and services it supplies
Financial institutions	Following sound marketing and corporate strategies which will produce guaranteed returns from lending and investment
Rank and file employees	Secure and interesting employment with good future prospects
Competitors	New developments that lead to competitive advantage
Consumers	Safe and effective treatments
Management	Control and influence over what happens in the firm

Illustrations of the impact of PEST factors on the growth of personal computers and on the insurance industry are shown in Exhibits 1.3 and 1.4 respectively. Political factors acting as market drivers are often more difficult to identify quite so easily. A good example, however, was the 1980s policy of the Conservative government of the time towards home ownership. In particular, the sale of council houses gave rise to a demand for mortgage loans from people who might not normally consider home ownership.

IMPACT OF COMPETITION

Competition is important in influencing how successful an organization's business venture can be. It is not simply a matter of producing a good product or service which matches with customer wants and needs and provides customer satisfaction. In one way or another, most firms are able to do this but some are much more successful in the marketplace than others. A firm must be able to position itself competitively in the minds of its customers so that its products and services stand out very favourably in important respects in relationship to competitors. Shell and Esso, for example, both sell essentially the same fuel oils, but both are able to carve out positions for themselves in the minds of their customers, so that they can both operate successfully in the marketplace. The nature and strength of competitors and how a firm jockeys for position are key aspects of marketing and business strategy.

Technologies and products have life cycles and so do markets and industries. There are different stages in the life cycle of markets and industries and these have important ramifications for marketing

EXHIBIT 1.3 PEST FACTORS RELATING TO THE PERSONAL COMPUTER MARKET

In the 1970s, the most sophisticated portable calculating device was a programmable hand-held calculator. In the mid-1970s it was regarded as sophisticated to possess such a machine. Personal computers as we know them today began to appear in the early 1980s. Clive Sinclair's ZX80 and ZX81 brought the power of real computer programming to the elbow of every buff who had an interest in the new technology. Of course, compared with modern-day personal computers such machines were comparatively primitive. The 1980s and the 1990s saw a rapid growth in the technology that was available. Not only did machines become much more powerful (the original ZX81, for instance, had only 1K of RAM!) but there was a phenomenal growth in the amount of peripheral equipment to go alongside the personal computer. CD ROMs, modems, colour printers, internal networks, the Internet, and so on. Technology provided an opportunity for the consumer to experience benefits that could only have been dreamed of by someone with an eye to the future at the beginning of the 1970s.

While technology made all these things available there were other factors at work which influenced the direction that the technological innovations should take. Socio-cultural factors have encouraged the growth of the Internet. Email was seen as a way of speeding up interpersonal communication. Letter writing has been a sociological phenomenon ever since people were able to write but the pace of modern life is so quick that even letter writing needed to be speeded up. Game playing has always been a sociological phenomenon. The need for amusement does not rest solely in children but is also characteristic of adult behaviour. Personal computers offered a real opportunity to participate in sophisticated simulations and games. The 1980s and the 1990s witnessed a rapid growth in the computer games industry in response to this socio-cultural need.

Computers are relatively expensive items to purchase. Since the 1980s there has been a concerted effort in the industry to bring out more and more sophisticated and high powered machines to provide the benefits required by consumers. Of course, in order to do this there have been economic considerations. In the first place, prices have had to be kept down in order to encourage consumers to purchase. From the producer's standpoint this has been achieved by shifting the locus of manufacture to those parts of the world (notably the Far East) where economies of scale in production can be best obtained.

strategy. Moreover, taken in conjunction with the number and strength of competitors that operate in a market or an industry at any one time in the life cycle, it poses a tight boundary within which the firm can design an optimal marketing strategy.

Some firms may be ideally suited to exploiting certain types of product market opportunities whereas others may languish and fail when trying to exploit the same ones. In another situation the reverse can easily apply. One cannot assume that every firm will be able to exploit the same situation to its advantage, even when the opportunity does appear to be very exciting and has much to promise. Having the necessary skills and assets, or having access to them, is critical in implementing successful marketing strategies. Without these assets and skills a whole series of strategies may fail.

EXHIBIT 1.4   PEST FACTORS AT WORK IN THE INSURANCE INDUSTRY

Political/environmental factors

Implications

Government retirement from welfare — Poor cannot pay for traditional life provision assurance

Self-help encouragement by government — Only middle-income groups can afford to pay

Increasingly severe pensions legislation — Driving up costs of compliance and complexity of selling

Economic environment factors

Widening gap between rich and poor — Poor will jettison life/savings costs – traditional market will be unprofitable

Socio-cultural factors

Major increases in working women in lower-income groups — No one at home to pay premiums

Fewer manual jobs/more office admin, jobs — Less need for home collection of life assurance

Lottery — Reduces disposable income

Higher expectations of middle-income groups — Better services and returns demanded

Demographic factors

Population shift to middle/old ages — Need for care and illness cover

Fewer young people — Falling market for life/savings products

Technological factors

New technology not easily accepted by lower-income groups — Benefits of automation (costs) not immediately available in traditional market

Growth in telemarketing/database — Key cost-cutting forces marketing

STRATEGIC WINDOWS

Abell (1978) introduced the concept of strategic windows. The principal idea behind the concept of a strategic window is that there are only limited periods during which the fit between the key requirements of a market and the particular competencies of a firm competing in that market is at an optimum. As a consequence it is recommended that investment in a product line or a market area is timed to coincide with periods during which a strategic window is open. Correspondingly, withdrawal should be considered where something which was a good fit, is no longer a good fit. The latter can arise, for example, if changes in market requirements exceed the firm's capability to adapt to such changes.

The argument put forward is that when changes in the market and the marketing environment are incremental in nature, firms can successfully adapt themselves to the new situation by modifying current marketing and other functional programmes. Such changes can be introduced through technological innovations, changes in customer tastes, changes in legal regulations, economic and financial constraints or any changes in environmental conditions. The nature of competition may also change and in particular the elements which make up the five forces of Porter's (1980a, 1980b) competition model. New entrants to the industry may appear; substitute products may become more attractive propositions to customers; both suppliers and customers may find their bargaining powers strengthened; and the balance of competition power between the incumbent firms in the industry may change as one firm develops a competitive advantage.

However, if the cumulative changes in the economic, technological, social, political and cultural environments remain unnoticed by a company's managers until it is too late to respond, the problems which they create for the firm may be overwhelmingly difficult to overcome (Large, 1992). Similarly, when the degree of market change is of such magnitude that the competence of a firm to continue to compete effectively is questioned, then the firm may be experiencing the closure of an important strategic window. Where change, leading eventually to the closure of a strategic window, is either very rapid or very slow the consequences may well be disastrous. In the first case, the window closes before an organization can respond and, in the second instance, it does not even notice that the window is about to close until it is too late to respond.

Entry to a new market constitutes an example of where the presence of a strategic window is critical to success. For example, in the tumble drier market in the 1970s, larger manufacturers delayed entry until the market was sufficiently large to generate the kind of return on investment they demanded (Proctor, 1989). Expenditure on plant, equipment and marketing represents another area in which the strategic window takes on importance. The question as to whether expenditure should be increased, diminished or maintained at the current level depends upon whether the strategic window is expected to remain open or to close in the near future.

The timing of exit from a market is also important. There are times when it is possible and advisable to divest business which one cannot operate profitably so as to profit from the divestment. For example, one may be able to reinvest the proceeds of a divested business in other opportunities where the strategic window is open. In such circumstances strategic windows are interdependent. Cunard, for example, successfully moved from being involved principally in passenger shipping to containerization – the strategic windows overlapped. The key seems to be being market oriented rather than product oriented in defining the business in which one is operating (see Exhibit 1.5).

It is important to examine not only where the firm is today, but how well equipped it is to deal with tomorrow. In particular, the task of predicting non-incremental changes in the market is of critical importance. Existing firms and their competitors can sometimes be replaced in a comparatively short space of time by a whole new range of competitors. Examples of this phenomenon have included products such as digital watches, women's tights, calculators, charter air travel, office copiers and scientific instruments.

By taking a market rather than a product view of what one has to offer new possible strategic windows may seem worthy of investigation. Newspaper producers, for example, might consider other ways of providing interesting information for people or may look more closely at the kind of information that they do provide. Travel agents might consider various ways of making people's dreams come true.

Firms which are oblivious to the opening and closing of strategic windows or firms which fail to utilize overlapping strategic windows to best advantage, or firms which are unable to divest when a window closes, risk disaster.

EXHIBIT 1.5 MARKET ORIENTATION VERSUS PRODUCT ORIENTATION

Product orientation	Market orientation
We are a night club	We offer an experience
We run an airline	We transport people and their goods anywhere in the world
We sell jewellery	We enhance your appearance
We sell houses	We create happy living environments for people
We sell newspapers	We provide interesting information for people
We run a university	We provide the opportunity for self development
We market personal computers	We bring a new dimension of interpersonal communication into people's lives
We are travel agents	We make people's dreams come true

EVOLVING MARKETS AND STRATEGIC WINDOWS

Strategic windows arise as a result of market evolution. Markets are not static unchanging entities but change substantially in nature over time. There are different ways in which a market can evolve. Four examples quoted by Abell (1978) are:

- the development of new primary demand
- the emergence of new competing technologies which cannibalize existing ones
- market redefinition
- channel changes.

Other sources include:

- restructuring of markets – removal of trading barriers
- creation of an internal market – the UK health service of the 1980s and 1990s
- creation of new industries and markets
- deregulation of markets
- entry of new highly competitive firms to an industry
- the changing structure of the retail trade and its impact on supplying firms
- impact of substitute products on an industry
- timing of withdrawal from a market
- managing products in times of high inflation or conditions of economic uncertainty.

The evolving patterns of markets imply that the resource requirements of a firm to compete effectively in a market may change radically with time. Unfortunately the resources and key competencies of incumbent firms cannot be so easily adjusted.

Strategic windows have implications for incumbent firms and for new entrants to a market. Incumbent firms have the following four options:

1   Assemble resources needed to close the gap between the new critical marketing requirements and the firm's competencies.
2   Shift their efforts to selected segments, where the fit between requirements and resources is still acceptable.
3   Shift to a low-profile approach cutting back on all further allocation of capital and deliberately milking the business for short-run profit.
4   Exit the market by liquidation or sale.

Abell (1978) noted that often the strategic window phenomenon is not recognized and the choices are not clearly articulated. Old approaches are continued long after the market has changed with the result that the market position is lost and financial losses accumulate. Alternatively, only lukewarm efforts are made to obtain the required resources or management thinks it can adapt where this is clearly unrealistic. The result is that firms become entrapped and are unable to move forward. They continue with lost causes in the hope that a change is around the corner. Ultimately, they fail or incur heavy losses or at the very best experience unrecoverable opportunity costs.

In the case of new entrants to an industry getting the entry timing right is clearly important (note the tumble drier example). In the case of incumbent firms, assessing the impact of new entrants on the market or industry is a major issue.

OPPORTUNITIES AND THREATS PRESENTED BY THE OPENING AND CLOSING OF STRATEGIC WINDOWS

Essentially we are looking at a multi-stage process. Organizations need to:

1   Identify the opportunities and threats posed by the opening and closing of strategic windows.
2   Analyse all the relevant internal and external environmental factors acting upon the firm in the context of the strategic windows.
3   Determine the best strategy or set of strategies that are likely to enable the firm to take best advantage of the strategic window while it is open.
4   Ensure that adequate resources are available to implement the chosen strategies.
5   Implement the chosen strategy to take best advantage of the opportunities presented by the strategic window and to minimize the risks posed by the threats.

In this book we will be systematically working through the process. Organizations should be conversant with the concept of the strategic window, noting that when the window is open an organization can prosper. This assumes that it is in touch with the market and operates in a profitable manner. However, it should also be noted that over time the strategic window may well start to close and the organization has to take cognizance of this and take appropriate action. It is the opening and shutting of strategic windows and how the firm might react to this that is the topic of interest. We discuss the nature and formulation of business and marketing strategy and point to the need for strategic marketing management in order to carry it out. We also outline the nature of the marketing management process that is involved.

The whole idea of strategic management is that the organization has to keep abreast of developments in its external and internal environments. It also has to ensure that a matching process between skills and resources is available to take best advantage of developments and opportunities in the environment and to avoid any threats that are posed. We look at the resources that the firm has available and at the developments in the environment that can take place that lead to opportunities and threats with which the firm has to get to grips. An analysis of the relevant factors which impinge on the opening and shutting of strategic windows needs to be undertaken by an organization prior to making strategic decisions.

Integral to ensuring that optimum use is made of the open strategic window is the notion of a sustainable competitive advantage. It is argued that an organization must develop such a sustainable competitive advantage to take advantage of the open strategic window. In essence, organizations should review the various generic strategies which lead to a sustainable competitive advantage, i.e. low cost, differentiation, focus, etc.

The next step in the process is to examine more closely the practicalities of how an organization may seek to establish a sustainable competitive advantage for itself in the market place. It is argued that this may be achieved through a systematic and imaginative approach to market segmentation, targeting and positioning. This involves analysis rather than action but the results of the analysis are put into action through a specifically designed marketing programme involving carefully constructed marketing mix strategies for individual target markets.

Markets and industries are of course dynamic and change over time. They have life cycles and attract competitors in different numbers and of different sizes and strengths according to the stage in the life cycle. Returning for a moment to portfolio models, it is argued that the products that businesses have in their portfolios make different contributions to profits and overheads. Moreover, given that an organization also has a long-term survival motivation, there is the impetus to look for ways of ironing out large fluctuations in profitability and ensuring long-term survival. In order to do this the firm has to constantly review its product market posture and look for ways of achieving its survival objectives. Organizations need to examine the strategic alternatives that are available. Essentially this involves the various strategies outlined in the well-known Ansoff grid (market penetration, product-market expansion and diversification) along with vertical integration strategies and to explore the rationale behind these strategies.

The first steps identify and analyse strategic options. Consideration will have been given to the matter of selecting an appropriate strategy. Organizations must also give attention to how strategy may be put into action to ensure that the strategic window(s) remain open. Organizations need to look at some of the ways in which conditions can be made easier for the implementation of strategies in general terms. In particular they need to pick out the notion of strategic alliances and networks as a means of gaining entry to new markets and businesses or rationalizing in terms of resource utilization so that profitability is improved. There is also the very important issue of customer service provision and maintaining good customer relations as a means of smoothing the process of implementing strategies. Emphasis is placed on the internal marketing process to ensure that all employees are motivated to be customer oriented and ensure that strategies are effectively put in place. Finally, organizations should consider the implementing of strategies and a system of systematic marketing planning to co-ordinate and plan the introduction of strategic moves.

First let us consider the nature of business and marketing strategy and how it is formulated.

NATURE OF COMPETITIVE STRATEGY

A competitive strategy is made up of six parts. The first four apply to any type of business whereas the other two are used when there is more than one business unit in an organization. It involves a determination of:

1 *The product market in which the business competes.* The scope of a business is partially determined by what products it offers, by the markets it serves, by the nature of other businesses with whom it chooses to compete, and by the extent of its vertical integration. The scope of the business is also affected by those same elements it chooses to avoid. Often the latter is more important because decisions regarding what to avoid, if acted upon rigorously, can conserve resources needed to compete successfully elsewhere.

2 *The level of investment.* Although there are variations and refinements, it is useful to see the options in terms of:
   (a) invest to grow
   (b) invest only to maintain the existing position
   (c) milk the business by minimizing investment
   (d) recover as much of the assets as possible by liquidating or divesting the business.

3 *The functional area strategies* required to compete in the selected product market. These are:
   (a) product line strategy
   (b) positioning strategy
   (c) pricing strategy
   (d) distribution strategy
   (e) manufacturing strategy
   (f) information technology strategy
   (g) segmentation strategy
   (h) global strategy.

4 *The strategic assets or skills* that underpin the strategy and provide the sustainable competitive advantage. A *strategic skill* is something that the business does extremely well such as manufacturing or marketing and which is strategically important to the business. A *strategic asset* is a resource such as a brand name or installed customer base that is strong relative to competitors. Strategy formulation should take into account the cost and feasibility of producing or maintaining assets or skills that will provide the basis for a sustainable competitive advantage.

   A single organization, firm or business, is usually made up of a number of business units. Most business units share an organizational framework with other business units which takes us to the remaining two points.

5 *The allocation of the resources among the business units.* Financial resources generated either internally or externally, plus non-financial resources such as plant, equipment and people, have to be allocated. The allocation decision is a key component in the strategy formulation process.

6 *Looking for synergies across the business*: that is the creation of value by having business units that support and complement each other. Where a firm has many businesses that can achieve

synergistic effects it will have an advantage over those firms that ignore such possibilities in their own organizations or who fail or are unable to achieve any synergy.

Essentially, competitive strategy is operationalized in terms of:

1 The product market investment decision that encompasses the product market scope of the business strategy, its investment intensity and the resource allocation over multiple businesses.
2 The functional area strategies – what to do.
3 The basis of a sustainable competitive advantage to compete in those markets. This core concept encompasses assets, skills and/or synergies matched with functional area strategies.

Armed with a knowledge of what is meant by competitive strategy we now look at how strategies are formulated.

THE CLASSIC APPROACH TO THE FORMULATION OF STRATEGY

Developing a competitive strategy means developing a broad formula for how a business is going to compete, what its goals should be and what policies will be needed to *attain* those goals. Competitive strategy is a combination of the ends or goals for which the firm is striving and the means or policies by which it is seeking to get there.

The Wheel of Competitive Strategy (see Porter, 1980a) is a device for articulating the key aspects of a firm's competitive strategy. At the hub of the wheel are the firm's goals – definitions of how the firm is going to compete; objectives for profitability, growth, market share, social responsiveness, etc. The spokes of the wheel are key operating policies with which the firm is seeking to achieve these goals – purchasing, R&D, finance and control, product line, target markets, marketing, sales, distribution, manufacturing, labour. Under each heading on the wheel a succinct statement of the key operating policies in that functional area should be derived from the company's activities. Like a wheel, the spokes (policies) must radiate from and reflect the hub (goals) and the spokes must be connected with each other or the wheel will not roll. The elements that make up the wheel are shown in Figure 1.2.

A competitive strategy requires the consideration of matters that determine the upper limits of what it can reasonably accomplish. An organization's strengths and weaknesses are reflected in its profile of assets and skills relative to competitors. This profile includes financial resources, technological posture, brand identification and so on. The personal values of an organization are reflected in the motivations and needs of key executives and other personnel who implement strategic decisions. Strengths and weaknesses along with values determine from an internal point of view what competitive strategy a company can successfully adopt.

An organization's industry and broader environment determine its external limits. Societal expectations reflect the impact on the company of such things as government policy, social concerns, evolving mores and many others. All of these factors must be considered before a business can develop a realistic and implementable set of goals and policies. Assessment of the appropriateness of a competitive strategy is achieved by testing the proposed goals and policies for consistency as follows.

Figure 1.2 *Elements of Porter's wheel of competitive strategy*

Internal consistency

- Are the goals mutually achievable?
- Do the key operating policies address the goals?
- Do the key operating policies reinforce each other?

Environmental fit

- Do the goals and policies exploit industry opportunities?
- Do the goals and policies deal with industry threats (including competitive response) to the degree possible with available resources?
- Does the timing of the goals and policies reflect the ability of the environment to absorb the actions?
- Are the goals and policies responsive to broader societal concerns?

Resource fit

- Do the goals and policies match the resources available to the company relative to competition?
- Does the timing of the goals and policies reflect the organization's ability to change?

Communication and implementation

- Are the goals well understood by the key implementers?
- Is there enough congruence between the goals and policies and the values of the key implementers to ensure commitment?
- Is there sufficient managerial capability to allow for effective implementation?

PROCESS FOR FORMULATING A COMPETITIVE STRATEGY

The process consists of three steps as follows.

1 What is the business doing now? Where are we now?

- *Identification*. What is the implicit or explicit current strategy?
- *Assumptions*. What assumptions about the company's relative position, strengths and weaknesses, competitors and industry trends must be made for the current strategy to be viable?

2 What is happening in the environment?

- *Industry analysis*. What are the key factors influencing competitive success? What are the important industry opportunities and threats?
- *Competitor analysis*. What are the capabilities and limitations of existing and potential competitors, and what are their probable future moves?
- *Societal analysis*. What important government, social and political factors will present opportunities or threats?
- *Strengths and weaknesses*. Given an analysis of industry and competitors, what are the firm's strengths and weaknesses relative to present and future competition?

3 What should the business be doing?

- *Tests of assumptions and strategy*. How do the assumptions embodied in the current strategy compare with the analysis indicated above? How does the strategy meet the tests indicated above?
- *Strategic alternatives*. What are the strategic alternatives given the analysis above? (Is the current strategy one of these?)
- *Strategic choice*. Which alternative best relates the company's situation to external opportunities and threats?

STRATEGY IDENTIFICATION AND SELECTION

There are three possible broad areas for consideration. The first is the selection of product markets in which the firm will operate and the question of how much investment should be allocated to each. The second is the development of functional area strategies and the third is the determination of the bases of sustainable competitive advantage in those product markets.

We will be considering these options in much greater detail later in the book. However, we will just mention them here for clarification purposes.

Product market investment strategies

Many strategic decisions involve products: which product lines to continue, which to add and which to delete. Markets need to be selected in which a competitive advantage will exist. It is crucial in strategy development to have a dynamic rather than a static focus. The concept of a product-market matrix (Ansoff matrix – see Ansoff, 1987) is helpful for identifying options and encouraging a dynamic perspective.

In the product-market matrix suggested by Ansoff there are four growth vectors. The first is to penetrate existing product markets (see Chapter 12). A firm may attempt to attract customers from competitors or to increase usage rates of existing customers. A second growth vector involves product expansion while remaining in existing markets. A third growth vector is to apply the same products in new markets, while the fourth growth vector is to diversify into new products. In addition, there is a third dimension to the matrix which is based on vertical integration.

Investment strategies

For each product market, a number of investment options are possible. The firm can reduce or control the investment in a business area by either a milking or a holding strategy. Alternatively, it can withdraw completely if prospects become very unattractive or if the business area becomes incompatible with the overall thrust of the firm. It can also invest to enter or grow.

Functional area strategies

The development of a business strategy involves the specification of the strategies in functional areas such as sales, brand management, R&D, manufacturing and finance. The co-ordination of various functional area strategies so that they don't work at cross-purposes can be difficult. The role of strategic objectives is to help in that task.

The strategic thrusts representing various ways to achieve sustainable competitive advantage can be implemented in a variety of ways. Differentiation, for instance, can be based upon product quality, product features, innovation, service, distribution or even a strong brand name. Low-cost strategies can be based on an experience curve which links cost reduction to cumulative production volume. However, it can also be based on factors such as no frills products or automated production processes.

Bases of sustainable competitive advantage

An effective strategy needs to involve assets and skills or synergies based on unique combinations of businesses. Thus, identifying which assets, skills and synergies to develop or maintain becomes a key decision.

STRATEGIC MARKET MANAGEMENT

Strategies have to be developed and implemented as part of the business management process. Most firms do have some form of regular cyclical planning. However, in an era of rapidly changing business environments such as those being experienced in the twenty-first century, the cyclical planning process does face many problems.

Strategic market management is motivated by the assumption that the planning cycle is inadequate to deal with the rapid rate of change that can occur in a firm's external environment. To cope with strategic surprises and fast-developing threats and opportunities, strategic decisions need to be precipitated and made outside the planning cycle.

It is useful to have a real-time information system rather than periodic continuous monitoring of the environment. In addition, efforts to develop strategic flexibility are likely to be helpful. The latter involves strategic options that allow quick and appropriate responses to sudden changes in the environment.

An important dimension to strategic market management is to be proactive rather than simply reactive to environmental change. The firm can itself bring about change in the environment. It is possible to make a sizeable impact on governmental policies, customer needs and technological developments. The goal is to develop market-driven strategies that are sensitive to the customer.

We look at the practical aspects of marketing planning in the last chapter of the book. The material in the previous chapters is highly relevant to the marketing planning process and many, if not all, of the topics which we look at are included in the marketing plan.

QUESTIONS

1　Some people view marketing in terms of a decision-making paradigm. How useful is such a perspective when marketing is viewed within the framework offered by strategic windows?

2　Discuss how overlapping strategic windows might be identified and exploited by an organization.

3　What is meant by competitive strategy? How should an organization set about determining its competitive strategy?

4　Given the nature of a rapidly changing environment where new developments take place very rapidly and firms need to react rapidly, is the idea of marketing planning still relevant? Why or why not?

5　Discuss how an organization should set about identifying and selecting competitive strategies. How might various stakeholder interests impinge on this process? Illustrate with an example.

CASE STUDIES

Mirela Fashions

In 1971, a highly ambitious young woman returned to Cyprus from Greece after obtaining a degree as a fashion designer. With the help of her parents, she bought a shop in the main shopping area in Limassol. The shop specialized in made-to-measure garments for women. The clientele at the time included relatives, friends and customers who wanted to select the design of their clothes and have them specially made. Gradually, the business gained a reputation for high quality and elegance. As the customer base increased, the need to employ more dressmakers became apparent. The owner decided to employ both qualified and untrained women, and according to their knowledge they were assigned to specific tasks.

Slowly the volume increased as more people came to the south part of Cyprus following the partition of Cyprus in the 1970s. At the same time the troubles and uncertainty in the Middle East brought wealthy Lebanese to the country, who transferred their businesses to Cyprus. As a result, boutiques started to emerge not only in Limassol but also in other towns, for example Nicosia and Larnaca. The owner identified a market opportunity that developed from various environmental changes: to become a supplier of women's clothes to different boutiques and shops across the country.

In order to cope with the high demand, the owner moved out of the shop to a specially converted area at the centre of the town. She bought more equipment, and hired more dressmakers as well as salespeople. The owner of the business also designed the clothes. The business was named 'Mirela Fashions'. Orders were placed after the owner exhibited designs to customers that varied according to the season.

More and more boutiques opened and the competition among them intensified. Subsequently, the owner had to develop different designs for each boutique. The business was booming and had gained a reputation acquired through word of mouth and participation at fashion shows across the country.

By the early 1990s the Lebanese had left Cyprus. At approximately the same time, as part of the preliminary stages of the entry requirements of Cyprus to the EU, the government gave permission to import foreign brands such as Benetton, Marlboro, Polo, Calvin Klein and Marks & Spencer. Cypriots became 'obsessed' with imported clothes. However, not all could afford them or were interested in buying them. Big clothes factories started closing down since the demand for local garments began to decrease. Local manufacturers could not export abroad since their prices were not competitive enough due to high labour costs. Many boutiques started closing as well. Some of those that remained built up stocks of both locally made clothes as well as imported brands. The owner had to dispense with the services of some people in order to keep its costs down. It was time to find a new niche for the business. And indeed, a new niche was found.

Despite the fact that Cypriots showed considerable interest in imported clothes, demand for made-to-measure garments was equally high. At the same time, the owner 'spotted' a new opportunity: the increasing demand for made-to-measure wedding dresses. The reputation of the business acquired over the years for high quality and attention to detail made it easy for the owner to attract customers from these two segments of the market. Meanwhile, the owner identified another opportunity: the big carnival festival in Limassol that lasts for two weeks in February. For two whole months the entire business operations are concentrated on the design, development and production of fancy dresses for shops, private organizations (e.g. the Rotary Club), big and small groups and individuals.

The accession of Cyprus to the EU in 2004 was marked by heightened competition in the local clothing industry by local and foreign businesses, and the increase in the imports of foreign fashion brands. Mirela Fashions has been in operation for 36 years, and during that time it has had to adapt in accordance to the market changes and fashion trends.

Contributed by Ioanna C. Papasolomou, Associate Professor, Marketing Dept, University of Nicosin

QUESTIONS

1 How is the organization trying to get to grips with the problems and difficulties presented by the opening and closing of strategic windows?
2 Does the organization appear to have a strategic marketing management function? Explain.
3 Do you think that Mirela Fashions' current competitive strategy is the correct one? Why or why not?
4 The strategic window of opportunity has remained open for some thirty years for this firm. It has met the changes in the market and the industry successfully. What kind of changes are likely to ensue with the accession of Cyprus in the European Union? How should the firm seek to meet these changes?
5 Identify the various stakeholder interests and how they might influence choice of strategy.

King Olaf's Hall

The Hall was built in the late eighteenth century, essentially to house the growing city's law courts and to provide a meeting place where merchants could enter into trading contracts with one another. It is a very fine imposing building close to the shopping centre of the city and is surrounded by a cobbled space to set it back from other buildings and the main road. The main entrance to the building is hidden behind a frontage of Classical Greek columns surmounting a series of stone steps. It has more the appearance of a Greek temple from times of Antiquity than a commercial or civic building. The Hall is very much in keeping architecturally with the museum, library and art gallery which are close by. King Olaf's Hall long since ceased to function as a commercial or civic building when the Law Courts fell into disuse in the middle of the twentieth century. At that time new law courts were opened close to the main commercial hub of the city. Subsequently, the Hall fell into disrepair in the later half of the twentieth century.

The shopping centre of the city has undergone a programme of improvement on a vast scale in recent times and boasts a major multi-million pound investment programme in a brand new shopping centre aimed to attract shoppers to the city. Recently, there has also been substantial improvements in rail and air transport links to the city and there are adequate on street and off-street parking facilities to cater for the growth in visitors and commuters.

Early in the 1990s the City Council agreed for a Trust to take over and manage the financing, maintenance, renovation and further use of the Hall. The Council agreed to make an annual contribution to the running of the Hall but it essentially devolved control and the raising of finances required to support the Hall to the Trust. The Trust had access to various funding sources and has just about managed to keep the Hall in a fair state of repair since that date.

19

The Hall contains a very large amount of floor space which can be used for such things as exhibitions, antique and collectors' fairs and to provide accommodation for the City Council's Annual Dinner. The Law Courts have been preserved in the same state as they were left after the last session in the 1950s. Below the Law Courts are the dungeons where people on remand and awaiting trial were held. The Hall possesses an upper floor mainly housing a number of small rooms but also featuring a small theatre/concert room capable of seating 200 people.

Early in the twenty-first century the building was designated as a World Heritage site and two years later the Trust was awarded £50 million by the EU to help renovate the building and put it in an excellent state of repair. Since that time much work has been put in hand to undertake essential repairs. However, the management of the Trust is concerned about maintaining the long-term viability of the Hall. With some 50 per cent of the EEC money still available it is looking at ways of how it can spend the money to make alterations to the building's internal structure to make it a self-financing project.

QUESTIONS

1 To what kinds of purposes do you think the Hall might be put?
2 To what extent do you think these purposes could make the Hall self-financing?
3 What might stakeholder interests in the building be and how might these impact on the desire to make the building self-financing?

Chapter 2

Portfolio analysis

INTRODUCTION

We might argue that organizations create their own environments rather than simply adapt to existing ones. They select the strategic windows of opportunities and threats through which they want to look out into the world and develop and market product and services to meet the needs of what they observe to be required in the face of environmental turbulence. Understanding how well these products and services meet the needs presented by the windows of opportunities and threats is a fitting start for exploring the subject of strategic marketing. It introduces the many factors that impinge on the firm's ability to operate in a strategically successful manner. These factors are both internal and external to the organization and form subjects in their own right which will be explored in subsequent chapters.

Organizations market a mix of products or services or both. These constitute the offering that is made through the strategic window. Central to the success or failure of a business is the health of its product (or service) mix. A starting point is the product life cycle concept. This is a useful conceptual framework within which to study how firms can vary their marketing strategies – though of course as we shall see in later chapters they do have to take other factors into account. There seems to be little doubt, however, that at different stages in the product life cycle certain marketing strategies seem to be more appropriate than others. The life cycle concept also points to the different earning patterns of products or services at various points in time. It indicates that it is necessary to have a balanced portfolio of products and services in terms of cash generating capabilities in order to ensure steady sales and profits at all times. Since products will generate different cash flows and profits over their lives it means that the firm has to constantly review its product mix, prune its product lines and introduce new products from time to time in order to maintain long-run profits and stay in business.

Several product portfolio models, perhaps the best known of which are the BCG (Boston Consulting Group) matrix, the GE/McKinsey matrix, and the Directional Policy matrix have been adopted by marketers to aid them assess the health of a firm's product mix. This chapter examines the use and limitations of such models. Portfolio models are useful diagnostic tools but more formal and detailed planning mechanisms are required to evolve and evaluate detailed strategies. Consideration of the product life cycle and the various portfolio models is essential when examining the implications of strategic windows for an organization. All these tools and methods give reasonably good indicators of when a strategic window is about to close.

THE PRODUCT LIFE CYCLE

The need for new products and new product markets has an important influence on strategy formulation. This is because there is evidence to show that most products have life cycles and progress through recognized stages. Every stage in the life cycle brings with it environmental threats and opportunities that require changes to be made in marketing strategy and have implications for marketing planning. In general, life cycles exhibit the following features:

- Products have a finite life span.
- The typical product life cycle curve, as reflected in the sales history of a product is 'S' shaped until it eventually levels off. It is at this point that market maturity occurs and when the maturity phase has run its course, a period of decline follows.
- In general terms, the stages in the life cycle are known as 'introduction, growth, maturity and decline'.
- The life cycle of a product may be prolonged by finding new uses or new users for the product or by getting present users to increase the amount they use.
- During its passage through the life cycle, the average profitability per unit of the product sold at first increases and then eventually begins to decline.

A typical life cycle of a successful product appears in Figure 2.1.

The length of the product life cycle

Product life cycles can vary considerably in terms of length. The steam locomotive made its début in the early nineteenth century and disappeared from regular service in the UK towards the end of the 1960s. One can still, of course, find enthusiasts using them in the twenty-first century in the UK and there are parts of the world – for example, Eastern Europe, Africa and China – where the steam locomotive is still in regular commercial use. In contrast, some women's and men's clothes come in

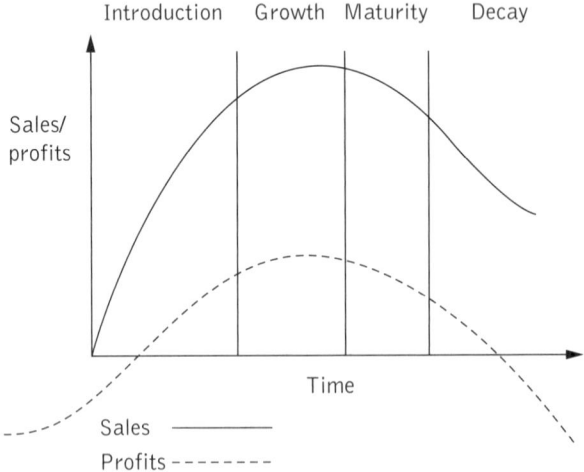

Figure 2.1 The product life cycle

and out of vogue with amazing alacrity. They can even become obsolete with the passing of the seasons, so they appear to have relatively short life cycles. However, fashions come back in vogue again from time to time and old products are introduced as new ones.

One problem that has been found in trying to make use of the product life cycle concept as a management tool is that many products do not appear to perform in the market place as it suggests. They seem to bypass some stages while getting stuck at other stages. Moreover, they may even come into vogue again after a period of going out of fashion. These observations have brought about criticisms of the product life cycle as a useful planning tool (Exhibit 2.1).

Experience shows that sales and profitability vary at every stage in the life cycle. Moreover, the comparative significance of, nature of, and interrelationship between price, promotion, distribution and the actual specification of the product itself change over the life cycle. The quality of the product is often important during the introductory stage, as inadequacies that appear during the trial of a product can end in long-term buyer lack of interest in the product. Advertising and marketing communications need to be informative during this period. Later, widening distribution or price reductions may become more important.

Awareness of the product life cycle concept can help a firm to take better advantage of the market position of the product or service. It can provide indicators of when new launches should be considered, when moving to new markets should be on the agenda and the need for diversification. The product life cycle concept can be used to analyse:

- product category (e.g. cars)
- product forms (e.g. small hatchbacks)
- product brand (e.g. Ford)
- product model (e.g. Fiesta).

Perhaps the most useful application of the product life cycle concept is with respect to product forms.

EXHIBIT 2.1   SWANSEA ENGINEERING: DIFFICULTIES IN USING THE PRODUCT LIFE CYCLE CONCEPT

Swansea Engineering makes wire for industrial uses. Applications range from wire for cables to carry high voltage electricity to wire for winding on small electric motors for incorporation in both industrial and domestic products. The firm has tried to use the life cycle concept to explain generic sales in the market and sales of its own products.

Difficulties encountered include the defining of product markets and the separation from natural growth and decline in the market and the effects of recession. Indeed, in recent years it has proved extremely difficult to assess exactly where many products and markets are in relationship to their anticipated life cycles.

Ironing out the fluctuations caused by economic recessions and mini-booms causes one of the major problems. In addition, since the life cycle has to be viewed within the context of individual markets the analysis can be quite complicated and sometimes difficult to perform. Not only are the markets country specific but they are also industry specific.

PRODUCT LIFE CYCLE STAGES

The introductory stage

Losses or at best low profits are experienced often during the introductory stage. This is because sales are low and promotion and distribution costs are relatively high. Obtaining distribution for a product requires substantial amounts of cash and promotional costs are greatest in relationship to sales during the introductory stage. In addition, extensive promotion is usually required to secure distribution. High margins can provide the cash for heavy promotional expenditure and this in turn produces high initial prices that may discourage rapid adoption of the product by certain customer segments.

Growth stage

New competitors enter the market attracted by the prospect of large-scale production potential and the large profits to be made as the market grows in size and economies of scale come into operation. There is little change in prices and promotional expenditure from the introductory stage, though both may be slightly reduced. There is also a decline in the 'promotion to sales ratio' – that is the amount of money spent on promotion in relation to the amount of sales generated, since sales are expanding during this stage. The net result of all this is that increased profits are generated as costs are spread over a larger volume and unit manufacturing costs decrease in line with the influence of the experience curve.

Growth eventually decelerates as fewer first-time buyers enter the market. This often means that a firm has to employ one of several strategies to keep up market growth as long as possible. These include:

- continually looking for new ways to improve product quality
- adding new features to a product or service
- refining the styling of a product
- introducing new models and flanker products
- entering new market segments
- switching the emphasis of advertising away from creating product awareness to producing conviction and purchase
- lowering price to entice price-sensitive buyers.

Maturity stage

The maturity stage follows on from the onset of decline in the rate of sales growth. The latter produces over-capacity in the industry which in turn leads to increased competition. It is a stage in which profits decline. During the maturity stage, firms implement frequent price reductions and increase advertising and consumer promotions. Emphasis is placed on product research and development to come up with product improvements and flanker brands. While the well established competitors do well, the weaker competitors may quit the market. Cash earned by strong competitors at this stage can be put into products that are at earlier stages in their life cycles.

Decline stage

Sales of most products eventually start to decline for one or more of several reasons. These include technological progress, shifts in consumer tastes and increased domestic and foreign competition. Over-capacity in the market is produced together with price cutting and lower profits. At this time some firms may withdraw from the market and those remaining reduce the number of products that they have to offer, pull out of smaller market segments and weaker trade channels, cut the promotion budget or reduce prices even further.

Consideration must be given to dropping products during this stage unless there are good reasons for retaining them. Weak products tend to occupy a disproportionate amount of management's time and resources. The products often require frequent price and inventory adjustments, short production runs and expensive set-up times. Moreover, they may need the kind of advertising and sales force attention which if it were to be spent on more lively products could produce greater profitability.

THE PRODUCT/SERVICE PORTFOLIO

Some products or services produce considerable amounts of cash while others do not. Where considerable cash is generated, it is often more than is required for essential operational expenditure and for additional investment in facilities and staff. In other cases, however, the cash generated may be insufficient to cover these kinds of expenditure. A firm might benefit if products that are not satisfactorily contributing to profits and overheads of the firm are dropped from the product mix. However, there may well be good reasons why the products are such poor cash generators at a particular moment in time. Indeed it may well be that some of these products will go on to be the big cash earners for a company in the future. Product portfolio models provide a means of rating products and/or services in order to assess the future probable cash contributions and future cash demands of each product or service.

PORTFOLIO MODELS

Portfolio analyses start by examining the positions of products. They consider the attractiveness of the market and the ability of the business to operate competitively within the market. The first of the portfolio models to be used extensively was the growth-share matrix – sometimes referred to as the cash-quadrants model. In this model, market growth rate was employed as the indicator for market attractiveness and relative market share was used to indicate competitive position. There have been a number of variations on the portfolio approach, but they all rely on the work of the Boston Consulting Group for theoretical and empirical underpinning.

The Boston matrix

The Boston approach maps products on to a two-dimensional matrix (Henderson, 1970). The method applies equally well to services or any form of strategic business unit. According to the Boston Consulting Group, the two most significant factors which govern the long-term profitability of a product are the rate of growth of its market and the share of the market that the product has relative to its largest competitor. The Boston Consulting Group presented the model in the form of a simple two-dimensional matrix. The two axes of the matrix are relative market share and market growth rate (Figure 2.2).

The relative market share of a product is assessed with respect to the market share of its largest competitor (or average of the leading companies as this was subsequently found to be more meaningful). The cut off between the high and low market share was originally judged to be equality with the leading competitor, and in the case of market growth rate was originally put at 10 per cent p.a. Both these dividing points were subsequently revised and the matrix was defined less mechanistically.

One interprets the strength or limitations of a product by its position in the matrix. Products falling into the high growth, high market share quadrant are termed 'stars'. They are tomorrow's cash earners. Being high market share businesses, they will be highly profitable and generate a lot of cash, but at the same time their high growth will also mean that they will require a lot of cash both to finance working capital and to build capacity. Thus, though profitable, stars might have either positive or negative net cash flow.

Products positioned in the low growth, high market share quadrant are designated 'cash cows'. These are the real cash generators, being profitable as a result of their high relative market share. It is quite likely that they will also create surplus cash not required to finance growth.

Products falling into the low growth, low relative market share quadrant are designated 'dogs'. These are inherently unprofitable and seem to possess no future, though their cash requirements are low.

Products in the high growth, low market share segment have been referred to as 'wild cats', 'problem children' or simply '?'s. They are unprofitable as a result of their low market share, and they consume a lot of cash merely to maintain their market position because of the high growth rate of the market.

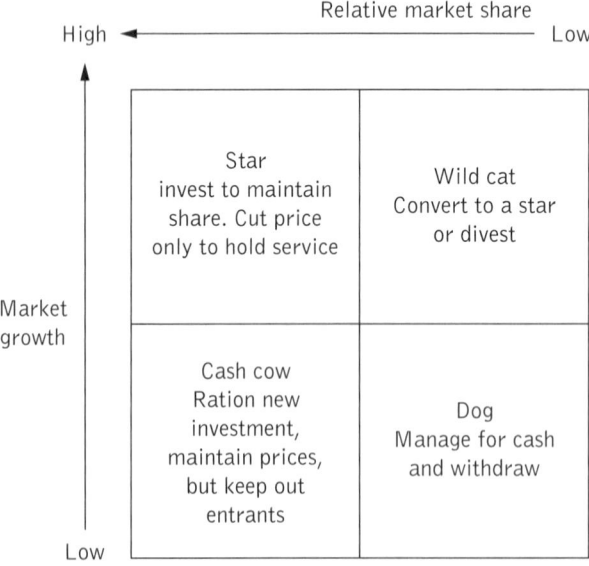

Figure 2.2   The BCG product portfolio matrix

The overall strategy is defined simply with regard to the management of cash flows in order to achieve a balanced portfolio over time. Cash is obtained from cash cows and invested in stars to convert them into tomorrow's cash cows. Dogs are divested and problem children are either converted into stars or liquidated. In this way a balanced portfolio should be achieved with an adequate succession of stars ready to take over from today's cash generators, the cash cows.

When drawing growth–share analyses, a number of matrices should be drawn. In the first place, growth–share matrices should be shown for the various stages of the planning cycle, i.e. now, in one year's time, two years' time, five years' time, etc. In this way an organization can track the projected progress over the planning horizon. It is also customary to circle the points on the matrix (see Figure 2.3). The size of circles should reflect the size of sales or profits for a particular product, product line or business unit. In addition to showing information about one's own organization on the matrix, it is also beneficial to show those of competitors on the same matrix. Matrices should not be too over-crowded with information or else they will be difficult to read. Business units, products or product lines shown on a matrix should also be comparable with one another. For example, a vehicle manufacturer might have three types of matrix – cars, vans and buses. One matrix might show a range of cars, another range of buses, and the third might show a range of vans. It would also be allowed to have a matrix showing the three broad categories of buses, cars and vans in aggregate form (Exhibit 2.2).

While the matrix is intuitively appealing, it has important shortcomings which limit its value as an analytical tool.

The Boston Consulting Group's original work from which the matrix resulted was founded on an analysis of 24 different commodities. Although this work has been replicated many times with other commodities it has not been replicated with differentiated or branded products. Its empirical foundations are founded entirely on an analysis of commodity products selling at market prices, whereas the substance of marketing is concerned with differentiating products for customers prepared to pay higher than base prices to satisfy their particular needs and wants.

The model is based on an implicit assumption that costs fall with experience and that the business that gains the most experience will have the lowest costs. In a young and rapidly growing market, experience is rapidly acquired, thus increasing the benefits of cost reduction and making it attractive to have a large market share. However, in low-growth, mature markets the cost benefits accruing from

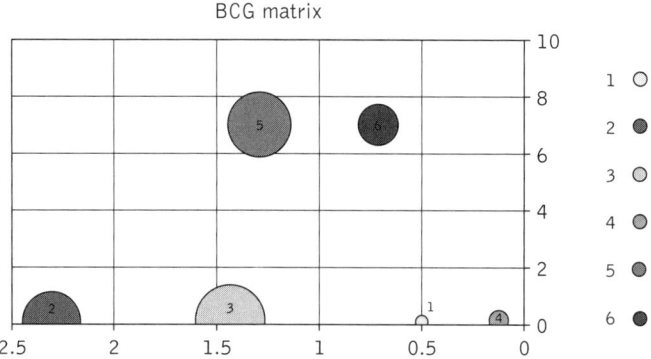

Figure 2.3 *Plotted Boston matrix (based on the data in Exhibit 2.2)*

EXHIBIT 2.2 ASSESSING MARKET GROWTH RATE AND MARKET SHARE POSITIONS IN SIX DIFFERENT SEGMENTS

	Colour of circles in matrix					
	Blue	Purple	White	Green	Violet	Red
Segment	1	2	3	4	5	6
Market growth rate	0.105	0.12	0.12	0.14	7	7
Sales	100	2,000	3,000	250	2,500	1,000
Average 3 largest competitors	200	867	2,083	1,967	1,933	1,400
Relative market share (Sales)	0.5	2.306805	1.44023	0.127097	1.293326	0.714286

experience are low and the benefits from increasing market share in order to gain cost advantages are small. The experience curve should not therefore suggest continuous cost reductions, but reductions during the growth phase, with cost increases occurring during the maturity stage.

A firm's relative market share was measured as share relative to its largest competitor and the division between high and low relative share was therefore set at unity. Thus in any industry there could only be one business with a high relative market share. Where industries are experiencing low growth, all but one competitor would fall into the low growth, low share dog quadrant for which Boston's prescription was simply divest.

The Boston prescriptions are restricted to versions of the buy, sell or hold type of decision. There is no qualitative substance in these statements and little to assist strategic management apart from investment/divestment. Nevertheless, the model has been used far beyond the strictly defined investment portfolio application. Corporate strategists have used the Boston portfolio to guide their investment decisions between businesses. Marketers, too, have misused the matrix to maintain a balanced portfolio of products and for them the limitations of the model are even more profound.

The Boston model has, of course, been widely criticized by strategists and marketers (viz. Proctor and Kitchen, 1990). Strategists have objected to the fundamental proposition that the strategic success of a business could be determined by just two quantifiable factors – market growth rate and market share. This seems too simplistic and could be true only if it was assumed that management itself could not make a difference.

Product life cycle portfolio matrix

To deal with specific criticisms aimed at the BCG matrix, Barksdale and Harris (1982) designed their own matrix. The specific criticisms of the BCG that they sought to address were:

1 that the BCG ignored products or businesses that were new, and
2 that the BCG overlooked markets with a negative growth rate.

As will be seen from the matrix below there is a specific focus on the growth and maturity stages of the product life cycle.

Using the same assumptions as are inherent in the BCG matrix, Barksdale and Harris bring out the additional issues that arise out of introducing new products (infants) and products in declining markets.

Warhorses

Cash cows develop into warhorses when an established market enters decline. The products still exhibit a high market share and can still be substantial cash generators. Marketing expenditure may still have to be reduced, or, selective withdrawal from market segments or elimination of certain models may still be necessary.

Dodos

Such products possess a low share in declining markets and there is little opportunity for growth or cash generation. Usually they should be removed from the portfolio, but if competitors are in the course of withdrawing from the market and look as if they will all have withdrawn fairly soon, it may be profitable for 'dodos' to remain.

Infants

These are high risk products not earning profits and using up considerable cash.

Limitations

As with the BCG there are still problems in defining products and markets or even rates of growth. In addition, other criticisms of the BCG can be levelled at this matrix too (see Figure 2.4).

The GE/McKinsey and Directional Policy matrices

Although potentially very powerful, the Boston matrix and Product Life Cycle Portfolio matrix can be difficult to use as both market growth rates and relative market shares may be difficult to measure accurately.

The GE/McKinsey matrix

A nine-celled multi-factor portfolio matrix was designed by General Electric working with McKinsey and company to overcome some of the limitations of considering only market share and market growth in accomplishing strategic marketing management. Once again, services or other forms of business unit can be plotted in place of products.

The GE/McKinsey multi-factor matrix (see *Business Horizons*, 28th April 1975) has two dimensions. Across the horizontal axis is industrial attractiveness and along the vertical axis, business strength. Both, as with the BCG matrix, increase toward the upper left corner of the matrix. The general

Relative market share			
High	Low		
Infants negative cash flow	Infants negative cash flow	Low	
Stars Modest + or − cash flows	Problem children Large negative cash flows	High	*Market growth*
Cash cows large positive cash flow	Dogs Modest + or − cash flows	Low	
Warhorses Positive cash flow	Dodos Negative cash flows	Negative	

Figure 2.4 *The product life cycle portfolio matrix*

Note: Based on data in Exhibit 2.2

categories of industry attractiveness and business strength permit additional factors to be considered in positioning product groupings in the matrix.

For example, GE originally considered size, market growth, pricing, market diversity and competitive structure as the major factors to describe industry attractiveness. In the case of business strength, attention was focused on size, growth, share, position, profitability, margins, technology position, strength/weaknesses, image, pollution and people. However, a company can use different factors in either the business strength or industrial attractiveness category, depending on the situation.

In order to construct a GE/McKinsey matrix, the factors have to be rated by their importance, each product has to be rated on each factor and the evaluations combined into a summary measure. Summary measures are obtained for each dimension of the matrix and thence plotted within the matrix.

Products or product groupings falling in different cells imply different strategic actions. For example, product groupings falling in the upper left three cells define those that should be invested in for growth; those falling in the lower right three cells of the matrix are harvested or divested. This leaves three cells, starting from the upper right corner, down to the lower left corner of the matrix. The general instructions for these three cells are to manage those products selectively for earnings.

Although the GE/McKinsey matrix offers a greater number of prescriptions than the Boston Consulting Group matrix, the general outcome is not much different to that produced by the latter. In all cases, products exhibiting a low share of a low growth market should be divested, a high share of a low growth market should be milked and a high share of a high growth market should receive investment (see Figure 2.5).

	Industry attractiveness			
High score		Low score		
Invest	Invest	Manage selectively for earnings	High score	Business strength
Invest	Manage selectively for earnings	Harvest or divest		
Manage selectively for earnings	Harvest or divest	Harvest or divest	Low score	

Figure 2.5 *The GE/McKinsey matrix*

Directional Policy matrix

The Shell Chemicals Directional Policy matrix is very similar to the GE/McKinsey matrix (see Robinson *et al.*, 1978). The major differences are greater precision in the assessment of factor ratings together with somewhat more explicit strategy guidelines. Rather than using single measures of success, i.e. market growth rate and relative market share, the DPM uses a multivariate approach where market growth rate is replaced by market attractiveness and relative market share by business strength.

Market attractiveness and business strength both comprise a set of Critical Success Factors (CSFs). The content of each of these sets of CSFs depends entirely upon the company and the competitive environment.

Market attractiveness

Market attractiveness should be measured in terms of the few key things one must get right in order to succeed. Some possible factors are listed below:

- *Market factors:* market size, market growth rate, cyclicality, seasonality, power of sellers and buyers, distributors, price sensitivity.
- *Competition:* number of competitors, type and power of competitors, ease of market entry, risk of product substitution, market share, image in market, possibility of new technology, volatility.
- *Technological:* sophistication of technology, patents, copyrights, maturity.
- *Economic:* financial strength and barriers, economies of scale, capacity utilization.
- *Socio-political:* social values, attitudes and trends, laws, etc.

Business strength

Business strength should also be measured in terms of the few key things one must get right in order to succeed and should enable a comparison to be made of a company relative to its major competitors. Some possible factors are listed below:

- *Market:* market share, company and market image, distribution channels.
- *Product:* pricing policy, product range, reputation for product reliability and quality standards, breadth of product line.
- *Capability:* managerial competence, design capability, ability to respond to changing circumstances, manufacturing strength, R&D, capital strength and finances.
- *Customer relations:* service levels, sales force coverage.

Selecting the business CSFs is not a trivial matter. The process should involve collective effort from key managers and executives in group meetings, and when done properly will result in consensus views which reflect organizational values. As the process is largely unscientific it is important that as many parties are involved as possible, including the most senior management.

Each factor is then assigned a range and given a score, from 0 to 10, relative to a firm's major competitors. Weightings can also be assigned to the factors to measure their relative importance, and the total combined score results in the market attractiveness or business strength score, which provides the two co-ordinates for the matrix plot (see Figure 2.6).

Position 1

This is equivalent to the question mark position in the Boston matrix. For products in this position the market potential is considered attractive, but they do not have the necessary strength in the market to do extremely well.

The options for this position are either to invest in the product to build market strength or to take as much as you can from the product. Focusing resources may be appropriate if investment is proposed

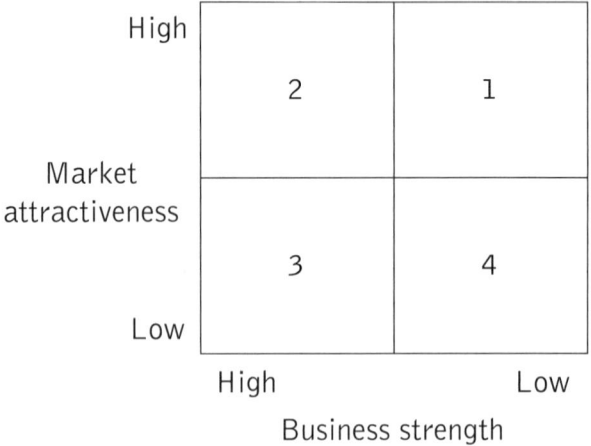

Figure 2.6 *The directional policy matrix (1)*

as a number of business functions may have to be developed because of the overall weak market position.

Position 2

This is equivalent to the star position in the Boston matrix. It is the most attractive position. The product has achieved a strong market position in a highly attractive market.

The continued development of this business deserves the best resources available to maintain the success.

Position 3

This is equivalent to the cash cow position in the Boston matrix. It is also a very attractive position. The product is dominant and in a strong market position in a market that has lost its future potential.

Position 4

This is equivalent to the dog position in the Boston matrix. It is not the most attractive of market positions and equates to low market potential for a product or products with few strengths.

Though these products may not generate as much profit as other more attractive products, they will obviously support the remainder of the product range and make a contribution to overheads. Figure 2.7 shows how a firm would portray its assessment of a product/service or business within different market segments.

Other portfolio models

The ADL (Arthur D. Little) multifactor portfolio model (Exhibit 2.3) is a widely used one (Patel and Younger, 1978). It is a hybrid of the BCG growth share matrix and a multifactor matrix. The two dimensions used to evaluate each business or segment are:

Industry maturity: four classifications

1 embryonic
2 growing
3 mature
4 ageing.
   and

Competitive position: five classifications

1 dominance
2 strong
3 favourable
4 tenable
5 weak.

	Wts	Acme	Corim	Solex	Tyma	Bertina	Dissot
Business strength							
Technology synergy	18	7	6	7	4	8	7
Production synergy	15	8	7	7	5	8	6
Marketing synergy	20	7	3	5	2	9	7
Competitive advantage	32	8	3	4	2	8	5
Resources required	15	6	4	5	4	7	5
	100						

	Wts	Acme	Corim	Solex	Tyma	Bertina	Dissot
Market attractiveness							
Size	23	3	3	3	3	3	3
Able to manage growth	19	9	5	7	5	8	6
Trends	9	8	8	8	8	8	8
Customers	17	7	3	3	4	8	3
Competition	14	9	3	4	4	8	4
Entrants	9	2	2	2	2	2	2
Firm's strategy	9	6	1	1	1	4	2
	100						

	1	2	3	4	5	6
	○ Acme blue	● Corim purple	○ Solex white	○ Tyma green	● Bertina violet	● Dissot red
Business strength	7.32	4.29	5.34	3.11	8.05	5.91
Market attractiveness	6.29	3.56	4.08	3.87	5.95	3.98
Revenues	2000	200	90	400	150	200

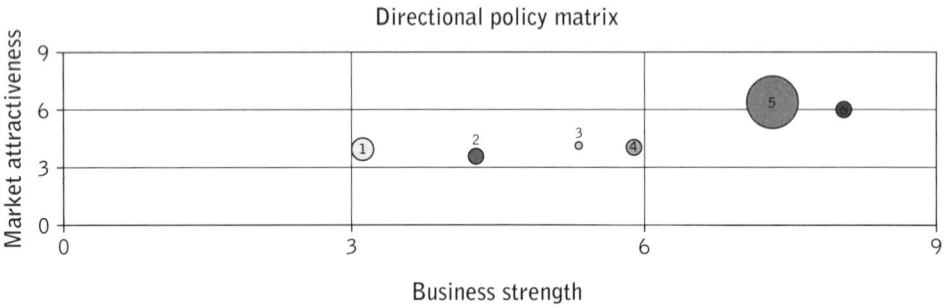

Figure 2.7 *The directional policy matrix (2)*

The ADL proposes basic strategy guidelines for each combination of industry maturity and competitive position. For example:

- *Industry maturity*: growing
- *Competitive position*: tenable
- *Guideline*: find niche and protect it.

EXHIBIT 2.3   ADL MATRIX

	Industry life cycle stage			
Competitive position	Embryonic	Growth	Mature	Ageing
Dominant	Hold position and seek to maximize share	Hold position and share	Hold position and expand with industry	Hold position
Strong	Attempt to improve position and maximize share	Attempt to improve position and be selective in attempts to improve share	Hold position and expand with industry	Hold position or harvest
Favourable	Selective attempts to improve position	Attempt to improve position and be selective in attempts to improve share	Find niche and attempt to guard it.	Harvest or phased out withdrawal
Tenable	Selectively push for position	Find niche and attempt to guard it	Find niche and hang on or phased out withdrawal	Phased out withdrawal or abandon
Weak	Improve or get out	Turnaround or abandon	Turn around or phased out withdrawal	Abandon

Positioning in the ADL matrix

Positioning in the matrix identifies a general strategy. When using the ADL approach, the line of business or SBU is not especially defined by a product or organizational unit. One has to look for discrete businesses by finding commonalties among products and business lines using the following criteria as guidelines:

- common rivals
- prices
- customers
- quality/style
- substitutability
- divestment or liquidation.

This assessment of the industry life cycle stage of each business is made on the basis of:

- business market share,
- investment, and
- profitability and cash flow.

35

The competitive position of a firm is based on an assessment of the following criteria:

- *Dominant*: Rare. Often results from a near monopoly or protected leadership.
- *Strong*: A strong business can usually follow a strategy without too much consideration of moves from rivals.
- *Favourable*: Industry is fragmented. No clear leader among stronger rivals.
- *Tenable*: Business has a niche, either geographical or defined by the product.
- *Weak*: Business is too small to be profitable or survive over the long term.
- *Critical weaknesses*.

Known limitations of the ADL matrix include the following.

- There is no standard length of life cycles.
- Determining the current industry life cycle phase is awkward.
- Competitors may influence the length of the life cycle.

Comments on portfolio model usage

Portfolio models are easy to use and the benefit of using such models is to gain some idea of the profile of strong/weak products or services in the mix. They may, however, cause an organization to put too much stress on market-share growth and entry into high growth businesses. They may also cause firms to pay insufficient attention to managing the current business.

Another problem is that the results produced by using the models are responsive to the weights and ratings and can be manipulated to produce desired results. Since an averaging process is taking place, several businesses may end up in the same cell location, but vary considerably in terms of their ratings against specific factors. Moreover, many products or services will end up in the middle of the matrix and this makes it difficult to suggest an appropriate strategy. The models do not accommodate the synergy between two or more products/services and this suggests that making decisions for one in isolation from the others may be shortsighted.

These and other criticisms gradually diminished the popularity of portfolio analysis. However, its rise and fall did have a lasting influence on subsequent work on competition and business strategy because it highlighted the need for more careful analysis of the two basic dimensions of portfolio–analytic grids: industry attractiveness and competitive position (Ghemawat, 2002),

QUESTIONS

1 Discuss the usefulness of the concept of the product life cycle as a planning tool. What are its major weaknesses?

2 Explain why firms need to have a balanced product/service portfolio with elements at different stages in the product life cycle to ensure long-term survival and growth.

3 Explain how the Boston Consulting Group (BCG) model might be used to assess the health of a firm's product mix and to suggest strategies. What are the limitations of the BCG model? Does the product life cycle portfolio matrix offer any real improvements on the BCG?

4   How might the GE/McKinsey matrix be used to assess the health of a firm's product mix and to suggest strategies? What are the limitations of the GE/McKinsey model. Does the Directional Policy matrix offer anything radically new? Explain.

5   Looking at the portfolio matrices discussed in the chapter, what are their limitations? What use can marketers really make of these matrices?

CASE STUDIES

Acme (A)

Acme markets a product in six different market segments. The information in Table 2.1 is available for the firm's product and five competitors who make up the remainder of the sales to each market segment.

On the basis of the information provided, comment on the probable state of health of the company from a product portfolio perspective. What other information would you deem necessary to facilitate an improved analysis of the situation?

Acme (B)

Acme identifies the business strengths and market attractiveness factors for its product and those of its competitors as shown in Table 2.2. In conjunction with the A case above evaluate the position.

Table 2.1 ACME (A)

	Sales (£000)					
Segment	Acme	Corom	Solex	Tyma	Bertina	Dissot
1	100	100	150	200	200	200
2	2,000	200	90	400	150	200
3	3,000	750	600	400	2,500	400
4	250	400	200	300	4,000	1,500
5	2,500	100	1,500	100	1,800	600
6	1,000	400	2,000	100	650	1,200

	Market share by unit sales					
Segment	Acme	Corom	Solex	Tyma	Bertina	Total %
1	0.3	0.3	0.5	0.7	0.7	3.0	3.5
2	6.6	0.7	0.3	1.3	0.5	3.2	10.0
3	9.9	2.5	2.0	1.3	8.2	3.1	25.2
4	0.8	1.3	0.7	1.0	13.2	4.9	21.9
5	8.2	0.3	4.9	0.3	5.9	2.0	21.8
6	3.3	1.3	6.6	0.3	2.1	4.0	17.6
							100.0

37

■ *Table 2.1* *continued*

	Market growth rates (%)	Development stage (now)	Development stage (in five years)
Segment 1	10.5	Early growth	Maturity
Segment 2	12.0	Growth	Maturity
Segment 3	12.0	Growth	Maturity
Segment 4	14.0	Growth	Maturity
Segment 5	7.0	Maturity	Decline
Segment 6	7.0	Maturity	Decline

■ *Table 2.2* *ACME (B)*

Business strengths	Weighted importance	Score (max 10)					
		Acme	Corom	Solex	Tyma	Bertina	Dissot
Technology synergy (poor–good)	18	7	6	7	4	8	7
Production synergy (poor–good)	15	8	7	7	5	8	6
Marketing synergy (poor–good)	20	7	3	5	2	9	7
Competitive advantage (none–distinct)	32	8	3	4	2	8	5
Resources required (difficult–obtainable)	15	6	4	5	4	7	5
Total	100						

Market attractiveness (Segment 1)	Weighted importance	Score max (10)					
		Acme	Corom	Solex	Tyma	Bertina	Dissot
Size (small–large)	23	3	3	3	3	3	3
Able to manage growth (poor–good)	19	8	5	7	5	8	6
Trends (declining–emergent)	9	8	8	8	8	8	8
Customers (fragmented–similar)	17	5	3	3	4	8	3
Competition (difficult–easy)	14	8	3	4	4	8	4
Entrants (many–few)	9	2	2	2	2	2	2
Firm's strategy (unlikely–likely)	9	4	1	1	1	4	2
Total	100						

Table 2.2 *continued*

Market attractiveness (Segment 2)	Weighted importance	Score max (10)					
		Acme	Corom	Solex	Tyma	Bertina	Dissot
Size (small–large)	23	3	3	3	3	3	3
Able to manage growth (poor–good)	19	9	5	7	5	8	6
Trends (declining–emergent)	9	8	8	8	8	8	8
Customers (fragmented– similar)	17	7	3	3	4	8	3
Competition (difficult–easy)	14	9	3	4	4	8	4
Entrants (many–few)	9	2	2	2	2	2	2
Firm's strategy (unlikely– likely)	9	6	1	1	1	4	2
Total	100						

Market attractiveness (Segment 3)	Weighted importance	Score max (10)					
		Acme	Corom	Solex	Tyma	Bertina	Dissot
Size (small–large)	23	5	5	5	5	5	5
Able to manage growth (poor–good)	19	9	4	4	4	8	3
Trends (declining–emergent)	9	8	8	8	8	8	8
Customers (fragmented– similar)	17	7	5	5	4	7	4
Competition (difficult–easy)	14	8	4	4	4	7	3
Entrants (many–few)	9	4	4	4	4	4	4
Firm's strategy (unlikely– likely)	9	7	3	3	3	6	4
Total	100						

39

Table 2.2 *continued*

Market attractiveness (Segment 4)	Weighted importance	Score max (10)					
		Acme	Corom	Solex	Tyma	Bertina	Dissot
Size (small–large)	23	3	3	3	3	3	3
Able to manage growth (poor–good)	19	3	5	4	9	9	3
Trends (declining–emergent)	9	5	5	5	5	5	5
Customers (fragmented–similar)	17	3	3	2	3	8	2
Competition (difficult–easy)	14	3	2	2	2	9	3
Entrants (many–few)	9	7	7	7	7	7	7
Firm's strategy (unlikely–likely)	9	3	4	3	4	8	3
Total	100						

Market attractiveness (Segment 5)	Weighted importance	Score max (10)					
		Acme	Corom	Solex	Tyma	Bertina	Dissot
Size (small–large)	23	7	7	7	7	7	7
Able to manage growth (poor–good)	19	9	2	8	2	8	5
Trends (declining–emergent)	9	5	5	5	5	5	5
Customers (fragmented–similar)	17	8	1	6	3	7	4
Competition (difficult–easy)	14	9	3	5	4	7	4
Entrants (many–few)	9	7	7	7	7	7	7
Firm's strategy (unlikely–likely)	9	8	1	8	1	9	3
Total	100						

Table 2.2 *continued*

Market attractiveness (Segment 6)	Weighted importance	Score max (10)					
		Acme	Corom	Solex	Tyma	Bertina	Dissot
Size (small–large)	23	6	6	6	6	6	6
Able to manage growth (poor–good)	19	7	2	7	1	3	8
Trends (declining–emergent)	9	5	5	5	5	5	5
Customers (fragmented–similar)	17	6	3	5	2	6	6
Competition (difficult–easy)	14	7	5	3	4	5	8
Entrants (many–few)	9	6	6	6	6	6	6
Firm's strategy (unlikely–likely)	9	4	5	8	2	4	7
Total	100						

Chapter 3

Analysis of the business enterprise

INTRODUCTION

Making the best of a strategic window opportunity not only involves identifying promising opportunities but also having the right kind of resources to make the best of the opportunity. In addition to an analysis of external threats and opportunities in the environment, strategy development must be based on objectives, strengths and capabilities of a business. Understanding a business in depth is the goal of self-analysis. It is similar to competitor analysis but it has a greater focus on performance assessment. The analysis is based on detailed current information on sales, profits, costs, organizational structure, management style and other factors.

There are a number of different approaches to self-analysis. First, there is the focus on marketing competencies and the resource-based view of the firm which is central to any thinking about self-analysis from a marketing perspective. Next there is value chain analysis which examines the elements upon which a competitive advantage can be based. Other useful frameworks include Kay's distinctive capabilities and the Balanced Scorecard. Then there is shareholder value analysis which provides a financial evaluation of a business. The scope of this book does not really provide an opportunity to work through examples of shareholder value analysis which is quite complex. Sales and profitability analysis are discussed along with the need to implement more qualitative measures of analysis which try to ascertain customer perceptions of the organization and its products or services. This then moves us along to the need to consider strategic options.

The second part of the chapter looks at the need for creativity in business and stresses the problems associated with negative mind sets and blocks to creative thinking. Being aware of such blocks and the damage they can inflict is crucial if one is to cope with the opportunities and threats provided by the opening and closing of strategic windows. Consideration is also given to some of the ways the organization can get around the problem of blocks to creative thinking.

MARKETING COMPETENCIES

Two main ideas characterize thinking about marketing in recent years. The first is market orientation and the second is the resource-based view of the firm.

Market orientation is central to marketing (see Figure 3.1). A firm characterized as market oriented might have:

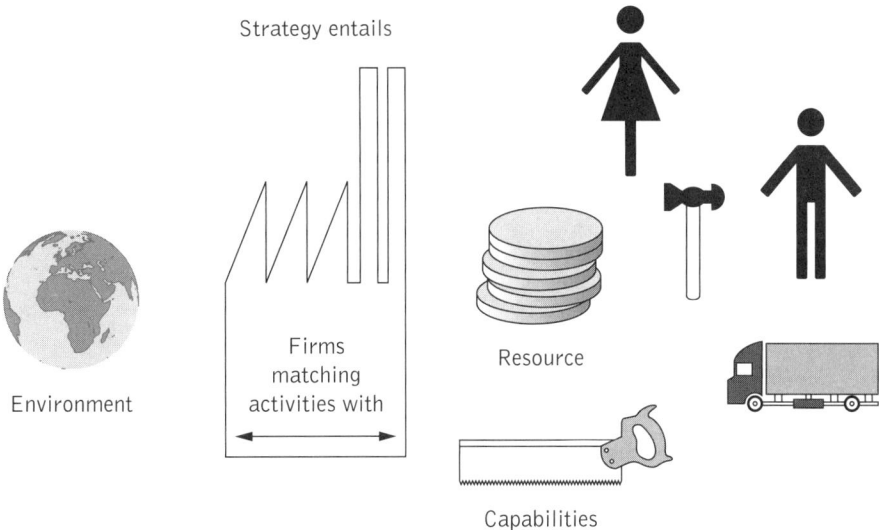

Strategy entails

Environment

Firms matching activities with

Resource

Capabilities

Figure 3.1 *Matching strategy with resources*

1 developed an appreciation that understanding present and potential customer needs is fundamental to providing superior customer value

2 encouraged the systematic gathering and sharing of information regarding present and potential customers and competitors as well as other related constituencies; and

3 instilled an integrated, organization-wide priority to respond to changing customer needs and competitor activities in order to exploit opportunities and circumvent threats (Hunt and Morgan, 1995; Kohli and Jaworski, 1990; Narver and Slater, 1990).

Market orientation places emphasis on the high performance of companies with high quality, organization-wide generation and sharing of market intelligence which produces responsiveness to market needs. The resource-based view of the firm, on the other hand, suggests that superior performance reflects, in the main, historically developed resource endowments. Both these approaches are required to ensure strategic success. Strategy selection must reflect the demands of environmental changes, but at the same time, it should develop a company's distinctive competencies. It is through competitive positioning that the benefits from both of these independent approaches are obtained. It enables firms to compete by identifying target markets and encapsulating the competitive advantage that will be sought in trying to reach these target markets. It recognizes that if the advantage is to be sustainable in the face of competition, it has to be based on the firm's distinctive resources and capabilities (see Figure 3.2).

Whereas the pursuit of a market orientation may well be a worthwhile aim, firms appear to significantly differ in the extent to which they exhibit traits associated with such an orientation. There are several reasons for this. For instance, firms may experience inter-functional rivalry (Fisher *et al.*, 1997) which can restrict market oriented activities and behaviours. They can also lack suitable processes, systems and procedures used to expedite strategic and tactical actions which can seriously limit the firm's responsiveness to necessary change (Jaworski and Kohli, 1993).

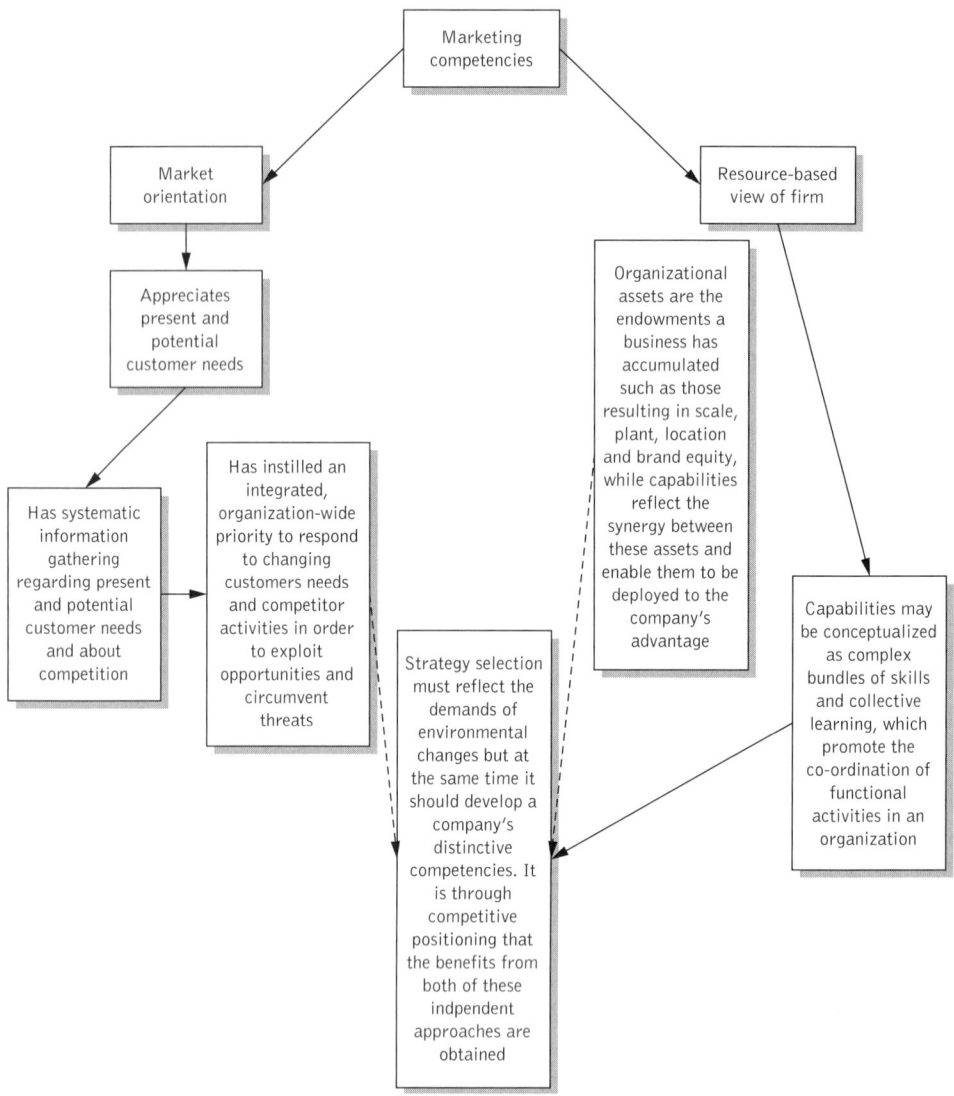

Figure 3.2 *Strategy selection and marketing competencies*

RESOURCE-BASED VIEW OF THE FIRM

For a strategy to be sustainable it has to be based on the firm's resources and capabilities. Day (1994) distinguished between a firm's assets and capabilities as follows. Organizational assets are the endowments a business has accumulated such as those resulting in scale, plant, location and brand equity, whereas capabilities reflect the synergy between these assets and enable them to be deployed to the company's advantage. Capabilities may be conceptualized as complex bundles of skills and collective learning, which promote the co-ordination of functional activities in an organization.

Organizational assets comprise things such as: *physical assets* – land, facilities, buildings, equipment; financial assets – cash, credit rating; *operations assets* – machinery, systems and processes; *human assets* – employees, their qualities and skills; marketing assets – distribution penetration, marketing expertise, market positioning, market knowledge, customer loyalty, brand name, reputation, relationships with distributors; *legal assets* – patents and copyrights; *systems* – management information systems and decision support mechanisms. Company capabilities refer to a firm's ability to deploy assets through organizational processes to achieve desired results.

There are a number of ways of analysing the strengths and weaknesses of the organization. These will be considered in the remainder of the chapter.

VALUE CHAIN ANALYSIS

Porter considered the value chain as a means of ascertaining the competitive advantage that a firm might possess. A value chain of this nature comprises two types of value-creating activities as follows.

Primary value activities

- *inbound logistics*: material handling and warehousing
- *operations*: transforming inputs into the final product *outbound logistics* – order processing and distribution
- *marketing and sales*: communication, pricing and channel management
- *service*: installation, repair and parts.

Secondary value activities

- *procurement*: procedures and information systems
- *technology development*: improving product and processes/systems
- *human resource management*: hiring, training and compensation
- *firm infrastructure*: general management, finance, accounting, governmental relations and quality management.

Each of the activities in the value chain is a potential source of competitive advantage and thus should be considered in undertaking self assessment. Value chain analysis facilitates working out how to create the value for customers, as well as maximizing benefits for the organization. Organizations take raw inputs, and 'add value' to them by turning them into something of worth to other people. In a manufacturing organization, the manufacturer 'adds value' by taking a raw material of little use to the end-user (for example, aluminium ore) and converting it into something that people are prepared to pay money for (e.g. window frames). The concept also applies in service industries, where people use inputs of time, knowledge, equipment and systems to create services of real value to the person being served – the customer. Customers aren't necessarily outside the organization: they can be other stakeholders in the organization.

As a rule, the more value that is created, the more people will be prepared to pay for a product or service, and the more they will they keep on buying from the organization. Value chain analysis helps

45

identify the ways in which an organization can create value for customers and other stakeholders. Value Chain Analysis is a three-step process:

1 *Activity analysis*: identifying activities undertaken in delivering the product or service
2 *Value analysis*: how to add value for the customer/stakeholder; and
3 *Evaluation and planning*: whether it is worth making changes, and then plan and implement changes.

Activity analysis

One needs to list or brainstorm activities that in some way contribute towards customers'/stakeholders' experience in dealing with the organization. At an organizational level, this would include the step-by-step business processes that are used to serve the customer – primary activities. These will include marketing; sales and order-taking; operational processes; delivery; support; and so on (this might also involve many other steps or processes specific to the industry). It could also be broadened to include:

- how one recruits people with the skills to provide the best service
- how one motivates organizational teams to perform well
- how one keeps up-to-date with the most efficient and effective techniques
- how one selects and develops the technologies that give a competitive edge to the organization; and
- how feedback is obtained from customers/stakeholders on how the firm is doing, and what can be done to improve further.

Value analysis

This involves identifying for each activity identified the things that customers/stakeholders value in the way that each activity is conducted. For example, with respect to a telephone order-taking process, the customer will value a quick answer to his or her call; a polite manner; efficient taking of order details; fast and knowledgeable answering of questions; and an efficient and quick resolution to any problems that arise. If one is thinking about delivery of a professional service, the customer will most likely value an accurate and correct solution; a solution based on completely up-to-date information; a solution that is clearly expressed and easily actionable; and so on. One then needs to work out what needs to be done or changed to improve value created for each value factor.

Evaluate changes and plan for action

This involves picking out those things which can be done quickly, easily, and cheaply in the first place, Next the more difficult changes have to be examined. Some of these may be impractical or may deliver only marginal improvements at a substantial cost. These latter ideas should be put aside and not considered further. The remaining ideas should then be prioritized and a plan evolved to introduce them.

SHAREHOLDER VALUE ANALYSIS

A business can be evaluated by examining the value it creates for its shareholders (see for example, Mills, 1994; Rappaport, 1986). A quantitative figure can be put on this value. It involves calculating the sum of the present values of future cash flows and residual value less the market value of any debt associated with the business. A positive value means that the business is creating shareholder value whereas a negative one means the shareholder value is being eroded. If a new strategy is to be considered, its value will be the difference between the value with the strategy option and the value without it.

Shareholder value analysis presents solutions to many of the difficulties attached to an analysis of business profitability using return on assets as a yardstick. By focusing on cash flow one eliminates many accounting problems such as distortions caused by depreciation and asset book values. Shareholder value analysis also considers future measures of profitability when evaluating a business. In theory, the method encourages executives not to be driven by short-term pressures of the stock market because of its forward-looking orientation. In addition, it focuses attention on financial analysis and cash flows. It does not pay attention to the development of creative, innovative strategic options and the underlying strategic competitive advantages that must exist to support them.

Such an approach requires the ability of executives to provide good objective estimates of future profits which can be very difficult. Executives tend to be overly optimistic about market acceptance of new ventures and to underestimate the time and investment required. In addition, there are many sources of uncertainty which affect the financial outcomes not the least of which are competitors' reactions.

The shareholder value-based management approach has encountered difficulties at middle management levels as and when attempts are made to incorporate the concept into operational plans. This should not be surprising. The low level of financial understanding among non-financial managers is not a recently discovered phenomenon and therefore attempts at introducing financially oriented planning and control systems were (and are) clearly problematic. However, the fact that difficulties exist should not prevent attempts at linking financially based performance systems with marketing and operations-based measures.

KAY'S DISTINCTIVE CAPABILITIES

Kay (1993) argued that added value could be created by successfully managing contracts and relationships. He envisaged three factors that would enable organizations to achieve a competitive advantage: *architecture*, *reputation* and *innovation*. In addition to these factors he also argued that a firm may have a competitive advantage through its control of strategic assets. He conceptualized *architecture* as a network of relational contracts within or around the organization, with employees (internal) and with suppliers and customers (external). His view was that this can add value because of the inherent knowledge it possesses and the routines it encompasses. He argued that it allows adaptable response to change taking place and promotes open exchange of information. However, Kay suggests *reputation* is a key way of communicating quality values to customers when it cannot easily be determined in other ways. *Innovation* too he considered to be the basis of competitive advantage.

Innovation, quality, customer relations, management capabilities, alliances, technology, brand value, employee relations, environmental and community issues taken together are important value creation drivers in an organization (Low, 2000). Monitoring and assessing these is important. Interest has developed in recent years in both the public and private sectors into how performance can best be measured and reported to management. This has led to the development of interest in measuring performance against goals. The 'balanced scorecard' (Kaplan and Norton, 1996) has been adopted widely for this use. However, the public sector requires a somewhat modified approach to that of the private sector. Below we will introduce the 'balanced scorecard' and a more recent addition, 'the public sector scorecard'.

The balanced scorecard

A balanced scorecard is a performance measurement technique that strikes a balance between financial and non-financial/operating measures, relating performance to rewards, and taking into account the multiplicity of stakeholder interests (Figure 3.3). The balanced scorecard examines the organization from four perspectives and requires one to develop metrics, collect data and analyse it relative to each of these perspectives:

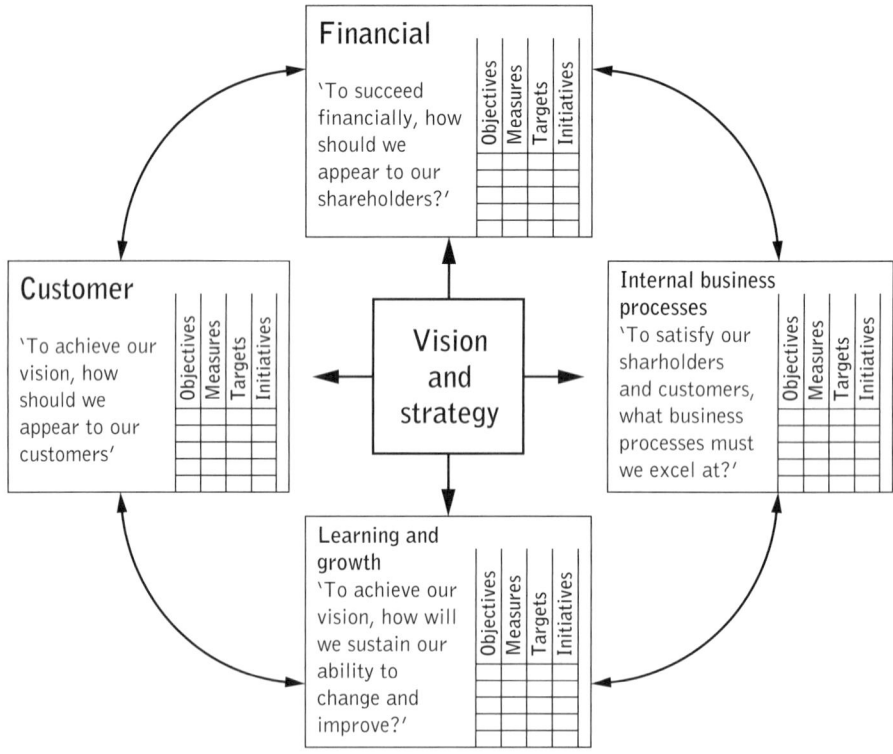

Figure 3.3 *The balanced scorecard*

Reprinted by permission of *Harvard Business Review*. From 'Translating Vision and Strategy – four perspectives' by R.S. Kaplan and D. P. Norton, Jan–Feb 1996. Copyright © 1996 by the Harvard Business School Publishing Corporation, all rights reserved.

- the learning and growth perspective
- the business process perspective
- the customer perspective
- the financial perspective

Use of the scorecard helps give a clear picture as viewed from different perspectives. Performance measures enable improvements to be identified. These measures relate to characteristics of products, services, processes, and operations and portray the factors that lead to improved customer, operational, and financial performance. Some possible measures are shown in Exhibit 3.1. The appropriateness of measures may depend on the type and size of the organization.

An alternative approach for the public sector is reported in Moullin (2002). It takes a strategic perspective, whereby the organization's performance is examined against its main objectives and key performance targets. In addition the term 'customer' is replaced with the term 'service user/stakeholder', the 'internal' perspective is renamed 'operational excellence' and the term growth is omitted in the innovation and learning perspective. In this last respect, while the meaning of growth in the balanced scorecard is more than just growth in physical or monetary terms, it can be confusing since growth in terms of more service users, may be something the organization wishes to avoid.

The public sector scorecard can be a valuable tool to use in assessing perceptions of performance held by different stakeholder groups either for the service as a whole or even for specific projects or activities. The method of construction can involve either a large number of different measures or a much smaller number, depending on needs and preferences. It utilizes simple data collection tools such rating scales collected by questionnaire and can be analysed and presented graphically with the aid of a standard spreadsheet package. The type of data used and how it is incorporated in the model is very much in the hands of the user since there are no hard and fast rules as far as this is concerned. In some cases hard data may be available and can be reflected in the scorecard rather than a subjective assessment based upon scale values subjectively estimated by stakeholders.

Specifically, the scorecard addresses:

- *Service user/stakeholder*. How they view the service and to what extent they have contributed to the service.
- *Operational excellence*. Effectiveness of processes and staff along with staff satisfaction.
- *Innovation and learning*. How the organization is continuing to improve and how it learns from others.
- *Financial*. How well the service keeps costs under control and creates value for money.
- *Strategic*. To what extent the service has met its key performance outcomes.

The public-sector scorecard can make use of simple rating scales filled in by various stakeholders or it can use hard data which is collected in other ways – for example, financial performance data or staff turnover ratios.

More complex and detailed collection of data for monitoring purposes

As noted in the last section, there is scope for more complex and detailed collection of data and monitoring of performance.

EXHIBIT 3.1 KEY PERFORMANCE INDICATORS FOR THE BALANCED SCORECARD

Perspective	Key performance indicators
Financial	
Profits	Return on investment, return on sales, ratio to industry/market/competitor average
Income to shareholders	Level of dividend, dividend cover
Business growth	Sales growth
Business stability	Debt/equity ratio, interest cover
Customer	
Satisfaction	Survey satisfaction data
Quality of products/service	Level/number/% of complaints
Level of service	Product/service delivery lead time in terms of time
Business development	
Innovation/creativity	Numbers of new products, new ideas, new sales leads,
Effectiveness	Sales/sales calls ratio
	Market penetration measure
	Repeat business rate
Investment	% retained profit for reinvestment
	Index of R&D expenditure (deflated)
	Trend (running annual average) in capital expenditure over previous five years.
	% marketing expenditure on new products/services
Internal	
Stability of workforce	Staff turnover rate
Staff development	Number training days given to employees/managers at different levels for different purposes
Performance	Productivity measures
Commitment	Absence levels
Communication	Survey of staff level of awareness of key recent issues relating to their work

Stakeholder satisfaction with the service and service quality can be assessed in much detail. In addition the competence of the service provider, commitment to the service provider, attitude towards the service provider and communication effectiveness with the provider can all be assessed in greater detail. Exhibit 3.1 summarizes some of the measures that can be used in this context. However, one does have to bear in mind the stakeholders involved and their interests.

Innovation and learning also offer a variety of possible ways for more detailed assessment. In the case of learning one might assess among other things:

To what extent

- Learning is linked to both organizational strategy and individual goals.
- Use is being made of new business and management concepts that can improve the organization's performance.
- Training is taking place to fill existing competency gaps.
- New or existing forms of competency training are being used – e.g. distance learning, self development or Internet-based programmes.
- The career reward system provides recognition of learning.
- How much learning takes place in teams.
- Use is made of learning from patients/customers in the form of satisfaction, complaints, changing needs, changing tastes, etc.).
- Knowledge is absorbed from outside, knowledge is diffused within, knowledge is generated within, and exploited within services (viz. Sprenger and Have, 1996).

Innovation assessment needs to be directed towards monitoring improvements in the processes, people and services which are offered to patients/customers. One might assess and monitor inputs, innovation process and outputs (viz. BCG, 2006) as follows.

Inputs

- *Financial resources being committed.*
- *People* committed to an innovation and how *key* people are being used.
- *The number of ideas generated and the expected payback for each.*
- *Key capabilities*. What and where are the shared resources – and potential bottlenecks.

Processes

- *Resources expended per individual project and on average.*
- *Cycle times for the entire process and specific parts*. How long it takes to get ideas turned into service offerings, etc.
- *The number of ideas that are moving from one stage of the process to the next.*
- *The difference between the initial expected value of an idea and the actual realized value.*

For outputs

- *The number of new products or services launched.*
- *Incremental savings in costs.*

Operational excellence involves measuring the effectiveness of processes and the satisfaction of staff with their work. It seeks to identify critical success factors in meeting with customer/patient requirements. The focus is on efficiency, streamlining, ensuring that resources are available as and when required and reducing organizational slack. Preventative maintenance and detailed inspection of processes are also aspects of operational excellence. Measures should seek to reflect these factors.

Staff are a key component in ensuring the effective and efficient delivery of a service. Indicators of job satisfaction include adequate levels of financial compensation for work performed, flexible working hours, opportunities for advancement, job security, an interesting job, staff working independently and staff feeling that they are useful to society. The measures here should reflect the extent to which these facilities are considered by management to be available within the organization or unit.

Financial aspects may be largely concerned with how costs are kept under control. Measures may reflect the extent to which managers feel costs have exceeded expectations and may be related to different areas of business activity and kinds of work. In this respect there may be several different sources or types of costs assessed and monitored. In terms of delivering value for money it might be advisable to ask the question 'value for money to whom?' Separate measures and assessment procedures might then be with the perceptions of different stakeholder groups.

FINANCIAL PERFORMANCE: SALES AND PROFITABILITY

Self-analysis starts with an analysis of current financial performance, measures of sales and profitability. Change in either of these can signal a change in the market viability of a product line and the ability to produce competitively. Most firms have sales and profitability targets as key elements of their objectives.

A reasonably sensitive measure of what customers think about a product or service is its sales or market share. If customers alter their views about a product or service, sales and market share should be affected. Increased sales can mean that a customer base has grown. Increased share can provide the potential to gain a strategic competitive advantage in the form of economies of scale and experience curve effects. The converse is also true when sales decline. Nevertheless, a difficulty with using sales as a measure is that it can be influenced by short-term promotional activities on the part of the firm or its competitors. An analysis of sales or share should therefore be viewed within the context of a study of customer satisfaction.

Profitability

Profits can be used for capital needed to pursue growth strategies, to replace obsolete plant and equipment and to absorb market risk. Return on assets is often taken as the measure of profitability. It is a product of *profit margin*, which depends on the selling price and cost structure, and *asset turnover* which depends on inventory control and asset utilization. Businesses should try to earn a return on assets that meets or exceeds the cost of capital, the weighted average cost of equity and cost of debt. Although such measures are helpful, ascertaining the relevant figures is not always as straightforward as one might assume. There are many difficulties surrounding their calculation, such as the distortions caused by depreciation and the fact that intangible assets such as brand equity are not included, just to mention two.

OTHER KINDS OF PERFORMANCE MEASUREMENT

It is difficult to measure performance indicators that really reflect long-term prospects. It is simpler to focus on short-term profitability measures and correspondingly to reduce investment in new products and brand images that will have long-term pay-offs. However, performance measures should reflect the long-term viability and health of an enterprise. Attention should be placed on assets and skills that underlie current and future strategies and their strategic competitive advantages. Such measures might include customer satisfaction, brand loyalty measures, product or service quality measures, brand or firm associations, relative cost, new product activity, and manager–employee capability and performance.

CUSTOMER SATISFACTION AND BRAND LOYALTY

One of the most important assets of many firms is the loyalty of its customer base. Measures of sales and market share are useful but crude indicators of what customers really feel about a firm. Measures of customer service and brand loyalty are more sensitive and provide diagnostic value as well. One way of accessing customer needs/wants is to examine customers' complaints and obviously try to respond to them. As far as measurement is concerned, the most important point is that the range of instruments used and their sensitivity are appropriate to the clients under scrutiny.

A number of difficulties can arise when taking measurements. The issues of validity and reliability are critical, as are sensitivity, timeliness, specificity, ambiguity, explicitness and accuracy. Timeliness refers to the extent to which the material can become available; capacity, the extent to which changes in direction and pace can be detected; and sensitivity, the extent to which small levels of change can be detected. The factor of specificity takes account of the relationship between variables and the extent to which they are related to each other. Ambiguity is concerned with clarity; and explicitness and accuracy are to do with which measurements are made and recorded. Finally, a number of issues affect the whole process of measurement in organizations, i.e. cost-effectiveness, feasibility and the effect that being measured has on the participants.

PRODUCT AND SERVICE QUALITY

A product or service and its components should be critically and objectively compared with both the competition and with customer expectations and needs. Quality is usually based on several critical dimensions that can be identified and measured over time – number of defects, conformance to performance specifications, durability, reliability, etc. We can contrast notional ideas about product quality with similar ideas about service quality (see Exhibit 3.2).

BRAND OR FIRM ASSOCIATIONS

Companies may become attractive takeover targets and the value of their stock may rise because of the strength of their brands (Sherrington, 1995). Moreover, some brands are even valued as assets in

EXHIBIT 3.2   PRODUCT AND SERVICE QUALITY

Product quality

1   *Performance* – how well a product performs the task it was designed to do?
2   *Durability* – how long the product will last?
3   *Conformance with specifications* – what is the incidence of defects found in the product on delivery; what is the incidence of defects which cannot be remedied?
4   *Features* – what special features does the product have which makes it superior to competitive offerings?
5   *The name* – can one associate the image of the firm and the brand name with concepts of quality?
6   *Reliability* – can one expect the same kind of quality every time that the product is used?
7   *Serviceability* – is the service system efficient, competent and convenient?
8   *Fit and finish* – does the product look and feel like a quality product?

Service quality

1   *Tangibles* – do the physical facilities, equipment and appearance of personnel associated with the service promote confidence in the quality of the service?
2   *Reliability* – is there evidence of an ability to perform the promised service properly the first time?
3   *Responsiveness* – is there a willingness to help customers and provide prompt service?
4   *Competence* – do the personnel possess knowledge and skill and have they an ability to convey trust and confidence?
5   *Credibility/trustworthiness* – is the organization trustworthy and does it always deliver what it promises to deliver?
6   *Empathy* – does the provider of the service provide its customers with individualized attention?
7   *Courtesy* – do customers perceive the service provided to be a friendly one?
8   *Communication* – are customers kept informed about the service offered in the language they can understand? Do the providers of the service listen to what the customers have to say?

the company balance sheet. Branding for consumers represents the mark of a given level of quality and value that helps them choose between one offering and another.

The development of a range of brands to cover different consumer segments enables a firm to benefit from changing consumer wants. From a marketer's point of view, brands allow the producer, and more recently the retailer, to target different groups of consumers or segments of the market, with different labels and product offerings. In fact, developing more than one brand enables a firm to segment a market and target different consumers. Moreover, as long as brands add more value than cost for these new segments, an improvement in overall profitability can ensue. The development of a portfolio of discrete brands permits a firm to insulate the problems of one product from the rest of the range and it can allow it to divest less profitable brands.

An important asset of a brand or firm is what customers think of it: its associations and perceived quality. The latter, of course, may be different to actual quality. It can be based on experiences with past products or services and quality cues such as retailer types, pricing strategies, packaging, advertising and typical customers. The product may be associated with expertise in a particular technological area or with innovativeness. Such associations can be an important strategic asset for a brand or firm.

Associations can be monitored through the regular use of questions posed in focus groups to describe user experiences. The identification of changes in important associations will likely emerge from such research. Further tracking information can be obtained through surveys.

RELATIVE COST

A careful cost analysis of a product or service and its components involves tearing down competitors' products and analyzing their systems in detail – reverse engineering (Exhibit 3.3). Such an analysis enables one to see where costs may be saved in product construction and material used. Alternatively, weaknesses in one's own designs can be improved. Where an advantage is held in the design of one's own product but the additional cost is only small, this may be promoted as a strategic competitive advantage if it is felt that the advantage can be sustained.

MANAGER/EMPLOYEE CAPABILITY AND PERFORMANCE

Organizations have to both obtain and sustain a team of talented individuals who can carry on the necessary management activities to sustain the organization's position *vis-à-vis* competitors. Moreover, an organization should be evaluated not only in terms of how well it obtains human resources but also in terms of how well it nurtures them. A healthy organization will consist of individuals who are motivated, challenged, fulfilled and growing in their professions. Each of these dimensions can be observed and measured by employee surveys and group discussions.

EXHIBIT 3.3   REVERSE ENGINEERING

Manufacturing organizations often have a team of engineers who buy products of their competitors, reverse engineer them and figure out how much they cost by the parts used. From that process of reverse engineering these firms can estimate the production cost, the quality and the capabilities of their competitors' machines. With this information they can improve their own machines' design and decrease their production cost. The needed information is not gained illegally. It involves the use of theoretical estimates based on the engineers' own knowledge of the industry and of the machines' hardware. The same principle also applies to organizations working in the service sector. In this case the steps in providing a service are analysed and costed and the quality of the service assessed.

OTHER PERFORMANCE FACTORS

Additional factors that could be considered include:

- customer loyalty management
- average order/purchase value
- the 'expected value' of a transaction period
- the cost of attracting customers
- the cost of retaining customers
- co-productivity – the involvement of suppliers and customers in creating value
- operational gearing
- financial gearing and corporate control
- strategic and operational cash flow
- capacity management availability and utilization.

It is arguable that each of these factors influences sales and/or costs, and should be considered within either sales growth rate or operating margin analysis. However, an equally justifiable case can be made for considering them as specific factors. Their inclusion in this way acknowledges their importance, together with the further acknowledgement that for specific organizations their influence can be significant.

Customer loyalty management is reflected in average order/purchase value and the distribution of order/purchase value sizes. It has to be borne in mind that the costs of order management and handling is not usually size related and a profile of order size across the current and potential customer base is a better indicator of value creation. The average period of customer loyalty and the expected value of the loyalty transaction may be a significant factor. This might be quantified by calculating the net present values of costs of acquiring and retaining customers. Such analysis is an important consideration in shareholder value creation; there can be quite different value results from similar levels of revenue.

Normann and Ramirez (1993) identify the importance of customer and supplier involvement in the 'value creating system'. They use the example of Ikea to illustrate the role the customer may take in creating value. They highlighted a number of tasks assumed by customers that are usually undertaken by the retailer. The approach can be used with suppliers and distributors using transaction cost analysis. Hence, customers, suppliers and distributors become involved in value creation and this co-productivity is an important value driver.

DETERMINANTS OF STRATEGIC OPTIONS

Another aspect to self-analysis is to consider the determinants of strategic options. One needs to consider the characteristics of a business that make some options infeasible without making major organizational changes. There may also be key criteria that are critical when exercising choice among strategic options.

Past and current strategies

Before beginning new strategies one should understand the basis and outcomes of past strategies that have been adopted. History repeats itself only too often and there is no point in making the same mistake twice. In addition, a strategy that has paid dividends in the past may work well in another situation. There is no point inventing the wheel twice over. However, care has to be exercised in not assuming that what has worked in the past will always work in future situations (see later in the chapter).

Organizational capabilities and constraints

Internal organization can affect both the cost and feasibility of some strategies. There has to be a fit between a strategy and the internal structure of an organization. If a strategy does not work well it may be expensive or even impossible to make it work. Later in the book (see Chapter 13) we will be looking at strategic alliances, i.e. where organizations co-operate in order to work together for mutual benefit. Internal organizational factors relating to all firms participating in such ventures have to be compatible with one another and the overall strategies being pursued by the consortia.

Financial resources and constraints

In the end, strategic decisions may well be based on access to funds to provide the necessary resources to get the best out of a perceived opportunity. Ultimately, judgements need to be made about whether or not to invest in a product, product line or service, or simply to withdraw cash from it. A basic consideration in all this is the firm's ability to supply investment resources. A financial analysis to determine probable, actual and potential sources and uses of funds can help provide an estimate of this ability.

CREATIVITY

Nowadays, the majority of organizations are fully aware of just how vital creativity is to their prosperity. Over time, considerable research has been undertaken which enables us to obtain a better understanding of creativity and become more innovative ourselves. Even in the 1970s it was reported that the 'accelerating pace of change is now widely accepted . . . Alvin Toffler found evidence that the pace of change was causing "Future shock" and social disorientation' (Rickards, 1985) and this change is an ever present phenomenon to which businesses of all kinds are forced to respond, if they want to stand the best chance of survival and prosperity. But how should they respond?

An increasing number of problems have no precedents and there are fewer tried and tested ways of approaching them. Many suggest that creativity is indeed the answer and as Majaro (1991) suggests: 'It is universally assumed that enhanced creativity can provide a company with a competitive edge.' A survey sponsored by Porter/Novelli among 100 executive readers of *Fortune 500* in 1993 found that people thought creativity was essential to ensure success in business. Indeed, Oldman and Cummings (1996) note that 'numerous commentators have argued that enhancing the creative performance of employees is a necessary step if organisations are able to achieve competitive advantage'.

The main problem in management according to James March (1988) is that:

Organisations face a large number of problems of about equal importance, but only a few solutions. Thus the chance of finding a solution to a particular problem is small.

In order to identify and so solve many of the problems that arise in business it is necessary to challenge the problem-solving capabilities of those in charge. In many cases the creative process which is used to approach problems has to be restructured and redeveloped in order to produce new ideas and perspectives.

Change is an intrinsic necessity for a company that wishes to perform well in the long term. As Sir John Harvey-Jones stated: 'Unless a company is progressing all the time, it is in fact moving backwards. It is quite impossible to maintain the status quo' (Rogers, 1996). Attempting to do things in the same way as they have always been done in the past can lead to difficulties in a business environment which is experiencing rapid cultural, economic or technological change.

The rapid growth of competition in business and industry is often quoted as a reason for wanting to understand more about the creative process (see for example, Van Gundy, 1988; Rickards, 1990). Many firms are experiencing pressure to continually enhance old systems and products. Growth and survival can be related directly to an organization's ability to produce (or adopt) and implement new products or services, and processes (Van Gundy, 1988). One of the key aspects of any organization's success or failure is its ability to stay ahead of the competition in a rapidly changing environment. The modern business with its emphasis on competition, building larger markets, strategic planning, team working, etc., has created the need for new problem-solving and decision-making strategies.

Another reason is that managers need to discover new and better ways to solve problems (Ackoff and Vegara, 1988). In particular, an increasing number of problems have few or no precedents, hence there are fewer tried and tested ways of approaching them with the anticipation of reaching a successful outcome. To stay in business a company has to respond creatively to the problems it faces. Problems may exist in both the external and internal environments. The former poses problems such as how to cope with slow economic growth, how to deal with new entrants to an industry, how to increase sales at the pace of competition in high-growth markets, how to deal with new technological developments and how to cope with shorter product life cycles. The latter poses problems to do with poor internal communications, financial problems, alienated or poorly motivated staff and inadequate planning.

Changes within a company, forced by either internal or external factors, create an unhappy climate for the company and its workers. Management needs to respond positively to such situations. Creativity is considered to be a vital asset for any person who is involved in a leadership situation (see, for example, Bennis and Nanus, 1985; and empirical evidence provided by Ekvall, 1988). Creative leaders actively hunt for new problems and are especially successful in handling new challenges which demand solutions outside the routine of orthodox strategies. They often possess significant vision and are able to inspire others by their creative talents.

HOW CREATIVE THINKING MAY BE USED IN MARKETING

Creative thinking benefits all areas and activities of management. It is required to dream up better ways of marketing goods, to devise new production methods, to find new ways to motivate people, and so on. Creativity turns up in every business situation where there is a chance that things can be done in a more business-like, more profitable or in a more satisfying way. Problems which require creative thinking are 'open-ended' problems. That is, problems for which there is not just one solution. Executives have to make decisions which require creative problem solving in planning, organizing, leading, and controlling their organizations, for example:

Planning

- Determining the mission of the organization
- Determining the organizational objectives
- Identifying strengths, weaknesses, threats and opportunities
- Adjusting the organization's behaviour and strategies to competitors' strategies
- Deciding how to implement competitive strategies.

Organizing

- Deciding what jobs need to be done within an organizational unit
- Deciding how various jobs within an organizational unit can be grouped together, etc.
- Deciding how much authority should be delegated to various organizational positions
- Determining how best to train people for their jobs.

Leading

- Finding ways of increasing productivity in marketing activities.

Controlling

- Deciding what systems of control are needed
- Setting standards
- Identifying why standards/objectives have not been achieved.

THE NEED TO BE READY FOR CHANGE

Executives must be ready for anything which requires having the necessary tools to proactively combat change. As Morgan (1989) states:

> Many organisations and their managers drive toward the future while looking through the rear-view mirror. They manage in relation to events that have already occurred, rather than anticipate and confront the challenges of the future.

If we were not at times 'blocked' in our thinking we would not need creative problem-solving methods. In this chapter we will first consider the nature of problem solving before going on to examine *individual* and *organizational* blocks to creative thinking. In addition, we will look at ways of dealing with both kinds of blocks. It is the existence of these blocks that gives rise to the need for a structured creative problem-solving process and for training to help overcome particular mindsets (Exhibit 3.4).

EXHIBIT 3.4   RONEX INDUSTRIES: OVERCOMING MINDSET

Ronex Industries is a large electronics distributor that has been in business since the 1950s and recently reinvented itself in a way that made it the talk of the entire electronics distribution industry. Ronex has 38 locations with about 1,300 employees, half of whom are salespeople. The CEO describes the organization as a junction box, selling and packaging the goods of over 100 suppliers to meet the needs of over 30,000 customers.

Until the early 1990s, Ronex was a master of MBO-based compensation plans. It was very proud of its elaborate system of incentives for everyone in the organization. Then, the CEO and other senior managers in the company were exposed to ideas about creative thinking. They began to realize that the MBO-system they were so proud of was actually a barrier to innovation as it discouraged full co-operation between business team members and increased sub-optimization.

Over a one-year period, Ronex eliminated all individual incentives, including sales com-missions and all supplier-sponsored promotions. This action created a flurry in the industry as it was labelled everything from 'communist' to 'visionary'. It turned out to be more on the visionary side as it set up an environment which has created a doubling in sales and earnings, a reduction in employee turnover of over 50 per cent, and the achievement of an ISO 9002 certification in every warehouse and value-added operation in less than six months, without using outside consultants.

MINDSET

Mindset is a condition where an individual is over-sensitized to some part of the information available at the expense of other parts. Mindsets can be useful:

- It helps to become sensitized to some important things and serves us well – for example, red lights act as warnings and alert us to impending danger.
- As a result of learning from experience, mindset sensitizes us to patterns that remind us of ways which have enabled us to solve past problems. We do not have to reinvent the wheel each time that we encounter the same problem. For example, if when dealing with an irate customer we have found an approach that seems to be satisfactory from the point of view of dealing with the situation, then when we subsequently encounter another irate customer we can deal with the situation using our acquired knowledge.

When mindset blocks us

Duncker (1945) investigated how past experience may block productive problem solving. He suggested the expression 'functional fixedness' to refer to a block against using an object in a new way that is required to solve a problem. Interesting real-life examples of functional fixedness are provided by Weizenbaum (1984). According to the latter, the steam engine had been in use for a hundred years to pump water out of mines before Trevithick had the idea of using it as a source of locomotive power

– it had only been seen as a tool to help pump water out of mines. The computer had also been used for a long time as a calculator before its use as a general symbol manipulator was envisaged.

It would seem that although mindset can provide us with substantial benefits, unfortunately there are times when it can stand in the way of progress. Mindset can create difficulties for executives when they are facing new or novel problems. When stuck on a problem, executives tend to follow their mindset and this may be counterproductive as far as previously unencountered problems are concerned. Mindset is often characterized by 'one right answer' thinking, always looking for reasons why something will not work and an over-regard for logical thinking (Exhibit 3.5).

Executives may have learned from past experience that a particular way of dealing with a problem usually leads to a satisfactory solution. Constant successful application of the approach reinforces the belief that this way is the correct way to approach the problem and even the only way to approach the problem. When a new problem arrives that defies solution by the learned approach, executives become stuck and do not know what to do.

BARRIERS TO INDIVIDUAL'S CREATIVITY

Many researchers have attempted to address the phenomenon of barriers to creativity. These include Arnold (1962), Adams (1974), Jones (1987) and Majaro (1991). All have produced detailed lists of the various kinds of barriers to creative problem solving. Some barriers limit an individual's creative output and are related to the people themselves. On the other hand, there are those that emanate from the environment in which people operate. Personal barriers may be subdivided into physiological barriers, such as the perceptual limitations of the senses or the brain's data handling capacity, and psychological barriers related to the person's behaviour or attitudes. Arnold (1962) suggested:

1 *Perceptual blocks*, which prevent a person receiving a true, relevant picture of the outside world.
2 *Cultural blocks*, which result from influences of society.
3 *Emotional blocks* such as fear, anxiety and jealousy.

EXHIBIT 3.5   FORD MODEL 'T' – THE MINDSET OF HENRY FORD

Henry Ford's model 'T' remained unchanged for years while General Motors (Chevrolet) was making changes often using new technology.

Henry Ford said: 'We'll give the customer any colour he wants as long as it is black.' It was an arrogant statement by an arrogant man who had been on top so long he thought nothing could dislodge him from the number one position.

In the late 1920s Ford nearly went out of business as a result of this myopic approach. General Motors (Chevrolet) took over as number one in the US and Ford did not catch up until the late 1980s.

Adams added a fourth category:

4   Intellectual and expressive blocks.

Dealing with individual blocks to creativity

Jones (1987) initiated a study designed to find out more about the factors which inhibit creativity. In reviewing the literature on the subject he found that several authors included perceptual, cultural and emotional blocks within their taxonomies while others mentioned factors such as errors in thinking and personal fears. He identified four typologies of blocks. These were derived from cluster analysis of self-reported items. The typologies are:

- *Strategic blocks*. 'One right answer approaches', inflexibility in thinking. These affect the approach taken to solve problems. They include the tendency to rely heavily on past experience or particular techniques without challenging their appropriateness; focusing on a narrow range of options for either problem definition or problem solving; and adapting an overly serious approach to problems which prevents the emergence of a playful, imaginative and humorous climate.
- *Value blocks*. 'Over-generalized rigidity influenced by personal values.' These occur when personal beliefs and values restrict the range of ideas contemplated. Values co-exist and failure to reconcile them contributes to difficult personal and organizational dilemmas.
- *Perceptual blocks*. 'Over-narrow focus of attention and interest.' These arise from a lack of sensory awareness at a physical level and therefore contribute to a lack of awareness of implications of situations.
- *Self-image blocks*. 'Poor effectiveness through fear of failure, timidity in expressing ideas, etc.' These reduce effectiveness in advancing ideas assertively. They arise from a lack of self-confidence in the value of one's own ideas. Individuals may be reluctant to seek help and talk about personal feelings. This barrier seems to be the greatest impediment to the successful implementation of new ideas.

Jones's approach has resulted in training applications which centre on personal feedback and counselling, including suggestions for the most appropriate mechanisms for developing improved skills. Strategic blocks can be challenged through creative problem-solving training. Values, however, are a more difficult problem – but creating an awareness of personal values in the individual offers some respite. Perceptual blocks can be freed through observation and self-image blocks can profit from assertiveness training.

BLOCKS TO CREATIVE THINKING IN ORGANIZATIONS

Some of the major blocks (see also Exhibit 3.6) are:

- Emphasis on managerial control – control can stifle creativity since autonomy and a degree of freedom are critical ingredients of creative thinking. Moreover, traditional financial controls are not appropriate for long-term innovation efforts.

EXHIBIT 3.6   BLOCKS TO CREATIVITY IN ORGANIZATIONS

People and organizations tend to fall into a variety of traps when trying to become more innovative:

1   Identifying the wrong problem
2   Judging ideas too quickly
3   Stopping with the first good idea
4   Failing to get the support of key personnel in the organization
5   Failing to challenge assumptions.

- Short-range thinking – there is a tendency to give priority to quick returns with financially measurable results.
- Analysis paralysis – ideas are often over-analysed and time is lost along with any competitive advantage.
- Rigid hierarchical structures – an unpredictable environment requires a responsive organizational structure and this is not characteristic of most organizations.
- There is a tendency to look for one project that is likely to generate a big pay-off, rather than a number of smaller projects with small to medium pay-offs. Good small projects can thus often be overlooked.
- Market versus technology-driven product planning – there tends to be an over-emphasis on market research, in line with the marketing orientation adopted by many companies. Although the marketing orientation is very important it is often implemented at the expense of good ideas which come out of R&D and which never get off the ground.
- Pressure to achieve and do more with less resources – R&D departments are often penalized for cutting costs; the more the department saves one year, the less it has to play with the next. Paradoxically, the more companies have to cut back on expenditure, the more creative they must become.
- Lack of a systematic approach to innovation – a lack of real ideas about how to innovate.
- The belief that some people are creative and others are not.

Ways of dealing with such blocks include:

- Encouraging prudent risk taking.
- Freedom of thought – some degree of autonomy.
- Linking rewards with specific performance.
- Encouraging different viewpoints on problems.
- Positive involvement of top management.
- Continual flow of ideas.
- Responding positively to new ideas.

ELEMENTS OF CREATIVE ORGANIZATIONS

One can divide the characteristics of organizational creativity into four distinct elements (the four Ps of creativity):

- *People*: teams or individuals
- *Processes*: how ideas are developed and innovation accomplished
- *Place*: creative environment
- *Product*: the output of the creativity.

One cannot treat each one of the four Ps in isolation from the other. They are interdependent. Perhaps the one to receive the least attention is Place. An organization concerned with creating a climate that influences effective creative activity (see Exhibit 3.7) should provide at least the following:

- *Resources*: these should be appropriate and sufficient
- *Security*: adequate salary and security of job tenure
- *Trust*: allow for mistakes
- *Reward/recognition*: feedback, recognition and reward.

QUESTIONS

1   What are the various quantitative and financial appraisals that a firm should undertake when undertaking a self audit?

EXHIBIT 3.7   QUIETSLEEP CORPORATION: CREATIVITY IN ACTION

Quietsleep Corporation is a small company that develops medical technology for treating sleep apnea. The company has created a unique, innovation-focused, risk-honouring environment that has helped it take a leading position in its specialized industry, competing with much larger firms. Its mission statement reads: 'Innovating to Help People' and its tag line is 'Where Sleep Technology Is Headed' since it is committed to staying at the forefront of innovation and technology.

In its application, Quietsleep lists the critical skills for innovation as being 'empathy and caring'. It calls the perfect innovation incubator the ability to empathize with customers, suppliers and team-mates and to genuinely care about their passions, fears, concerns and needs. Quietsleep's environment of innovation has allowed it to dominate a profitable market niche in spite of competition from much larger organizations.

2 What kinds of non-quantitative, non-financial analyses should a firm undertake when making a self appraisal?

3 Creativity in strategy formulation is important. How might organizations deal with the various blocks to creative thinking that can arise?

4 How would you measure creativity in an organization?

5 How would the various kinds of self appraisals that a firm could undertake be used in the course of formulating strategies? Examine each aspect of self appraisal in detail.

CASE STUDIES

Barrington Breweries

Barrington Breweries has increasing volume sales and market shares for most of its brands. It recognizes that there are opportunities for expansion in Europe, the US and Pacific Rim countries. Nevertheless, there are some ominous threats appearing on the horizon. Foreign competition, price war – eroded margins, retail shakeout – lack of capital investment, increase in trade purchasing power, commodity pricing and perception of lager, and market wrecking by existing competitors have all figured of late.

In analysing its own internal strengths the company feels that it has a good mission statement with focus/vision/clear objectives. It also considers that it has a comprehensive distribution network, with tied houses. The brewery is a market leader in many segments. This, it believes, it has achieved mainly as a result of being a low-cost producer – economies of scale and experience it has gained in the trade.

At the same time, the firm recognizes that it has many internal weaknesses. It is a bureaucratic super-tanker – traditional conservative approach to business – predominantly hierarchical in structure. In some market sectors it is losing ground and the company also feels that it is perhaps too dependent on tied estate. Moreover, despite being a low-cost producer, no price leadership exists in the business. Perhaps even more serious is the inertia in the company and internal resistance to change – especially among shareholders.

QUESTIONS

1 What kind of mindsets is the firm most likely to experience?

2 What kind of self-analysis ought the firm to undertake?

Avila Batteries

Avila Batteries was founded in the late 1950s by Fernando Bracamente to make starter batteries for cars and trucks. Situated around 50 kilometres or so to the west of Madrid, Avila is in a very convenient position to serve central and northern Spanish towns and cities. Moreover, no difficulties are presented in gaining access to the remaining parts of Spain, the whole of Portugal and much of the south and southwest of France.

The firm grew slowly in size during the 1950s and 1960s. In the 1970s it stabilized its share of the Spanish market at around 5 per cent of national sales and earned as much again in sales from exports to Portugal and France. This was a position it held on to until the late 1990s when market share, sales and profits in all markets began to slip. The family management of Avila Batteries had always taken the view that it didn't want to outgrow the family membership and that a priority was to keep ownership of the firm in the family. In the past, it had forgone large growth opportunities for fear of losing control of the business.

The change in fortunes in the early 2000s accompanied Fernando's retirement. His successor, his son-in-law, took over the business at a time when competitors were making a big drive to capture larger shares of business on the Iberian peninsular. Juan Fernandez, the new supremo of Avila Batteries, was keen to expand the business. He had waited nearly twenty years for the opportunity to take control and on succeeding to the business was extremely perturbed to learn that it was at a period when the firm's business was declining for the first time in its history.

Juan did not suffer from blinkered thinking. He knew exactly what was going on in the business environment and he wanted to take action that would put the firm on a strong footing for the twenty-first century. As a priority he saw the need to undertake some creative thinking with respect to dealing with the situation.

QUESTIONS

1   What kind of self-analysis ought the firm to undertake?
2   How should Juan set about the task of getting some creative ideas?
3   What suggestions have you got regarding creative courses of action he might pursue in order to remedy the situation of falling sales, market share and profits?

Chapter 4

Industry analysis

INTRODUCTION

Organizations operate within markets and these markets are within industries. The strategic window of opportunity opens out on a market within an industry. Understanding the nature of the industry and how it changes is thus crucial to understanding the process of how strategic-windows can be opened and closed by external forces.

Industries and markets are different entities. Whereas markets can be looked upon as groups of customers with similar buying needs, industries are collections of organizations with common products and technologies. Vehicle makers are an example of an industry, whereas car products represent a market – the products and services customers use to maintain their cars. Both a knowledge of markets and industries helps to identify competition.

Industries, like products (see Chapter 2) have life cycles. As with products, industries progress through their life cycles and as they do so the nature of competition and consumer demand changes. Naturally, this has implications for the opening and closure of strategic windows. In this chapter, we examine the implication of the different stages in the industry life cycle for the marketing activities of the organization. In addition to the progression through a life cycle, the entire nature of industries can be different or even change from one stage in the life cycle to the next. Many industries are fragmented – a state where no one firm predominates the others. The chapter also introduces the notion of strategic groups. These are groups within an industry which follow similar strategies and serve similar customers. The chapter also gives consideration to SPACE analysis which like portfolio analysis (see Chapter 2) summarizes a large number of strategic-issues in a few dimensions. It relates industry strength to competitive advantage and the financial strength of a firm. The Boston Consultancy Group competitive advantage matrix is also introduced and examined. This recognizes that strategic groups within an industry have different levels of profitability and it helps to classify the competitive environments that coexist within an industry.

The material in this chapter presents an understanding of the kinds of strategies and problems that firms adopt or encounter when operating in different stages of the industry life cycle or in different types of industrial settings. Understanding the stage of the industry life cycle in which a firm is operating is a key factor in marketing planning. As will be seen below it has implications for other kinds of marketing analysis that have to be undertaken. Although the emphasis of these early chapters is on analysis, in this chapter analysis must go hand in hand with understanding the dynamics of the industry and the strategies that firms can pursue.

INDUSTRY LIFE CYCLES

In the same way that products have life cycles so too do industries. It has to be remembered that initially the concept of the product life cycle was based on the notion that technologies have life cycles and that it was the technologies incorporated in products that gave the latter life cycles. Of course, other factors are also relative to the product life. However, since industries are about products and technologies it is not too surprising that they too should have life cycles. The three key stages which we shall look at below are growth, maturity and decline (see Figure 4.1). We shall also look at two other relevant aspects of an industry – the amount of hostility that exists in an industry and the amount of fragmentation that has taken place. In both cases we will relate this to strategy.

ANALYSIS OF EMERGING AND DEVELOPING INDUSTRIES

Emerging industries are either newly formed or reformed industries that have been produced by technological innovations, shifts in cost relationships, emergence of new consumer needs, or other economic and sociological changes that make a new product or service a potentially viable business opportunity (Porter, 1980a). In such a situation, from the viewpoint of formulating strategy there are no preconceived ideas on how to operate competitively.

Considerable uncertainty exists about the technology and the strategic approaches adopted by industry participants. There is little or poor information about competitors, their customers and what is happening in the industry. Often there is ignorance regarding which firms are actually competitors and reliable industry sales and market share data are often unavailable (Exhibit 4.1).

In the case of producers, the initial small production volume and lack of experience with the product often combine to produce high costs relative to those the industry can potentially achieve. Often there is a steep learning curve in operation and ideas come rapidly in terms of improved

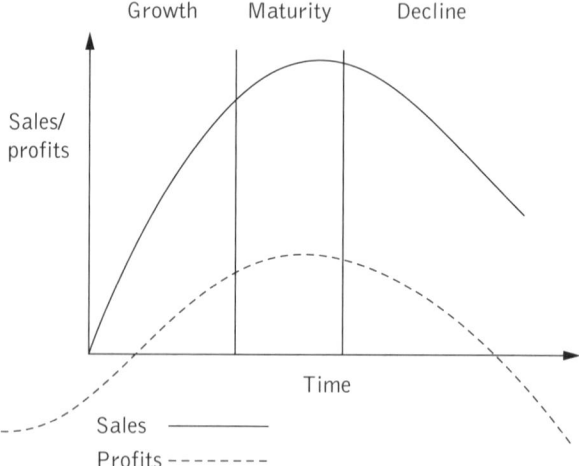

Figure 4.1 *Industry life cycle*

EXHIBIT 4.1   CHARACTERISTICS OF EMERGING INDUSTRIES

1   Emerging industries are either newly formed or reformed industries that have been produced by technological innovations, shifts in cost relationships, emergence of new consumer needs, or other economic and sociological changes that make a new product or service a potentially viable business opportunity.

2   Uncertainty exists about the technology and the strategic approaches adopted by industry participants. There is little or poor information about competitors, their customers and what is happening in the industry and reliable industry sales and market share data are often unavailable.

3   The initial small production volume and lack of experience with the product often combine to produce high costs relative to those the industry can potentially achieve.

4   From the customer's point of view, changeover costs from what they currently use can be expensive.

procedures, plant requirements for changeover engineering, or R&D costs of changeover, costs in modifying interrelated stages of production, or related aspects of the business.

From the customer's point of view, changeover costs from what they currently use can be expensive. There is also the cost of obsolescence. For some buyers, where successive generations of technology in the emerging industry will make early versions of products obsolete, all the benefits they require may be obtained from the first generation. Others, however, will be forced to acquire successive generations of the new product to remain competitive.

Given the nature of the situation, under such circumstances, analysis of the situation has to be based on primary research and data collection. Although information collected in this way may seem to be relatively expensive, it can pay dividends by enabling firms to establish themselves early in such developing industries with the benefit of possibly being a market leader. Good marketing information systems need to be put in place to collect and assimilate whatever sparse data can be collected about customers, competitors and other relevant factors.

ANALYSIS OF MATURING INDUSTRIES

Growth in evolving industries slows down with time, but maturity does not occur at any fixed point in development. It can be delayed by innovations or other events that maintain continued growth, and strategic breakthroughs may even lead mature industries to recover rapid growth. Industries can experience more than one transition to maturity. In many ways this is similar to the concept of the product life cycle where the cycle can be extended by product face-lifts and so on. Any analysis of an industry aimed at assessing whether or how the transition to maturity is taking place has to take account of these factors.

Clues concerning the transition to maturity may be obtained by studying the significant changes that take place in the competitive environment during this stage of development. Analysis should try to identify those competitors that do not perceive the need for such changes very clearly or may perceive them but be reluctant to make the often substantial changes in strategy that are required. Such firms, their markets and customers are obvious targets to attack when formulating marketing strategy. The reason that they are myopic in their thinking may go beyond strategic considerations and have its roots in the organizational structure and leadership of those competitors. It is these implications which may underpin the reluctance to make appropriate strategic changes.

Decline in industry growth rate means that firms cannot keep up their own growth rate in the industry simply by holding their market share. Maintaining growth rate in sales requires that market share has to be increased at the expense of competition. Competitors who have so far coexisted amicably may regard such a change in strategy as aggressive and irrational. Moreover, it may lead to substantial retaliation. Price cutting, new forms of promotional activity and new additional services may be the order of the day. Firms need to monitor their growth rates and market share very closely and analysis should take into account the likely reactions to competitors of any new strategic moves that the firm is likely to take and any proactive moves that competitors themselves are likely to make.

As customers get used to the product they become more critical in their appraisal of what firms have to offer and also become more brand conscious. Customers' attention moves from deciding whether to purchase the product to making choices among brands. This change means that the firms supplying the goods must reassess their strategy. Slower growth, more knowledgeable customers and greater technological maturity means that competition is based more upon level of service and cost control. Key questions that the analyst has to answer here relate to responses the firm should make to changes in customer appraisals of the product offerings and suggesting ways of improving customer service and at the same time keeping costs under control.

During times of growth and expansion, capacity additions to the industry will have been continual and regular. As growth reaches maturity, *over-capacity* can occur. Scaling down operations or at least careful monitoring of any further demands for increasing capacity may be required. Over-capacity can lead to over-production and thence to price warfare to take up the production capacity. Forecasting the rate of industry growth and being able to identify turning points and distinguish them from the impacts of recession is of paramount importance. Understanding whether what is being experienced is a true transition to maturity is extremely important. In hi-tech industries this can be quite difficult since new technologies may appear rapidly and extend the growth phase of hi-tech industries.

The ability to find new products and applications diminishes as maturity is attained and where they can be found they tend to be more risky and costly. As a consequence, a reorientation in terms of approach to R&D is required. Given the high rate of new product failure (see Chapter 11) this puts more pressure on marketing analysts to determine more accurately the demand for new products. It underlines the importance of marketing research activities to do with identifying and testing out new product ideas.

Some international competitors possess radically different cost structures and this means that those who are most favourably placed can often enter foreign markets with a decided advantage over the country's domestic producers. Entry can take the form of exports or foreign investments. The aluminium foil wrappings market is an example of this. For many years Bacofoil has dominated this market. Then came the advent of private label branding by supermarkets and more recently imports from highly competitive overseas producers. Competitor analysis has to be undertaken to identify and evaluate the offerings of both actual and potential entrants to the industry (Exhibit 4.2).

EXHIBIT 4.2   CHARACTERISTICS OF MATURING INDUSTRIES

1   Growth slowing down but maturity does not occur at any fixed point in development.

2   It can be delayed by innovations or other events that maintain continued growth and strategic breakthroughs may even lead mature industries to recover rapid growth. Industries can experience more than one transition to maturity.

3   Significant changes that take place in the competitive environment.

4   Decline in industry growth rate means that firms cannot keep up their own growth rate in the industry simply by holding their market share.

5   Maintaining growth rate in sales requires that market share has to be increased at the expense of competition.

6   Competitors who have so far coexisted amicably may regard such a change in strategy as aggressive and irrational. Moreover, it may lead to substantial retaliation.

7   Price cutting, new forms of promotional activity and new additional services may be the order of the day.

8   As customers get used to the product they become more critical in their appraisal of what firms have to offer and also become more brand conscious.

9   Competition is based more upon level of service and cost control.

10   Over-capacity can lead to over-production and thence to price warfare to take up the production capacity.

11   The ability to find new products and applications diminishes as maturity is attained and where they can be found they tend to be more risky and costly.

12   Some international competitors possess radically different cost structures and this means that those who are most favourably placed can often enter foreign markets with a decided advantage over the country's domestic producers.

IMPLICATIONS OF THE TRANSITION TO MATURITY

Rationalization of the product mix and correct pricing become key issues and place a considerable amount of emphasis on cost analysis. Whereas broad product lines and the introduction of new varieties and options may have characterized the growth phase, at the maturity phase this may no longer be a viable strategy. Emphasis on cost control may accentuate the need to prune and find less risky ways of maintaining market share. The maturity phase puts pressure on the advantage of being able to measure costs of individual items and to set the prices accordingly. Many firms use average cost pricing methods during the growth stage and this means that there will have been some cross-subsidization of products. However, continuing this approach will invite price cutting or new product introductions by competitors against the items that are priced artificially high.

At this stage the emphasis may be on trying to get people to buy more of the product both in terms of amount and frequency of purchase rather than trying to attract new customers. Sales can often be increased by offering additional services or peripheral equipment, or by upgrading and widening the product line. Some degree of diversification of product market scope may result. However, it is a more economical strategy than that of finding new customers since the latter means winning market share which can be costly.

A further point is that more than one cost curve can exist in an industry. Even where a firm is not the overall cost leader it can sometimes find cost curves which will make it a lower-cost producer for certain types of buyer, variety of product or order sizes – this is the key to implementing a *focus strategy*.

The effects of industry maturity may be circumvented by competing internationally. Sometimes goods which are obsolete in the home market may not be so in international markets. Alternatively, the industry structure, within an international context, may be favourable with fewer competitors and less sophisticated and powerful buyers.

Not all firms will attempt the transition to operating in a mature industry. Choice reflects not only availability of resources but also what competitors intend to do and how long it will take to adjust to the new conditions and the long-term profitability during the maturity phase. Disinvestment can be an attractive alternative for some firms. Even the industry leaders may not necessarily be in the best position to make the transitions required if they have substantial inertia built into their growth stage strategies. Indeed, it may well be the smaller firms who have the necessary wherewithal to manage best. The latter may be able to segment the market more easily. Moreover, a new entrant to the industry may possess the requisite resources and be able to establish itself in a strong position.

ANALYSIS OF DECLINING MARKETS

Although one is apt to think that declining markets are ones from which firms are anxious to exit, in fact, they represent good opportunities for firms that tailor their strategies successfully to the demands of the situation. This is because declining markets are not as attractive as growing markets to many competitors and sooner or later scale economies may cause the larger firms to consider withdrawal, thereby leaving an often relatively large market without major forces within it. Moreover, it may be possible for a firm to revitalize an industry. This may be achieved by creating new markets, new products, new applications, revitalized marketing methods, government-assisted growth and/or the exploitation of sub-markets (Figure 4.2). Analysis of the industry in these circumstances has to point to the direction that a firm might take.

New markets are characterized by moves into neglected or ignored market segments with potential for new growth. Sometimes a dormant industry can be revitalized by a new product that makes existing products obsolete and accelerates the replacement cycle. A new application for a product can stimulate new industry growth. A product class can be revived by a revitalized marketing approach. Government-stimulated growth can take the form of tax incentives or legislation giving rise to a new industry or market. Some firms have been successful in declining or mature industries because they have been able to focus on growth sub-areas, pockets of demand that are healthy and even expanding.

Be the profitable survivor

The essence of this strategy is to provide the impetus to encourage competitors to leave the industry so that as the surviving firm a very strong position can be held. In order to do this a firm may:

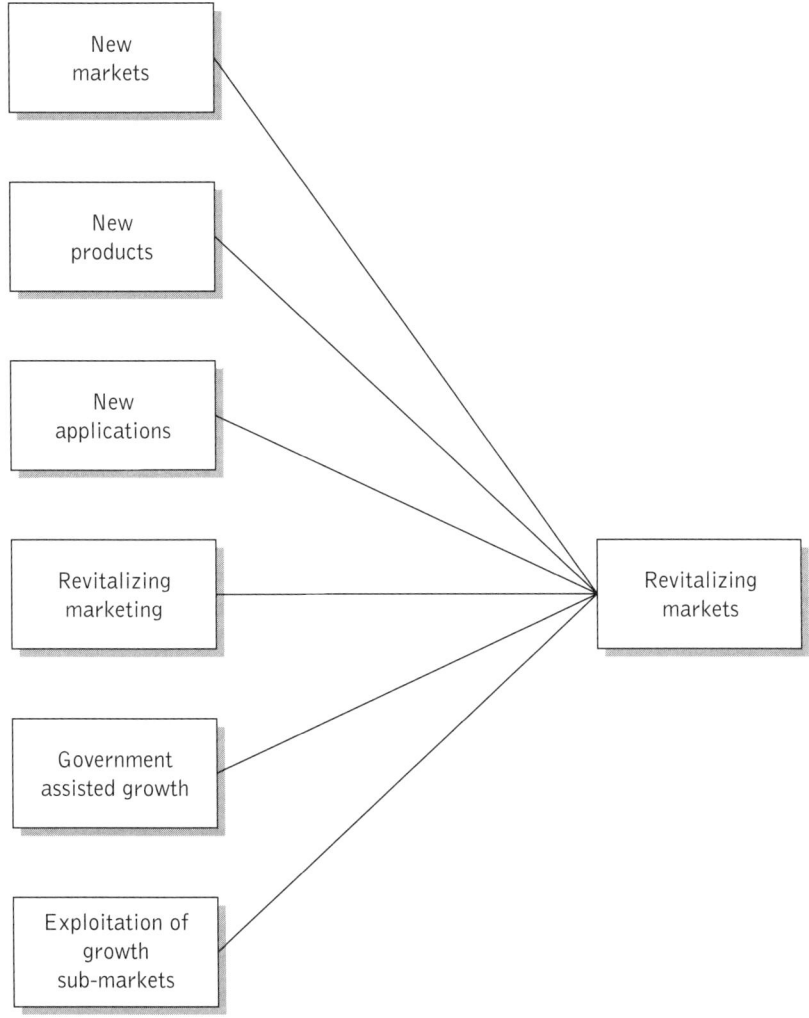

Figure 4.2 *Ways of revitalizing markets*

1 Make it clear to all that it intends to be the surviving leader of the industry.
2 Reduce prices or increase promotions to make the industry less attractive to competitors.
3 Introduce new products and cover new segments so as to deter competitors from finding a profitable niche.
4 Reduce competitors' exit barriers by assuming their long-term contracts, supplying spare parts and servicing the product in the field or even by supplying them with products.
5 Create a national dominant brand.
6 Purchase a competitor's market share or its production capacity.

Milk or harvest

This strategy aims to generate cash flow by reducing investment and operating expenses, even if it causes a reduction in sales and market share. It assumes that the firm has better use for the funds and that the business is not crucial to the firm in any way and that a milking strategy is feasible because sales will decline in an orderly fashion.

Fast milking involves sharp reductions in operating expenditures and even price increases to maximize short-term cash flow and to minimize the possibility that any additional money will be invested in the business. The strategy accepts the risk of a sharp sales decline that could precipitate a market exit. Slow milking involves sharply reducing long-term investment in plant, equipment and R&D, but only gradually reducing expenditures in operating areas such as marketing and service. The latter attempts to maximize the flow of cash over time by prolonging and slowing the decline.

Conditions favouring a milking strategy

1   The decline rate is pronounced and is unlikely to change, but it is not excessively steep and pockets of lasting demand ensure that the decline rate will not suddenly become precipitous.
2   The price structure is stable at a level that is profitable for the efficient firms.
3   The business position is weak but there is enough customer loyalty, perhaps in a limited part of the market, to generate sales and profit in milking mode. The risk of losing relative position with a milking strategy is low.
4   The business is not central to the current mission of the firm.
5   A milking strategy can be successfully managed.

Milking may be preferred to divesting products because the strategy can be reversed if it turns out to be based upon incorrect premises regarding market prospects, competitor moves, cost projections, etc.

The hold strategy

The strategy is a variant of the milking strategy and involves avoiding growth-motivated investment but maintaining an adequate level of investment to maintain product quality, production facilities and customer loyalty. It is appropriate when an industry is declining in an orderly way, pockets of enduring demand exist, price pressures are not extreme, the firm has exploitable assets or skills, and a business contributes by its presence to other business units in the firm (Figure 4.3). It is preferable to an investment strategy when an industry lacks growth opportunities and a strategy for increasing share would risk triggering competitive retaliation. It can be a long-term strategy for managing a cash cow or an interim strategy employed until the uncertainties of a situation are resolved. One problem with the hold strategy is that if conditions change, reluctance or slowness to reinvest may result in lost market share.

Divestment or liquidation

When a business environment and business position are both unfavourable, then divestment or liquidation is called for. Exit decisions may be triggered by:

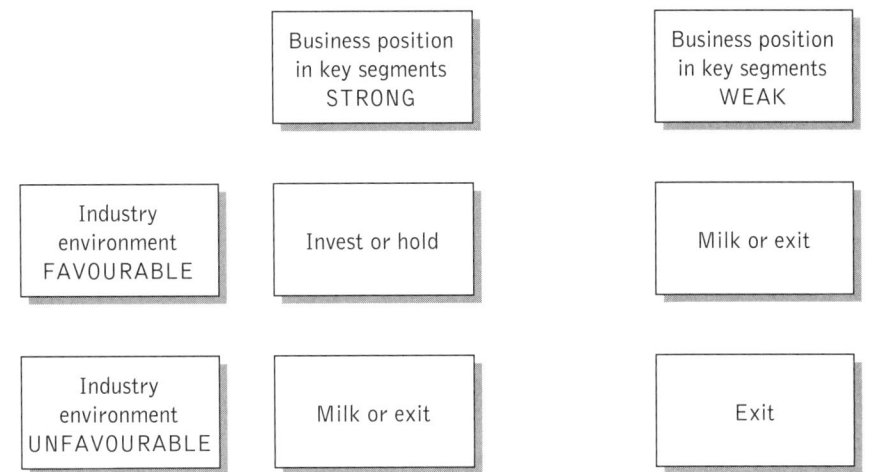

Figure 4.3 *Strategies for declining or stagnant industries*

1 a rapid and accelerating decline rate
2 extreme price pressures
3 a weak business position: the business is incurring losses and prospects are bad
4 the role of the business being superfluous or unwanted
5 exit barriers which can be easily surmounted.

HOSTILE MARKETS

Hostile markets are those with over-capacity, low margins, intense competition and management in disarray. Decline in demand and competitive expansion both contribute to the creation of a hostile market. Declining markets may produce hostile markets often associated with over-capacity, low margins, intense competition and management in turmoil. Hostile markets can also occur in other situations, for instance in growth markets where there is over-capacity as a result of too many competitors.

ANALYSIS OF FRAGMENTED INDUSTRIES

Many firms compete in industries where no one firm has a significant market share and is able to impose a strong influence over the industry. Small and medium-sized firms are often to be found in such industries. The essential feature of such industries is the absence of a market leader having the power to shape the industry. Fragmented industries occur across a broad section of different types of business.

Industries are fragmented for a wide variety of reasons some of which involve underlying economic causes. These include:

- low overall entry barriers
- absence of economies of scale or experience curve

- high transportation costs
- high inventory costs or erratic sales fluctuations
- no advantages of size in dealing with buyers or suppliers
- diseconomies of scale in some important aspect of business
- diverse market needs
- high product differentiation, particularly when based upon image
- exit barriers in place.

Overcoming fragmentation represents a very significant strategic opportunity. The rewards can be high because entry costs are low and there tend to be small and relatively weak competitors who offer little in the way of threats or retaliation. Overcoming fragmentation needs an attack on the fundamental economic factors leading to the fragmented structure. Some common approaches include:

- *Creating economies of scale or experience curve benefits*: process innovations may consolidate an industry.
- *Standardizing diverse market needs*: product or marketing innovations can achieve this.
- *Overcoming those aspects most responsible for fragmentation*.
- *Making acquisitions for a critical mass*: making many acquisitions of neighbouring firms can be successful provided that the acquisitions can be integrated and managed.
- *Spotting industry trends early*: in effect this means examining the impact of market drivers such as political, economic, social, technological and business trends as they impact on the industry.

High personal service and close control are commonly found in fragmented industries so the strategy should involve keeping individual operations small and autonomous. The approach should also feature tight central control with an emphasis on rewarding performance.

Fragmented industries often produce products or services that are difficult to differentiate from one another. An effective strategy can be to increase the added value of the business by concentrating on the nature of the augmented product or service.

When there are numerous items in the product line, an effective strategy for achieving good results focuses on a tightly constrained group of products. This is a kind of *focus* strategy. Another focus strategy is to specialize on a particular category of customer. Customers with the least bargaining leverage are most attractive since they purchase small annual volumes or because they are small in absolute size. Alternatively, a firm may specialize in terms of customers who are the least price sensitive or who most need the added value that the firm can provide along with the basic product or service. Another approach is to service only small orders for which the customer wants immediate delivery and is less price sensitive. Another is to service only custom orders to take advantage of less price sensitivity or to build switching costs.

There can be substantial economies of scale in densely covering a given geographic area by concentrating facilities, marketing and particularly sales activities in those areas. It permits the efficient use of the sales force, effective use of advertising and allows for a single distribution centre, among other things.

The first step is to conduct a full industry and competitor analysis to identify the sources of competitive forces in the industry, the structure within the industry and the position of the significant competitors (Figure 4.4). With this analysis as a background the second step is to identify the causes

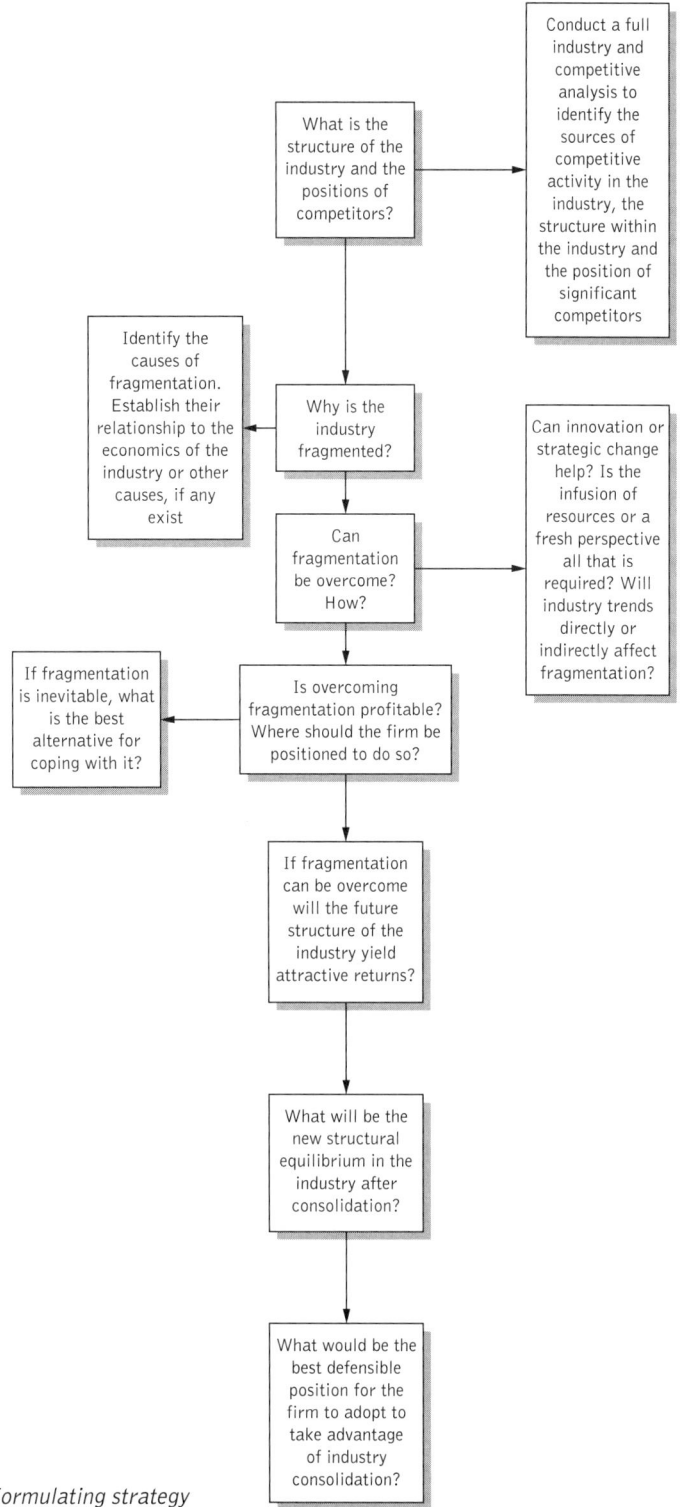

Figure 4.4 *Formulating strategy*

of fragmentation within the industry. It is important to list the causes and establish their relationship, if any, to the economics of the industry. If there are other reasons these too should be identified.

The third step involves examining the causes of fragmentation and establishing whether any of these sources of fragmentation can be overcome through innovation or strategic change. Or whether the infusion of resources or a fresh perspective is all that is necessary. In addition, one should assess whether any of the sources of fragmentation will be altered directly or indirectly by industry trends.

The next step depends upon a positive answer to one of the preceding questions. If fragmentation can be overcome, the firm has to assess whether or not the implied future structure of the industry will yield attractive returns. For the answer to this question the firm has to predict the new structural equilibrium in the industry once consolidation occurs and then it must reapply structural analysis. If the consolidated industry does offer attractive returns then the firm must determine what is the best defensible position for it to adopt to take advantage of the new situation.

If the chances of overcoming fragmentation are unfavourable then the best alternative from those available has to be selected, bearing in mind the particular resources and skills of the firm.

STRATEGIC GROUPS

A strategic group is comprised of firms within an industry following similar strategies aimed at similar customers or customer groups. The identification of strategic groups is fundamental to industry analysis since, just as industries can rise or fall despite the state of the overall business environment, so strategy groups with distinctive competencies can withstand and even defy the general fluctuations within an industry. Understanding the dynamics of existing strategic groups can be productive in understanding their vulnerability to competitive attack.

The separation of strategic groups within a market depends on the barriers to mobility within the industry, i.e. their ability to compete in all markets. Strategic groups often share common competitors because they are often competing to fulfil similar market needs using similar technologies.

The inability of companies to understand the differences in strategic groups is one that causes the frequent failure of companies entering a new market through acquisition. Although the broad business definition, products being sold and customers may be similar within the acquired and the acquiring firm, when the two are in different strategic groups there can be major misunderstandings.

SPACE ANALYSIS

Strategic Position and Action Evaluation (SPACE) (Rowe et al., 1989) analysis extends environmental analysis to consider industry strength and relates this to competitive advantage and financial strength of a company. Similarly to the portfolio models it summarizes a large number of strategic issues on a few dimensions. It plots dimensions of the firm (its financial strengths and competitive advantages) against industry dimensions (environmental stability and industry strength).

Environmental turbulence is seen as being counterbalanced by financial strength – a company with high liquidity or access to other reserves being able to withstand environmental volatility. Industry strength focuses upon attractiveness of the industry in terms of growth potential, profitability and the ability to use its resources efficiently. A firm operating in the industry needs to have a competitive advantage. SPACE analysis involves rating a firm (and its competitors) on all the factors and drawing up a profile as shown below (see Figure 4.5).

The firm illustrated has a predominantly aggressive quadrant posture and enjoys significant advantages, nevertheless it is likely to face threats from new competition. It has to guard against complacency which may prevent it gaining further market dominance by developing products with a definite competitive edge.

A competitive posture is typical of a company with a considerable advantage in an attractive industry. However, the company's financial strength is insufficient to balance the environmental instability it faces. Such a firm clearly needs more financial resources to maintain its competitive position. The need to raise capital or consider a merger is on the horizon.

A conservative posture is typical of a company operating in mature markets where the lack of need for investment has generated financial surpluses. The lack of investment can mean that such a firm will compete at a disadvantage and a lack of opportunities within existing markets may augur long-term vulnerability. They must therefore defend existing products to ensure a continued cash flow while they seek new market opportunities.

A firm with a defensive posture is clearly vulnerable. It has little residual strength to combat competition and needs to foster resources by operating efficiently and being prepared to retreat from competitive markets in order to concentrate on ones it has a chance of defending. The outlook of such a firm is poor.

Aggressive strategies might entail

- market penetration
- market development
- product development
- integration
- diversification.

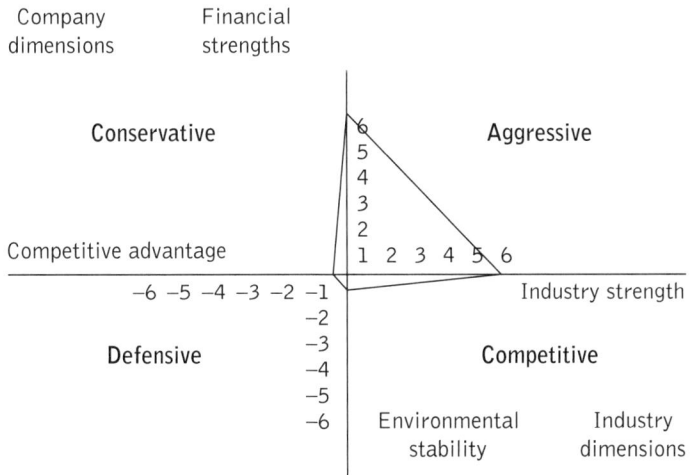

Figure 4.5 *SPACE analysis (1)*

Conservative strategies might entail

■ market penetration
■ market development
■ product development
■ concentric diversification.

Defensive strategies might include

■ retrenchment
■ divestment
■ concentric diversification.

Competitive strategies might include

■ integration
■ market penetration
■ market development
■ product development
■ joint ventures.

An illustrative example of SPACE analysis is shown in Figure 4.6.

THE COMPETITIVE ADVANTAGE MATRIX

Strategic groups within a market have differing levels of profitability. Recognition of this led the Boston Consulting Group (1979) to develop a matrix which helps to classify the competitive environments that can coexist within an industry. The framework identifies two dimensions: the number of approaches to achieving advantage within a market and the potential size advantage.

The stalemate quadrant represents markets with few ways of achieving advantage and where potential size advantage is small. Firms in such a strategic group find trading something akin to a commodity market. The products themselves can be complex, yet the product designs can all converge despite technological improvements. Competitors are forced to compete mainly on the basis of efficient manufacturing and distribution.

The volume quadrant represents the situation where opportunities for differentiation remain few, yet where no potential size advantage exists. It results in industries where large economies of scale can be achieved by a few dominant suppliers.

Specialized markets occur where firms within the same markets have differing returns to scale.

Fragmented markets occur when the market's requirements are less well defined than the stalemate, volume or specialized instances. Success depends on finding niches where particular product specifications are required. Since the opportunity to grow in a single niche is limited, multiple niches are sought (Table 4.1).

Company dimensions

Financial Strength (1)	
Return on Investment	4
Leverage	5
Liquidity	4
Capital required/available	3
Cash flow	4
Exit barriers	4
Risk	4
Average	4.125

Industry strength (2)	
Growth potential	4
Profit potential	3
Financial stability	4
Technological know-how	3
Resource utilisation	5
Capital intensity	5
Market entry ability	5
Productivity	4
Average	4.125

Industry dimensions

Environmental stability (3)	
Technological changes	-5
Rate of inflation	-4
Demand variability	-3
Price range of competing products	-2
Entry barriers	-1
Competitive pressure	-4
Price Elasticity of Demand	-3
Average	-3.142857

Competitive advantage (4)	
Market share	-4
Product quality	-3
Product life cycle	-3
Product replacement cycle	-4
Customer loyalty	-4
Competition's capacity utilisation	-3
Technological know-how	-3
Vertical integration	-3
Average	-3.375

	4	Financial Strength	4
	5	Industry Strength	4.125
	4	Environmental Stability	3.142857
	3	Competitive Advantage	3.375

SPACE analysis

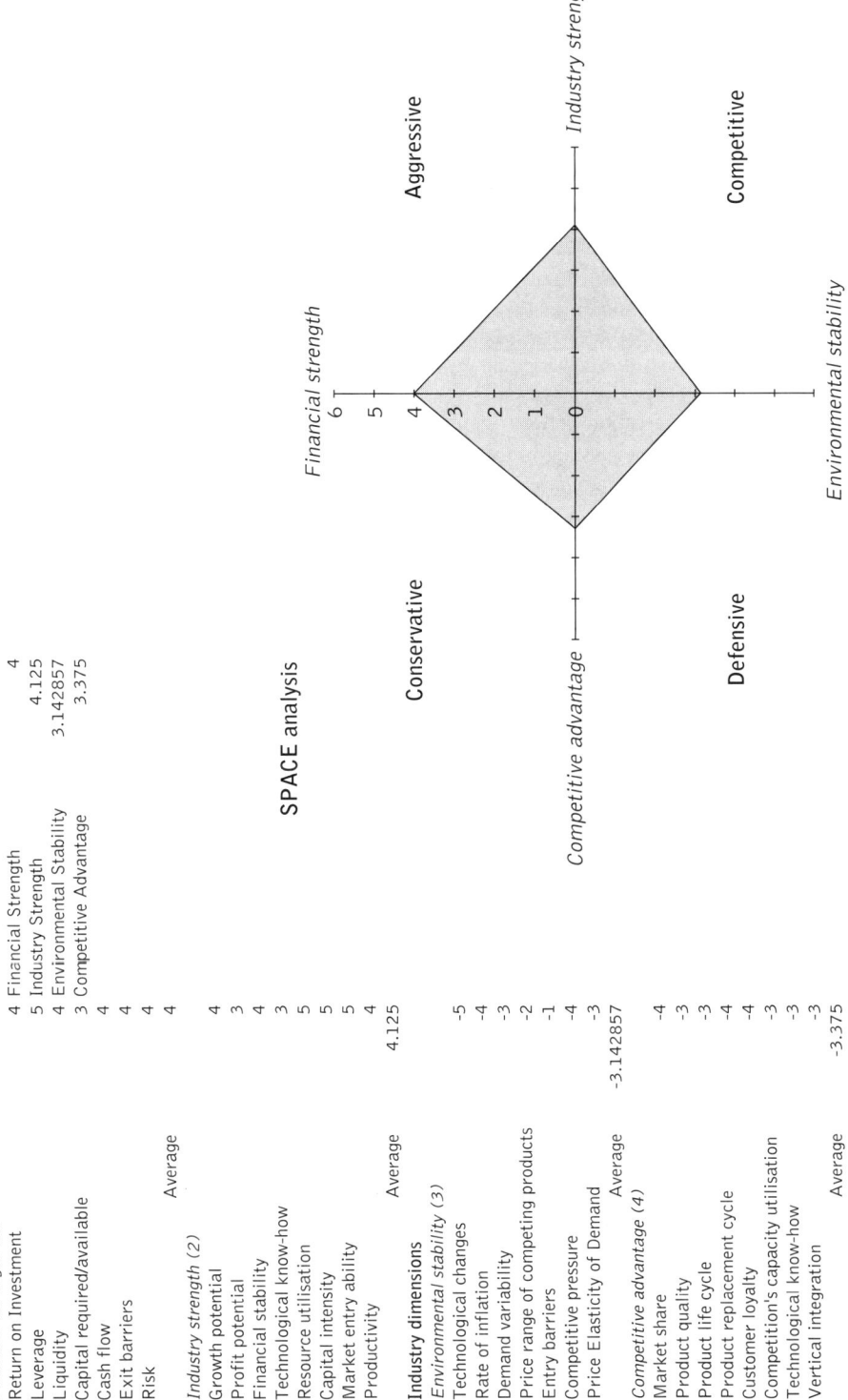

Figure 4.6 SPACE analysis (2)

Table 4.1   *The BCG competitive advantage matrix*

Number of ways to achieve an advantage	Many	Fragmented	Specialized
	Few	Stalemate	Volume
		Small	Large
		Potential size advantage	

QUESTIONS

1   Why is it useful to differentiate between industries at the different stages of their life cycles?
2   How would you determine the stage of the life cycle that a particular industry is at?
3   Discuss the value of SPACE analysis.
4   Indicate how you might use the competitive advantage matrix. What do you regard as its main advantages and disadvantages in terms of being a useful analytical approach?
5   Discuss the relationship of the industry life cycle to the concept of the strategic window.

CASE STUDIES

Stelco

Analysis of past experience shows that firms have sought to protect both supply and demand problems through a series of mergers, acquisitions and takeovers which has led to vertically integrated companies. The belief has been that a high degree of backward and forward integration offers a high degree of security. Vertical integration, however, poses problems for some of the key problems associated with the opening and closure of strategic windows. Concentrating all one's efforts on protecting existing businesses can limit possibilities of exploiting new opportunities in new industries.

Stelco manufactures and sells stainless steel products under well-known international brand names throughout the world. It has a considerable amount of vertical integration with operations ranging from iron-ore extraction, through steel rolling mills to manufacturing products for consumer, industrial and business markets. It also makes castings and components to assemble into its finished products for consumer and business/industrial markets. The organization owns coal-mines, iron-ore mines and transportation companies and owns firms that manufacture finished products and components for consumer and industrial/business customers.

In the case of an industry that is in a long-term growth phase, vertical integration is an excellent strategy. But once the industry matures, and growth begins to flatten out – or even if the growth pattern changes as a result of technology – there is a downward trend and vertical integration does not help the business. The organization does not have the advantage of volume but still has the expense at each level of integration.

Stelco is in an industry that has reached maturity. It has factories all over the world and it argues that it is participating in a global business. This strategy it feels will allow it to provide a more competitive product to different markets. The firm can put together a product for a given market that is far more competitive than it could if it were a fully integrated business building one single product.

QUESTION

Consider what the future may hold for such a company and suggest how it might alter its strategies in the future.

ABC Ltd

ABC Ltd considers itself to be a successful organization operating in a very competitive industry. It earns a better than industry average for its return on investment and returns exceptionally good leverage and liquidity figures. The organisation regularly retains large proportions of its profits for investment in new projects and products and can readily access further capital if this is required. Moreover cash flow in the organization is extremely good and there are few bad debtors.

While the industry in which the organization operates is highly competitive it is not a capital intensive industry in which there are high sunk costs of any description, risks are comparatively low and both exit and entry to the industry is fairly easy. Because of the high growth and profit potential in the industry it does attract new entrants which increases the amount of competition year on year. Because the firm is well established in the industry it is financially stable and has also managed to develop its technological knowhow to keep it well ahead of both existing competition and any would be new entrants to the industry. The organization prides itself on its high productivity which it considers to be critical to its success in the face of strong competition from companies in the Far East with which it has to compete both at home and abroad. Bearing in mind its experience of the industry and strength both in financial terms and technological terms the organization feels well placed to enter into any new markets that can be found.

Despite the industry's growth potential and apparent profit potential it is necessary to keep abreast of the rapid technological changes that beset the industry. While demand and inflation are not considered a problem, competitive pressure is intense and keen pricing of goods is the order of the day. The industry is price elastic so that it is important to ensure that prices are very much in line with those charged by competitors.

The organization is one of the three leading companies in terms of market share in 7 of the 10 markets in which it operates. In the remaining 3 markets it has only very small market shares. In all instances, however, the organization's product quality is rated as very good .

EXERCISE

Conduct a SPACE analysis for the organization.

Majestic Tobacco Company

The Majestic Tobacco Company was set up in the nineteenth century as a result of several smaller companies merging their resources to take advantage of what was to become a rapidly growing industry. Eventually it was to have customers throughout the world with producers operating in many different countries.

During the twentieth century the Majestic Tobacco Company expanded its activities in international markets largely through the acquisition of successful smaller enterprises operating in both developed and developing countries. To ensure a guaranteed source of raw material a substantial programme of backward integration was undertaken. In addition, the firm acquired road transport companies and other shipping facilities to facilitate movement of the raw material and finished products.

Towards the end of the twentieth century consumers started to respond to the growing mountain of evidence which pointed to the health risks associated with consuming tobacco products. By the end of the twentieth century many of the developed countries were actively engaged in trying to find ways of dissuading users from using such products.

Some of the firms in the industry responded to the subsequent decline in demand for tobacco products by trying to find new markets or increase demand in those countries where there were no active attempts being made to discourage consumers. A few companies began to think about moving into other product markets where there were no such health risks involved.

In the early years of the twenty-first century the Majestic Tobacco Company felt that it needed to consider very carefully how it should evolve its future strategy. In particular, it was concerned whether it should try to protect the business that it had built up for over a century or whether it should concentrate on finding new products and opportunities.

QUESTION

How would you advise the company?

Chapter 5

Market analysis

INTRODUCTION

The strategic window opens out upon a market. Market analysis builds on customer and competitor analysis to allow strategic judgements to be made about a market and its dynamics. One of the primary objectives of a market analysis is to assess its prospects for participants. Another key purpose of market analysis is to understand the dynamics of the market. One needs to identify emerging key success factors, trends, threats and opportunities and to develop strategic questions that can guide information gathering and analysis.

Measuring the size of the market, identifying the trends and being able to predict how the market is going to develop in the future are critical factors in understanding the state of strategic windows. Organizations need to have a firm grasp of the methods of assessing market size and forecasting the size to which a market will grow. Both short- and long-term forecasts are important. Long-term forecasts are most useful for medium- and long-term strategic planning purposes, whereas short-term forecasts enable organizations to monitor the effectiveness of earlier long-term forecasts. Market size and projected market growth rates are not the only important dimensions of market analysis. One also needs to understand the factors which influence the profitability of a market at its various stages of development.

Trying to understand the key factors which govern a firm's success are very important. This moves us on from simply looking at the profitability of a market to consideration of cost structures, distribution systems and related trends and developments.

DIMENSIONS OF MARKET ANALYSIS

This varies somewhat according to the context (Figure 5.1). However, the following are often included:

- actual and potential market size
- market growth
- market profitability
- cost structure
- distribution systems
- trends and developments
- key success factors.

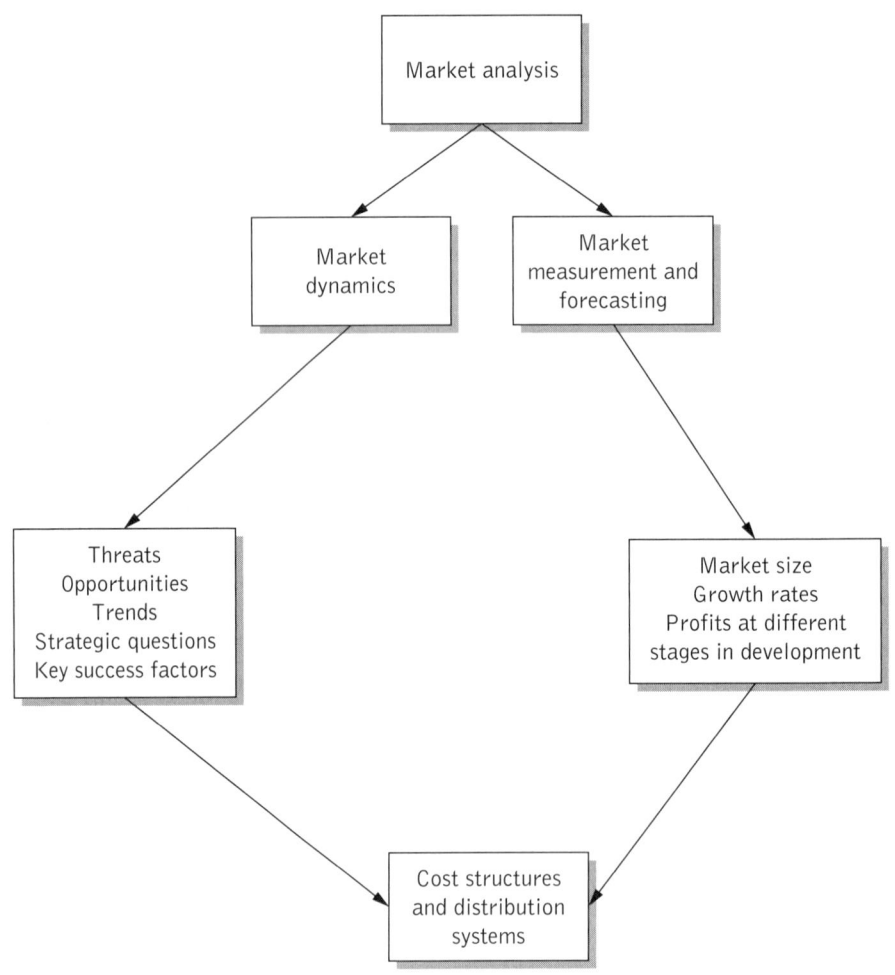

Figure 5.1   Market analysis

ACTUAL AND POTENTIAL MARKET SIZE

A starting point is always the level of sales. Estimates of market size can be based on government sources or trade association findings. Another approach is to obtain information on competitors' sales from published financial sources, customers or even competitors. Still another, though more expensive option, is to survey customers and project their usage to the total market.

The potential market is also of interest. A new use, new user group or more frequent usage could change dramatically the size and prospects for the market.

MARKET GROWTH

After the size of the market and its important sub-markets have been estimated, the focus turns to estimating trends in growth rates or decline rates.

Identifying driving forces

Often the most important strategic question involves the prediction of market sales and identifying the factors that will drive sales directly or indirectly.

A VARIETY OF FORECASTS

There are different types of forecasts. All are useful when trying to establish how the market will grow and what expected sales might turn out to be. These include:

- *Economic forecasts* which help to understand the changes in the business environment that are likely to take place as a result of government fiscal policies in particular. They include predicted changes in the gross domestic product (GDP), inflation, unemployment, balance of payments, money supply, consumer spending, public sector borrowing and so on. The use of such forecasts provides a context to understanding what may take place in the firm's industries and/or markets that it serves. The financial press regularly publishes economic forecasts from specialist forecasting organizations (e.g. National Institute of Economic and Social Research), the treasury and the merchant banks.
- *Environmental forecasts* which relate to political, social, technological, environmental and legal changes as they may affect the firm, its industries and markets. Along with economic forecasts they provide a good starting point for analysis and forecasting demands. Such influences may be viewed and considered as part of different scenarios for the present and for specific points in time in the future.
- *Market and product/service forecasts* which relate to specific sectors and are applied to predictions about the end-user markets into which products are sold. The forecast of end-user demand is an important input in the product forecast.
- *Sales forecasts* which are used to assess what will happen to a company's sales as a result of changes in the market environment and to different levels of sales and promotional effort.

Forecasts can be made for any number of time periods. Usually there are:

- short-term forecasts concerned with periods up to a year
- medium-term forecasts which look beyond a year as far as three years
- long-term forecasts which are predictions beyond three years.

The forecasts of the economic environment and the market enable the organization to steer its future course. They highlight general opportunities and identify unprofitable moves and areas of decline.

SELECTING THE FORECASTING METHOD

Forecasts should be expressed in terms which are appropriate to their purpose. Monetary values should be inflation free and possibly converted to an index. It is usual to qualify a forecast by using different predictions, based on different assumptions and showing an upper and lower limit either side of the best estimate. This should be accompanied by a statement of the assumptions that are made and how they will influence demand. Forecasts should be made using several approaches.

Long-term forecasting can be difficult since so much uncertainty is associated with many of the factors involved and the difficulties surrounding long-term forecasting are often tackled by firms using scenario planning methods.

Defining market demand

Demand can be measured at several levels:

- *product levels*: product item sales, product form sales, product line sales, company sales, industry sales, national sales
- *space levels*: sales to individual customers, sales by territory, area or country, world sales
- *time levels*: short-range, medium-range, long-range sales.

There are 'penetrated markets', 'potential markets', 'available markets' and 'served markets'. The current number of users of a product or service and the sales volume they generate constitutes the 'penetrated market'. There may be figures readily available which indicate this or it may be necessary to establish it by sample survey.

These estimates do not take account of those people who have an interest in buying the product or service, but who currently do not do so. The latter people are important since in looking at future demand they provide a measure of the 'potential market'. Customers must be able to afford the product or service, so in assessing the 'potential market' this must be established. This will redefine the market size.

Opportunity to use the product or service also cuts down on the size of the market. If it is not possible to use a product, then this will obviously restrict the market size. Taking this into account will define the 'available market'. A company has only a limited amount of resources at its disposal and so selects only certain market segments where it feels that it has the capacity to compete effectively and where the market size is sufficiently attractive. This becomes the 'served' or the 'target market'.

Predicting future demand

A company's production schedules, planned manning levels and financial budgeting are all related to the sales forecast. A too optimistic forecast can lead to excess stocks being accumulated, over-production and too high manning levels, and over borrowing or inefficient deployment of financial resources. A pessimistic forecast can lead to large opportunity costs and the creation of frustration among potential buyers of the company's products because delivery is late or not forthcoming.

Firms adopt a variety of approaches to sales forecasting but the basic approach is to:

1 make an environmental forecast regarding inflation, employment, interest rates, consumer spending and saving, business investment, etc.
2 make a forecast of sales and profits to be earned by the industry using the data in stage 1 together with other information which links industry figures to environmental trends
3 make a company sales forecast using the data in stage 2 and assuming a given market share.

Often, however, firms may not know the industry sales level. In such cases sales forecasts are made at the company level at stage 2, and stage 3 is not used.

There are two basic approaches to forecasting sales for established products, both of which have a number of variants. On the one hand there are the methods which rely on asking people questions, and on the other hand there are those which involve the statistical or mathematical analysis of historical data.

Asking people questions

Surveys of buyers' intentions
There are market research organizations which conduct periodic surveys of buying intentions. Using the results of regular sample surveys, predictions of the likely demand for various items are then prepared. Firms can of course carry out the surveys themselves, provided that they have the resources to do so. It is a method which can be applied effectively by producers of industrial plant, machinery and supplies.

Composite of sales force opinion
The sales force is in constant contact with the market and is in an excellent position to provide estimates on potential sales demand. When making use of estimates of the sales force one has to take into account any bias that may exist. For one reason or another the sales force may be biased either in the direction of pessimism or optimism. Another difficulty is that the sales force often may not really appreciate the larger economic factors which may influence sales. Providing one can identify sources of bias and adjust for them in interpreting predictions it is possible to make use of these estimates.

Expert opinion
Expert opinion is another method of forecasting. Experts may include dealers, distributors, suppliers, marketing consultants and even trade associations. A key factor which influences patterns of sales in a country is the state of its economy. Various economic experts can provide their opinions and a government produces its own forecast for the economy.

Analysing past data
Firms tend to base their forecasts on what they have achieved in the past. This approach to forecasting offers few opportunities for mistakes except where there are large variations in sales from one year to the next.

Historical data can provide a useful perspective. However, the strategic interest is not on projections of history, but rather on the prediction of turning points which in turn requires lead indicators. Sales of related equipment or patterns of demographic data can often provide useful lead indicators. In both cases, of course, a reasonable lag between the change in the lead indicator and its impact on the sales of the firm or industry is required in order for it to be of use. Government forecasts of economic activity, provided experience shows them to be reasonably accurate, have a similar effect.

Market sales forecasts, especially of new markets, can be based on the experience of analogous industries. Of course, one has to be able to identify markets with similar characteristics.

Detecting maturity and decline

One particularly important set of turning points in market sales is when the growth phase of the product life cycle changes to a flat maturity phase, and when the maturity phase changes into a decline phase. These transitions are important to the health and nature of the market. Often they are accompanied by changes in key success factors. Historical sales and profit patterns of a market can help to identify the onset of maturity or decline, but the following are often more sensitive indicators:

1 *Price pressure* caused by over-capacity and the lack of product differentiation. When growth slows or even reverses, capacity developed under a more optimistic scenario becomes excessive. Furthermore, the product evolution process often results in most competitors matching product improvements. Thus it becomes more difficult to maintain a meaningful differentiation.

2 *Buyer sophistication and knowledge*. Buyers tend to become more familiar and knowledgeable as the product matures and thus become less willing to apply a premium price to obtain the security of an established name. As a result, the value of big names recedes.

3 *Substitute products or technologies*.

4 *Saturation*. When the number of first-time buyers declines, market sales should mature or decline.

5 *No growth sources*. The market is fully penetrated and there are no visible sources of growth from new uses or users.

6 *Customer disinterest*. A reduction of the interest of customers in applications, new product announcements and so on.

FORECASTING METHODS

Forecasting amounts to estimating some future event that is outside the control of the organization and which provides a basis for managerial planning. The estimates produced often form the basis of production planning, sales force planning, setting advertising appropriations, estimating cash flow, and assessing the need for innovation. Moreover, marketing plans are only useful if the size of current and future markets is carefully measured and estimated. Such information is a useful starting point from which to determine how resources should be allocated among markets and products or services.

Methods which adopt a solely time dependent approach

Classical time series analysis

The first set of methods are those which are based on time series analysis. In this case, it is assumed that sales simply vary as a function of time. The time effects are divided into:

- *cycle*: fluctuations every few years (e.g. the effect of trade cycles as various major economies in the world are hit by booms and slumps)
- *trend*: a general upward, downward or static (no trend) pattern (e.g. upward trend of sales of video recorders during the growth phase of the life cycle)
- *seasonal*: systematic variations at certain times of the year (e.g. additional sales of bathing costumes in the summer months)
- *erratic*: unpredictable or random variations (e.g. demand interrupted by an industry-wide strike).

Erratic variation is taken into account when making forecasts, but one does not attempt to predict it exactly. One merely expresses it as the error one attaches to the sales forecast. This method is most suitable for forecasting sales of products where the unexplained variation is small.

The trend component results from developments in a population, the formation of capital and developments in technology. It is evidenced by a general upward or downward shift in the pattern of sales. If there is no such pattern then there is assumed to be no trend.

The cycle depicts the wavelike flow of sales over a number of years and is most useful when examining data for use in intermediate range forecasts (3–7 years). Traditionally, the cycle represents swings in economic activity.

The seasonal component refers to recurrent sales patterns that may exist within the period of a single year. This will reflect things such as weather factors, holidays, seasonal buying habits and so on.

Erratic variation comprises such things as strikes, fashions and other unforeseen circumstances. These factors are unpredictable and need to be removed from past data in order to inspect the other three elements. Time series analysis consists of deconstructing the original sales data into its trend, cyclical, seasonal and erratic components. The series is then recombined to produce a sales forecast.

Demand for period t is:

$$D = [A + T_t]/(S_t) + \text{Erratic variation}$$

where A = Average level

T_t = Trend component

S_t = Seasonal factor

Example

Imagine Table 5.1 represents quarterly data on shipments of a particular commodity.

There is more than one way to forecast time series data such as these, but perhaps the best method is to use dummy variables and multiple regression analysis. Multiple regression is a statistical tool that can be applied to past data to discover the most important factors influencing sales and their relative influence. The dummy variables in this particular case represent the factors influencing sales. The approach consists of creating a variable for each of the four quarters (Table 5.2) and the following equation is then estimated by multiple linear regression analysis:

$$\text{Sales} = B_0 + B_1 \text{ Time} + B_2 \text{ Winter} + B_3 \text{ Spring} + B_4 \text{ Summer}$$

Table 5.1 *Quarterly data on shipments of a particular commodity*

Period	Year	Sales (tons)
1	2006	436
2		291
3		357
4		529
5	2007	386
6		304
7		333
8		471
9	2008	383
10		336
11		365
12		539

Table 5.2 *Dummy variables and multiple regression analysis*

Time	Sales	Winter	Spring	Summer	Autumn
1	436	1	0	0	0
2	291	0	1	0	0
3	357	0	0	1	0
4	529	0	0	0	1
5	386	1	0	0	0
6	304	0	1	0	0
7	333	0	0	1	0
8	471	0	0	0	1
9	383	1	0	0	0
10	336	0	1	0	0
11	365	0	0	1	0
12	539	0	0	0	1

It should be noted that one of the dummy variables has to be left out so that the regression can be solved by computer – in this case 'Fall' is omitted. The values obtained are:

$$B_0 = 510.5 \quad B_1 = 0.3125 \quad B_2 = -110.396$$

$$B_3 = -202.042 \quad B_4 = -161.021$$

Substituting values into the equation for subsequent periods enables a forecast of sales to be made. For example:

Period 13 forecast sales $= 510.5 + 0.3125 \times 13 - 110.396 \times 1 = 360$

Moving average

This is one of the simplest methods and usually trend seasonal or cyclical patterns are not included in this method, although in the more advanced methods it is possible to do so.

The average demand is the arithmetic mean of demand from a number (N) of past periods.

$$A_t = [D_1 + D_2 + \ldots + D_{t-N+1}]/N$$

The forecast demand for period$_t$ + 1 is a projection of the past average demand. The number of periods included in the average can be increased to give more importance to past demand (referred to as damping). Moreover, in order to fine tune the sensitivity of the moving average to certain periods, a weighting factor W_t can be applied to those periods:

$$F_{t+1} = A_t = W_1 D_1 + W_2 D_2 + \ldots + W_N D_{t-N+1} \text{ where } W_1 + W_2 + \ldots + W_N = 1$$

Exponential smoothing

Many businesses produce many hundreds or thousands of products. Notable examples are the firms operating in the pharmaceutical industry. For such firms a simple forecasting technique is required which requires the minimum of data. In its simplest form exponential smoothing requires only three pieces of information:

1   the period's actual sales, Q_t
2   the current period's smoothed sales, q_t
3   a smoothing parameter, a, a value between 0 and 1.

The sales forecast for the next period is given by the formula:

$$q_t + 1 = aQ_t + (1 - a)q_{1t}$$

Forecasts of this kind are handled by computer. Using an iterative procedure (trial and error), the computer program can regularly determine that value of a which gives the most satisfactory results in making forecasts. The value is the one that gives the best fit to past sales. Once the system has been set up, all that one has to do is to add new sales figures to the database as and when they occur. There are a number of more sophisticated variants on this approach, e.g. double exponential smoothing, and exponential smoothing incorporating seasonal and trend components.

Statistical demand analysis

So far, the statistical or mathematical approaches we have considered treat the factors that seem to influence sales as regularly recurring phenomena. The difficulty with this approach is that some patterns do not reappear at regular intervals. For example, although there are economic booms and slumps from time to time, their patterns are not so precise as to enable accurate forecasts to be made.

Statistical demand analysis attempts to identify the source of all influences on demand so that more accurate forecasts can be made. The basic statistical method to take account of such factors is multiple regression analysis. Experience seems to indicate that the factors most commonly considered are price, income, population and marketing promotion.

The first stage in a regression analysis is to build a causal model in which one tries to explain sales in terms of a number of independent variables. For example, we might conjecture that industry sales of umbrellas are related to their relative price (P), personal disposable income (I), relative advertising expenditure and the absolute level of rainfall (R). We would express this relationship in the form of an equation:

$$S = a_0P + b_1I + b_2A + b_3R$$

What one has to do is to estimate the parameters for a_0, b_1 . . . b_3 and apply them to quantifications of P, I, A and R for the period of the forecast.

In principle, demand equations of this variety are acquired by fitting the best equations to historical or cross-sectional data. The coefficients of the equation are estimated according to what is called the 'least squares criterion'. According to this criterion, the best equation is the one that minimizes a measure of the error between the actual and the predicted observations. The better the fit, the more useful will be the equation for forecasting purposes.

Although this is a popular technique, one has to use it with care. There must always be an adequate number of observations – in making annual forecasts, 10–15 years' data is not unreasonable, where there are four independent variables. Another problem is that what seem to be independent variables turn out to influence each other and are not very independent at all. For example, relative price and relative advertising expenditure may well influence each other, since advertising costs can be reflected in the selling price. In addition, there are other pitfalls to be watched for.

Building a model

Building a model for sales forecasting purposes can be time consuming and has an inherent problem in that there is an in-built assumption that historical relationships between variables in the model will remain the same in the future. Actually building the model itself can also be a challenge. For example, suppose we are interested in forecasting market demand in units for cars and have data available over the past 30 years which records actual car sales. A first step might be to conjecture what factors might influence sales (market demand) in any one year. Suppose we adopt a fairly simplistic view that demand will be influenced by price, incomes and interest rates. Measuring and representing all these variables may present difficulties. For example: should we represent sales in absolute unit terms or as an index? Should we construct a price index for all cars sold or should we show an average price? How should we represent income – as an average income per household or as an index? Finally, how should we measure interest – as an average interest rate for the year or as an index? Finally, how easy is it to get any of this data if it is available at all? In the developed countries it may not be too much of a problem but in others it may be difficult.

Suppose we can obtain suitable data and decide to represent it in the way shown in the Table 5.3. One question we should ask is whether there are any lagged effect relationships. That means whether it is the influence of a variable in a previous period rather than the current one that influences demand in the current period. If this is the case then we need to set up a table which reflects the lagged effect. Suppose in this case that we argue that there are no lagged effects and proceed on this basis.

Table 5.3 Car sales data

Year	Sales	Price index	Income	Interest (%)
1978	6,996,148	38.2	25305	7.82
1979	8,339,631	39.1	28343	5.45
1980	8,945,623	39.6	28765	5.12
1981	9,145,356	40.7	31654	8.78
1982	7,228,437	44.6	30567	11.03
1983	6,876,523	48.9	31003	8.12
1984	7,334,823	53.4	31987	7.09
1985	8,999,991	58.4	32674	7.05
1986	9,227,325	60.5	34375	8.88
1987	7,943,769	71.4	35278	12.34
1988	6,225,337	82.5	37654	13.34
1989	6,118,349	91.8	37112	17.98
1990	2,875,345	96.3	37882	13.45
1991	5,228,146	98.4	38889	9.65
1992	7,991,342	101.5	41098	11.78
1993	8,117,118	105.2	42065	8.82
1994	8,000,010	104.8	43123	8.80
1995	7,063,214	105.3	44766	8.30
1996	7,152,469	107.9	46987	9.12
1997	6,448,226	112.3	48234	10.07
1998	6,347,432	121.4	50023	10.00
1999	5,778,123	122.5	50034	8.12
2000	6,115,209	125.7	51098	6.12
2001	6,114,889	129.5	51123	5.78
2002	6,783,456	131.2	52224	6.97
2003	6,457,325	138.7	55765	7.99
2004	6,876,543	143.5	56123	8.13
2005	6,558,776	144.2	57678	8.56
2006	6,453,876	142.5	60004	8.22
2007	6,453,777	145.1	64897	8.11

Next we will try to assess the parameters to our model using multiple regression analysis using one of a number of computer statistical packages that are available (though one can do this using a spreadsheet). Let us assume that we adopt the 'least squares' option approach to estimating the parameters and that the computer package (Figure 5.2 and Table 5.4) produces the following data output as a result of reading in and analysing the data in Table 5.3.

The printouts show that the model produced, indicated in the section 'Parameter estimates', only accounts for some of the variation in demand (see the section indicated 'summary of fit' and the R squared values relating to the amount of variance explained). The graphs give a good picture of the margins of error in predicting values. In addition in the 'Actual by predicted plot' graph (Figure 5.3) there is one point in particular that does not lie close to line of best fit. Removal of the data from the table which relates to this point from our original table would improve the fit of the model. It might well be that we can explain the reason why this 'outlier' point has occurred and that it is not typical of what would normally have occurred – strikes and natural disasters and their impact on production output might be examples. The graph entitled 'Residual by predicted plot' gives a good picture of

95

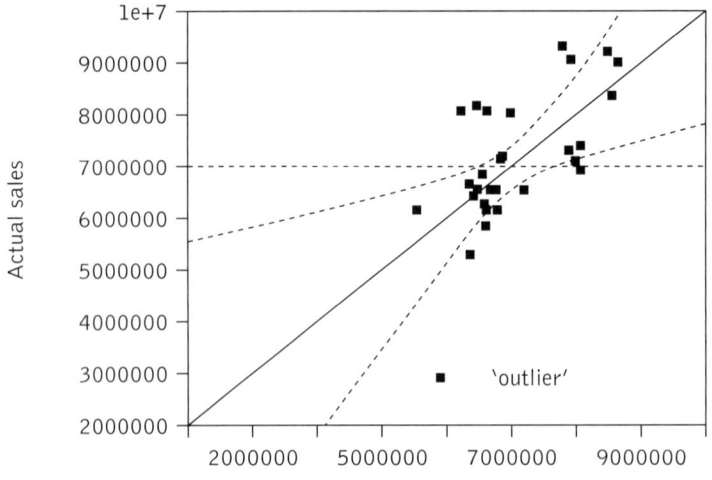

Sales predicted P = 0.0032 RSq = 0.41 RMSE = 1.07e6

Figure 5.2 *Response sales: whole model, actual by predicted plot*

Table 5.4 *Response sales*

Summary of fit

Rsquare	0.406192
Rsquare adj	0.337675
Root mean square error	1067949
Mean of response	7006553
Observations (or sum wgts)	30

Analysis of variance

Source	DF	Sum of squares	Mean square	F ratio
Model	3	2.02842e13	6.7614e12	5.9284
Error	26	2.96534e13	1.1405e12	Prob > F
C. Total	29	4.99376e13		0.0032

Parameter estimates

Term	Estimate	Std error	t ratio	Prob >|t|
Intercept	7863684.6	1841435	4.27	0.0002
Price	−49709.72	23163.12	−2.15	0.0414
Income	114.44439	80.3331	1.42	0.1662
Interest	−11217909	8302976	−1.35	0.1883

Effect tests

Source	Nparm	DF	Sum of squares	F ratio	Prob > F
Price	1	1	5.25278e12	4.6056	0.0414
Income	1	1	2.31473e12	2.0296	0.1662
Interest	1	1	2.08189e12	1.8254	0.1883

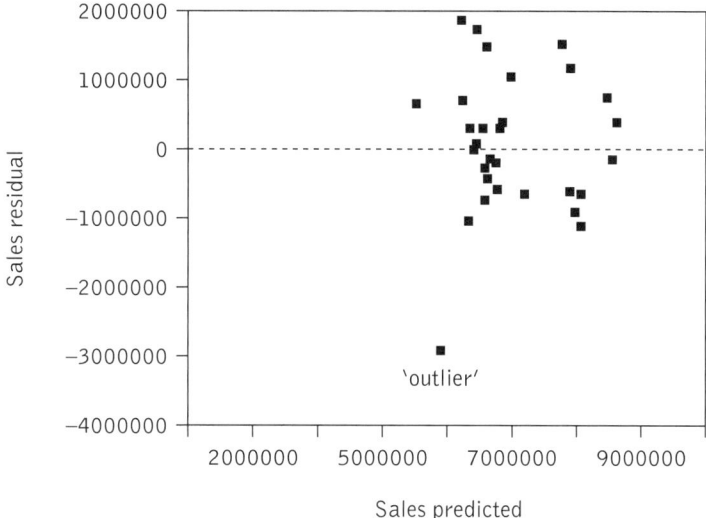

Figure 5.3 *Residual by predicted plot*

the goodness of fit of the model to the data. The addition of more explanatory variables could improve the explanatory value of the model thereby improving its predictive ability and make it more useful for forecasting

In simple terms the forecasting model based on the regression analysis undertaken above would be:

7863684.6 − 49709.72 Price + 114.44439 Income − 11217909 Interest

Thus given the expected price, income and interest levels for the next year we could predict the expected sales of cars. Bearing in mind the standard error the estimates shown in the 'Parameter estimates' table (5.4) we could also indicate upper and lower margins of error in our forecast with different degrees of confidence.

System dynamics

This approach offers an approach to forecasting via computer simulation. It was originally founded in the early 1960s by Jay W. Forrester of the MIT Sloan School of Management with the establishment of the MIT System Dynamics Group. Sytems dynamics feedback loops and stocks and flows are the basic building blocks of a system dynamics model. They are helpful in portraying how a system is connected by feedback loops which create the nonlinearity so often found in problems. Computer software is used to simulate a system dynamics model of the situation being studied.

The use of a system dynamics approach can provide a framework for investigating the likely outcomes of policies if certain initiatives are implemented. Hence, system dynamics modelling may help in assessing the likely impact of different initiatives and in the subsequent formulation of a policy, by providing a model of the major influences. Once developed, it can aid policy-makers by allowing them immediate feedback and analysis of how different policies may or may not work.

In Figure 5.4, use is made of the computer simulation package Vensim which facilitates systems dynamics modelling. The model presented is a very simple one depicting how a population size changes over time without the intervention of any extraneous factors. One can develop this model into quite an elaborate representation of real world populations of products, people, services, etc. and build in the various extraneous factors that will impact upon how the size of the population will vary over time. Indeed, one could substitute 'demand' for a product or service for the 'population' and so assess the impact of extraneous factors on demand itself. The method enables different scenarios and forecasts to made by varying assumptions about population factors that influence growth or decline.

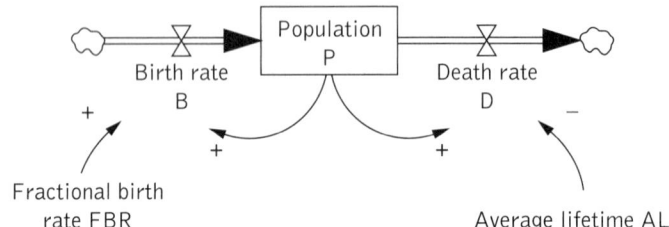

Figure 5.4 *A simple systems dynamics model of population movement over time*

Forecasting sales of new products

To forecast sales of new products, one needs some initial sales figures with which to work. Given that early sales data are available, it is then generally possible by using one or other of a variety of mathematical models or 'curve fitting routines' to make some prediction for sales over a specified period of time. Alternatively, it may be possible to look at sales histories of similar new products and make predictions by analogy. There are numerous examples of these models (see, for instance, Kotler and Lilien, 1983).

Example
The epidemic model of initial sales is a useful tool to have to hand when trying to make sales prediction for certain kinds of new products. The model developed by Bass (1969), which he specifically tested out on a range of consumer durable goods, is illustrative:

$$P_t = p + q/m(Y_t)$$

where

    P_t = probability of purchase given no previous purchase was made

    Y_t = total number who have tried

    m = total number of potential buyers [saturation level]

    q = parameter reflecting the rate of diffusion of the model

    p = initial probability of first-time purchase

Table 5.5 Sales model

Year	Sales$_t$ (000s)	Y_t (000s)	Y_t^2
1	1	0	0
2	2	1	1
3	4	3	9
4	10	7	49
5	20	17	289
6	36	37	1369
7	48	73	5329
8	58	121	14641
9	–	–	–

The model (Table 5.5) can be estimated by running a regression of current versus past sales:

$$\text{Sales}_t = c_0 + c_1 Y_t + c_2 Y_t^2$$

Analysis of the above sales gives the forecasting model:

$$\text{Sales}_t = 2.06 + 1.016\, Y_t - 0.00464\, Y_t^2$$

Forecasting sales of new products in retail outlets

Large retail chains often add new lines to their stock. Most of these retailers have benchmarks against which to judge whether a product is likely to be successful or not. A common practice is to offer the product for sale for a limited period in one of its shops. If the product fails to achieve a certain level of sales within the specified period it is withdrawn from sale and not put on sale in other outlets.

LONGER-TERM FORECASTING

Marketing strategy is an essential input into the overall corporate strategy (Johnson and Scholes, 1988) and usually determines the most important elements of that strategy. Typical approaches to the production of such marketing strategy, however, focus on the relatively short term. These are achieved, for example, through the use of matrices balancing the impact of current actions (Ansoff, 1987), or derived from existing forces such as competitive pressures (Porter, 1985), or – even stressing the short-term nature of decisions – derived from incremental and emergent strategies (Mintzberg and Quinn, 1991).

There is, of course, the conventional corporate strategy process (Taylor, 1984), optimizing performance in the shorter term; and the traditional marketing strategy is a valuable contributor to this (McDonald, 1989). In addition, however, there should also be a separate, presently well hidden, process of producing 'robust' plans which underpin survival over the longer term (Taylor, 1984).

There are two quite distinct approaches to the strategy process. The two sets of strategies should have different objectives. Corporate (short-term) strategy is typically about optimizing current performance, 'matching the organization's activities to the environment and to its resource capability' (Johnson and Scholes, 1988, 1993).

On the other hand, 'robust' strategies are about survival in the longer term, ensuring that all the potential threats are covered (Pfeffer and Salancik, 1978). They demand that multiple, and often divergent, objectives are met; in order to exploit the potential emerging from changes in the (external) environment, and especially to guard against the whole range of threats which might endanger survival in the longer term, with the aim of understanding what these might be. In general, these focus on critical developments in the external environment; typically not just the marketing environment but the wider social environment, rather than on the manipulation of internal resources.

Scenario forecasting

The overall process starts with a simple form of scenario forecasting. The techniques have been derived from those traditionally used, most notably from those publicized by Shell (Wack, 1985; Van Der Heijden, 1996). Whatever approach is adopted, this is the most complex part of the overall planning process. On the other hand, the simpler it is, the better it works; not least because those involved understand what is happening. One focuses on the key 'drivers' for change – things that affect the industry being investigated, over a two-decade time scale – without exploring the complications. As a result, we may lose some 'accuracy'; especially in terms of the fine detail about the future the process reveals. On the other hand, we are able to detect almost all the key developments, certainly all those which have surfaced by other methods, covering the great majority of expected 'drivers'. This part of the overall planning process can be undertaken in as little time as half a day. It might involve a management team of six to eight members, using a variation on well understood focus group techniques combined with some from scenario forecasting – and with little more than Post-It notes stuck on a wall to facilitate their thinking. Even so, this is a critical aspect of the process; since only if the key turning points are identified in these scenarios will the (robust) strategies developed in response be valid.

There are just a number of simple steps to producing a long-range marketing plan.

Definitive statement

The starting point of the plan itself must be a definitive statement of what has emerged from the scenario work. The output of this process should be a formal 'map' of some kind concerning of the issues, the turning points, which will decide the long-term future of the organization. Although many of these key turning points may revolve around conventional marketing issues, especially those relating to the core relationships with customers, quite a few of them bring into play factors in the social environment (as well as those in politics and economics). Possibly the greatest benefit, therefore, is that the process brings into consideration factors that would be otherwise overlooked by more conventional (marketing) planning processes.

Develop the robust strategies

What is needed is a set of strategies to protect against (or to capitalize on) what has emerged from the previous step – in terms of effectively addressing the key turning points.

Comparison with 'corporate' strategy

Exactly what form this comparison takes will depend upon what form you have adopted for presenting these strategies. The essence, however, is that each (robust versus corporate) should be compared statement by statement.

Decide strategic changes

Emerging directly from the comparison with corporate strategy will be a clear definition of the divergences, if any, between the two types of strategy. This will, therefore, immediately highlight the nature of any changes to be made. These should then be addressed, again statement by statement, in terms of the changes which will be accordingly made in the overall corporate strategy statement.

Translate to action

The final stage of any planning process should always be to do something (McDonald, 1989). It may be that, here, the action is to positively incorporate these changes in the overall corporate plan. In this case, a single sentence, stating that this has happened may be enough. The more thorough alternative is to produce a separate action plan where the shorter-term (more certain) elements of the revised strategy are translated into the necessary actions (and related time scales).

MARKET PROFITABILITY ANALYSIS

According to Porter (1985), the attractiveness of a market or an industry is measured by the long-term return on investment of the average firm. This in turn depends on five factors that influence profitability:

- the intensity of competition
- the existence of potential competitors who will enter if profits are high
- substitute products that will attract customers if prices become high
- the bargaining power of customers
- the bargaining power of suppliers.

Competitors

The intensity of competition from exiting competitors will depend on several factors, including:

- the number of competitors
- their relative size
- whether or not their product offerings and strategies are similar
- the existence of high fixed costs
- the commitment of competitors
- the size and nature of exit barriers.

As a first approximation, the more competitors there are, then the more competitive intensity exists. However, the nature of the competitors can have a sizeable impact. The relative size of the competitors will affect the competitive intensity. If a market is dominated by a few firms of equal size then the market is likely to be highly competitive.

Potential competitors

Barriers to entry obviously act to encourage or to deter potential entrants to a market. In projecting the level of competitive activity in a market, an understanding of the relevant barriers to entry is important. The following are the main barriers to entry to consider:

- *capital investment* required
- *economies of scale*: in production and promotion
- *distribution channels*: the cost of gaining distribution can be difficult and costly
- *product differentiation*: established firms may have high levels of customer loyalty produced by protected product features, a brand name and image, customer service and established and accepted promotion methods.

Substitute products

Substitute products comprise those sets of products that are identified as competing with less intensity than the primary competitors. They are still relevant, however, and can influence the profitability of the market and can in fact be a major threat. Substitutes that show a steady improvement in relative price/performance and for which the customer's cost of switching is minimal are of particular interest.

Customer power

When customers have relatively more power than sellers, they can force prices down or demand more services and therefore influence profitability. A customer's power will be greater when their purchase size is a large proportion of the seller's business, when alternative suppliers are available and when the customer can integrate backward and make all or part of the product.

Supplier power

When the supplier industry is concentrated and sells to a variety of customers in diverse markets, it will have a relative power that can be used to influence prices. Power will also be enhanced when the cost to the customers of switching suppliers is high.

COST STRUCTURE

An understanding of the cost structure of a market can provide insights into present and future key success factors. The first step is to conduct an analysis of the value chain to determine where value is added to the product or service. The proportion of value added attributed to one value chain stage can become so important that a key success factor is associated with that stage. It may, for example, be possible to develop control over a resource or technology. An alternative is that competitors will aim to be the lowest-cost producer in a high-value added stage of the value chain. Advantages in lower-value added stages will simply have less leverage. Where transportation costs are high, for example, location close to a market will have significant advantages.

It is most important to be able to anticipate changes in key success factors. This may be approached by examining the changes in the relative importance of the value added stages.

Another market cost structure consideration is the extent to which experience curve strategies are feasible.

DISTRIBUTION SYSTEMS

One needs to consider alternative channels, the trends that are taking place in choice of channel and what new channels are likely to be emerging in the future. One also has to take account of who has the power in the channel and how that is likely to change in the future. Access to an effective and efficient distribution channel is often a key success factor.

Related to power in market profitability analysis is channel power. In industries without strong brand names, retailers usually have relatively high power and can hold down the price that the manufacturers are paid. The enhanced power of supermarkets, caused in large part by the explosion of transaction information and the importance of promotions, has altered the way in which packaged goods are marketed.

KEY SUCCESS FACTORS: BASES OF COMPETITION

These are assets and skills that provide the basis for competing successfully. There are two types:

- *strategic necessities*: if these are absent then they will create a substantial weakness
- *strategic strengths*: those at which the firm excels and are assets or skills that are superior to those of the competition. They can provide a competitive advantage.

Key success factors differ by industry in a more or less predictable way.

RISKS IN HIGH-GROWTH MARKETS

There are a number of conditions that need to be considered when evaluating whether a high growth market is really as attractive as it might seem. These are:

Whether the number of competitors serving the market is really greater than can be sustained by the growth opportunity

The following conditions are found in markets in which a surplus of competitors is likely to be attracted and a subsequent shakeout is likely:

1 the market and its growth rate are highly visible to all and therefore unlikely to be overlooked by any firms which may have an interest
2 very high initial and forecast growth
3 seemingly very few threats to the sustainability of the growth rate
4 few initial barriers to entry
5 products make use of an exiting technology rather than a risky or protected technology
6 some of the potential entrants have low visibility and their intentions are unknown or uncertain.

The shakeout itself often occurs over a relatively short period of time. The trigger is likely to be a combination of:

1 an unexpected slowing of market growth rate, either because the market is close to saturation or a recession has intervened
2 aggressive late entrants buying their way into the market by cutting prices
3 the market leader attempting to stem the erosion of its market position with aggressive product and price retaliation
4 the key success factors in the market changing as a result of technological development, perhaps shifting the value-added structure.

Whether a competitor may enter with a superior product or low cost advantage

The late entry of low-cost products from the Far East has occurred in many industries including radios, TVs, VCRs and computer components and peripherals.

Whether the key success factors in the market are likely to change in a way that is incompatible with the evaluating firm's capabilities

Many product markets have experienced a shift over time from a focus on product technology to process technology. A firm that might be capable of achieving product-technology based advantages may not have the resources or skills required to develop the process-technology based advantage that the evolving market requires.

Whether the technology in the market might change

Developing first-generation technology can involve a commitment to a product line and production facilities that may become obsolete, and to a technology that may not survive. A safe strategy is to wait until it becomes clear which technology will dominate and then attempt to improve it with a compatible entry.

Whether the market growth may in fact fail to be commensurate with expectations

Many shakeouts occur when market growth rate – even though it is good – falls below expectations. Competitors may have built their capacity to meet expectations.

Whether resources are inadequate to maintain a high growth rate

Financing requirements are frequently increased by higher than expected product development and market entry costs, and by price erosion caused by aggressive or desperate competitors.

The organizational pressures and problems created by growth can be even more difficult to predict and deal with than financial strains. Many firms have failed to survive the rapid growth phase because they were unable to obtain and train people to handle the expanded business or to adjust their systems and structures.

Whether distribution may be inadequate or not available

Most distribution channels can support only a small number of brands. For example, most distributors are unwilling to carry more than four or five brands of a household appliance because of the limited amount of shelf-space available. Given the limit on the number of brands that can be distributed, some brands may find it impossible to gain distribution at all or at the very least the distribution level will be unacceptably low.

As market growth rate begins to slow, distributor power is increased. Their willingness to use this power to extract price and promotion concessions from manufacturers or to drop suppliers is often augmented by their own problems in maintaining margins in the face of extreme competition for their own customers. Many of the same factors that draw in an overabundance of manufacturers also contributes to over-crowding in subsequent stages of a distribution channel. The eventual shakeout at this level can have equally serious repercussions for suppliers.

QUESTIONS

1 One of the primary objectives of a market analysis is to assess its prospects for participants. Another key purpose of market analysis is to understand the dynamics of the market. Indicate how these objectives might be achieved.
2 There are two basic approaches to forecasting sales for established products, both of which have a number of variants. On the one hand, there are the methods which rely on asking people questions, and on the other hand, there are those which involve the statistical or mathematical analysis of historical data. Discuss the various merits of these methods and indicate under what circumstances they might be used in practice.
3 Why is long-range forecasting important? How might an organization tackle the problem of long-range forecasting.
4 Outline a practical method of ascertaining the profitability of a market.
5 What are key success factors? How might they be identified in practice?

CASE STUDIES

Cometex

Door-to-door selling is something which always seems to have been with us. The tinkers of the Middle Ages still have their counterparts today. In modern times, door-to-door selling seems to have come in and out of fashion. In the 1950s, for example, even vacuum cleaners were sold in this way. More usual has been the bric-à-brac type of salesman carrying a range of household utensils in an often large case or encyclopaedia salesmen with their well rehearsed sales chatter. One of the most popular forms of door-to-door selling has been the Avon representative selling a variety of beauty aids to the appearance-conscious housewife.

Cometex, the door-to-door home cleaning company, is planning an expansion strategy into emerging markets, as the firm has suffered drops in sales in the home UK market. The firm said it would invest £5 million in expanded joint ventures with a door-to-door cosmetics group. The managing director said sales from the joint ventures could reach 'several hundred million pounds' in ten years. Cometex is launching in five East European countries beginning with Hungary, and three Asian countries including Japan.

The overseas expansion follows joint ventures with the same cosmetic group in Latin America during the past few years. South American turnover is expected to rise sharply, with its recent launch in Brazil. Cometex has also begun local manufacturing in Mexico, where margins are 10 per cent higher than in western Europe.

In the UK, however, Cometex suffered from recruitment problems which affected its network of door-to-door distributors. The company blamed low levels of unemployment, although it added that its customers were spending on average 6 per cent more than last year. Cometex has tremendous growth prospects with the cosmetic group's management in emerging markets which have yet to show through in its results.

QUESTIONS

1 Is door-to-door selling in mature markets and developed economies a dying craft? Why or why not?
2 Do you consider that the strategy being followed by Cometex is the right one? Why or why not?
3 How might Cometex undertake market analysis for its products? Be specific.

Ecoprods

Ever since environmental pollution came on to the political and business agendas, firms have been steered, voluntarily or otherwise, towards 'green' or 'eco' products. Indeed, it has now become part of the appeal of products that they are environmentally friendly and the 'eco' label is as familiar to the consumer as any brand label. Non-reusable batteries are an example of where environmentally friendly chemical constituents have been used to replace the undesirable mercury content which polluted the environment when batteries were disposed of. However, these days, defining exactly what is or what is not an 'eco' product has become increasingly more difficult and boundaries are becoming blurred.

A firm called Ecoprods has produced a prototype battery charger that does not require a mains source for its power. In fact, the product is essentially a solar car battery booster. The charger uses the latest type of solar cells to trickle charge a car battery while the car is left standing for long periods of time. It simply sits on the dashboard and plugs into the cigarette lighter socket. Even on dull or cloudy days it can convert enough energy from available sunlight to keep the battery charge satisfactorily topped up. When one is away on holiday it is an ideal way to ensure that the battery is well charged.

Ecoprods needs to assess the market for such a product. In particular, it is keen to assess the potential market size and the likely price that it should charge. In addition, it needs to identify the best way of seeking to distribute the product, should the market seem large enough, and to establish what is needed in the way of promotional expenditure.

QUESTIONS

1 How would you undertake a market analysis for this product?
2 What do you consider to be the main problems or difficulties in undertaking such a market analysis?

Forecasting demand for university part-time MBA courses

A textbook publisher is interested in getting an idea of how the market for MBA courses is likely to develop over the next five years. It has been suggested that the data collected in Table 5.6 might be useful in enabling the publisher to get some idea of how the market is likely to develop.

QUESTION

Comment on how useful you think this data would be.

Table 5.6   *Part-time MBA courses*

Year	Places taken up	Price index for MBA Study	Average annual income (managers) £	Number of institutions offer-ing MBA places
1978	1,024	48.2	25305	43
1979	1,076	49.7	28343	43
1980	1,098	48.6	28765	43
1981	982	53.8	31654	43
1982	1,075	54.1	30567	43
1983	1,145	54.6	31003	43
1984	1,456	54.5	31987	45
1985	1,789	54.3	32674	46
1986	2,090	57.2	34375	47
1987	2,150	58.9	35278	48
1988	2,065	62.7	37654	48
1989	2,213	62.1	37112	48
1990	2,456	63.6	37882	48
1991	2,519	64.5	38889	48
1992	2,785	66.8	41098	49
1993	2,845	68.1	42065	49
1994	3,013	69.5	43123	50
1995	3,256	70.7	44766	52
1996	3,789	71.3	46987	54
1997	4,056	73.2	48234	58
1998	4,112	74.6	50023	58
1999	3,987	80.5	50034	58
2000	4,067	83.6	51098	58
2001	4,234	85.8	51123	58
2002	4,345	88.4	52224	58
2003	4,678	91.5	55765	60
2004	4,754	94.6	56123	60
2005	4,019	100.0	57678	60
2006	4,245	102.3	60004	60
2007	4,658	104.3	64897	60

Chapter 6

Analysing competition

INTRODUCTION

All firms have strategic windows and some of these windows open out on to markets that are shared with other firms. Where windows share views over the same market, competition exists. It is important to understand how different firms view the same market since their perceived and actual windows of opportunity will not all be the same.

The nature of competition and the factors which influence it are explored along with how firms identify competitors and how they use product positioning to obtain a competitive advantage. Attention is paid to how firms define their marketing strategies and analyse the competitive positions of rivals. Consideration is given to the various sources of information available to firms that enable them to gauge competitors' strengths and weaknesses.

Success in the market place depends not only on an ability to identify customer wants and needs but also upon an ability to be able to satisfy those wants and needs better than competitors are able to do. This implies that organizations need to look for ways of achieving a differential advantage in the eyes of the customer. The differential advantage is often achieved through the product or service itself but sometimes it may be achieved through other elements of the marketing mix.

Attention in this chapter is given to Porter's five forces model to portray the various factors which influence competition and how this influence is effected.

Actually identifying competition may not always be quite straightforward. It is important to be able to correctly identify different types of competitors so that suitable reaction to their marketing strategies and tactics can be put into practice as and when required.

The various bases of competitive advantage are discussed and reference is made to Porter's strategic thrust typologies. This is then followed by a discussion of the various typologies of competitors that can be identified and the kind of strategy each one employs. Finally, the chapter ends by looking at how to assess competitors' strengths and weaknesses and the sources of information that should be consulted to make this possible.

Attention is also given to ways and methods of obtaining information about competitors' actual and planned activities. In particular, attention is given to market signalling actions and their interpretation.

NATURE OF COMPETITION AND IDENTIFICATION OF AN ORGANIZATION'S COMPETITORS

Competition is the process of active rivalry between the sellers of a particular product as they seek to win and retain buyer demand for their offerings. The operational definition of competition, however, hinges upon the meaning of 'a particular product'.

The identification of an organization's competitors may not be as simple or as obvious as it might at first sight appear. The most obvious competitors are those which offer identical products or services to the same customers. However, substitute products and services highlight the nature of indirect competition which must also be taken into account. Five levels of competition have been suggested: direct competition, close competition, products of a similar nature, substitute products and indirect competition.

Factors influencing competition

Industries have distinctive idiosyncrasies of their own and these idiosyncrasies alter over time. They are often referred to as the dynamics of the industry. No matter how hard a company tries, if it fails to fit into the dynamics of the industry, ultimate success may not be achieved. Porter (1985) sees competition in an industry being governed by five different sets of forces (Figure 6.1).

Citing these five 'forces' is rather arbitrary, since a sixth force, government regulation, is often the most significant influence in determining the profitability of an industry. In fact, when Porter studied the pharmaceuticals and airline industries he discovered that government regulation and deregulation were important factors relating to profitability in both (Porter, 1988). However, we will look at the five forces of the model in more detail.

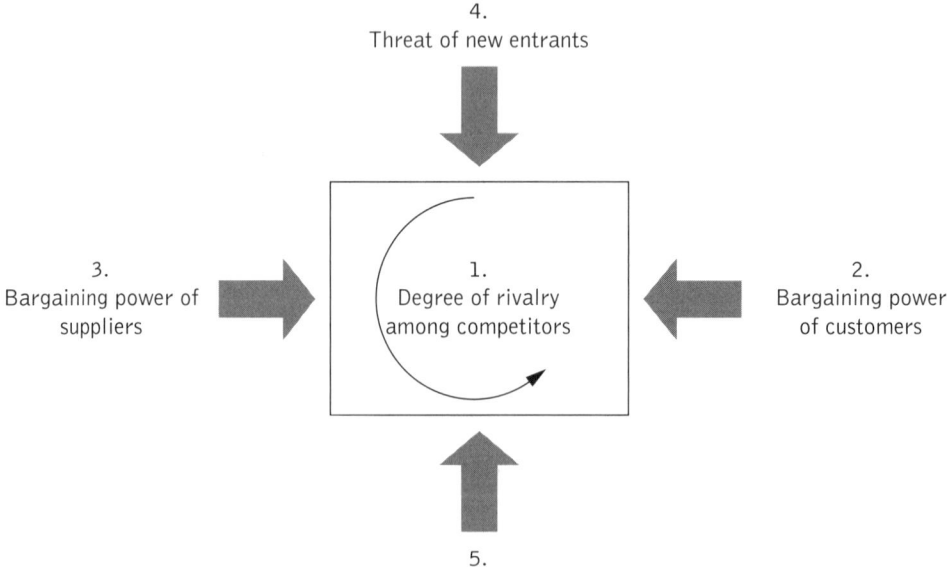

Figure 6.1   Forces of competition (1)

Rivalry among competitors

Competition in an industry is more intense if there are many comparable rivals trying to satisfy the wants and needs of the same customers in the same market or market segment. Moreover, competition increases where industry growth is slow, costs are high and there is a lack of product differentiation. High exit barriers from a market or industry contribute to increased competition. Firms may find it difficult to get out of a business because of the relationship of the business with other businesses in which they are engaged. An organization may also have considerable investments in assets which are used for the specific business and for which no valuable other use can be found.

Bargaining power of customers

Customers can exert influence on producers (Exhibit 6.1). Where there are a small number of buyers, for example, or a predominant/single buyer, the producer's opportunities for action are limited. In the situation where one customer accounts for a significant proportion of a supplier's business, then the one customer can exert considerable influence and control over the price and quality of the products that it buys. Such firms can demand the highest specification in products, with tight delivery times (for just-in-time manufacturing and hence reducing the cost of raw material inventories) and customized products.

Buyers exert pressure in industries by hunting for lower prices, higher quality, additional service and through demands for improved products and services. In general, the greater the bargaining power of buyers, the less advantage sellers will have. Not all buyers have equal bargaining power with sellers; some may be less sensitive than others to price, quality or service. For example, in the clothing industry, major manufacturers confront significant customer power when they sell to retail chains like Marks & Spencer and Burton. However, they can get much better prices selling to small owner-managed boutiques.

Bargaining power of suppliers

Suppliers can exert pressures by controlling supplies. A powerful supplier is in a position to influence the profitability of a whole industry by raising prices or reducing the quality of the goods it supplies.

EXHIBIT 6.1 CUSTOMER POWER IN THE AEROSPACE INDUSTRY

When there is a downturn in the market for planes, supplying firms are affected by the power of their customers. Plane makers, producing for the world's major airlines, are very dependent on the state of the world economy. When demand is low and margins are tight, they have to look for cost savings, irrespective of production costs. Many companies have large investments in plant and cannot exit from the market. They know, however, that when the economic climate improves, demand will recover, forcing prices back to more profitable levels. The bargaining power of the customer is greater when demand is low and reduces when demand rises.

A firm that has few or only one potential supplier may exert little influence over the prices it pays for bought-in materials and components. It may also experience difficulty in influencing the quality of its raw materials and resources. If it is the only purchaser and constitutes an important part of the supplier's business, however, it can exert a great deal of influence over both prices and quality. Another form of supplier power is 'lock-in'. This involves making it difficult or unattractive for a customer to change suppliers. It can be put into effect, for example, by offering specific services or product attributes that a competitor finds difficult to match.

Powerful suppliers can have the same adverse effects upon profitability as powerful buyers. Suppliers can exert bargaining power on participants in an industry by raising prices or reducing the quality of purchased goods and services. Powerful suppliers can thereby squeeze profitability out of an industry unable to recover cost increases in its own prices.

Threat of new entrants

The threat of new entrants can increase competitive activity in a market. Outsiders will be tempted to enter a market or an industry if they feel that the opportunity is sufficiently appealing in terms of profitability and sales. Markets which have grown to a substantial size become potentially attractive to large powerful firms provided that the level of competitive activity enables them to achieve the kind of market share and profits and sales volume they expect.

This provides an incentive for the firms already operating in the market to make the prospects appear less attractive to would-be entrants by increasing the level of competitive activity. For example, lowering price levels would increase the competition between firms within the market and it might also deter other firms from entering because it would be more difficult to obtain high profitability levels. Much depends, however, on the cost structure of a would-be entrant.

Where a market is seen to be profitable, it may attract new entrants. Suppliers may expand downstream, or buyers may move upstream. This can cause increased competition and a likely reduction in margins. Methods to discourage entry include raising the cost of entry into a market. This may be achieved by developing new products through R&D which the competition find hard to match, or introducing new marketing initiatives, such as long-term contracts with customers, or raising the cost of entry through economies of scale. Raising the cost of entry has long been practised within many industries. In such cases, larger, more expensive plants are continually built to gain competitive advantage.

Threat of substitute products or services

Substitutes, or alternative products that can perform the same function, impose limits on the price that an industry can charge for its products. The presence of substitutes is not obvious and may not be easily perceived by firms operating in an industry. Substitutes may even be preferred by customers and incumbent firms may only be noticed when it is too late to arrest their dominance.

An example which illustrates the rise of a substitute product is the current increasing proliferation of low-cost microcomputers coupled with low-cost easy-to-use business packages in areas such as accounting, database management and word processing. This 'product' adversely affected the 'industry' of specialist programmers and specialist computer bureaux. The threat of substitutes depends on technical comparability of substitutes, the relative price of substitutes, the speed of technological development in 'substitute' industries and the cost of switching. Substitute products that deserve the most attention strategically are those that:

1 are subject to trends improving their price-performance trade-off with the industry's product, or
2 are produced by industries earning high profits.

Figure 6.2 illustrates how one might assess the degree of competition that may exist within an industry or market.

Reactions to strong competition

Where competition among existing firms in a market or industry is strong a good policy is to try to differentiate the product or service from what the competition has to offer. Re-segmenting the market can also be an effective approach. A fundamental competitive advantage, however, may reside in being able to offer a product or service at a low cost to the buyer while maintaining the same level of quality. Looking critically at costs and cutting these where possible can help considerably to hold and maintain a competitive stance where competition is strong. Where threats of new entrants to an industry or market are high the best approach may be to try to create barriers to entry certainly to react very strongly to new entrants when they make a bid to enter. Threats of substitute products can be parried by researching for substitutes oneself and by constantly re-engineering and improving existing products or services. Keeping in touch with customer preferences and staying at least one step ahead of competition in terms of being able to anticipate customers' requirements is also an effective strategy. When looking at the bargaining power of buyers and suppliers then it may be worthwhile considering integrative strategies. Forward integration in the case of buyers and backward integration in the case of suppliers.

Competitive strategy and profitability

A question of considerable general interest relates to how a business can maximize its profitability, or at least become the most profitable performer in its industry. Maximum profitability can, in principle, only be achieved in one of two ways: either by minimizing costs or by maximizing prices. Thus any useful business strategy must aim to follow one or other of these aims: to be the lowest-cost producer or the highest-price seller.

Porter (1988) argues that failure to make the choice between cost leadership and differentiation means that a company is 'stuck in the middle', with no competitive advantage. This results in 'poor performance'. There is no doubt that there is a danger of this happening and it has long been emphasized by many other writers' (e.g. Drucker, 1964) assertion that concentration is the key to real economic results). Moreover, the basic concept of strategic direction seems to suggest much the same thing. Many companies which have a clear direction and a distinct position are also demonstrably either cost leaders or differentiators, but not both. Names like Rolls-Royce, Bic, Cartier and KwikSave, for example, can be immediately classified in one camp or the other. Some researchers have even suggested that the most effective strategies for some situations comprise systematic oscillation between cost leadership and differentiation (Gilbert and Strebel, 1988).

Porter Competition forces

5= strongly agree
0= strongly disagree

Competition among existing firms

Even distribution in terms of strength of competitors	4
The growth within the industry is slow or declining	4
Capital intensity / fixed costs are high	4
Switching costs for buyers is relatively easy / cheap	3
Incremental costs of increasing production /service delivery costs are high	4
Staying in the market / industry is very important to the incumbent firms	4
Average	3.833333

Threat of new entrants

Low economies of scale exist in the industry/market	5
Few or no cost disadvantages independent of scale	4
Low brand loyalty	3
Low customer loyalty	4
Easy to gain access to distribution	4
Little differentiation of products/services	3
Low expenditure on capital equipment in the market/industry	3
Low technological, regulatory or competence barriers	3
No excess production / supply capacity existing in market/industry	3
High industry /market growth	5
Low entry deterring price	2
Defensive retaliation threats low	4
Average	3.666667

Bargaining power of suppliers

Few substitute products / services exist	4
Limited number of suppliers or available supply	5
Industry unimportant as a customer for the supplier	4
Supplier's product is an important input	4
Suppliers can differentiate products	3
Threat of forward integration exists	3
High costs of switching to an alternative supply	4
Average	3.833333

Bargaining power of Buyer

Limited number of buyers	4
Purchases make up a significant proportion of buyer's costs	3
Products / services have little differentiation	3
Easy to switch to alternative suppliers	4
Threat of backward integration	2
Purchases are of low importance	5
Buyer has full information on costs and performance	2
Average	3.285714

Threat of substitute products

Buyers can easily change to buying the substitute without penalty	3
Buyer acceptability of substitutes is high	2
Price/performance of substitute is comparatively high	1
Average	2

Competition among existing firms	3.833333333
Threat of new entrants	3.666666667
Bargaining power of suppliers	3.833333333
Bargaining power of Buyer	3.285714286
Threat of substitute products	2

Forces of competition

Figure 6.2 Forces of competition (2)

When 'focus' was introduced initially as a generic strategy it obscured the simple structure of the model which argued that profits could be maximized either by achieving lowest costs or highest prices. Competition reduces profits by the introduction of substitutes, new entrants, etc. as suggested by Porter. Moreover, perfect competition erodes profitability perfectly. Minimizing competition would minimize erosion of profits and this could be done by focusing on areas of the market where there are the fewest competitors. This in turn is a recommendation for the adoption of the 'focus strategy'. However, it is debatable as to whether 'focus' is really a strategy in its own right – at the end of the day all strategies are focused to some extent. Even Ivory Soap (Clifford and Cavanagh, 1985), which has a very broad appeal, is carefully positioned as a multi-dimensional brand aimed at a fully researched customer profile.

STRATEGY TYPOLOGIES

While Porter's typologies represent one important way of looking at how firms behave in the market place there are other ways of looking at what firms do. Various suggestions have been put forward to account for the strategies adopted by firms. A commonly adopted framework is to consider firms according to the role they play in a market. The suggestion is that firms act as:

1 market leader
2 market challenger
3 market follower, or
4 market nicher.

These roles are discussed below.

Leader

The market leader is the enterprise that has the largest market share. Leadership is exercised with respect to price changes, new product introductions, distribution coverage and promotional intensity. Because of their large volume sales, market leaders enjoy the benefits of economies of scale and accumulated experience which helps reduce costs and bolster profits. Not surprisingly, dominant firms want to stay in the leading position and this requires them to:

1 find ways of expanding total market demand
2 protect market share
3 even increase market share.

The market leader is conscious of economies of scale of operation and is happiest when making inroads into large and substantial markets. Small specialist markets (niches) are not the prime interest of market leaders.

For example, the Ford motor company produces a range of cars for high-volume markets, e.g. the Ka for the small car market. Ferrari, on the other hand specializes in producing high-performance sports saloons, etc. for a very small market segment that is prepared to pay a very high price for such a car.

Challenger

Another group of competitors are referred to as market challengers. These companies aspire to become market leaders, recognizing the benefits of holding such an exalted position. Challengers attack the leader and other competitors in order to try to gain market share. It is uncommon for market challengers to attack the leader directly. They usually try to gain market share by attacking markets in which the smaller and less efficient firms operate. Such markets, of course, do have to be of a substantial size and not be too small or specialized to deter the larger firms.

There are a variety of strategies that challengers can adopt. One strategy is to produce an enormous variety of types, styles and sizes of products including both cheaper and more expensive models. This was a strategy adopted by the Japanese Seiko company when it attacked the watch market. It accompanied this strategy with another which involved distributing its watches through every possible channel. The wide variety of models it had available (over 2,000) meant that it could supply different types of channel with different models and thereby avoid the adverse effects of channel conflict.

Follower

A third role that firms can adopt is that termed market follower. Firms which undertake a good deal of innovation often have to recoup massive investment costs. Market followers are able to copy what the leading firms produce and save themselves the burden of massive investment costs. This means that they can operate very profitably at the going price in a market. Such firms will obviously have to forgo the market share which comes from being first into the field.

Providing they can stay cost efficient and obtain a reasonable share of the market they can survive. Less efficient ones, however, are open to attack from the market challengers.

Market niching

Most industries include smaller firms that specialize in producing products or in offering services to specific sectors of the market, i.e. in specific segments. In so doing they avoid the competitive thrusts of the larger firms for whom specialization does not offer attractive economies of scale, that is, the segments are too small to generate the kind of return on investment that the larger firms require. This is a strategy called market niching.

Market niching is a strategy that is not only of interest to small firms but is also of interest to the small divisions of larger companies. The latter firms seek some degree of specialization. In cases where the latter occurs the position of small firms is not quite so secure. From a firm's point of view, an ideal market niche is:

1 of sufficient size to be profitable to a firm serving it
2 capable of growth
3 of negligible interest to major competitors
4 a good fit with the firm's skills and resources.

Specialization is the corner-stone of market niching.

There is strong evidence to show that a strong brand in a niche market earns a higher percentage return than a strong brand in a big market. In the case of large markets, competitive threats and retailer pressure can hold back profits even for the top brand.

COMPETITION RESEARCH

Many of the same factors that a firm considers under self-analysis are also relevant when looking at competitor analysis. Among these the components of the value chain need to be considered in the context of evaluating competition (see Chapter 3). In addition to this the following is relevant to competitor analysis.

UNDERSTANDING COMPETITORS' STRATEGIES

Understanding competition is central to making marketing plans and strategy. A firm has to be regularly comparing its products, prices, channels of distribution and promotional methods with those of its competitors in order to ensure that it is not at a disadvantage. In so doing it can also identify areas where it can gain a competitive advantage.

In order to establish a sustainable competitive advantage in the market place it is necessary to know and understand the strategies adopted by competitors. This is more than noting in which markets/segments the competition is operating and their respective market shares and financial performance. In addition, it is important to consider how competition will develop in the future and thus to ascertain the focus of the strategies that competitors are pursuing.

Firms need to monitor competition continually. The main need is for information regarding:

- sales
- market share
- profit margin
- return on investment
- cash flow
- new investment.

in addition, knowledge of competitors' financial performances is useful.

Such information enables firms to gain comprehensive impressions of their rivals that may be useful in predicting short-term strategies to be adopted by competitors. A knowledge of competitors' specific objectives would be very welcome since these would give clues as to future strategies that competitors are likely to pursue. This kind of information may be difficult to obtain but may be inferred from present or past activities.

IDENTIFYING COMPETITORS

The first step, however, is to identify the competition. This may seem a simple question for most firms to answer. For example, at first sight a book publisher's main competitors might appear to be other book publishers. This is, of course, correct. However, product substitution also has to be considered. This involves looking more broadly at the types of business in which the firm operates. If this is done one can identify many producers of goods and services that people use for leisure, education and other informational needs. Many of these products could be potential competition for the publisher. Many of these products could be used instead of the publishers' books, i.e. they can be substituted.

SOURCES OF INFORMATION ABOUT COMPETITORS

Decision-making can be improved by an adequate supply of relevant information and a knowledge of good sources of information is an important first step. A suitable starting point is to examine what competitors say about themselves and what others say about them. Sources of information fall into four categories:

- public
- government
- trade
- investors.

Public sources

Advertising, promotional materials and press releases are prime sources of information on what competitors have to say about themselves. Articles and newspaper reports provide a good source of information on what others have to say about them. Nonetheless, one does have to be wary of the information gleaned since it may be biased or even distorted.

Trade and professional sources

Courses, seminars, technical papers and manuals prepared by competitors can give detailed insights into competitors' activities. However, it can take a considerable amount of time to distil and analyse this information. Distributors, the trade press and even customers can be good sources of information about what others have to say about competitors.

Government

In the UK, firms have to lodge their annual reports at Company House in London and the contents of these reports provide insights into the operations of competitors. In particular, lawsuits, government ministries and national plans are useful sources of information.

Investors

Annual meetings, annual reports and prospectuses are primary sources of what competitors have to say about themselves. Credit reports and industry studies provide an outsider's viewpoint.

BENCHMARKING

There are several notions about what benchmarking is. Here we will adopt the view that benchmarking is the continuous process of measuring products, services and practices against the toughest competitors or those companies recognized as industry leaders with a view to stimulating performance improvement. Camp (1989) identified four types of benchmarking:

- benchmarking against internal operations
- benchmarking against external operations of direct competitors
- benchmarking against the equivalent functional operations of non-competitors
- generic process benchmarking.

These approaches all involve comparison of the performance and management of processes. A fifth category could be added – that of product benchmarking which compares the features and performance of products.

Competitor benchmarking involves performance comparisons between organizations which are direct competitors. Some competitor comparisons are possible from public sources, but these are often of limited detail and hence limited value.

MARKET SIGNALS

A market signal is any action by a competitor that provides direct or indirect indications of its intention, motives, goals or internal situation. Some signals are bluffs, some are warnings and some are serious commitments to a course of action. Market signals are indirect ways of communicating in the market place and can be interpreted so as to assist competitor analysis and strategy formulation. A prerequisite to interpreting signals correctly is to develop a baseline competitor analysis – an understanding of a competitor's future goals, assumptions about the market and themselves, current strategies and capabilities. The ability to read market signals rests on subtle judgements about competitors relating to known aspects of their situations with their behaviour.

TYPES OF MARKET SIGNALS

Market signals have two different functions: they can be truthful indicators of a competitor's motives, intentions or goals or they can be bluffs. Bluffs are signals designed to mislead other firms into taking or not taking action to benefit the signaller. Discerning the difference between the two can often involve subtle judgements. Market signals take a variety of forms, depending on the particular competitive behaviour involved and the medium employed. The important types of market signals are as follows:

Prior announcement of moves

This is a formal communication made by a competitor that it either will or will not take some action, such as instigating a price change. Such an announcement does not mean with certainty that the action will be taken. Announcements can be made that are not carried out, either because nothing was done or a later announcement nullified the action.

In general, prior announcements can serve a number of signalling functions that are not mutually exclusive:

- *Pre-empting other competitors*. They can be an attempt to indicate a commitment to take action for the purpose of pre-empting other competitors. For example, indicating that it is going to launch a new product well before it is ready for the market place, seeking to get customers to wait for the new product rather than buy a competitor's product in the meantime.

- *Threats to competitors*. Announcements can be threats of action to be taken if a competitor follows through with a planned move. For example, a firm might hear that its competitor is about to lower its price. The firm might then announce that it too is to introduce a price reduction below that indicated by its competitor. Such an announcement would indicate that the firm is quite happy to engage in a price war and this may well deter the other firm from making the first price reduction.
- *Tests of competitors' feelings*. A firm may be contemplating the introduction of a new type of after-sales agreement but is unsure whether competitors will view this with pleasure or displeasure. By making an announcement about the new scheme the firm can test competitors' reactions to its proposals.
- *Minimizing the provocation of a forthcoming strategic adjustment*. This kind of approach seeks to minimize unwelcome retaliation and warfare resulting from a strategic adjustment. It usually takes the form of announcing the strategic adjustment and providing full information as to why the firm believes that the adjustment is necessary. Caution has to be exercised when interpreting such signals since the firm may simply be trying to disguise an aggressive move.
- *Internal marketing*. Announcements can sometimes serve the purpose of seeking internal support for a move. Committing the firm to do something publicly can be a way of extinguishing internal debate about its desirability.

One of the most difficult tasks is to determine whether a prior announcement is an attempt at pre-emption or a conciliatory move. One can attempt to assess this by studying the lasting benefits that might accrue to competitors from pre-emption. If such benefits exist then it could well indicate announcements prelude pre-emption. Conversely, if the competitor acting in its own narrow self-interest could have done better through a surprise move, then conciliation may be indicated. An announcement that discloses an action much less damaging than it otherwise might have been, given the capabilities of the competitor, may usually be viewed as conciliatory. Announcements much in advance of a move tend to be conciliatory.

Announcements can be bluffs because they need not always be carried out. As such they may simply be viewed as mechanisms designed to produce some response from competitors not to continue with a line of action they may be contemplating instigating. Occasionally, it can be a bluff designed to trick competitors into expanding resources in gearing up to defend against a non-existent threat.

The medium in which a prior announcement appears may be a clue to its underlying motives.

Announcement of results or actions after the fact

These often take the form of announcements about sales figures, additions of capacity and so on. They ensure that other firms know about the data released and this may in turn influence the latter's behaviour. Such announcements can be misleading, though this is not always the case.

Public discussion of the industry by competitors

Competitors often comment on industry conditions and on prospects for the future. These commentaries are often full of signals which testify to the commenting firm's assumptions about the industry and presumably by implication the strategy they are developing. In addition to commentary on the industry generally, competitors sometimes comment on their rival's direct moves. Such commentary can signal displeasure or pleasure with a move.

The manner in which strategic changes are implemented

When introducing a new product it can be initially introduced to a peripheral market or it can immediately be aggressively sold to the key customers of its rivals. A price change may be made initially on products that represent the heart of a competitor's product line, or the price changes can be first put into effect in product or market segments where the competitor does not have any great interest. A move can be made at the normal time of the year or it can be made at an unusual time. Of course there can be bluffs.

Divergence from past goals

If a competitor has historically produced products exclusively at the high end of the product spectrum in terms of quality, its introduction of a significantly inferior product is an indication of a potential major realignment of its goals or assumptions.

Divergence from industry norms

A move that diverges from industry norms is usually an aggressive signal.

The cross-parry

When one firm initiates a move in one area and a competitor responds in a different area with one that affects the initiating firm, the situation is referred to as a cross-parry. It occurs where firms compete in different geographic areas or have multiple product lines that do not completely overlap. It represents a choice for the defending firm not to counter the initial move directly but to counter it indirectly. In responding indirectly, the responding firm may well be trying not to trigger a set of destructive moves and counter-moves in the encroached-upon market but to clearly signal displeasure and raise the threat of retaliation at a later date. If the cross-parry is towards one of the initiator's important markets it may be interpreted as a strong warning. If it is towards a lesser market then the warning will be less severe.

   The cross-parry is an effective way to discipline a competitor if there is a great divergence of market shares. If, for example, a price cut is involved then the cost of meeting this price cut will be greatest for the firm with the largest share. If the firm with the largest share in the cross-parry market initiated the first move then this may increase the pressure on the firm to back off.

The fighting brand

A form of signal related to the cross-parry is the fighting brand. A firm threatened or potentially threatened by another can introduce a brand that has the effect of punishing or threatening to punish the source of the threat. Fighting brands are warnings or deterrents to absorb the brunt of a competitive attack. They are also introduced with little push or support before any serious attack occurs, thereby serving as a warning. Fighting brands can also be used as an offensive weapon as part of a larger campaign.

Recourse to legal action

Large firms sometimes force smaller ones to yield ground by threatening to take legal action for a variety of patent and other infringements – even if no such infringements actually exist. Such firms force the weaker firm to comply because it does not want to bear the extremely high legal costs which it can incur in order to make its case.

Historical analysis of signals

Studying the historical relationship between a firm's announcements and its moves, or between other varieties of potential signals and the subsequent outcomes can greatly improve the ability to read signals accurately. Searching for signs that a competitor may have given in the past before making changes can also help to reveal types of unconscious signal unique to that competitor.

QUESTIONS

1   Discuss the usefulness of Porter's five forces model in helping an organization to develop its business strategies.
2   Porter argues that failure to make the choice between cost leadership and differentiation implies that a company is 'stuck in the middle', with no competitive advantage. How can this point of view be reconciled with the success of those firms which apply both of these strategic thrusts?
3   Differentiate between:
    (a) market leader
    (b) market challenger
    (c) market follower
    (d) market nicher
    and discuss the various strategies which might be pursued by each one of the four categories.
4   How might a firm set about trying to collect information on a continuous basis about its competitors?
5   Discuss the usefulness of market signals in the context of trying to understand competitors' moves.

CASE STUDIES

Cyproswim Ltd

A brief history of the company

Even if the swimming pool industry in the US and in Europe has a long history, in Cyprus there were no swimming pools until 1967. The first pools that were constructed were those of the Ledra Palace

(Nicosia), Hilton (Nicosia) and Forest Park (Limassol) hotels, between 1966 and 1967. However, there was no specialized business responsible for the construction and maintenance of swimming pools. The construction of the pools mentioned above was undertaken by air-conditioning businesses. The significant increase in tourism in the country created the need for more hotels. The founder of the first swimming pool business in Cyprus realized the high market potential and decided to establish its business under the name of Cyproswim Ltd, undertaking the construction of the swimming pools at the Apollonia (Limassol), Golden Sands and Salamis Bay (Famagusta) hotels.

The demand for swimming pools was high, people responded positively and the local government was supportive towards the import of swimming pool equipment and chemicals. The first equipment was imported from the US. The installation of swimming pool equipment, maintenance and the chemical treatment were among the key business activities undertaken by the company. The company's efforts were not only supported by the government of Cyprus but also by the Cyprus Tourism Organization.

The lack of availability of skilled labour, and the rapid increase in the demand of services were the key problems encountered by the company. The electrical and plumbing installations that are essential for the construction of a swimming pool could not be carried out due to the lack of professionals that had the knowledge and knowhow. Cyproswim took the initiative to organize a seminar given by American specialists at the American Embassy. The company's manager also realized the importance of attending exhibitions and trade shows.

Apart from the above problems, the partition of Cyprus had a negative impact on the company which at the time possessed more than 95 per cent of the market. Most business was located in the north of Cyprus and hence was lost. Also, machinery that had a value of CP5000 at the time and was delivered to the Dome Hotel in Kyrenia was never paid for.

However, new business opportunities were explored in the Greek Cypriot part of the island since new hotels were built. Swimming pools were also built by wealthy individuals at their houses. For many years the company was operating in a monopolistic market, which enabled it to achieve economies of scale.

A few years later, another swimming pool business under the name Poseidon entered the market. However, to this day the firm does not undertake the construction of swimming pools but only chemical treatment. A third company entered the market offering the same services as Cyproswim. In the late 1980s two more companies were established that marketed prefabricated pools. Prefabricated pools are often preferred by individuals rather than hotels. By the late 1990s, there were 12 swimming pool companies operating in Cyprus. Although the company owned the highest market share, it realized the importance of not losing sight of its competitors.

The company's competitors have managed to take a significant market share. In view of the strong competition, the management has started to consider marketing as a factor that plays an important role in the firm's success. Every year more and more effort is placed on marketing, and a higher proportion of the company's budget is absorbed by marketing activities, with the intention of satisfying the company's customers in the best possible way.

Contributed by Ioanna C. Papasolomou

QUESTION

What kind of competitor analysis would be of most benefit to Cyproswim? How might this analysis be reflected in its marketing strategy?

Cartech

A firm that innovates can steal a competitive advantage over other firms in its industry. Nevertheless, there are many innovations that fail in the market place. They fail to meet the expectations of the firms that launch them and quite often achieve abysmally low sales by any standard. Some of these products are good, whereas others are just gimmicks or fads. However, one thing does seem to be clear, if a new product does not stand out sufficiently well from other existing products in the market place then its chances of success are diminished.

Perhaps the best way to beat competition is to be so innovative that potential customers won't even see a product as having any potential substitutes. It has long been known, for example, that some people just adore the personification of inanimate objects. Children's toys are a good example. Toys with a repertoire of songs and sayings are always a favourite when displayed in most children's toy shops and attract considerable attention from passers by – both young and old. There have also been some more practical applications of voice technology in products. Most notable among these have been talking watches which have been a great help to the blind and partially sighted.

Cartech has extended voice technology to car alarms. It has produced a product which can be fitted in five minutes without tools or drilling. The alarm contains a deafening 130dB siren and also literally talks. When the alarm is activated by the remote control key-fob the alarm announces to all and sundry 'alarm armed' in confirmation. If someone sets off the alarm's built-in vibration sensors (with anything from a sharp jolt to a light tap) the alarm will react with the spoken words 'Stand back! This vehicle is alarmed'. When the alarm detects a change in electrical current (such as that produced by a door opening) the product will again emit an urgent spoken warning, followed by the siren if the words are ignored. Other voice command functions include an emergency panic button, activated by the remote control from either inside or outside the car ('Please help! Please help!' plus siren), a handy car finder button for crowded car parks ('Your car is here') and step by step vocal instructions for setting the sensitivity of the car alarm sensors.

Cartech feels that it has a unique product which is sufficiently different from anything else on the market to mean that it has no competition. It intends to set a premium price on the product, but before marketing the product is interested to analyse it in the context of competitive offerings just to confirm its own feelings.

QUESTIONS

1   Does the product really stand out from what competitors have to offer? Why or why not?
2   If the product is a success what other products might the firm also consider?

3 How should the firm set about marketing the talking alarm so as to maximize its prospects for success?

4 What kind of competitor research should the firm have undertaken prior to considering the development of such a product?

Evaluating competitive forces

A firm is evaluating the competitive forces at play within its primary market. Using a five-point scale it assesses points shown in Table 6.1.

QUESTION

How would you interpret these evaluations?

Arnos Group

The 'Popular Savings Bank of Arnos' was established with the aim of encouraging saving among the general public. Since its establishment, the corporation has emerged as one of the most competitive financial service organizations with operations expanded in nine countries. The company's long-term goal is the expansion and differentiation of its sources of income through the internalization of its operations with the focus being on Greece and countries with strong presence of Greek expatriates. In 1980, it opened its first branch in the UK, and in 2008 it started its operations in Australia. Today the corporation has six representative offices in Johannesburg, Toronto, Montreal, Belgrade, New York, and Moscow. The representative offices play a major role in its international activities and contribute significantly in the opening of new accounts and customer investments.

In 1995, the corporation introduced a new life insurance company, with the aim of providing innovative insurance schemes to customers. In 1998 the group introduced the first Internet banking service in the country, and in 1999 marked the creation of the Arnos Telebank, the first call centre in the country.

In 2000, the bank launched its new Corporate Identity. The name changed to 'Arnos Group'. In 2008 it celebrated its 100th anniversary and an e-bank was launched in Greece. In the same year it launched full banking services in Australia with five branches offering innovative products. In 2002, a new corporate image was established through the promotional message 'a lifelong assistance'. In 2005 the group proceeded with important strategic moves to support its efforts for the internalization of its operations. It founded a bank in France, and it expanded its operations to Croatia.

A milestone in the history of the group was the change in the composition of its share capital in 2006, with the acquisition of a strategic share by an investment fund. Subsequently, the company has been renamed into Arnos Popular Bank. The bank was in fact created by the merger of three groups: A Financial Group, Arnos Group, and another bank. The emergent corporation is characterized by dynamism, efficiency and a competitive advantage. The bank has been a pioneer of new technology and

Table 6.1 *Porter competition forces*

Competition among existing firms

Even distribution in terms of strength of competitors	1
The growth within the industry is slow or declining	2
Capital intensity/fixed costs are high	1
Switching costs for buyers is relatively easy/cheap	1
Incremental costs for increasing production/service delivery costs are high	2
Staying in the market/industry is very important to the incumbent firms	1
	Average

Threat of new entrants

Low economies of scale exist in the industry/market	5
Few or no cost disadvantages independent of scale	3
Low brand loyalty	4
Low customer loyalty	4
Easy to gain access to distribution	3
Little differentiation of products/services	2
Low expenditure on capital equipment in the market/industry	5
Low technological, regulatory or competence barriers	5
No excess production/supply capacity existing in market/industry	3
High industry/market growth	2
Low entry deterring price	4
Defensive retaliation threats low	3
	Average

Bargaining power of suppliers

Few substitute products/services exist	1
Limited number of suppliers or available supply	2
Industry unimportant as a customer for the supplier	4
Supplier's products is an important input	2
Suppliers can differentiate products	2
Threat of forward integration exists	2
High costs of switching to an alternative supply	1
	Average

Bargaining power of Buyer

Limited number of buyers	1
Purchases make up a significant proportion of buyer's costs	2
Products/services have little differentiation	3
Easy to switch to alternative suppliers	5
Threat of backward integration	2
Purchases are of low importance	2
Buyer has full information on costs and performance	2
	Average

Threat of substitute products

Buyers can easily change to buying the substitute without penalty	1
Buyer acceptability of substitutes is high	2
Price/performance of substitute is comparatively high	1
	Average

Notes: 5 = strongly agree; 0 = strongly disagree

was one of the first banks to recognize the value of technology within financial services and focuses on pioneering electronic banking services in the region.

The bank has received many awards for its achievements in banking and technology over the years. In 2005, the group received the following awards:

- 'Bank of the year'.
- 'Best in class' for custody services, from an internationally renowed finance magazine.
- 'Best private banking in Europe'.

The group focuses on expanding its operations in south-eastern Europe and offering higher service quality, more competitive products, and increased shareholder value. The company's approach to improving its international presence is founded on plans to acquire new banking units in Russia by purchasing local retail banks in order to be able to offer full banking services.

The main competitor of the bank is the Bank of Arnos Group. The bank is a leading financial services organization with a strong presence in Greece, the UK and Australia. The group provides a wide range of financial products/services which include banking services in the following countries: Crete, Greece, UK, Australia, Romania, Russia and the Channel islands. The corporation operates six branches in the United Kingdom and since 2000 its international operations have been enhanced with a wholly owned subsidiary bank in Australia. In 2007, the bank expanded its operations in Romania with the provision of leasing services and it also acquired the relevant banking license from the Central Bank of Russia for the provision of banking services in the country. The group is also the first corporation from the regions financial services world to set up full banking operations by opening up local branches in ex-Soviet bloc countries.

The country has emerged as a major international financial centre due to the following factors: the legal framework, the infrastructure, the highly educated workforce, the comparative tax, and other fiscal incentives offered to international companies. As a result, many foreign businesses have established operations there. The financial services sector has grown significantly since accession into the European Union, which has steadily grown by over 50 per cent annually. The regulatory requirements regarding international businesses comply fully with the relevant European Union directives and other international requirements especially in terms of money laundering.

Contributed by Ioanna C. Papasolomou

QUESTIONS

1 Discuss the usefulness of Porter's five forces model in helping an organization such as the Arnos Popular Bank to develop its business strategies.
2 What types of information are required in order to monitor competitors continually?
3 What types of information source can financial service organizations use about competitors?

Chapter 7

Analysing the business environment

INTRODUCTION

While strategic windows open out on to markets within industries, these same markets and industries are dynamic and changing. To understand the causes and predict the consequences of the changes that take place, an organization needs to appreciate the broader business issues that are involved and the factors in the business environment which bring about such changes. Firms operate in changing and at times hostile business environments. Increasing environmental turbulence (O'Regan and Ghobadian, 2002; Dreyer and Gronhaug, 2004), has presented a variety of challenges for the strategic management of organizations.

The environment does not always accommodate the interests of the firm. An organization in its environment might be likened to a ship at sea. Sometimes the sea is rough and the ship has difficulty in making progress on its journey, sometimes it is calm and the weather is clear so that the ship can make steady progress. Sometimes the weather is malevolent: there are thick fogs and icebergs which create risk for the very survival of the ship. Organizational environments present the same kinds of opportunities and threats for the organization as the sea does for the ship.

Organizations need to respond and adapt to changing environmental conditions if they intend to survive. They can even instigate changes in the environment which are in their own interests. Both demand an understanding of those factors and forces which bring about change in the environment. Ideally, an organization should adapt to changes as they occur, even anticipate them in advance or systematically instigate changes to its own advantage. An inability to do so can put organizations in positions where their short- and long-term survival is jeopardized. The business environment is the setting within which a business operates, formulates policies and makes decisions. It is usual to distinguish between the internal and the external environment. The former usually comprises the various assets and resources possessed by the organization. That is, its workforce, plant and machinery, knowhow, financial resources, etc. The latter refers to people, institutions and developments, etc., which exert an external influence on how the organization performs. Of course, with the emergence of strategic alliances and networks such a definition of boundaries does tend to become more blurred.

Firms need to know all about the business environment in which they operate. It is essential that they can anticipate the changes that are likely to take place in the marketing environment in the foreseeable future. However, as noted above, it is not simply a matter of adapting to change. Organizations can also exercise their own influence on the environment. Among the ways that this can be achieved is the development and commercialization of new technological ideas. These new technologies then become part of the business environment and in their turn have an impact upon what other organizations can do.

Considerable control can be exercised over its internal environment by a firm, but a firm cannot exert control in the same way or to the same extent over the external environment. It can only attempt to influence it. There are various ways of influencing events in the external environment. These may include activities such as lobbying among legislative groups. The latter is what organizations often do when trying to influence the formulation of European Union directives which can have an impact on such things as product design safety standards, etc.

CHANGING PATTERNS AND CHANGING STRATEGIES

Marketing policies, plans and decisions are implemented in the context of an ever-changing external environment. The nature of this environment and the changes occurring within it present opportunities, threats and constraints to an organization's activities.

The changing nature of markets requires entirely different marketing strategies to be adopted for the same products from time to time. There are fragmented markets and mass markets. Mass markets are markets in which there is a large volume demand for a standard product. Fragmented markets are based upon distinct niches and segments.

There are many examples of changes in the marketing environment that impact heavily upon organizations and what they have to do in order to survive and prosper. For instance, from the point of view of technological change, the introduction of the microchip has had a major impact on many types of consumer durables, e.g. washers, cookers, etc. and on home entertainment, home-based office work and computer-based learning in education.

Since the 1980s there have been many changes in people's shopping habits as a greater emphasis has been put on convenience shopping. Since joining the EU, British firms and people have been influenced by the ideas expressed in other EU countries and enacted through the European parliament. Indeed all the forces of the marketing environment have made an impact on what firms and people want and do throughout the world (Figure 7.1).

There are a variety of different environmental variables which affect consumers and firms. Social and cultural factors, political, fiscal and economic policies, and changes in technology all have an impact on customers' wants and needs for products and services and the kind of products and services that are produced. Customers and competitors, too, exert an influence and we will look at both of these two factors in detail in later chapters.

In the next section we will look specifically at social and cultural factors.

THE CHANGING NATURE OF SOCIAL AND CULTURAL ASPECTS OF CONSUMERS

We will look here at demography, the nature of cultural values, and changes in values and attitudes and how they impact upon the marketing activities of organizations.

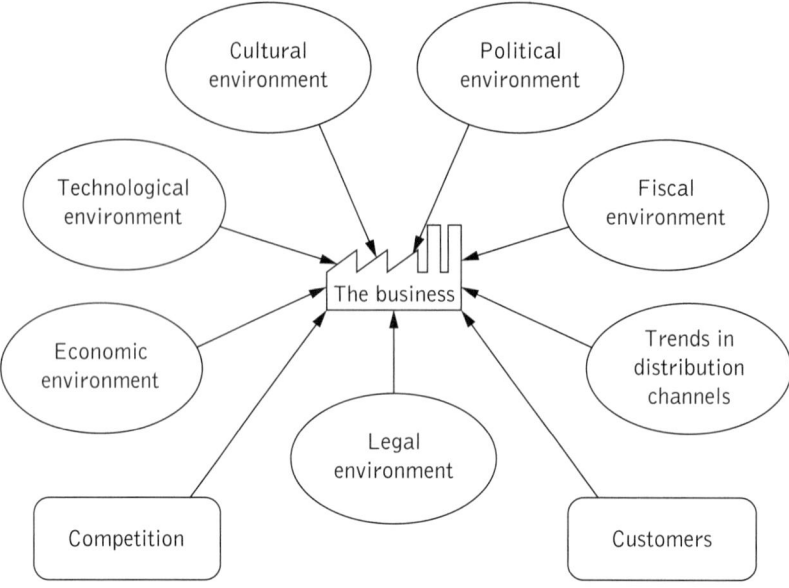

Figure 7.1 *The marketing environment*

Demography

Demographic and cultural factors make up society-wide influences and changes that can affect the marketing environment. In terms of demographic factors, the following are of interest to marketers:

- population: size, growth rate, distribution by gender, birth rates, death rates, life expectancy
- density: location, geographical/regional shifts
- household/family: size, make-up
- income/wealth distribution
- socio-economic groups: occupations, ethnic groups.

These factors change slowly over time and exert powerful effects on the volume and nature of demand for most products and services. Some influences are obvious: the demand for children's products and services will be related to birth rate patterns. The demand for products and services to meet the wants and needs of the elderly will be related to characteristics and trends of an ageing population.

In European countries in recent times there has been a slowing down of the birth rate. Along with this, an extension of life expectancy has resulted in a shift in the profile of the population to that of an ageing one. In addition, many changes have taken place in the make-up and size of family households. Fewer marriages and fewer children coupled with an increase in the labour force of married women have changed the basic nature of the family household. Career couples with no children are now quite common and are a target group of interest to many marketers because of their relatively high disposable income.

Another characteristic seems to have been a growth in non-family households. Some of these are made up of single, career people, whereas others are made up of divorced or widowed adults. There has also been an increase in single parent families. These changes in the structure and characteristics of households have had a major affect on the pattern of demand for a wide range of everyday goods and services.

As far as income and wealth are concerned, the total gross domestic product of Europe is now greater than that of the US and accounts for over one-third of world GDP and much of world trade (Haliburton and Hunerberg, 1993). Within Europe there are disparities in terms of relative wealth. In the case of Switzerland, for example, per capita GDP is many more times that of Portugal. These differences seem to be widening because of the unequal effects of the recent recession and the relatively higher population growth in the poorer countries.

There are also marked disparities of wealth distribution within individual countries in Europe. For example, northern versus southern Italy, the southeast of England versus the peripheral UK regions and, to an extent, regional differences in Germany. It is not appropriate therefore to regard Europe as a single economic region for products which are directly influenced by the level of economic development.

The nature of cultural values

Often, different regions of a country exhibit different buying preference patterns that seem to reflect different cultural and traditional values. In addition, because many towns and cities throughout the world are now very cosmopolitan in nature, it is quite common to find large ethnic groups living in fairly large concentrations in urban areas. These groups have distinct cultural values which are reflected in their buying preference patterns. For example, ethnic minorities make up a very small proportion of the population of the UK. But in the Greater London area, in the West Midlands and in West Yorkshire it is significantly greater.

Culture is reflected in the prevalent core beliefs and values of people. These beliefs and values are declared in family and friendship relations, in social conventions and rites, in social institutions and in social order itself. They take a long time to change since they are inextricably linked to such things as family upbringing, the education system, national history, religion and various other institutional phenomena.

A variety of secondary beliefs and values which are less durable and more situationally determined are also to be found. For example, while belief in law enforcement may be rooted in core values, attitudes towards private law enforcement and vigilantes reflect secondary values and beliefs. These beliefs are more likely to vary within society and to change over time. They may also be recognizable in sub-cultures within society. Sub-cultures evolve for a variety of reasons and commonly involve a grouping of people with common interests, experiences and motivations. Cultures may also be identified with age groupings, regional affiliations, religious or ethnic associations, or even situational facets of life-style (e.g. students).

From the point of view of international marketing, language is an important aspect of culture which is particularly relevant to marketing communications. Barring the Swiss, the Dutch and, to a lesser extent, the Scandinavians and the Germans, Europeans experience major language hurdles. However, among the younger generation of Europeans the situation is improving and 'international English' is growing in popularity. Another aspect of culture which has an influence on consumers is religion. Religious beliefs, both at home and abroad, have a major influence on consumer attitudes and purchase behaviour. This is often reflected in the kinds of food that people consume, the drinks they purchase and even their manner of dress. Moreover, even business practices can vary considerably between different areas and countries.

Marketers have to understand cultural values in all aspects of implementing the marketing concept and managing the marketing mix.

Changes in values and attitudes

The 'permissive' society of the 1960s and the effects of its aftermath reflecting individualism exerted considerable influence on values and attitudes in the 1970s and 1980s. However, it would seem that these changes may now be undergoing a reversal. Today, people have in some respects returned to the social norms of the pre-1960s. Nevertheless, there are still many ways in which attitudes are considerably different to those of the pre-1960s.

Attitudes towards credit have changed substantially since the 1980s. Traditionally, credit purchasing was something which people tended to avoid. Indeed, there was at one time a social stigma against purchasing on credit except for major purchases such as homes and cars. This may have been a carry over of so-called 'Victorian' values or even a product of the hardships of debt which ensued during the years of depression – particularly in the 1920s and 1930s. Credit purchasing started to develop in the late 1950s as consumer confidence began to be restored following the hardships and rationing which existed in Britain in the immediate post-war period.

The Conservatives' message of 'You have never had it so good' which was popular in the late 1950s and early 1960s had a ring of truth about it. For many people, more affluent times have continued and today, credit has become an intrinsic part in the marketing of many products.

Changes in society's attitudes towards health over a similar period of time have resulted in a multi-million pound industry developing and the supply of health products and services. People are now more weight conscious, exercise conscious and conscious about their diets. Moreover, smoking which at one time was regarded a social sophistication is now considered to be anti-social.

There have been many changes in attitudes over the years which have had implications for marketing. One of the most far-reaching of these concerns the role of working women in western society. At one time British women tended to stay at home and rarely held jobs with substantial incomes. This situation has undergone considerable change and a high proportion of the workforce are women. This may have contributed to the acceptance of convenience foods and the widespread adoption of home freezers and microwave ovens as well as one-stop shopping.

THE INFLUENCE OF POLITICAL, FISCAL AND ECONOMIC POLICIES

Having examined one aspect of the environment, consumers and culture, and its impact on marketing activities, we now turn to examine those usually exerted by government: political, fiscal and economic policies.

Political and fiscal policies

Governments are in a position to take actions which can substantially alter a company's marketing environment. In the UK, privatization of the public utilities has created new terms and conditions for their suppliers and subcontractors. The creation of an internal market within the health service has had a substantial impact on the way in which hospitals and other health service units go about their work. The sale of Jaguar in the car industry and of British Airways has created commercially competitive companies which have had a substantial impact on the competitors in their respective industries. Deregulation in the EU has created opportunities and threats across borders. In the case of car manufacturers, their ability to restrict certain models to specific countries has been swept aside.

Legislation over such things as labelling, packaging, advertising and environmentalism all have to be taken into account when designing packaging and formulating advertising messages.

To discourage demand for certain imported goods, governments impose tariffs on them. Firms wanting to import such goods then must find ways of getting round the problems that this creates. For example, a government may impose low tariffs on sub-assemblies and firms may prefer to import sub-assemblies instead of fully assembled goods on which high tariffs have been placed. The lower tariffs may have been placed on sub-assemblies because local people can be employed to assemble the sub-assemblies into finished goods and this provides jobs which the government wants to encourage.

Political instability in a country can also have a marked effect on marketing methods used by exporters in accessing that country's markets. Under such circumstances it may be preferable, for example, to sell the licence to manufacture the product to a producer in the country concerned for a once-only royalty fee. Licences may be granted to produce or market goods and services. In the former case, the licence relates to knowhow. Royalty payments can be one-off payments or they can be fixed as a percentage of subsequent sales.

The economic cycle

Traditionally, the economy has been considered to follow a cyclical pattern consisting of four stages: boom, recession, slump (depression) and recovery. Various industries, markets and organizations can, of course, break this trend, either demonstrating a decline in growth during a boom, or an expansion during a slump.

In each stage of the cycle there are different business patterns (Figure 7.2). In times of prosperity, consumer spending is high. Organizations normally exploit this by extending product lines, increasing promotional efforts, expanding distribution and raising prices, on the presumption that consumers are often willing to pay more for well known and well established products and have the means to do so.

In times of recession, the purchasing power of consumers declines and may even stagnate when the economy enters into recovery. During a recession, consumers may shift their buying patterns to purchasing more basic, more functional, less expensive products and spend less on non-essential products. This means that decisions on the purchase of luxury items, such as cars or new homes, may be postponed. Not surprisingly, it is the producers and marketers of luxury goods who are most affected by an economic recession. The strategy for marketers during times of recession is usually to reduce prices, and prune the size of product lines.

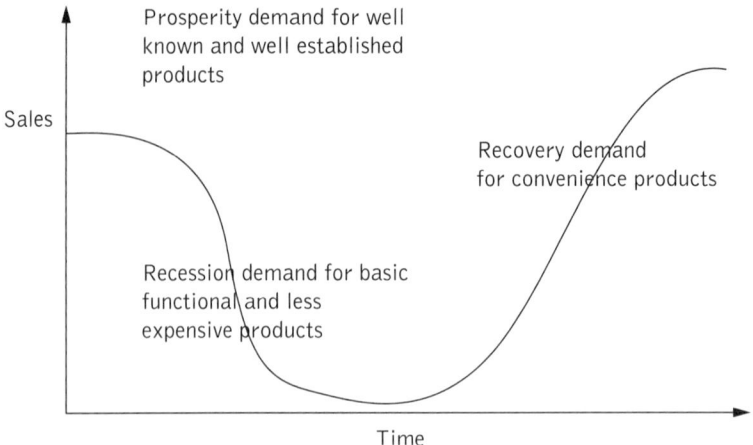

Figure 7.2 *Effects of booms and slumps in the economy*

As recovery starts to be felt, consumers begin to buy convenience products and higher priced goods and services. Assessing the strength of a recovery is difficult and organizations have to assess how quickly consumers are making the transition from recession.

Inflation

One of the most difficult phenomena to deal with during the economic cycle is inflation. Inflation is an increase in the general level of prices in an economy that is sustained over time. Inflation has two main causes:

- *excess demand* beyond the output capacity of the economy to supply goods and services
- *increases in input costs*: wages, raw materials and components.

Inflation, produced by rising prices and resulting in reduced consumer buying power, creates problems for the marketer. Not only is uncertainty introduced into the market through the effect of inflation on costs and sales forecasts, but it also makes it difficult to determine the price to charge during the next budgeting period.

Inflation is not welcomed by the business community. It is administratively expensive to constantly change prices in line with inflation and it can affect a firm's competitive positions in both domestic and foreign markets. High rates of inflation effectively make imports cheaper but make exports more expensive.

Next we will consider another of the environmental forces acting upon firms – technology.

THE INFLUENCE OF TECHNOLOGY

In modern times the influence of technology in the marketing environment has come to the fore. Technology has always been important but the rate of innovation has increased so rapidly in recent years that the impact of technology has become a principal driving force in business activity. In this section we examine the increasingly important role that technology has to play.

Technology is a major driving force for change everywhere. Major changes created through developments in technology have increased the potential losses or rewards associated with commercial success and failure. Technological progress depends on a process of successful innovation which involves commercialization of ideas and an understanding of market needs (Figure 7.3). The role of marketing is to guide development efforts and facilitate commercialization. The Sony Walkman presents an example of a product that matched customers' wants. In terms of technology sophistication it was basic and unexciting but the key element of its success was that it met a latent market need for a cheap, portable cassette player.

Technological advances and improvements are a feature of modern-day business. The obsolescence of products within a relatively short period from their introduction is commonplace. Personal computers are a good example of where product obsolescence can be very rapid indeed. Moreover, it is increasingly the case that tomorrow's products are no longer news by the time they are put on the market. During the lead time between an announcement of a new product and the time it can be made available to the consumer, competitors may already have announced improved or better versions of the same product.

Organizations which do not react to technological advances which are relevant to the kinds of products they produce run the risk of rapid product obsolescence and going out of business.

Another important aspect of the environment which impacts on marketing activities is changes in distribution patterns. In the next section we will examine this important topic in some detail.

CHANGES IN DISTRIBUTION PATTERNS

Distribution is part of marketing and the patterns of distribution have changed substantially since the 1960s. The impact of changes in distribution patterns is perhaps felt most in the case of consumer goods marketers, particularly in retailing.

In the UK, the growth in car ownership, the trend to a high percentage of husbands and wives both working, together with increasing standards of living has led to less time being available for shopping plus greater mobility of the shopper. All of these factors, in turn, have led to the need for one-stop

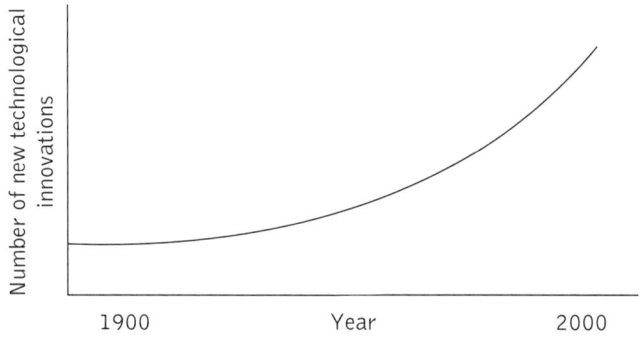

Figure 7.3 *Rate of technological change*

shopping facilities and thence to the development of supermarkets to provide this facility. Many of the traditional retail outlets have suffered severe competition as a result – fishmongers, butchers, pharmacists, etc.

With the passage of time, some of the chain stores such as Boots and Marks & Spencer have increased the range of products they offer to customers – for example, Marks & Spencer's move into food retailing and more recently into furniture. Large specialist retailing establishments (superstores) are now emerging to meet the needs of specific market segments – for example, Texas in the do-it-yourself home-care market.

HOW FIRMS ARE RESPONDING TO ENVIRONMENTAL CHANGE

Firms have adopted a number of ways of coming to grips with the ever-changing complexity of the environment. Foremost among these is the implementation of an effective marketing information system and the use of ongoing market research so that reaction time to change can be speeded up. These will be considered in more detail in later chapters on marketing information systems and marketing research. Another approach involves what is called 'fast track' marketing. Increasing rates of technological change and the shortening of the life of products mean that companies have to act quickly when they are introducing new products to the market (the process of new product development is discussed in a later chapter).

Late entrants to a market with a new product may find that the product does not offer attractive financial prospects since the product's commercial life is much shorter than might have been typical in the 1980s. This is obviously most applicable to those industrial markets where product development times can be counted in years, e.g. military and commercial aircraft. The response is to look for ways of reducing the amount of time in developing and testing a product. The implication of this is that organizations have to 'manage in parallel' and not sequentially. This means that instead of one stage following on from another, wherever possible the two stages take place at the same time. Spending more money to speed up the process of innovation is another strategy, while spending more effort on planning things before something is put into action also appears to bear dividends.

Another area which is receiving considerable attention is preservation of the physical environment. Public awareness of the damage that processes and products can do the physical environment has increased the pressure on firms to act in a way which preserves the physical environment rather than destroys it. We explore ways in which firms are reacting to this challenge in the next section on 'green' marketing.

GREEN MARKETING

Green principles relate to the preservation of the environment. There are a number of issues which have important implications for marketing. These issues are now being tackled and in many cases firms take advantage of the fact that they are producing environmentally friendly products when they are promoting the products. The kinds of problems which exist and how firms are tackling these problems are discussed below.

It was found that damage was being caused by chloro-fluoro-carbons (CFCs) to the Earth's ozone layer. This led to the gradual removal of CFCs from all products and, in particular, aerosol products.

Chemicals are a major force in environmental pollution. In an effort to make more productive use of land, intensive farming methods make use of artificial fertilizers and pesticides. Unfortunately, these can have a detrimental effect on the environment. The use of phosphates and bleaches in household detergents and the dumping of waste into rivers and the sea can also damage the environment. Organizations are changing their working practices to prevent such occurrences.

Another problem is that caused by the disposal of waste. This too can create environmental pollution. Packaging materials in which goods are shipped are a major contributor to waste. Over-packaging is being discouraged and the use of reusable or recyclable materials encouraged.

Greenbelt countryside is rapidly disappearing in many parts of the world as urban expansion occurs. Along with the disappearance of greenbelt countryside has been the encroachment of commercial and industrial developments on the natural habitats of animals. More and better use of existing urban retailing and manufacturing sites has provided a partial answer to this problem.

Animals have been the object of abuse and cruelty for a wide variety of purposes. Steps are being taken to create awareness, interest, desire and action to prevent this continuing unabated.

People may become increasingly more aware of the damage that can be caused to the environment by products, packaging, by-products and production processes. They may gradually learn to adopt more environmentally friendly products and, in particular, reject throwaway products.

Green labels

The UK government's plans for an official eco-label on green products were outlined in a Department of the Environment (as it was then) white paper in November 1991. The kind of products covered by the eco-labelling scheme were those where there was a significant impact on the environment or where there was a high degree of consumer confusion about the environmental claims.

Green issues are increasingly seen as important by consumers and this is being reflected in the types of products consumers want to use. Organizations are having to change the nature of their products to meet these requirements. Although many firms do appear to possess a social conscience or see the benefits of meeting the demands of green issues, this is not always the case. The legal infrastructure provides a remedy for this kind of abuse and many other kinds of business bad practices. In the next section we will examine this in more detail.

THE LEGAL ENVIRONMENT AND ITS INFLUENCE ON MARKETING ACTIVITIES

Although most firms willingly collaborate to act in the interests of society and behave in a reputable way, unfortunately there are firms who do not. In this section we will look at how the legal dimension of the marketing environment acts to preserve the best interests of customers and ensure fair competition in the market place.

Sometimes, goods are bought that are not of merchantable quality and it is not apparent at the time of purchase. The law exists to protect customers from unscrupulous manufacturers and dealers who produce shoddy, defective or dangerous goods. This also applies to the purchase of services.

Legislation may also be passed to curb unfair trading practices. This can occur when companies engage in trading practices which are not in the best interests of the customer. In the UK a variety of important Acts of Parliament have been passed which have either a direct or indirect effect on marketing in the UK. Similar kinds of laws may exist in other countries but this is not always the case.

Acts of Parliament pertinent to marketing which have been passed in the UK cover such things as requirements with respect to the labelling and advertising of foods; the provision of remedies where goods or services purchased do not match with the descriptions given for them; and making it an offence for anyone to demand payment for goods or services that have not been ordered.

There are also Acts concerning products offered at 'sale' prices; goods bought on credit; guarantees or conditions of sale; liability of traders for death or personal injury arising from negligence or from breach of duty; defects in products that give rise to damage; and the provision of a regulatory framework for the financial services industry. Legislation also covers anti-competitive practices in both public and private sectors.

ETHICS AND CODE OF PRACTICE

Laws are enacted to deal with behaviour which is generally considered to be illegal. Defining the boundary between what might be considered lawful and what is not lawful can sometimes be a difficult task. For instance, something might not technically be considered illegal, yet it might be considered undesirable and even immoral. In this section we pay attention to actions which although not against the law may be considered to be undesirable and not in the best interests of the consumer.

Ethics is a study of the principles of morality. In the setting of marketing, ethics relates to activities which although not actually illegal raise moral questions about their use. It is important to differentiate between practices which are illegal and those which are unethical. It is necessary to make these distinctions because of the way in which society reacts to violations of good behaviour. Where something is deemed to be illegal, the remedy is to seek redress through the law. Where something is considered to be unethical, one can only seek redress through pressure groups such as 'watch-dogs' (see below).

The practice of marketing can give rise to many ethical issues. There is a view that marketing creates wants that did not previously exist and which perhaps are not needed. Adherents to this philosophy argue that this is not in the best interests of society since it can lead to all kinds of undesirable social consequences. In the case of products such as drugs, legislation exists to outlaw trading in such goods except under medical supervision. However, there are a range of other products that are more difficult to deal with since the products themselves are not illegal. Cigarettes, alcohol and pornography are among the products which are the subject of contention.

Ethical issues arise also in connection with how organizations market their products. Advertising which makes misleading claims about products or services and advertising which operates at a subliminal level are examples. Price fixing, although legally outlawed, may still operate since its existence may be difficult to substantiate. Moreover, distributors may fail to live up to agreements they have made with producers without the latter's knowledge.

Because ethical problems arise in business and because they cannot often be dealt with inside the legal framework, other ways have to be found for dealing with them. In the next section we look at the various ways in which these problems may be properly addressed.

PRESSURE GROUPS, WATCH-DOGS AND CONSUMERISM

Pressure groups have come into being in response to the perpetration of unethical or undesirable practices. The purpose of such groups is to influence how decisions that result in socially unacceptable consequences are made and to bring to the attention of the public and governments the need to outlaw such practices.

Watch-dog organizations exist to deal with complaints about public sector organizations. Complaints received from users of these services are publicized. Another kind of group, environmental watch-dog organizations, look out for matters relating to protecting the environment. They seek to oppose plans to build factories or houses in the open countryside in some cases, and watch for environmental pollution caused by factories.

Consumerism is an organized movement established to guard the economic interests of consumers by compelling companies to behave in a socially responsible manner. Many organizations have produced voluntary codes of practice relating to matters which may give rise to environmental pollution as a result of pressure from consumerism. The government has established the Office of Fair Trading to encourage competition between organizations that is fair to each of them and fair to the consumer. There are various bodies which exist to protect the customer.

The Consumer Protection Advisory Committee was set up to deal with such things as terms and conditions of sale; prices; advertising, labelling and promoting goods and services; and selling methods. The National Consumer Council deals with presenting the opinions of consumers to industry and the government. The County Council Trading Standards/Consumer Protection departments deal with complaints from members of the public. The District Council Environmental Health departments enforce offences against particular Acts, such as food and drink which is not fit for sale and any other matters relating to shop hygiene.

Another body, the Advertising Standards Authority monitors the standard of advertising in the UK. Complaints can be made by members of the public direct to this body. A monthly report is issued which lists complaints received and the action taken by the Advertising Standards Authority.

PREDICTING ENVIRONMENTAL TRENDS AND EVENTS

Scenario writing

This is a tool developed and used originally in long-term planning and technological forecasting. It is a particularly useful method for speculating on the likelihood of new paradigm shifts.

Scenario writing is a method of looking ahead and forces an organization to be receptive to the need for change and creative thinking. It is an experience which involves considering new possibilities and opening up one's mind to considering what might happen.

The method involves all members of a team of co-workers and requires a leader or facilitator who introduces and co-ordinates sessions and who has the responsibility for producing a final report. Members of the team are referred to as scenario writers and each member is usually an expert in his or her own field. One needs to make sure that there are experts in the group whose expertise is relevant to the problem under study.

At the start of the exercise, the scenario writers are briefed with the task of considering the developments in their area of expertise over the next 5 to 10 years. When they have done this individually they are brought together under the guidance of a leader to examine the situation collectively. Participants need to be reminded that they should be tolerant of the views of others because a consensus of informed opinion has to be reached.

The procedure adopted is as follows:

1 *Briefing*: here the scenario writers are requested to consider what developments will take place in their area of specialization over the next 5 to 10 years. They are also asked to provide supporting evidence for this and to assess the likely impact of these developments on the organization (see Exhibit 7.1).
2 *Individual scenario writing*: scenario writers spend up to two weeks preparing their individual scenarios independently.
3 *Collective scenario writing*: here the scenario writers meet up to present their individual papers and viewpoints and to reach a consensus viewpoint on possible developments. The output of the meeting is usually the report.

Scenario writing can be extremely useful and productive where the situation under review is a very complex one. It is, however, extremely time consuming.

Although scenario writing is a formal procedure it is still speculative in nature since it aims to predict the future of an organization thus aiding the strategic planning process. The exercise can be conducted over a fairly lengthy time period (say two weeks) for its participants have to prepare a written report explaining their view of the future. The participants will be experts in the various functions of the organization. The benefits of bringing together experts from various functions enables an integrated vision of the future to be examined with documentary evidence to support each argument. An awareness of the future environment (internal and external) and the change which may take place in it will provoke more creative responses to current situations.

Scenario daydreaming

Like scenario writing, this method also looks into the future and tries to assess the impact that trends will have on the organization. It is, however, less formal in its approach and it is not the custom and practice to produce a report. It is usual for the entire process to take up only a couple of days and is an ideal activity for an 'away day' venue, provided there are at least two away days available.

Scenario daydreamers are not expected to substantiate their contributions. The purpose is to stimulate people's imaginations to think in the broader context and to consider more unusual ideas. A good group size is 8 to 10 people, but of course much depends on the size of the organization and the complexity of its business.

Again there is a leader or facilitator whose role it is to plan the sessions in detail, advise on the selection of participants, brief the participants about the sessions, lead the sessions and help summarize the conclusions which are reached. Minutes of the session also need to be taken by someone. The procedure for the session is summarized below:

- preparation
- the nature of the proceedings are explained
- the scenario daydreaming session.

EXHIBIT 7.1   CROSS-IMPACT MATRIX

Product	Existing	Planned	Possible	Total
Environment	6	12	14	32
Technology	-2	3	2	3
Regulation	1	2	3	6
Economic	2	2	3	7
Cultural	2	2	3	7
Demographic	3	3	3	9
Market	6	2	-2	6
Europe	3	3	-2	4
Far East	3	-1	0	2
Competitor	2	0	-8	-6
Alpha	1	0	-4	-3
Beta	1	0	-4	-3
Customer	-5	6	6	7
Wholesalers	-3	3	3	3
Large retailers	-2	3	3	4
Total	9	20	10	39

Cross-impact analysis

One of the first things one has to do in strategy formulation at any level in an establishment is to examine how the organization relates to the environments around it. In particular one must focus on the impact that these environments can have on the enterprise's future prosperity.

Cross-impact analysis is a technique that helps in examining the impact that a mixture of external threats and opportunities can have on the undertakings of an organization. In implementing the technique one has to obtain data from a range of sources including customers, competitors, the market and the environment. The procedure involves assessing the impact that changes or trends in these factors are likely to have on present, proposed or potential activities of the organization. Anything that threatens the prosperity of the organization is viewed as having a negative effect on the establishment whereas opportunities are reasoned to have positive effects.

One records the various impacts on a grid and on a scale ranging from + 4 to −4, where 0 specifies a lack of impact. The sum of various extraneous threats and opportunities on each one of the identified business/organizational activities is then noted. In addition the total scores of opportunities and threats facing each activity of the organization are recorded. All ratings are a matter of the subjective opinions of executives.

Procedure

1 The session has to be divided into a beginning, a middle and an end.
2 It is helpful to have a warm-up session prior to the main session.
3 The first step is to identify the various factors that are likely to affect the future of the organization. These factors usually reflect aspects of the environment such as economic trends, cost of commodities, political and governmental policies, changes in demography, technology, social structure, consumer requirements and competitive activity.
4 The main factors should be summarized on a flip-chart and possibly entered into a cross-impact matrix to indicate their importance.
5 Those present are then split into groups and each group is given several of the factors to consider in depth and arrive at a future scenario for each factor. Group members should have the expertise to be able to scenario daydream effectively for the factors they have been allocated. Roughly half an hour per scenario should be taken.
6 Groups should then reassemble to present their scenarios to one another. The entire group should discuss each scenario in turn and reach a common consensus.
7 All the scenarios presented should be integrated into a single comprehensive vision of the future.
8 Groups break into syndicate again and consider how the organization can respond to the opportunities and threats that are presented. Brain-storming and the use of the TOWS matrix (see Exhibits 7.2 and 7.3) are useful tools to use at this point.
9 The whole group reconvenes and the leader should review the proceedings, summarizing how the group sees matters and how the organization can try to meet future challenges.

The TOWS matrix presents a mechanism for facilitating the linkages between company strengths and weaknesses and threats and opportunities in the environment. It also provides a framework for identifying and formulating strategies. Opportunities, threats, strengths and weaknesses have to be identified and listed in the matrix. Next, various combinations of opportunities and strengths, opportunities and weaknesses, threats and strengths, and weaknesses and threats are examined in order to generate possible strategies. It should be observed that in generating strategies one seeks to maximize on strengths and opportunities and minimize on weaknesses and threats. Brainstorming may be used effectively in helping to identify factors and generate strategies.

EXHIBIT 7.2   THE TOWS MATRIX (1)

	Strengths	*Weaknesses*
Opportunities	Maximize on strengths and opportunities	Maximize on opportunities, minimize on weaknesses
Threats	Maximize on strengths, minimize on threats	Minimize on weaknesses, minimize on threats

EXHIBIT 7.3 SWOT ANALYSIS AND THE TOWS MATRIX

SWOT analysis is a technique specifically designed to help with the identification of suitable business strategies for an organization to follow. It involves specifying and relating together organizational strengths and weaknesses and environmental opportunities and threats. In practice this is often an activity that is not carried out well. It is all too easy, having identified all the important points, not to know what to do with the data generated. Although intended as a mechanism to explain strategy rather than to facilitate its generation, the TOWS matrix (Weihrich, 1982) presents a mechanism for facilitating linkages and presents a framework for identifying and formulating strategies. Implementing the TOWS matrix requires that the following steps are carried out:

1   Pin-point and assess the impact of environmental factors: economic, political, demographic, products and technology, market and competition on the organization.
2   Make a prognosis about the future.
3   Undertake an assessment of 'strengths and weaknesses' in terms of management and organization, operations, finance and marketing.
4   Develop strategy options.

Working systematically through this process enables internal and external factors to be entered on a grid and different combinations to be studied. For example, the entry to one cell of the grid could involve maximizing opportunities and maximizing strengths. This would amount to putting together at least one strength and one opportunity to produce a strategy that capitalizes upon this combination.

Any kind of organizational unit can benefit from this type of analysis as well as any situation that involves strategic decision-making. Originally, Weihrich (1982) illustrated a conceptual application of the TOWS matrix to the strategic dilemma facing Volkswagen in the USA during the 1970s. His account demonstrated how the TOWS matrix could be used as a structuring device for analysing strategic problems. For the writer, this raised the interesting question of whether the use of the TOWS matrix could lead to the identification of appropriate strategies for an organization. In pursuing this question the writer has examined over 50 cases in which the TOWS matrix has been employed in commercial organizations (see Exhibit 7.4). In all of these cases the users of the technique have felt that the method has enabled them to gain a deeper insight into the process of strategy formulation, has helped to structure their thinking and has often enabled them to come up with good new strategic ideas.

EXHIBIT 7.4   THE TOES MATRIX (2)

Product: plastic bags

Strengths	*Weaknesses*	
	1 Brand name	1 Exports
	2 Distribution	2 Sales force
	3 Low costs	
Opportunities		
1 Need for robust rubbish	Use existing distribution and	Strengthen sales force
disposal bags	brand name to market scented	and export skills. Look
2 European markets	bin-liners (S1, S2, O3)	to European markets
3 Scented bin-liners		(W1, W2, O2)
Threats		
1 Substitute materials	Capitalize on brand name,	Develop capability in
2 Imports	distribution and low costs to	substitute materials
	meet competition from imports	particularly for products
	(S1, S2, S3, T2)	that can be sold to export
		markets (T1, W1)

QUESTIONS

1 What factors might give rise to inhospitable environments?

2 Why should some firms react only slowly to changing environments?

3 Discuss the various ways in which an organization can try to change its external environment.

4 How does society try to cope with deviant behaviour in the business environment? How does this affect what firms can and cannot do?

5 Discuss how techniques such as scenario writing and scenario daydreaming may be useful in assessing the impact of environmental change on the fortunes of a business.

CASE STUDIES

Union Assurance Company

The Union Assurance Company is reviewing its strategies to take account of current trends in the business environment. It observed the following:

■ *Political/environmental factors.* Government withdrawal from welfare provision: self-help encouragement by government may restore welfare ethos

- *Economic environment factors.* Widening gap between rich and poor
- *Socio-cultural factors.* Substantial increase in working women in lower income groups; less manual jobs/more office administration jobs; the lottery of higher expectations of middle-income groups
- *Technological factors.* New tech not easily accepted by lower income groups; major growth in telemarketing/database marketing
- *Demographic factors.* Population shift to middle/old ages; fewer young people
- *Legislative factors.* Expenses/commission disclosure to every customer; increasingly severe pensions legislation

An industry analysis using the Porter framework indicated the following:

- *Bargaining power of suppliers.* Distribution is powerful; forces vertical integration; costs high to acquire/train
- *Threat of substitute products.* None for life assurance; money for savings; gambling increasing (lottery); low switching costs; no economies of scale; little differentiation; experience not a barrier – buyable
- *Bargaining power of customers.* Middle market strong; largely undifferentiated; switching relatively easy; disclosure law gives power of comparison on costs; cashing in is routine in lower market
- *Threat of new entrants.* Unlikely in home service market; significant in middle market; non-financial players with good reputations (e.g. Marks & Spencer, Virgin, etc.); new technology/lower costs
- *Degree of competitive rivalry.* Fragmented industry; over-capacity; few big brands/shares; high costs; worsening expense/profit position; high exit barriers; traditional life products declining; undifferentiated; poor reputation

Shifting to:

- *Rapid rationalization/consolidation for attractive growth and returns.* New players; big trusted brands; high tech/low cost; direct sales/low cost; low entry barriers; low cost driving low price; greater competition; new competencies; marketing/service

A SWOT analysis revealed the following:

- *Internal strengths.* Financial – major reserves which could be accessed for development/improving returns to customers; with profit fund – no new player has or can build one, a good capital barrier; loyalty and awareness among industrial branch customer base; investment income and track record (steady); national (locally based) distribution
- *Internal weaknesses.* Poor sales track record Inefficient, inaccurate and untimely administration/processing; uncompetitive returns/high expenses; management culture; low awareness levels/market profile; reliance on single distribution channel
- *External opportunities.* Older population – needs care and illness cover; government encouragement of self-help welfare provision; new database/telemarketing technology and cost benefits; growing prosperity of middle income/age group; service/marketing emerging as new competencies

- *External threats.* Increasing poverty of traditional customer base; reducing need for home collection of premiums for life and savings products (more in town office working and more women out all day); fewer young people – reducing market for savings and life products; cost-reducing technology – not acceptable to traditional low income groups; legislation driving up costs and cost competition – lower margins; substitute expenditure on lottery; political uncertainty – next government

QUESTION

Suggest possible strategies that the firm might pursue.

The Foldaway Company

Modern houses are getting smaller and much more compact. They are placed closer together, have smaller rooms, use sliding windows in kitchens instead of back doors and do without vestibules or lobbies altogether. It isn't that people necessarily want smaller houses – they want houses that are cheap and easy to run. However, the trend towards smaller houses does bring with it storage problems. Take, for example, Tony's house. It has a living room with an open-plan staircase leading to three upstairs bedrooms and a bathroom. The kitchen is at the back of the house and has a sliding glass window in place of a back door. There is no vestibule and the front door opens straight into the living room. There is a cupboard under the stairs but apart from a small airing cupboard outside the bathroom there are no other cupboards apart from those in the kitchen. Space is at a premium.

Tony runs a small firm which produces and markets a number of fold-away products. First, there is the clothes rail with fold-away convenience. This is a clothes rail with an unusual space-saving feature. Not only does the product provide masses of storage but it also folds down to a compact width of 15 cm when not in use for easy storage. It comes in handy for ironing, for storing out of season clothes and for use in spare bedrooms. The rail height is adjustable between 96.5 cm and 165 cm and can hold up to 40 kg of garments. It is fully mobile and runs on castors.

Second, there is a product which provides instant extra hanging space. Placed over the top of a door, the smart and sturdy steel hooks create hanging space for several garments or clothes hangers. They are perfect for the bedroom, bathroom or utility room (particularly for wet outdoor clothing and for ironed clothes). The hooks require no fixing and can be easily moved from door to door.

Third, there is the instant hanging rack. This is excellent for towels and robes in the bathroom (also ideal for extra hanging/airing space in the utility room/bedroom). The rack fits instantly over the top of any door and four heavy-duty suction cups also fix it on to the door for complete stability or can even attach it directly on to a shower screen. The rack comprises five bars, the top one pre-fitted with four sliding hooks for hanging garments. It measures $65 \times 121 \times 12$ cm.

Fourth, a mobile trouser rack which can increase the storage capacity of any wardrobe substantially. In most wardrobes something like 50 per cent of the space is wasted (i.e. below the hanging garments). This compact mobile rack ensures that no space remains unused. It is designed to hang 12 pairs of trousers and measures only $67 \times 53 \times 34$ cm, fitting into any standard wardrobe to create double-decker storage.

Tony has experienced considerable demand for the products and sales and profits of the firm are booming. He is keen to introduce new lines into the business which respond to the changing nature of the home.

QUESTION

What other kinds of products do you think Tony could introduce which respond to the changing environment?

Chapter 8

Analysing the customer in the market place

INTRODUCTION

The markets that are seen through strategic windows are not abstract concepts – they contain people. In order to understand how changes in the market occur, not only does an organization have to understand the broader issues in the business environment and the views of the market perceived by competitors, but it also has to understand the buying behaviour of the people themselves.

In studying buyer behaviour, a distinction is made between complex decision-making situations and those in which little consideration is given to the purchase being made. Where a product is relatively expensive and possibly technologically complex, prospective purchasers often go through a complex search and evaluation process prior to making a purchase. Various models of consumer behaviour have been developed over the years. The models reflect the different buying situations in which consumers find themselves.

Factors influencing consumer behaviour must be considered as well as similar factors influencing the buying decisions in business to business transactions. An understanding of these factors and how they influence the buying decision are extremely important when putting together a selling strategy (Exhibit 8.1). Market research also plays an important part in helping to identify relevant facts about

---

EXHIBIT 8.1   WHY IT IS IMPORTANT TO UNDERSTAND THE MAJOR FACTORS INFLUENCING CONSUMER BEHAVIOUR

In order to be able to function effectively in the market place firms need to know:

1   Who constitutes the market?
2   What does the market buy?
3   Why does the market buy?
4   Who participates in the buying?
5   How does the market buy?
6   When does the market buy?
7   Where does the market buy?

Source: Kotler (1988)

---

buyer behaviour (consumer or organizational) and provides all kinds of information which forms the basis of strategy formulation.

MODELS OF CONSUMER BEHAVIOUR

The marketing strategist needs to appreciate that consumers approach the purchase of different goods in different ways. The approaches taken have been thoroughly investigated and a number of situations have been identified. Four main purchase situations are considered here (see also Assael, 1987):

- habitual purchases
- impulse buying
- limited decision-making
- complex buying decisions.

Habitual purchases

Frequently purchased items at the supermarket are often bought out of habit and consumers do not undertake an extensive search for information nor do they engage in extensive evaluation prior to making a purchase. Consumers search for cues as to what the product is like. Colour of the packaging, for example, may be perceived by consumers to imply a given level of quality. The task of the marketing strategist has to discover the nature of these cues and ascertain the best way of making the product stand out on the shelves *vis-à-vis* competing products. In this sense, the products may then be seen to be 'putting themselves forward' to gain the attention of the consumer.

Repeated use of a product raises the confidence people have in using certain cues and scanning becomes cursory in nature. Cues can stem from the product itself (intrinsic cues) – taste, texture, etc. – or can be produced by other attributes than the product (extrinsic cues) – brand name, packaging, advertising, etc. People develop confidence in the reliability of certain cues and learn to choose with the help of extrinsic cues.

The manner in which consumers organize their perceptions helps to compensate for their limited information processing ability. To make it easier to get to grips with their own understanding of several competing brands consumers may categorize them according to several characteristics along a few dimensions. When confronted by a new brand, consumers will consider its likeness to each one of their mental categories and then judge its probable characteristics. In-store choice is predominantly based on the comparative assessment of rival brands.

Consumers purchase a particular brand because it is familiar and the familiarity is accentuated by different types of advertising. The main job of marketers of competing brands is to persuade the consumer to switch brands. Trying out a new brand is the key, for then there is the possibility that the behaviour of repeatedly buying the same brand will be transferred to the new brand. Price and value for money are the principal factors which consumers consider in buying goods of this nature. Price and sales promotion are the key marketing variables for marketing strategists to use in such circumstances.

Impulse buying

Impulse buying for many people may well be the main method of purchasing and it can create emotional friction in the mind of the consumer. This happens frequently where the price of goods is substantial relative to the purchaser's resources. The main task for the marketing strategist here is to allay cognitive dissonance. This may be achieved through advertising which is intended to specifically reassure purchasers that they have made a sensible choice in purchasing the product concerned.

Limited decision-making

Consumers engage in this form of pre-purchase activity when they buy products only occasionally and when information is required regarding an unfamiliar brand. People spend a moderate amount of time gathering information and deliberating upon it prior to making a purchase. For example, if a new improved version of a brand of shampoo is introduced consumers will perhaps ask a friend who has used the product about its performance or even watch a commercial before they consider trying the product for themselves. Marketing strategists need to pay attention to advertising that is informative in nature and which provides the potential purchasers with the kind of information they need to aid them in their decision-making.

Complex buying decisions

Many people have studied consumer behaviour and a five-stage model of the buying process has been distilled from these researches (see Engel *et al.*, 1986). The implication is that consumers actually pass through all the stages in buying a product or service. In actual fact, of course, as we have seen in the case of habitual purchases, this is not necessarily the case. However, it is a useful framework from within which to view the purchase of many of the more expensive types of durable products and services. Let us look in more detail at each of these stages in turn (Figure 8.1).

Problem recognition

First the prospective purchaser has to experience a need to buy a certain product, for example, a new hi-fi system. The need can be triggered by a variety of things, for instance the unsatisfactory performance of the current hi-fi system or the fact that a neighbour has bought a new one. The marketing strategist needs to identify the factors which give rise to the recognition of the problem and use these to advantage in marketing communications about the particular product, service or brand.

Information search

Once the problem has been recognized, prospective purchasers search for information about the product in question. A person who has recognized a need for a new hi-fi system, for example, may scan many hi-fi magazines for information on what is available and at what price. This scanning helps to identify locations where the products or service may be purchased and the intending buyer may well visit these locations to obtain more information and possibly to listen to a number of different hi-fi systems.

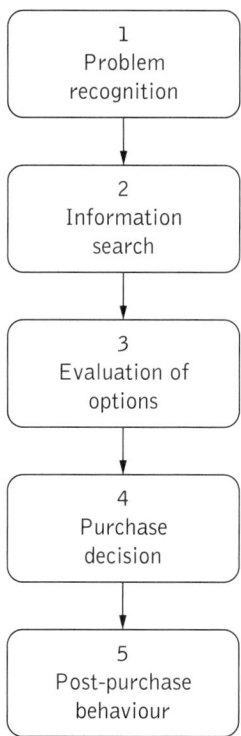

Figure 8.1 Complex buying decision

The amount of search undertaken varies with individuals, the amount of time available and the availability of suitable products and services. From the marketer's point of view, key interest is shown in the sources of information that the prospective purchaser will consult and the kind of information which is likely to sway the consumer into buying one particular brand over another.

Evaluation of options

There is an assumption that consumers make decisions on a conscious or rational basis, but this may not necessarily always be true. However, assuming a rational model of consumer choice, the process would seem to take account of the following:

- Products are thought of as a bundle of attributes, e.g. bicycle: lightweight/heavyweight, sports/touring, etc.
- Relevant attributes vary from one product or service to another, e.g. size and speed are important with cameras whereas the variety and container are emphasized in the case of chocolates.
- Some product attributes are more important to consumers than others, e.g. dependability and convenience may be considered more important than price when considering a business trip or an airline.
- The degree of importance of different product attributes to different consumer groups can form the basis of market segmentation, e.g. fast, courteous service at a restaurant.

151

- Consumers develop beliefs about products with respect to their various attributes – this forms a brand image, e.g. Volvo cars are safe.
- Consumers have utility functions with respect to each one of the attributes. Product/service satisfaction varies according to the fit between the product's performance on the attribute and the consumer's expectations, e.g. a small car's petrol consumption is satisfactory provided that it is more than 10 km per litre.
- Attitudes towards brands are formed through the process of evaluation, e.g. Seiko watches are better value for money than competing brands because they offer the same product features and have equally elegant designs.

Marketing strategists need to understand what criteria consumers use to evaluate their products and services. If it is discovered that a product or service does not meet with consumer's expectations then the marketer can try one or more of a number of options.

- Change the product so that it fits with consumer expectations.
- Change people's beliefs about the product or service.
- Change people's beliefs about competing brands and demonstrate that they are no better than the company's brand.
- Change people's perceptions of the importance of different brand attributes – if the product is considered weak on one attribute then the marketer could play down the importance of this attribute and stress the importance of others.
- Move the consumer's perception of what comprises an ideal product more in the direction of the existing brand's profile of attributes.

Purchase decision

The attitudes of other people often influence intending purchasers. Other factors may also arise which prevent the purchase intention being put into practice. Unfortunately, the marketer of the product can do little to counter these problems unless they make a thorough study of the likely sources of influence. This is clearly a job for marketing research provided that it is feasible and cost-effective to study the sources of influence involved.

Post-purchase behaviour

Post-purchase cognitive dissonance is often experienced by consumers after making a relatively expensive purchase. There is a tendency to ask oneself whether one has done the right thing in making the purchase or whether one would have been better off to have purchased a different brand, product or service altogether. Consumers need to be reassured. If the marketer has exaggerated the benefits of the product then the consumer will more than likely experience dissatisfaction. This in turn can lead to poor word of mouth communication about the product to the consumer's circle of friends, relations and acquaintances.

Marketing people can do much to allay dissonance. Some of the methods include:

- Directing specific advertising at people who have already bought the product, featuring contented, happy customers.

- Writing booklets which are dissonance-reducing to accompany the product or service.
- Arranging speedy redress of customer grievances.

Formal models of consumer behaviour help firms to establish a framework within which to both understand behaviour and formulate communication strategies to take advantage of their understanding. However, one also needs to have an appreciation of the various factors that influence the consumer decision-making process. The major factors influencing consumer behaviour are marketing factors (promotion, distribution, price and the product specification), environmental factors and buyer characteristics. We consider the marketing factors at some length throughout the book, so we will restrict ourselves to mentioning environmental and buyer characteristics here.

Environmental factors

A consumer goods market comprises all individuals or households purchasing goods or acquiring goods or services for personal consumption. Each market can be subdivided into 'sub-markets' or 'segments' each one of which could be regarded as a 'market' in its own right. There are many different ways in which 'sub-markets' or 'segments' can be defined.

Markets can be defined in geographic terms, but there is usually so much variation in terms of purchase behaviour within markets defined in this way that further segmentation is often required. The purchasing behaviour of individuals and groups within a market reflects different consumer characteristics, buying power, and wants and needs. Consumers vary considerably from one region of a country to another in terms of age, income, educational level, mobility patterns and taste. Moreover, climatic conditions vary substantially in different countries. However, it is possible to distinguish groups of consumers who have much in common with respect to wants and needs. As is indicated above, these groups make up market segments and marketing strategists need to develop products and services to serve the needs of these market segments.

Situational factors

The time available to make a purchase often plays an important role in determining what is purchased. For example, a last minute purchase of a book to read on an air journey may involve very little consideration of what alternatives are available and one may simply take the first reasonably appealing front cover that one sees. Even substantial purchases like houses and cars can be subjected to the influence of time pressures. If one has already sold one's house and has to move out quickly, but the new house one had previously chosen has been bought by another buyer in the meantime, the time to search for an alternative may be very limited.

Apart from time, there are several other situational factors that may influence purchases. For example, fear of unemployment may force would-be buyers of expensive domestic appliances to postpone their decisions, or inclement weather may create an unseasonal demand for waterproof clothing.

Level of involvement

Highly priced goods that are visible to others often cause consumers to undertake considerable search for information before effecting a purchase. Such goods are known as high involvement goods. Clothing, furniture, cars and houses are products which fall readily into this category. Curiously, the degree of involvement for the same products may vary across people. Some people, for example, undertake an extensive search when purchasing a birthday card for a particular person. Another person buying a birthday card for the same person may undertake very little search. Nor is this necessarily just a function of the relationship that each person has with the recipient of the card. One person may simply put less value on the card than the other.

BUYER CHARACTERISTICS: PSYCHOLOGICAL FACTORS INFLUENCING THE BUYING DECISION PROCESS

No two individuals are entirely alike in their behaviour and individual psychological processes intervene. People do not see the same event in exactly the same way. People differ in their perceptual processes of selective attention, selective distortion and selective retention (Figure 8.2).

Selective attention implies that people only pay attention to a small proportion of what is going on around them all the time. For example, when going about their daily work it is quite possible that they are exposed to hundreds of advertising messages but only actually 'perceive' a few of them. In all probability, people would screen out all of them except for the odd one or two which are in some way related to their current thoughts. Certainly, it is quite possible that they would be unable to recall any of them! The real test for the advertiser is to present messages in such a way that people will pay attention to them.

Selective distortion refers to how people assimilate incoming information so that it fits in with their preconceptions. It is possible, for example, that in showing horrific accidents resulting from drink

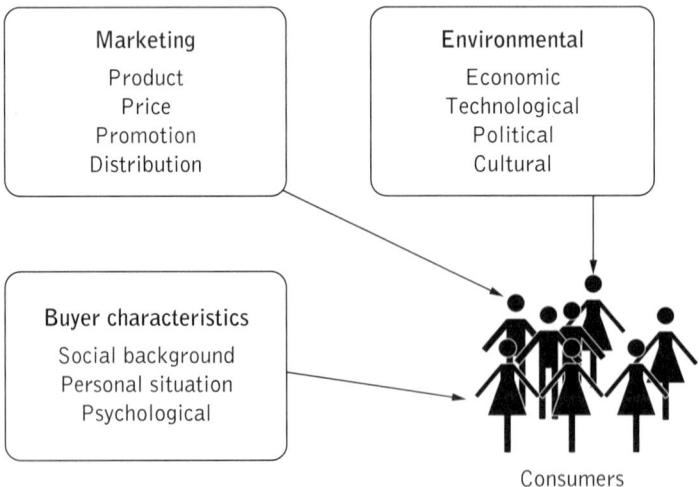

Figure 8.2 Factors influencing consumer behaviour

driving, people will not take notice of it because they feel that they cannot relate themselves to such a situation. For instance, they might assume that horrific accidents only really happen to people who are habitually very drunk.

Motivations

Marketers need to know what motivates people to buy particular brands or services. Given this information it may be possible to gain a competitive advantage in the design and/or marketing of a product. This can be done through persuading consumers that a product is better able to satisfy their wants and needs on account of the benefits it offers. There are various theories of motivation; two of the most important, as far as marketing is concerned, were put forward by Freud and Maslow respectively. Freud suggested that people may be influenced at an unconscious level. Thus it may not be possible to get people to talk rationally about why they make certain purchases. Freud makes us aware of these veiled motivations. As a consequence, different methods of research have been developed to get at these hidden kinds of motives. Maslow suggested that human needs are ordered in a hierarchy of importance. The most important needs are those to do with physiological needs, whereas the least important ones are to do with self actualization. Maslow contended that people would not seek to satisfy the less important needs until the more important ones were satisfied. This theory helps us to clarify how various products may fit in with people's purchase plans. For example, a person may consider buying a home before purchasing a motor car. A householder who has a car, a refrigerator, cooker, freezer, telephone and washing machine may next be interested in purchasing a dishwasher.

Learning

Most human behaviour is acquired as the result of learning from experience. This also applies to the purchase of goods and services and so learning is perhaps the most important factor underpinning consumer behaviour. Drives, stimuli, cues and responses and reinforcement are the key elements of learning. A drive is a force inside people that pushes them towards certain actions. Drives become motives when they are directed specifically towards a stimulus which will reduce the drive. Cues are minor stimuli which establish when, where and how a person will respond.

Marketers build up demand for a product or service by linking it with strong drives, using cues to motivate people and providing positive reinforcement to people who respond. In effect, this is really the whole basis of the marketing concept. Marketers seek to identify unsatisfied customer wants and needs (where there is a strong drive which is not fulfilled). The firm provides the product or service (stimulus) together with appropriate promotional messages (cues). The consumer responds by purchasing the product and the marketer follows this up with after-sales service or promotional messages to reinforce the fact that the consumer has made a good choice.

Beliefs and attitudes

People have beliefs and attitudes which affect their purchasing behaviour. Brand images are related to the beliefs and attitudes of people and as a result of these images, people make purchase decisions. Attitudes are associated with the way in which people behave and act. Marketing communications tries to inform customers that a product or service meets with their attitudes or corrects mistaken beliefs about a product or service.

Personality

A person's life-style is an expression of an individual's personality. Some people may have a life-style which people might describe as being *avant garde*. Other people may be described as conservative, and yet others as liberal-minded. Marketers have to look for relationships between their products and life-style groups that they can identify. They can then link this to images they wish to portray through marketing communication vehicles.

Life-style

Life-style that different occupations engender is thought to influence actual buying behaviour. There have been many different attempts to use life-style classification systems in market segmentation studies. Taylor Nelson's Applied Futures typology, which is used widely in marketing research and for segmentation purposes, has types of life-style ranging from the *belonger* who places great store in home, family, country, the establishment, etc., to the *aimless* who is uninvolved and alienated and is aggressive towards the system and resentful of its failure to provide employment. The life-style approach usually involves presenting respondents with a series of statements and asking for their degree of agreement with each (Likert scale). Such life-style data is then cluster analysed to produce groupings in terms of activities, interests and opinions. As indicated above, a name or type is then attributed to each grouping. If we can identify a group which corresponds to a market segment or sub-segment of the market for a product or service, appropriate features can be built into the product or service that will appeal to this segment. In addition, a promotional message that is congruent with the segment's life-style can be developed.

BUYER CHARACTERISTICS: SOCIAL FACTORS INFLUENCING THE BUYING DECISION PROCESS

Social factors exert an influence on the purchase behaviour of consumers. Several people may have a part to play in making a purchase. For example, in talking with friends, someone may prompt us into deciding that it is time we did something about buying a new house. Someone else suggests that we should visit a new estate where some individualistic houses are being built. Finally, we decide to buy a new house on the estate in question.

Each one of the persons, including ourselves, has played a role in the decision-making process. A friend was the initiator, another friend the influencer and we were the decider, buyer and actual user. A firm needs to be aware of the different influences since they have implications for the various marketing communications that have to be made.

Roles and status symbols

People often buy products that relate to or reflect their role and status. Status symbols vary for different social groupings and it is the job of the marketer to recognize what the status symbols are for different groups of people (Figure 8.3).

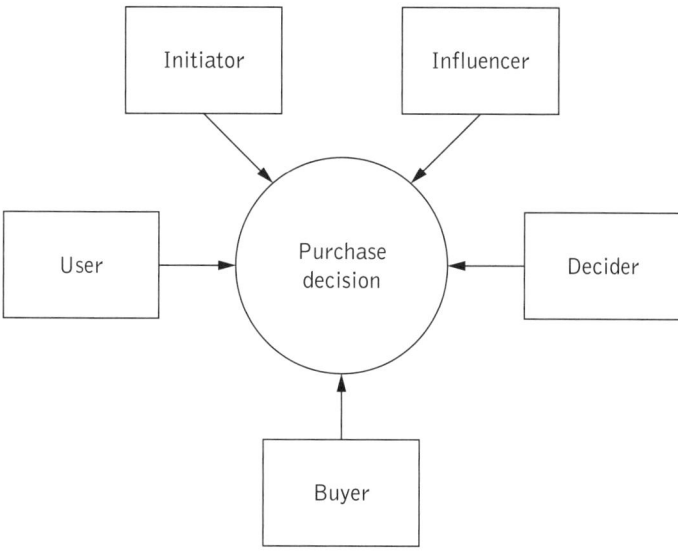

Figure 8.3 *Roles in the purchase decision-making process*

Family influence

Perhaps the strongest reference group which influences consumer behaviour is the family. As a consequence, marketers are interested in the roles and relative influence of the various members of a family in the purchase of a large variety of products and services. Traditionally, the wife or female partner in a family has tended to purchase the weekly shopping and buy small value items. Nevertheless, where there are children in a family the children may exert considerable influence over what is actually purchased during a trip to the supermarket. In the case of expensive items there is generally joint decision-making. The marketer's main task is to identify which member of the family has the greatest influence in choosing various products.

Age and life cycle

People pass through various stages in their life cycles. People have different life cycles according to whether or not they decide to establish a family unit. Exhibit 8.2 illustrates life cycle concept, assuming that people decide to build a family unit. Different buying patterns are exhibited at every stage in the life cycle.

The major weaknesses of the concept include the exclusion of those couples who never have children, lack of account taken of one-parent families, undue emphasis on the age of children and the changing role of the father/husband but not of the mother/wife.

The concepts here have been extended and applied in practical market analysis programmes such as Sagacity, which combines an abbreviated version of the family life cycle with income and occupation.

EXHIBIT 8.2 STAGES IN THE FAMILY LIFE CYCLE AND ASSOCIATED BEHAVIOURAL BUYING PATTERNS

Stage in the family life cycle	Buying interests
1 Single and young – away from home	Fashion clothes, sport and leisure products, cars, music centres and records, holidays
2 Young married couples – no children	Cars, consumer durables, holidays, furniture
3 Married – small children	Washers, driers, baby items, economy food
4 Married – children mainly under 13	Children's toys, education products, domestic appliances, many foods
5 Married – children mainly teenagers	Consumer durables, better furniture, hobby items
6 Married – children left home – both/ one still employed	Travel, recreation, self-education, investments, luxuries
7 Older – retired	Cheaper holidays, value for money goods
8 Solitary survivor	Economy living

REFERENCE GROUPS

Reference groups are made up of people who directly or indirectly influence a person's attitudes or behaviours. Teenagers, for example, may be influenced by a pop-star cult. Marketers try to identify the reference groups of their target customers and make use of opinions reflected by such groups in their marketing communications.

Social class

Social class reflects societal stratification. Members of a social class have similar values and attitudes in common. These are different to those of members of other social classes. The identification of the social class to which a person belongs can be a rather involved business but in general it is based upon the recognition of such points as job, pay, wealth, education and value orientation.

Research appears to indicate that social classes have distinct product and brand preferences in areas such as clothing, leisure activities, home furnishings and motor cars. There are also signs that social classes have leanings with respect to media preferences. Lower classes show a preference for television whereas upper classes favour magazines and journals. Moreover, within the media division itself, such as TV, we find upper classes favouring news and drama whereas lower classes like soap operas and quiz shows.

Social background

People's social background is reflected in their culture. Culture consists of values, perceptions, preferences and behaviours. Although many western societies put value on achievement, success and materialism which is good for the sale of goods and services which enable consumers to demonstrate their success and achievement through the kinds of products which they purchase, other societies have a somewhat different set of values. Materialism is not altogether absent in these other cultures but it has not been as prominent as it is in Europe and the US. Much of what is revered in western societies is not generally revered in such countries. Nevertheless, we live in a changing world and there are signs of some western artefacts being adopted in countries which have hitherto been slow to show an interest in western ideas, values and goods.

Sub-culture reflects nationality groups, religious groups, racial groups and geographic areas. One can observe its effects in the way consumers form preferences or tastes. Promising material success may sell some products but there is also a 'market' for what is apparently anti-materialist. One of the most rapidly developing business sectors at the present time is the occult 'mind and spirit' sector with its crystals, UFOs, alternative medicines and meditation. These are profit oriented businesses despite the image of antimaterialism.

POSTMODERNISM IN CONSUMER BEHAVIOUR

One of the central themes of postmodernism relevant to marketing concerns consumer behaviour. In the twenty-first century, organizations operating in developed countries are supposedly dealing with well educated and informed audiences. More to the point is that many consumers, irrespective of their level of educational attainment, are informed and well able to judge the merits of the variety of products and services and the advertising messages that accompany them. Moreover, in what today are comparatively affluent societies even by standards of the 1970s, consumer choice has burgeoned and lessened the scope for market suppliers to dictate what consumers should buy. The consumers' main choice at the beginning of the twenty-first century is one of how to spend their money or wealth. Brand choice will always exist when consumers finally make up their minds how to spend their money but it is persuading people to make up their minds in the first place that is now one of the predominant issues. Presented with a large variety of choices, consumers are beginning to question what they really want. In many cases, consumers may not really know what they want, but only how to reject the unwanted alternatives.

Postmodern marketing has five key features according to Firat and Venkatesh (1995) which may serve to underpin and facilitate the process of exchange. These are:

- hyperreality
- fragmentation
- reversed production and consumption
- decentred subjects
- juxtaposition of opposites.

Hyperreality

Hyperreality is the most widespread sign of postmodernism on the current marketing scene. It is evidenced by such things as fat-free fat, beefless beef, decaffeinated coffee, alcohol-less alcohol, and sugar-free butter (Brown, 1999). It is found in the virtual worlds of cyberspace and in the pseudo worlds of theme parks, hotels and heritage centres. It involves the creation of consumption sites and marketing phenomena at surrealistic geographic places. The Valley of the Kings, for example, might be recreated in a theme park just some distance from a European capital city. In some respects this would be superior to the real thing since the negative aspects of the real thing would be absent – extreme heat for example. Hyperreality offers the customer previously new, creative and innovative experiences. While at the turn of the twenty-first century such opportunities are relatively limited in scope there seems little doubt that they can be developed in all kinds of different ways in the future. The whole concept of shopping may be adapted to the needs of providing a 'hyperreal' experience. For example, if one wants to experience the ambience of the bazaars in the Near East, why should it be necessary to travel all the way to places such as Istanbul?

Fragmentation

Fragmentation of markets into smaller and smaller segments, each with its own complement of carefully positioned products is apparent everywhere (Brown, 1999). It reflects the fact that marketing in postmodernity is rapid, rabid, frenetic and volatile. It is often reflected in shopping at speed and its very disjointedness is in part peculiar to the activities of practitioners with their ceaseless proliferation of brands, increasing number of outlets and preparedness to accept any form of payment for goods and services provided. It also mirrors consumers' disconnected postmodern life-styles, behaviours and moods. The postmodern consumer adopts a multiplicity of roles from DIY enthusiast to pseudo-academic and leads a correspondingly fragmented existence among a proliferation of products and brands.

Reversed production and consumption

Reversed production and consumption concern consumers' loyalty to images and symbols that they produce in the process of consumption. Consumer loyalties cannot be fixed because they are constantly changing and consumers are correspondingly unpredictable in their behaviour. The shifting nature of the symbolism of consumer wants and needs makes it seem apparent to marketers that consumers do not know what they want, but only what they do not want. Moreover, what is symbolic today may not be symbolic tomorrow or alternatively it may symbolize something that is unattractive. The task for marketers is to predict what will be a fashionable symbol tomorrow, and equally important, when tomorrow will be.

Decentred subjects

Decentred subjects means that individuals cannot be unambiguously defined by their occupation, social class, demographics, etc. Although traditional segmentation criteria may be applied and marketing strategies formulated, it is increasingly accepted that these capture the target market only for a relatively short time. The consumer of the twenty-first century is always just beyond the reach of marketing strategists. However, if one accepts decentredness as a truism this would lead one to conclude that the strategic tools of marketing are too crude to be of any effective use. Since segmentation, targeting and positioning make up the centrepiece of modern marketing strategy, marketers should accept that the target may be moving, that target composition may be changing and thus that target positioning is inconstant. When communicating with target market audiences these factors take on a new significance and demand a highly creative approach to marketing communications.

Juxtaposition of opposites

Juxtaposition of opposites concerns the attempt to appeal to the difficult-to-target postmodern consumer. The approach involves adopting an open, untargeted, ill-defined, imprecise appeal which permits imaginative consumer participation, e.g. ironic advertising treatments where the purpose, pitch or intent is unclear, and sometimes the product or service too. This may be achieved through messages containing elements of entertainment or bribery and which feature combinations of contradictory symbols, themes and references. Many advertisers are now using these types of messages. Such advertisements often leave the consumer wondering what the advertisements were about. The messages stimulate the consumers' curiosity and challenge them to relate the messages to their own experiences and desires and to produce creative insights about their meaning.

A postmodern view of consumer behaviour emphasizes knowledge interpretation through metaphor, constructed truth, semiotics and symbolic, as opposed to actual, realities (Brown, 1994). From this perspective, the idealized image of consumers as rational cognitive analytical decision-makers, falls into disarray. If correct, marketers and marketing communication professionals would be well advised that the postmodern route of continuous offerings of ambivalent but still decodable messages is the way forward.

Postmodern consumption has major implications for the practice of marketing. The old idea of finding out what customers want and delivering it to them in an efficient, timely and profitable manner no longer seems apt. People often do not know what they want – though they may recognize it when they see it and certainly seem to know what they do not want. Perhaps the latter bears a pointer towards what marketing should be doing – finding out what people don't want and giving them a less unacceptable alternative.

SOCIETAL MARKETING AND CONSUMER BEHAVIOUR

Many firms are blending communications activities with public purpose marketing or enlightened capitalism with their economic marketing strategies (Handelman and Arnold, 1999). Such marketing practices are indicative of firms starting to practice, for economic reasons, corporate social responsibility (Brown and Dacin, 1997). Moreover, the emphasis on consumerism and an increasing awareness of environmental and ethical issues all have their implications for marketing strategists. The fact that business depends on reputation and image as much as upon products, services or pricing suggests that firms must not ignore social responsibility.

ORGANIZATIONAL BUYING DECISIONS

Organizational buyers are those purchasing goods and services for some tangibly productive and commercially meaningful purpose. They purchase on behalf of organizations operating across a wide spectrum of markets. Organizational buyers operate in:

1 *Producer markets*. These are profit-making businesses that purchase products and services and use them to make other products. These include raw materials, components, semi-finished and finished goods manufacturers.
2 *Reseller markets*. These consist of distributors such as wholesalers and retailers who buy finished goods for resale.
3 *Government markets*. These comprise national and local governments seeking to provide the public with education, water, energy, national defence, road systems and healthcare.
4 *Institutional markets*. These are often organizations that seek to achieve the charitable, educational, community or other non-business goals that make up institutional markets. They include churches, some hospitals, libraries, museums, universities and charitable organizations.

Demand for industrial goods is derived from the demand for consumer goods. For example, in the car industry, firms specialize in the production of electrical components for motor vehicles. The demand for the electrical car components depends upon the demand for the cars to which the components are fitted. If the motor industry is depressed then the demand for electrical components for the motor industry will also be depressed. If the demand for a particular motor vehicle manufacturer's cars is depressed but the rest of the industry is buoyant, then only the demand for electrical components for that manufacturer's vehicles will be depressed.

The total demand for many industrial goods is relatively price inelastic. For example, in the instance of the electrical components for the car industry introduced above, if the price of one or two components is increased then this will not reduce the demand for those components. This is because the added cost of incorporating them in the final consumer product – a motor vehicle – is negligible. Where the added costs are substantial in relation to the final consumer product and the price rise is substantial, then demand may well be reduced.

Models of business to business buying behaviour

In the same way that there are models of the consumer decision-making process there are also models of the business to business buying behaviour process. Robinson *et al.* (1967) identified eight buying phases in the buying process:

- problem recognition
- proposal solicitation
- general need description
- supplier selection
- product specification
- order-routine specification
- supplier's search
- performance review.

The model fits well where a product or service is being bought for the first time, but appears to be less applicable in other situations.

Organizational buyer behaviour is a complex process. Although the job of buyer may exist in a firm, there may be many people concerned in the purchase decisions. Marketers have to identify the various roles played and then influence the various actors in the decision-making process.

Influences on organizational buying decisions

Industrial goods are bought by organizational buyers. In reality, however, more people actually influence business buying decisions than consumer buying decisions. Indeed there may be a buying committee consisting of technical experts and senior management personnel. These are often found in the purchase of relatively expensive industrial goods. Even if this is not the case, the same people may be involved or consulted in the course of making buying decisions. Webster and Wind (1972) provide a detailed account of the various influences on industrial buyers.

Industrial buyers respond to both rational economic and personal appeals when participating in buying decisions. There are various influences on industrial buyers and these may be classified as follows:

- *environmental*: economic recessions and resurgence, technological developments, legal constraints, competitive activities, etc.
- *organizational*: reflecting objectives, procedures, structures and systems
- *interpersonal*: arising from status differences between people associated with the purchasing decision
- *individual*: associated with the age, income, education, job position, personality and attitude to risk of the buyer.

Characteristics of organizational transactions

There are various differences between the customers in business to business markets and consumer markets. In particular there are:

- fewer buyers
- larger buyers
- geographically concentrated customer groups.

Generally, such purchases are made less frequently than consumer goods sales. The contract regarding the terms of sale of such items is often a long-term agreement requiring re-negotiation from time to time. In addition, purchasing decisions are often made by a committee and several people or departments in the organization will be involved in the negotiations.

Attributes of organizational buyers

Some organizational buyers simply place orders. People occupying these jobs require little or no skill. More often, however, the importance that organizations give to the role of the buyer is much greater and the buyer needs to know all about the products and services on offer. Indeed, some buyers often have a great deal of autonomy in the extent to which they can purchase on behalf of the organization. Buyers are also proactive rather than reactive and watch out for information which can enable them to make better purchase decisions.

Primary concerns of organizational buyers

The primary concerns of organizational buyers are:

- delivery
- service
- price.

It is common to purchase goods on the basis of specifications. If a supplier fails to deliver goods to a specification this often terminates the agreement to supply goods to a firm.

Delivery time is of paramount importance. Failure of a supplier to make promised deliveries can hold up production and cause considerable lost sales to a company. Reliability in terms of keeping to promised delivery dates is an important concern of organizational buyers since it can help to reduce the level of safety stocks kept and hence free-up working capital.

Specific services required vary in terms of importance. Market information, technical assistance, inventory maintenance, on-time delivery, repair service and credit facilities are commonly sought-after services.

Price influences operating costs and costs of goods sold. These in turn affect the customer's selling price and profit margin. When purchasing major equipment, for example, an industrial buyer looks upon the price as the amount of investment necessary to obtain a certain level of return or savings. This leads to a comparison of the price of a machine with the value of the benefits that the machine will yield.

Buying decisions

A firm that centralizes buying decisions has a different approach to purchasing than one where purchasing decisions are made at distinct locations. Centralized purchasing involves giving a separate organizational unit authority to purchase at a regional, divisional or headquarters level.

Centralization of purchasing is more likely where:

1 two or more purchasing units within the organization have common requirements
2 there are opportunities to strengthen bargaining position, obtain lower prices through the aggregation of a firm's total requirements and achieve economies in inventory control
3 there is opportunity to consolidate purchasing power and secure favourable terms and service when a few large sellers dominate the supply industry
4 engineering involvement is high and the engineering group is in close organizational and physical proximity.

SIMILARITIES OF ORGANIZATIONAL BUYER BEHAVIOUR WITH CONSUMER BEHAVIOUR

Similarities with what we have outlined earlier in this chapter relating to consumer behaviour do in fact exist. As is the case of consumers making purchase decisions, there are a variety of people who actually exert an influence on the decision:

- *users*: who will use the product or service
- *influencers*: often technical persons whose expertise is requested prior to making decisions
- *deciders*: those who actually have authority to take decisions
- *approvers*: those who hold the purse strings
- *buyers*: who select the supplier and arrange the terms of purchase
- *gatekeepers*: who can screen out information before it ever gets into the decision-makers' in-trays.

Firms marketing products should be aware of the various influential roles in decision-making. Moreover, they need to identify the key influential people and to persuade them that the product will meet a felt need.

ROLE FOR MARKET RESEARCH

Customer or market research can produce quantitative facts about particular markets and market segments (Exhibit 8.3). For example, the size of the market both in terms of unit sales and value. When these data are collected over time it allows one to identify trends and helps to predict future sales. It can also provide information on where customers are located, their spending patterns, earnings and creditworthiness. It can also explain why customers prefer one brand to another and what price they are willing to pay for a brand. Market research can also provide information about market share of all the firms operating in a market or market segment.

Firms undertake marketing research to help identify why people buy or do not buy products and services. It also provides information for making marketing mix decisions (pricing, product, distribution and promotion).

EXHIBIT 8.3   CUSTOMER MARKET RESEARCH

Customer market research provides information on:

- market and market segment sizes
- trends in the market which can be used for forecasting
- brand shares
- customer characteristics and motivations
- competitors' brands' shares.

Research can be undertaken both in-house and by specialist marketing research companies. Where the latter are involved, research can be tailor-made to a client's requirements or bought 'off the peg' if a suitable omnibus research report is available. There are a variety of other sources which provide research data that are useful to companies. These include trade associations and government departments.

The research process involves: problem definition, consulting company records and published data sources, deciding whether field work is required and if so what is the best research method, specifying the location and size/type of sample, collecting the data, analysing the data, evaluating the results and setting down recommendations for action.

Various methods are used in marketing research, including surveys, experiments and observational methods. Since virtually all research involves working with sample data, a key aspect of research concerns how the sample is taken from the population. Quota sampling and simple random sampling methods are widely used in practice.

The bulk of marketing research carried out is actually market research which relies very much on survey methods. Questionnaire design and analysis along with sampling are key aspects of survey methods. There are costs and risks involved in undertaking research. The implications of these have to be fully appreciated before entering into research.

NATURE OF MARKETING RESEARCH

Marketing research uncovers facts about both buyers and non-buyers of products. It involves ascertaining the nature of wants and needs and assessing the current and potential demand for products and services. Information can help to reduce the element of uncertainty and guesswork in making marketing decisions. For instance, information on income levels and customer perceptions of a fair price can be used to advantage in setting prices.

INFORMATION SOURCES

Sources of information are of two varieties – company records and outside sources.

Company records

Firms have useful marketing information filed away in their internal company records. These include customer sales records, salespersons' reports and correspondence with individual customers. In addition, there are the company's own sales statistics and competitive information gleaned from a variety of sources.

Outside sources of information

Sources include trade associations which produce reports, surveys and other statistics for companies which belong to the association. Independently published reports and surveys on specific markets are also produced by organizations such as Mintel and the Economist Intelligence Unit. Other sources of useful information include government statistics (census data, family expenditure surveys, national income statistics, etc.) and company reports and accounts of competitors. The latter provide insightful information about competitors' future strategies and plans and can be obtained from Companies House in London.

Marketing research services

Management consultants can help with strategy formulation and advise on marketing problems. Such firms will survey the market to measure consumer attitudes or identify consumer wants and needs. In addition, because of the wealth of knowledge that they have accumulated, they are able to offer expert advice on marketing strategy.

The companies undertake research on behalf of clients and also carry out omnibus surveys. These cover a wide range of products and services and probe into people's attitudes and opinions about the products and other related matters. Information obtained in these surveys is sold to client companies on request. Omnibus surveys contain both relevant and irrelevant information as far as client companies are concerned. This means that although they are comparatively cheap to obtain, their value is somewhat limited. Specific surveys relating to a company's products and those of its competitors may also be commissioned and in this case the results are made known only to the clients sponsoring the research. However, the latter kinds of surveys are more expensive than the omnibus surveys.

THE PROCESS OF RESEARCH

Research is carried out systematically to ensure that problems are dealt with properly and that nothing is overlooked. There are a number of stages to the research process (Figure 8.4). These are:

- problem definition
- consulting company records and published data sources
- deciding whether field work is required and if so what is the best research method
- specifying the location and size/type of sample
- collecting the data
- analysing the data
- evaluating the results
- setting down recommendations for action.

Problem definition

The first stage in the research process is problem definition. This is an initial statement of the research objectives. Research objectives are usually to provide information on people's

- opinions
- knowledge
- attitudes
- behaviour

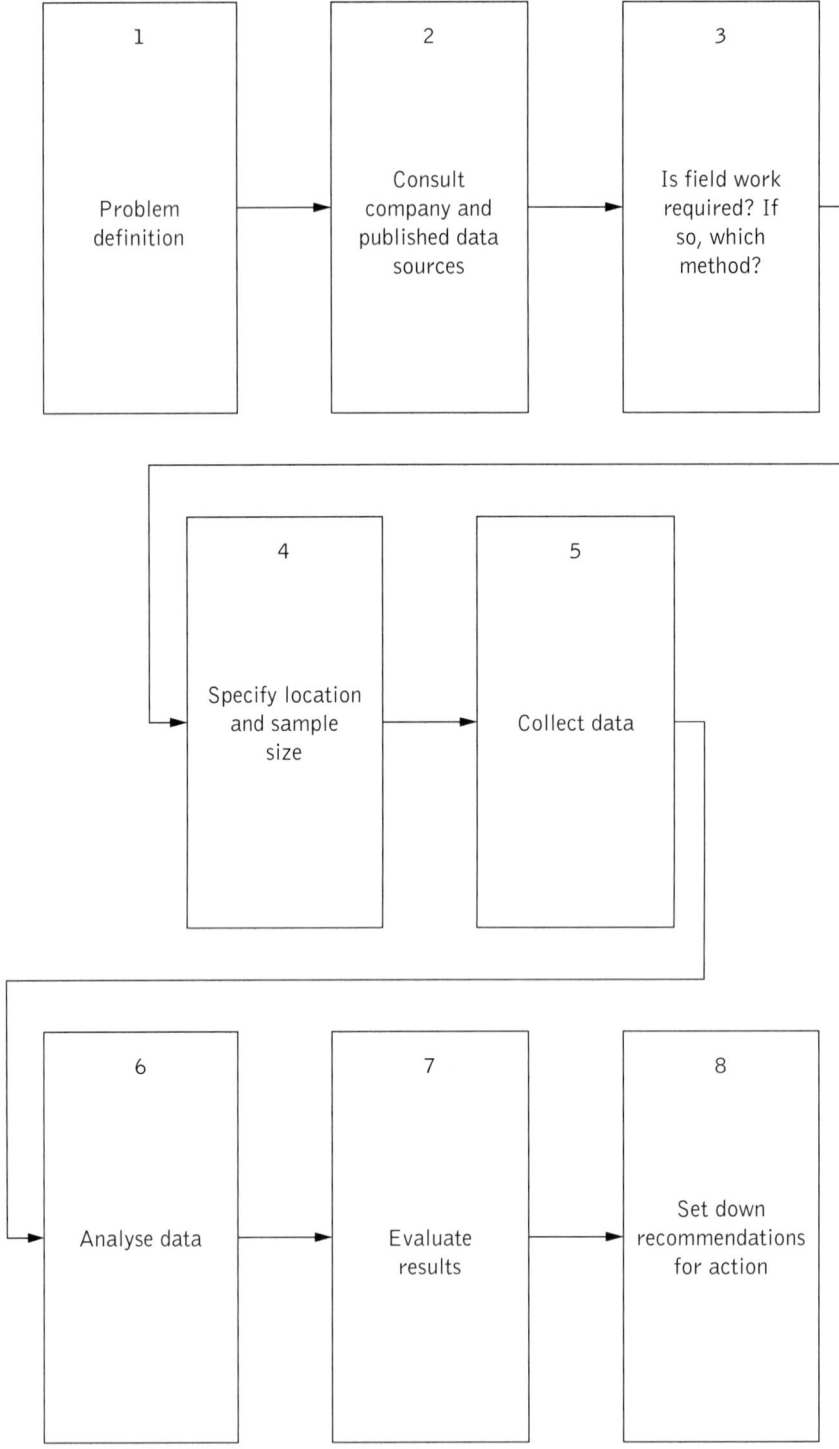

Figure 8.4 *Stages in the marketing research process*

- beliefs
- social background.
- intentions.

Consulting company records and published data sources

Following problem definition, the next step is to consult published data sources such as company records and previous reports provided by outside bodies and/or information in relevant periodicals. Some of these sources of data may provide answers to all or some of the aspects of the problem which has been identified. One cannot expect to obtain answers to all aspects of a problem in this way and it is often necessary to undertake field research to find out more specific information. Field research involves finding things out by asking questions, doing experiments, making observations, etc., all of which generate 'primary data'.

When field research is necessary, the next step is to choose whether to commission consultants to undertake the research work or whether to undertake the work oneself. Much will depend on the size of the firm and its resources. Small firms usually do not have the resources to conduct their own marketing research. The research method has also to be decided. From the point of view of the do-it-yourself approach to market research this will probably mean that a survey of one kind or another will be undertaken.

ANALYSING INFORMATION

The best method of analysing data varies according to the kind of study that has been undertaken and the kind of data that have been obtained. In this section we will illustrate the application of data analysis to data which have been collected by survey research. The same methods will sometimes be applicable to both observational and experimental research and there may also be other forms of data analysis which can be used on survey data which are not covered here. Readers interested in a comprehensive review of data analysis methods in marketing research should consult a specialized text (viz. Proctor, 2000).

MARKETING RESEARCH ON THE INTERNET

The Internet offers marketers a unique opportunity to gather vast amounts of demographic and usage-related marketing data with which to better understand their customers. Marketers can gather secondary data on the Internet by accessing government sources, such as census data, or by going to private information providers. Researchers can also access data from organizations about current events, trends, target markets and competitors, and much more may be found in the many newspapers and trade magazines available online. The web also gives marketers an excellent opportunity to conduct competitive analysis by visiting competitors' websites to gather information about their product offerings, services, prices, etc.

Web users can also be asked for information. Many websites encourage visitors to register in order to maximize their use of the site or to gain access to premium areas; some even require it. Registration forms typically ask for basic information such as name, e-mail address and age, from which marketers can build user profiles for their own use or to sell to other companies. Marketers can conduct surveys to learn more about the people who access their pages, offering prizes as motivation for participation.

Marketers also gather intelligence and communicate internally through *intranets*, which employ the infrastructure and standards of the World Wide Web. Special software called 'firewalls' permit employees to access their firm's intranet while barring unauthorized users. Through intranets, employees can develop their own web pages and share details of their operations and projects with other company employees, whether they are across the hall or around the world. Intranets provide an opportunity for organization-wide marketing intelligence to permit the co-ordination and integration of efforts to achieve a true market orientation. When various departments and functional areas of a firm can quickly share vital internal information about inventories, production or even quality tests, the whole company improves its ability to serve both internal and external target markets.

QUESTIONS

1 'When deciding on the purchase of a new watch I am the only person who has any influence on the decision regarding which make or brand I will buy.' How generalizable do you feel this statement is? Justify your answer.
2 Many consumer-purchasing situations involve complex buying decisions. Describe some situations which illustrate this point and explain how the 'five stages in the buying process' model is relevant to these situations.
3 'The goods and services people buy represent an extension of their own personalities.' Discuss.
4 How does postmodernism impact on marketing activities in the twenty-first century?
5 'In the same way that consumers are subjected to various influences on their buying behaviour, organizational buyers are also subjected to a variety of influences.' Expand on this statement.
6 Market research is merely a qualitative approach to ascertaining customer preferences. To what extent would you agree with this statement?

CASE STUDIES

Choosing a holiday: part of a focus group discussion

First Class tour operators based in the West Midlands are trying to find out more about consumer choice as far as choosing a holiday destination is concerned. As part and parcel of the marketing strategy the firm is keen to develop an augmented service package that will appeal to its regular customers as well as pull in new customers. First Class has commissioned a small market research bureau to carry out research for this purpose. The market research bureau initially set up a number of focus group discussions at different locations in the West Midlands for this purpose. The samples of respondents taken were essentially convenience ones comprising people of various ages in different settings, e.g. in youth clubs, social clubs, further education centres, etc., and comprised anyone who was prepared to give an hour or so of their time. Part of the discussion that took place in one such session with a group of people at a social club is shown below.

'I like the sea and the sun. I like to laze on the beach, to dance all night at a disco and do it again and again,' Cheryl smiled.

'That's because you're young. When I was your age, I wanted to do the same thing.' Yvonne spoke with a tone of nostalgia. 'Now it's seeing different places that I like. I like going with John on tours. Last year we took the pilgrimage tour route to Santiago in Spain. We started in France and followed the well known route, stopping at different places on the way. There was a party of thirty of us and we had a whale of a time.'

'Everyone has their own tastes,' Bill grinned. 'I watched *Wish You Were Here* on Granada TV and ended up getting away from all the traditional holiday destinations altogether. I went on my own to Thailand. I saw the bright lights and did some exploring of the ancient temples at Ankor Wat.'

'Some of us have never been abroad and never will,' Old Mike commented. 'I can't see what all the interest is in going to foreign parts when there is so much to see and do in England. It's expensive to go abroad – and all that foreign food! Not to talk about different languages and the fact that you can't make yourself understood. I like to go to Blackpool at Easter, Blackpool in the summer, Blackpool in September and Blackpool at Christmas. I never get bored of Blackpool.'

'Flying puts me off going a long way,' Fiona joined in. 'I tried it once. I went with a friend to Paris for a weekend and was sick on the plane. I am just so afraid of flying. If I can't get there by land and sea I do not go. Of course, that has not stopped me visiting places on the continent. I have been to Belgium and France quite often. But that is all.'

'I like doing something really different, but the cost deters me', Wendy broke into the conversation cautiously. 'A couple of years ago I joined a singles party on a trip to Antarctica. I flew to Tierra del Fuego and a boat took a party of us to the Antarctic coast. I didn't like all the people. I also had to share a cabin with an older woman. She was alright, but it would have been difficult if we had not got on well. I regard myself as a bit adventurous but not way out.'

'I go bungee-jumping in New Zealand. That is really exciting. It's a craze over there,' Tom butted in.

'What I like is a cruise. I have done the Caribbean, the Mediterranean, the Baltic and cruised off the coast of Alaska and enjoyed them all. You find all kinds of people on these cruises, make all sorts of friends and thoroughly enjoy yourself,' Winnie put in.

QUESTIONS

1   How would First Class make use of such data in formulating marketing strategies?
2   What else might the market research bureau do by way of research?

Office Improvements

Office Improvements is a marketing company offering a wide range of office products and services on behalf of its clients to a wide range of businesses and organizations. The firm defines its business as finding ways of making offices in organizations more efficient, more employee-friendly and more economical to run. John Grant, the CEO of Office Improvements, believes that this gives the firm the widest scope possible in terms of the kinds of products he can market. 'Of course,' he says, 'this means we have two kinds of customer. Those whose products and services we market and those who buy the products and services which we market.' The firm does not experience too much difficulty finding businesses which would like to make use of Office Improvements' marketing skills. The main difficulty encountered by the firm is in its marketing to organizations that want to make use of the products and services it has to offer. As John Grant says:

'When you are a small company trying to make your way in the world, you encounter all kinds of problems when it comes to getting new contracts. In our case it isn't a case of hiring salespeople to call on wholesalers or retailers, you have to actually get out yourself and talk to your customers. Finding the right person to talk to can often be a nightmare. We define our business as that of helping firms to create healthy working environments for their employees. This means that we actually sell industrial solvents and cleaning materials as well as a variety of different types of equipment – ranging from fans and air extractor units to heating appliances for offices and work shops. We are essentially a marketing outfit and get our products from a variety of sources both in this country and abroad. We do not sell in small quantities but aim to equip other organizations as comprehensively as we can.

'Our major difficulty is locating the decision-makers. When you want to get a local authority as one of your customers, whom do you approach? I can tell you it is not that easy. It is not always straightforward when you are dealing with a central buying office. Often the person you approach cannot make the decisions and has to consult with other people. You have a real job on your hands I can tell you.'

QUESTION

What steps do you think John Grant could take to ensure that his approach to users of the products and services he has to offer is optimal?

Chapter 9

Sustainable competitive advantage and generic strategies

INTRODUCTION

Keeping the strategic window open involves maintaining a sustainable competitive advantage. In consequence, we argue that competitive advantage should be market led. We examine the nature of core competencies and interpret their importance as the basis of gaining a sustainable competitive advantage in the market place. Along with these core competencies are a number of generic strategies that an organization can seek to follow or implement. We will look at each of these generic strategies in turn.

First we will look at low-cost, focus and pre-emptive strategies and differentiation strategies. The latter leads us to consider product and service quality, customer focus and relevant issues relating to brand management.

COMPETITIVE ADVANTAGE SHOULD BE MARKET LED

It can be argued that an organization's products and services constitute the main focus of competitive strategy. In this context the aim is to offer a competitive bundle of benefits, or value, to the customer. Competitive advantage is achieved through the positioning of one firm's offering relative to another. An alternative view suggests that it is superior resources and processes designed to utilize such resources efficiently that will create a competitive advantage. Both approaches are not mutually exclusive and can be complementary (viz. Hunt and Morgan, 1995; Verdin and Williamson, 1993). Indeed, such a view is in keeping with the view of keeping open the strategic window of opportunity.

CORE COMPETENCIES AND COMPETITIVE ADVANTAGE

It seems reasonable that competitive advantage should be developed on the basis of core competencies. Through the identification of its distinctive competencies and the relating of them to its core products, a firm can develop strategies and plans which make best use of those capabilities. New capabilities might then be sought after in order to achieve greater sustainable advantage. If a firm identifies its core competencies incorrectly this will result in the firm overlooking attractive opportunities and lead it to pursuing poor ones.

In searching for a competitive advantage, businesses often develop capabilities in key functional areas (Prahalad and Hamel, 1990). To be sustainable, these capabilities must be difficult to imitate and should support the organization's business strategy (Day and Wensley, 1988; Day, 1994). Organizations that stress the development of key capabilities are better able to achieve and maintain a position of advantage despite turbulent environmental impacts on the business (Achrol, 1991).

The development of key marketing capabilities has been identified as one of the primary ways firms can achieve a competitive advantage (Day and Wensley, 1988; McKee *et al.*, 1989; Day, 1990, 1994). In this context, firms must develop processes that allow them to collect information about market opportunities, develop goods and services to meet the needs of targeted customers in selected markets, price these products according to market information, communicate product advantages to potential customers and distribute products to customers (Day, 1993, 1994).

Organizational capabilities assist in the process of achieving a competitive advantage. Organizational capability is 'a firm's ability to perform repeatedly a productive task which relates either directly or indirectly to a firm's capacity for creating value through effecting the transformation of inputs to outputs' (Grant, 1996, p. 377). Such capabilities are produced as a result of the integration of the knowledge and skills of the organization's employees (Grant, 1991, 1996). To develop marketing capability repeated experience in applying knowledge and skills to transforming marketing inputs to outputs is required. In practice, marketing capabilities are the integrative processes designed to apply the collective knowledge, skills and resources of the firm to the market-related needs of the business, enabling the business to add value to its goods and services, adapt to market conditions, take advantage of market opportunities and meet competitive threats (Day, 1993, 1994).

Core competencies

Selznick introduced the concept of 'distinctive competence' to explain how a particular business obtains a competitive advantage (Selznick, 1957). Selznick's argument was not entirely unique. Drucker developed a parallel theme of business leadership: a business must be the leader in something – it mattered not what that something was, so long as the customer genuinely wanted it and was prepared to pay for it (Drucker, 1964).

Prahalad and Hamel (1990) put forward the idea of 'core competencies' as the basis upon which to build strategies. This approach differed from the ideas of both Selznick and Drucker and resulted from studies examining the way successful firms, mainly Japanese, appeared systematically to acquire and exploit combinations of fundamental technologies in order to develop generic or core products with which to dominate global markets. Core competence is a combination of technological and managerial capabilities which provide the firm with a leadership position in the development of certain generic or core products. A firm's existing core competencies reflect the fundamental skills and knowledge behind its successful products. They may relate to world leadership in specific technologies or they may be related to particular organizational or managerial skills.

Acquiring and nurturing competencies which are not 'core' is wasteful of resources and effort. It is better to buy in non-core competencies (Quinn *et al.*, 1990) and focus all internal efforts on the acquisition and development of what really matters. A firm's capacity for competitive innovation reflects its ability to acquire relevant core competencies and to apply them effectively in the development of core products. Capability is not constrained by the competencies already possessed, nor by the resources available, but can be extended by the careful definition of the competencies required and the means of their acquisition and development.

Missing competencies can be painstakingly developed internally through focused investment in R&D or acquired externally through various forms of collaborative arrangements. However, internal development is expensive and beyond the means of all but the largest organizations. In an era when the diffusion of technology is rapid, the resultant competitive advantage may be short lived. Much new technology cannot be protected and there is no real commercial benefit in being the holder of patents the essence of which is immediately copied by competitors. As Ouchi and Bolton (1988) suggest, internal development is not the best way to progress in areas where the intellectual property may be 'leaky'.

The strength of a business should not be seen in terms of a particular product, sector of the market or distribution channel, but in terms of the underlying capability to generate a range of rapidly evolving products or markets. The rationale for structuring an organization as a collection of strategic business units is questionable. More important is the development and acquisition of common strands of expertise which cut across products, markets and business units. This may lead to some apparently strange combinations of business activities. For example, 3M's products include Post-It notes, magnetic tape, photographic film, pressure sensitive tapes and coated abrasives. These all have quite different production technologies, end consumers and channels of distribution. The rationale is based on the core competencies in substrates, coatings and adhesives.

Prahalad and Hamel (1990) quoted several such examples of the use of core competencies. The success of NEC, for example, resulted directly from this approach (Exhibit 9.1). In similar vein, between 1980 and 1988 Canon grew very rapidly to beat Xerox with a range of core products including image scanners, laser printers, copiers and cameras, based on core competencies in precision mechanics, fine optics and microelectronics.

Core competencies apply also in the services sector, though in this case the competencies may be related to technology imported from manufacturing. For example, fast cycle times are a critical factor in providing customer service in many industries (Exhibit 9.2).

EXHIBIT 9.1   NEC'S USE OF CORE COMPETENCIES

NEC adopted the core competencies approach by systematically exploiting the convergence of core competencies in computing and communications (C&C). A C&C committee oversaw the development of these core competencies and resulting core products. This was supported by other co-ordination groups and teams which cut across the traditional organization structure and ensured that each member of the organization knew and understood the strategic intent. They developed competencies internally and also through over a 100 purposive collaborations and alliances with other organizations. Between 1980 and 1988 NEC's sales grew from $3.8bn to $21.9bn and the company became the world number one in semiconductors and a leading player in telecommunications and computers. Over the same period, its American competitor GTE, enjoyed sales growth from $10bn to $16.5bn and had to withdraw from several of its major business areas.

Source: Prahalad and Hamel (1990, pp. 79–91)

EXHIBIT 9.2   SOURCES OF COMPETITIVE ADVANTAGE

Skills

- specialized knowledge of market and needs customer service orientation
- design expertise
- applications experience
- trade relationships
- utilizing relevant technologies
- systems design capabilities
- ability to respond rapidly and with flexibility.

Resources

- coverage of distribution
- availability or access to capital
- business contacts
- low cost manufacturing and distribution systems
- production capability or capacity raw material ownership
- knowledge or access to sources.

The scale and grid shown in Figure 9.1 can be used to assess competitive advantage. In the example a firm operates in six market segments. It assesses its skills and resources for each market segment using a 9-point rating and assigning different weightings to each of the scale item that make up the two dimensions of the scale, Skills and Resources. Segments scoring highly on both dimensions are those in which the firm has the most favourable competitive advantage.

STRATEGIC INTENT

Strategic intent concerns the direction in which a business is headed in the long term. If identified simply and succinctly it can have a profound effect on the firm's stakeholders, both internal and external. Employees know what they are trying to achieve and therefore how they should make their greatest efforts; customers know what the firm's products and services embody; suppliers understand what the key elements are when dealing with the firm.

Przybylowicz and Faulkner (1993) argue that strategic intent creates a sense of urgency, requires competitor focus, searches for weaknesses in competitors' positions that can provide competitive advantage if properly addressed, and is stable over time while remaining flexible as to the means used to achieve the intended goals. Core competencies have to be leveraged across business unit boundaries in order to promote efficiency and effectiveness in research and development. The strategic intent process facilitates the attacking of horizontal market opportunities that might be missed in a business unit structure.

Achieving market leadership and following the path of 'strategic intent' is not without dangers. Prahalad and Hamel argue that market share leadership typically yields shareholder wealth. However,

	SEGMENT						
		1	2	3	4	5	6
Skills	Wts						
Market knowledge	12	7	6	7	4	8	7
Customer service	15	8	7	7	5	8	6
Design expertis	14	7	3	5	2	9	7
Applications experience	12	8	3	4	2	8	5
Trade relationships	15	6	4	5	4	7	5
Technology utilisation	16	3	4	5	6	4	3
Systems design capability	6	7	7	7	4	5	6
Able to respond rapidly and flexibly	10	5	6	4	4	7	8
	100						
Resources							
	Wts						
Distribution coverage	19	3	3	3	3	3	3
Access / availability of capital	19	9	5	7	5	8	6
Business contacts	19	8	8	8	8	8	8
Low cost mfrg. and distribution	17	7	3	3	4	8	3
Production capability/capacity	14	9	3	4	4	8	4
Raw material access to sources	12	2	2	2	2	2	2
	100						

SEGMENT	○ 1	● 2	○ 3	◉ 4	● 5	● 6
Skills	4.88	3.15	3.82	2.35	5.43	4.07
Resources	6.49	4.21	4.73	4.52	6.33	4.54
Size	1	1	1	1	1	1

Sources of competitive advantage

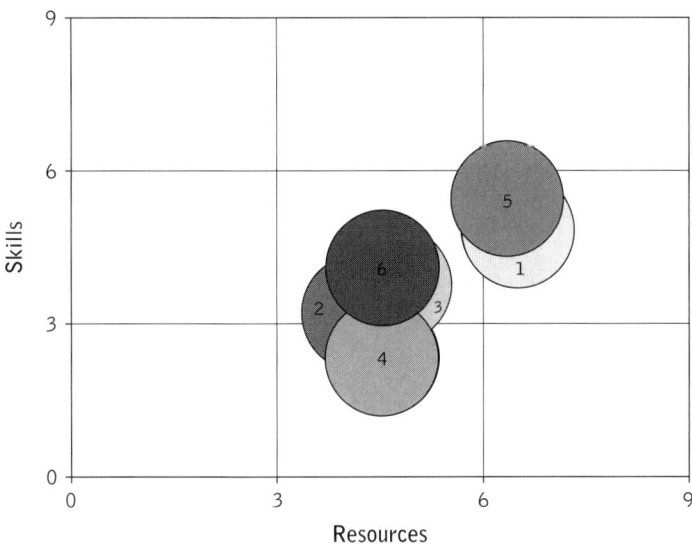

Figure 9.1 *Sources of competitive advantage (1)*

nearly all companies pursue market share, but few achieve exemplary performance for their shareholders. Moreover, Kontes and Mankins (1992) suggest that one of the weaknesses of the strategic intent proposition is the absence of an economic framework for making investment decisions. In following a strategy of global market leadership, it is assumed that competitors will not respond in ways that drive investment returns to or below the cost of capital. However, this does in fact often happen when all players try to lead all markets.

Strategic intent needs to be defined with precision and it also needs to be supported by indications of how fast the firm proposes to travel and how far. Thus milestones along the route need to be spelled out and progress at each stage monitored and the people involved rewarded according to progress.

'Become the leading world producer of photocopiers' is a statement of strategic direction which could be a powerful organizing and motivating concept. The strategic intent of 'beat Xerox' is still more powerful, focusing as it does on the major competitor and thus identifying standards to be beaten, or mechanisms to be avoided, right across every aspect of the business.

GENERIC STRATEGIES

Low-cost, focus and pre-emptive strategies

Porter (1985) suggested the alternatives of a low-cost strategy, a differentiation strategy and a focused strategy. The low-cost strategy involves the sacrifice of some quality, fashion and even product innovation in order to keep costs low – the lowest in the industry. With this strategy there is also an assumption that the achievement of production economies of scale is a significant factor in success. This contrasts with a differentiation strategy which focuses on the factors ignored by the low-cost strategy such as product variety, quality and service, but again implicit is the notion that size matters to achieve successful differentiation. Smaller firms are advised to move towards strategies which target small sub-segments of the market to avoid competition with larger businesses for whom these segments are too small and specialized to be of interest (Figure 9.2). Variants on the Porter model exist, with some writers suggesting a more detailed categorization of options, but the notion of a set

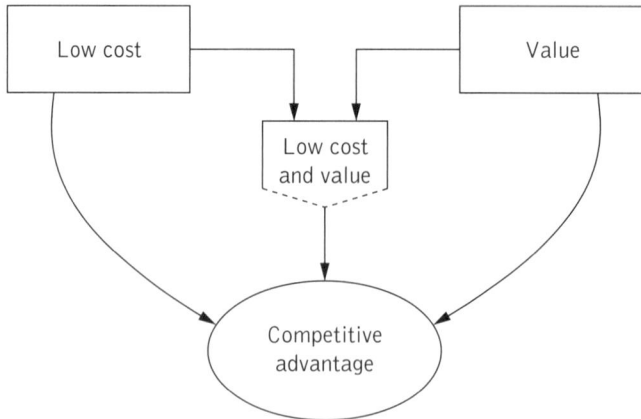

Figure 9.2 *Sources of competitive advantage (2)*

of generic strategies of this type among which choice must be made was the dominant strategic paradigm of the 1980s and early 1990s.

Low-cost strategies

Although there is a tendency to think of low-cost strategies as a single approach such as scale economies, low-cost labour, or production automation, it is important to recognize that there are many methods of obtaining a low-cost advantage. The successful low-cost firms are those that can harness multiple approaches.

No frills product/service

A direct approach to low cost is simply to remove all frills and extras from a product or service. A major risk, especially in the service sector, is that competitors will add just a few features and position themselves against a no-frills firm. The goal is to generate a cost advantage that is sustainable for one of two reasons. First, competitors cannot easily stop offering services that their customers expect. Second, competitors' operations and facilities have been designed for such services and cannot easily be changed. A firm with an inherent cost advantage has a good chance of success with a no-frills approach.

Product design

A product's design or composition can create cost advantages. A variant is to augment a product with relatively high-margin accessories or extra features and thus provide a higher perceived value to customers. Product downsizing is another approach that can be helpful when price pressures inhibit alternatives.

Cost advantages can also be achieved in other ways. Some of these include:

- obtaining good access to raw materials
- when a major cost component is distribution, the use of a different channel
- in some labour-intensive industries, access to inexpensive labour
- government subsidies or other special treatment
- the best retail locations are obtained by those who enter early into a market
- innovations in the production process, including automation
- reduction of overheads: especially where there is a bloated workforce.

Differentiation

A differentiation strategy is one where wide product ranges and higher quality products are offered for the convenience of customers as well as added services such as delivery, information services, etc. A differentiation strategy is one in which a product offering is different from that of one or more competitors in a way that is valued by the customers. The value added should affect customer choice and ultimate satisfaction. Most successful strategies that are not based entirely on a low-cost advantage will be differentiated in some way.

There are many ways to differentiate by adding value. There might be something which can be done much better than competitors, or an extra product feature or service that can be included. Value can be added to any aspect of a business.

Successful differentiation strategies

A successful differentiation strategy should:

1 generate customer value
2 provide perceived value
3 be difficult to copy.

Generating value

A differentiation strategy needs to add value for the customer. A distinction is needed between apparent value and actual value. Too often a point of difference with apparent value is not valued by the customer.

A key to a successful differentiation strategy is to develop the point of differentiation from the customer's perspective rather than from the perspective of the business operation. In particular, one needs to assess how the point of differentiation affects the customer's experience of buying and using the product. Is there a cost saving or added performance, for example?

Marketing research, too, can often provide an insight into customers that leads both to a better understanding of customers and an opportunity to test out ideas and assumptions. One role of such research is to ensure that the value added will justify the price premium involved. A differentiation strategy is often associated with high price because it usually makes price less critical to the customer and because differentiation usually costs something.

Provide perceived value

The added value must be perceived by the customer. If that is not the case, the problem may be that the value added has not been communicated or at least not communicated effectively. Branding the added value is one way to make it more memorable, meaningful and believable. The perceived value problem is particularly acute when the customer is not capable of evaluating the added value. The task is to manage the signals or cues of value added. User associations and endorsements can help.

Difficult to copy

Differentiation needs to be sustainable and thus difficult to copy. When it involves a total organizational effort with a complex set of assets and skills it is difficult and costly to copy, especially if there is a dynamic and evolving quality to it. A creative organization with a heavy R&D investment can inhibit investment. In addition, if there are multiple points of differentiation this too can inhibit investment since duplication will be expensive.

Over-investment in a value-added activity can have a long-term pay-off by discouraging duplication. For instance, the development of a superior service back-up system might discourage competitors.

The same logic applies to a broad product line. Some elements in the line may be unprofitable, but if they plug holes that competitors could use to provide value, then the analysis looks different.

Many approaches to differentiation

There are many approaches or strategic orientations that can lead to sustainable differentiation strategies. These include the use of strategic information systems, global thinking, being innovative, customer driven or employing a unique distribution system. Employing quality and building strong brands, however, are two of the most important approaches and these will be considered in some detail next.

The quality option

The prototype of differentiation is a quality strategy in which a business will deliver and be perceived to deliver a product or service superior to that of competitors. A quality strategy can mean that the brand, whether it is a hotel, car or computer, will be a premium brand as opposed to a value or economy entry. A brand can also be a quality option within a group of value or economy brands.

Total quality management

To be the quality option, a business must distinguish itself with respect to delivering quality to customers. What is required is a quality-focused management system that is comprehensive, integrative and supported throughout the organization. The system consists of a host of tools and precepts, including:

1   the commitment of senior management to quality
2   cross-functional teams that focus on quality improvement projects and have the power to make changes
3   a process rather than results orientation
4   suggestion, measurement and recognition systems
5   a focus on the problems and underlying causes of customer complaints and areas of dissatisfaction
6   the tracking of key quality measures
7   the involvement of suppliers in the system with supplier audits, ratings and recognition, as well as joint team efforts
8   the importance of the customer – quality is defined in terms of customer satisfaction.

The quality option is designed ultimately to improve customer satisfaction. It follows that a customer focus will be part of a successful effort. One indicator of a customer focus is the involvement of top management. A hallmark of most customer-driven organizations is that the top executives have regular meaningful one-to-one contact with customers. Another indicator is the link to the compensation and measurement system. It is crucial to understand not only what is important with respect to quality but also what drives those quality perceptions.

Building strong brands

Differentiation can also be accomplished by building strong brands to create brand equity. This strategy is likely to prove sustainable since it creates competitive barriers. Brand equity generates value to the customer that can emerge either as a price premium or enhanced brand loyalty. Brand equity is a set of assets and liabilities linked to a brand's name and symbol that add to or subtract from the value provided by a product or service to a firm or that firm's customers. The assets and liabilities on which brand equity is based differ according to the situation. They come under four headings:

- perceived brand quality
- brand identity
- brand awareness
- brand loyalty.

We have already looked at quality so we will now look at the other three categorizations.

Brand awareness

Brand awareness gives the product or service a sense of familiarity. In the case of low involvement products, such as soap, this familiarity can be an important influence in the purchase decision. In market research taste tests, a recognized name can affect evaluation of a product even if the brand has never been purchased or used. Awareness of the name can be a signal of presence, commitment and substance, attributes that can be important even to industrial buyers of big ticket items and consumer buyers of durables.

High recognition of a strong name is an enormous asset. The asset becomes stronger with the passage of time as the number of exposures and experiences grows. As a result, a challenging brand, even with an enormous advertising budget and other points of advantage, may find it difficult to enter the memory of the customer.

Brand identity

A brand identity reflects the associations attached to a firm and its brands. These associations are usually those of product attributes or customer benefits. A brand's associations are assets that can create confidence and trust, affect feelings towards a product and provide the basis for brand extensions. They can provide an important basis for differentiation, especially in product classes where it is difficult to distinguish objectively between various brands.

Brand loyalty

For many businesses the loyalty of the installed customer base is a coveted asset. Competitors may copy or improve on a product or service but they still have to make the customers switch brands. Brand loyalty or resistance to switching can be based on lack of motivation to change from the existing brand, a genuine liking for an existing brand or the actual cost of switching. Switching costs reflect the sunk investment that has to be sacrificed in order to switch from one brand to another. Switching costs will be lower for fast-moving consumer goods but clearly higher for durable consumer white goods. An existing base of loyal customers provides an enormous sustainable competitive advantage.

It reduces the marketing costs of doing business since existing customers are relatively easy to hold whereas getting and retaining new ones is more difficult.

The loyalty of existing customers represents a substantial entry barrier to would-be competitors. Excessive resources are required when entering a market in which existing customers must be cajoled away from an established brand with which they are well satisfied. The profit potential for the tentative entrant is thus reduced.

Brands and strategy

It has been remarked that companies become attractive takeover targets and the value of their stock rises because of the strength of their brands (Sherrington, 1995) and some brands are even valued as assets in the company balance sheet. Branding for consumers represents the mark of a given level of quality and value that helps them choose between one offering and another. The development of a range of brands to cover different consumer segments enables a firm to benefit from changing consumer wants. From a marketer's point of view, brands allow the producer, and more recently the retailer, to target different groups of consumers or segments of the market with different label product offerings. In fact, developing more than one brand enables a firm to segment a market and target different consumers. The development of a portfolio of discrete brands enables a firm to isolate the problems of one product from the rest of the range and it can enable it to divest less profitable brands.

Brand trends at the retail level

The preparedness of branded goods producers to supply own label products for retailers stems partly from a need to take up spare production capacity but it is also indicative of the need to prevent complete erosion of the existing sales base. The willingness of leading producers to supply own-label products has also reduced the quality gap between own labels and producer brands.

The sophistication of retailers' own marketing communications, particularly packaging and promotion styles, has strengthened their credibility in terms of ability to deliver satisfying products. Retailers have used advertising to create a brand image which has been reinforced by unique design features applied to store layouts, staff training and their own-label product ranges. They have also begun to use product-specific advertising to promote own-label brands.

It is as a result of being able to gather precise consumer information more quickly through EPOS technology that retailers have been able to become innovative in terms of their own label products. Retailers have begun to develop differentiated ranges of own-label products to meet segmented customer needs. But own-label activity is not restricted to grocery products and supermarkets. Mitchell (1995) indicated that the travel business is becoming retailer driven rather than tour-operator driven, with some travel agency companies offering their own packages alongside tour-operator brands.

Porter's model of competitive forces provides a useful framework within which to look at the competitive forces at work in this instance. Seen from the point of view of producers, it can be argued that the power of the buyer (the retailer) has been strengthened by the product-market strategies which the retailers pursue. In addition, retailers also represent new entrants to the markets themselves. Strictly speaking, own brands do not meet the formal definition of substitute products, but they certainly perform the function of such products.

Counter-strategies available to producers

Producers use database and direct marketing to try to get closer to the consumer. Producers also meet the new challenge from own label brands by investing in the development of innovative products which can be shown to have demonstrably different advantages over own label products. Producers are also able to take advantage of their more focused image – since retailers supply such a wide range of products – and producers may very well benefit from developing products in partnership with one another.

Producer–retailer partnerships

Problems created by the emergence of own brands may be circumvented by producers and retailers getting together and co-operating. Partnerships, where both sides are working for mutual advantage, seem to be fruitful avenues for exploration. The extent to which a producer can obtain co-operation from a retailer does depend upon how much value the latter places on its supplier's marketing and product development expertise. In general, retailers are in the more powerful position since they have gained leverage in the retailer–producer bargaining interface. Faced with the increasing power of retailers, producers need to gain and take notice of the needs and views of retailers.

There is a need for joint product development projects and joint marketing ventures between producers and retailers. Moreover, producers can augment their product offerings with product add-ons, including services to retailers and consumers with respect to delivery, after-sales contact, financing and promotion. A producer's strength will be defined not just in terms of the brand strength, but in terms of the skills of staff assigned to managing brands, retailers and consumers, and the flexibility and effectiveness of the organization structure within which they operate.

Category management

The concept of managing categories rather than specific brands involves co-operation between manufacturer and retailer in the development of a product. An alliance is formed to develop the entire product category. Here there is scope for sharing consumer and market data, especially where both parties are developing consumer databases. For example, in 1997, the Consortium Jigsaw looked at the possibility of linking data from Unilever, Bass, Kimberly Clark and Heinz (Evans and Moutinho, 1999).

Ethical branding

Ethics are a potentially powerful influence on consumer decisions. Companies such as Shell have found out with its environmental policies and its treatment of indigenous peoples, that if a brand gets its ethical stance wrong, it can have an adverse effect on the company wherever it goes and whatever it does. Nor is Shell alone in this, among the big brand names for Nike, with its cheap labour sourcing policies, has also experienced similar problems. Brands such as the Body Shop and the Co-op Bank on the other hand have demonstrated the power of taking an ethical stance. There are certainly many consumers who would prefer to choose ethically safe products and companies. It is reflective of a deep shift in public expectations of what brands do and what they stand for. Increasing marketing literacy, the rise of pressure groups and the development of the consumer press are making people realize that ethical issues are deeply embedded in society. Moreover, relative prosperity in developed countries is affording the consumers in these countries the luxury of worrying about these things and the opportunity to express their approval or disapproval in how they spend their money.

Brands have to take an ethical stance in ethical matters whether it relates to matters which impact on the environment – for instance, the disposal of toxic waste or pollution of the atmosphere – or contributions to society in the form of charitable donations. Of course, the key issue is judging the acceptable price that consumers are willing to pay for adhering to their ethical principles. Consumers are price conscious though the existence of an affluent society can shift the upper boundary to their discretionary purchasing activity and hence allow some degree of ethical consideration to enter into their purchasing decisions.

With this trend towards ethical branding the question that consumers tend to ask is not whether they can trust the brand to deliver attributes X and Y but whether the people who bring the brand to the market are the sort of people they can trust to do X and Y. Clearly this has a considerable impact on the image that firms need to project towards their audiences and this is accomplished through promotional strategy.

FOCUS STRATEGIES

The focus strategic thrust, whether it involves differentiation, low cost or both, concentrates on one part of the market or product line. A focus strategy avoids strategy dilution or distraction and is more likely to lead to competitive advantage. When the internal investment programmes and culture have all been directed towards a single end and there is buy-in on the part of everyone in the organization, the result will be assets, skills and functional strategies that match market needs. In most cases the product line or market is expanded, compromises are made in advertising, distribution, manufacturing and so on. Moreover, the strategic competitive advantage and associated entry barriers will be diluted.

A business that lacks the resources to compete in a broad product market must focus in order to generate the impact that is needed to compete effectively. A focus strategy provides the potential to bypass competitor assets and skills. It can also provide a positioning device. Although pay-off of a small niche may be less than that of a growing market, the competition may often also be less intense. Large growth markets attract many competitors and stimulate over-capacity whereas this is unlikely to occur in niche markets to the same extent.

Nevertheless, a focus strategy does limit the potentials of a business. Profitable sales may well be missed and the business may have to compete with firms that enjoy scale economies.

Focusing the product line

Focusing on part of a product line can enhance the line's technical superiority. In most businesses, the key people have expertise or interest in a few products. As the product line broadens, however, the products tend to be 'me too' products which do not provide value and detract from the base business. This may spur on the need to remain focused and resist product expansion.

Targeting a segment

The same argument applies as in focusing the product line mentioned above.

Low-share competitors

In many industries there is a dominant firm with substantial scale advantages. A key to competing against such firms is usually to use some variant of focus strategy. One approach is to look for a portion of the market in which the dominant firm is making high profits which may be used to subsidize other parts of its business. Another is to focus on a part of the market that has been neglected and develop an offering and strategy to capture it.

THE PRE-EMPTIVE MOVE

This is the implementation of a strategy new to a business area that, because it is first, generates a skill or asset that competitors are inhibited or prevented from duplicating or countering. A sustainable first-mover advantage can result from technological leadership, pre-emption of assets and/or buyer-switching costs. Pre-emptive moves can be directed at supply systems, products, production systems, customers or distribution and service systems.

A business can gain advantage by pre-empting access to the best or least expensive sources of raw materials or production equipment. Like many pre-emptive moves, those oriented toward the supply system are risky. If supply commitments are made and business does not materialize or other superior supply sources emerge, such a strategy could backfire.

The first product to be introduced in a market can enjoy the substantial advantage of occupying a desirable position. It allows the first entrant the opportunity to adopt whatever positioning strategy it wants. A new competitor is almost forced into another positioning strategy. A key in some industries is to become the industry standard. A first mover can develop customer loyalty by creating switching costs.

A retail chain can pre-empt locations by committing early to an area and selecting prime outlets. It can also discourage competitors by reducing the profit potential. In many industries, distribution channel capacity limits exist. There is limited shelf space or warehousing capacity available. Getting access to the limited capacity makes it much harder for competitors to make inroads.

QUESTIONS

1   How are core competencies related to strategy formulation?
2   How relevant are Porter's generic strategy typologies in the twenty-first century?
3   Given the increasing power of retailers in consumer goods marketing how has this affected producers' brand strategy?
4   How might ethical branding issues be featured in the way in which organizations promote and otherwise market themselves?
5   Are focus strategies becoming more important? Why or why not.
6   In what way should strategy be market led?

CASE STUDIES

Barney Malone

Barney Malone's parents emigrated from Ireland to Australia in the late 1950s. Eventually they settled in Adelaide in the far south-east of the country. Barney was brought up and educated in the suburbs of Adelaide and following a number of 'career offering' jobs in banking insurance, he opted to take up something much more practical in the 1980s by going into partnership in his mother's beauty salon business.

Molly Malone had started a beauty salon in Adelaide soon after landing there in 1958. She had worked for several beauticians back in Dublin and knew the trade well. Business was brisk and by the time Barney joined the business in the early 1980s, Molly Malone owned three salons in Adelaide. It wasn't long, however, before Barney learned the skills of the trade and he had an eye for business too.

Barney decided that providing a straightforward beautician service was not enough and that the business might consider some form of diversification. Moreover, it was in the diversified areas that he himself was more interested. While his mother Molly was a skilled beautician, she lacked the business acumen to explore other things as well. Barney on the other hand was only too keen to try. Recently, he decided to move into offering hairdressing-related products and contacted an importer of such items in Adelaide. The importer obtained the items from a variety of suppliers in the Far East who were only too keen to get into the growing Australian market. Initially, Barney had decided to take on four different products. The products were sold from each of the three salons in Adelaide. The four products were as follows:

1 *An electric cordless hair cutting set retailing for around A$50.* The cordless cutter set brought the users everything they needed for effective home haircutting. The rechargeable mains powered clipper came with six attachments which enabled the user to cut hair to pre-selected lengths. The pack also came with a choice of barber's scissors, a comb, clipper, lubricating oil and cleaning brush, plus a zippered leather-look storage/travel pouch. There was also a colour booklet containing step-by-step tips to haircutting.

2 *An electric hot air brush and styling system retailing for around A$45.* The product was a hot air paddle brush which included a series of flow vents to enable the warm air to be directed on to the hair as it is brushed through. The product was considered to be ideal for controlling and smoothing the hair as well as creating 'flick ups' at the ends. The styling handle came with a set of additional accessories and attachments for creating height, volume, waves and curls plus an exclusive styling booklet to give instructions on use.

3 *A big-power but small-sized hair dryer which fitted in the palm of the hand.* Its high power and micro air concentrator attachment dries thick hair fast and is compact enough to fold down into a small bag. The product has two speeds and the low speed can also be used for drying finger and toe nails after varnishing. The product has dual voltage for worldwide travel and an extra-long power cord, plus a travel pouch.

4 *An epilator that retails for around A$60.* The epilator removes hair as short as 0.25 mm by the root and does the job efficiently and almost painlessly The whole unit fits into the hand and its curved micro tweezers glide smoothly over the contours of the body. The product is cordless and comes with a smart storage pouch, cleaning brush and full instructions.

Sales of the products have been extremely good over the past three years and have made a healthy contribution to the sales and profits of the business (around 5 per cent of sales). Barney now faces an important decision. Molly has decided to retire and Barney is unsure as to whether he wants to retain the beauty salon business. Apart from Molly and Barney there are no other members of the immediate family in the business. Barney's brothers and sisters all have other interests and none have expressed any interest in the business. Barney's wife runs a knitware shop with one assistant and although she has experience of retailing, she has no experience of the beauty trade. While she is not against the idea of getting involved in the beauty business she is somewhat worried whether she would have the necessary skills and experience to make a really effective contribution.

Each of the beauty salons is directly managed by Molly. There is a senior, very experienced assistant at each salon who works alongside two or three juniors. However, when one of the seniors leaves it usually means that Molly has to get involved in the day-to-day operation of the business and deal with clients and their needs. Barney's role has been essentially that of business manager, looking after the accounts, purchases, tax returns and expenses.

QUESTION

Given that Molly is going to retire, what do you think Barney's best options are?

Singapore Stan

Stan runs an antiques and curios shop in Singapore. Most of his clientele are visitors who take away relics or copies as souvenirs of their visit. They want something which seems to be genuinely oriental in nature to remind them of their visit to the Far East. Stan's shop is not far from the city centre in a shopping mall. It is easily accessible and many passers-by gaze at the various artifacts he has on show.

Stan did a degree in England where he took computer science as his principal subject. He is a proficient programmer and an expert in both software and hardware. However, Stan's first love was antiques and curios and following a five-year spell with a large multinational computer company with large offices in Kuala Lumpur after he returned with his degree from England, he decided to return home to his native Singapore and develop a small business of his own specializing in antiques and curios. That was six months ago and in the meantime the business has started to develop but it has not really taken off in a big way. Stan can just about make ends meet but still lives at home with his parents in their small suburban flat.

Stan's interest in antiques and curios goes back to his childhood when he read books that were given to him by an uncle and which contained many pictures of such items. It is a passion he shares with his girlfriend May. She helps from time to time in the shop while Stan is out looking for new items in the suburbs of Singapore or further afield in Kuala Lumpur. He also has contacts in Hong Kong and Shanghai – the latter being the place from where his parents originated. The suppliers in both these places regularly ship him items that he has ordered after perusing their 'lists'. The lists are sent out monthly along with photographs or sometimes sketches of the items concerned. Stan and May hope to marry in the near future but money is something of a problem and a place of their own hard to even think about. In Singapore living accommodation is at premium prices.

May went to secretarial college in Singapore and has good secretarial qualifications. She worked for a bank for three years before deciding to give this up to help Stan run his business. The business has therefore to provide incomes for both Stan and May.

QUESTIONS

1 What are the business's core competencies? Are they the same as those possessed by Stan and May?
2 How can Stan develop a sustainable competitive advantage for his business?

Chapter 10

Segmentation, targeting and positioning

INTRODUCTION

The market that the organization sees through the strategic window is a very complex entity. In evolving strategies to take advantage of the opportunities that exist within it, the organization has to divide it into manageable chunks at which it can direct its relevant resources and capabilities.

Market segmentation was seen as one of the top-tier priorities for marketing research according the US Marketing Institute. There is no doubt that it is of great importance to practitioners and it is often viewed by managers as a means of adopting relatively efficient use of marketing resources (McDonald and Dunbar, 2004).

Segmentation, targeting and positioning are three of the pillars of modern marketing strategy. There are few markets these days in which an undifferentiated approach will pay dividends. The approach today is to accept that there are different demands in the market place and that a product or service needs to be tailored-in specifically to meet these differing demands if it is to stand the best chance of success. The first step in the process of achieving this is to research the market to identify how it might best be segmented into buying groups that are significantly different from one another in terms of their buying behaviour and product or service requirements. Having analysed the market along appropriate lines so that there are identified segments to the market, the next step is to decide which represent financially viable propositions as far as the organization is concerned. Some may be too small or others too competitive. It is the task of targeting to define those that promise the kind of returns on investment that will help the organization achieve its objectives. Lastly there is the question of how to place or position oneself in the minds of the users in the targeted segments so that the product or service the organization has to offer stands out from those of competitors. Competitive positioning is the last of the three steps.

SEGMENTATION

Products can be designed and marketed so as to have a more or less general appeal to most customers in a market. However, customers have varying wants and needs and firms are likely to achieve a greater competitive advantage by producing a number of different offerings to meet the needs of specific groups of people making up segments of the market. Attention needs to be given to procedures for identifying market segments, choosing the best market segments in which to operate and deciding the strategy to effect in entering market segments.

Market segmentation is a technique which can help firms find ways of establishing a competitive advantage. A market segment is a section of a market which possesses one or more unique features that both give it an identity and set it apart from other segments. Market segmentation amounts to partitioning a market into a number of distinct sections, using criteria which reflect different and distinctive purchasing motives and behaviour of customers. Segmentation makes it easier for firms to produce goods or services that fit closely with what people want.

Segmentation can be put into effect in a variety of ways. Markets comprise buyers of products and services who differ in their purchase behaviour from one another in various respects. The differences point to varying buyer wants and needs, the different resources at the buyers' disposal, their place of residence, buying attitudes and buying practices. Any combination of these differences can be used as a basis for market segmentation. The important thing that has to be remembered, however, is that a market segment exists only when people have common characteristics as buyers.

There are classes of buyers, or market segments, where the difference is only slight in terms of product requirements. In such circumstances, the appropriate approach may be to identify the broad classes of similar requirements and the common characteristics of people who share these require-ments. Products can then be offered which meet the common wants of the identified segments, and marketing communications relating to the products can be directed through suitable media to appeal to people possessing the identified characteristics. Some travel companies, for example, offer packaged holidays (flight, intermediate travel, hotel accommodation and excursions) which appeal to groups of people who have slightly different ideas on how they will spend their holiday. There is sufficient commonality of interest in what such companies have to offer, however, to attract these different groups to make use of the same packaged holiday.

Segmentation is a powerful component of marketing strategy. Failure to segment the market at all, when competitors are doing so, can lead to almost catastrophic consequences (Figure 10.1).

MARKET SEGMENTATION RESEARCH

A segment is a unique group of customers (or potential customers) who share some common characteristics which make them different from other groups of customers. Different segments may have different needs; they may require different versions of the same product; they may pay different prices; they may buy in different places; they may be reached by different media.

In consumer markets, customers and prospective customers can be grouped together, or 'segmented' by: attitude, life-style, age, gender, stage in the family life cycle, or by job type, level of income and many other relevant variables. In industrial markets, customers and prospective customers are generally grouped together and allocated into a particular segment depending on the customer type, customer size, customer culture, customer location. Customers and prospective customers can be further segmented according to whether they are heavy or light users of a particular product or service and whether they are very loyal to a particular competitor.

Segmenting and selecting the optimum market segments is called target marketing. This is a vital marketing skill. Target marketing requires an ability to:

1 Find the key characteristic/s that break a market into relevant 'actionable' segments.
2 Identify and quantify which customers fall into which segments.
3 Target the best segments most likely to give the best results.

191

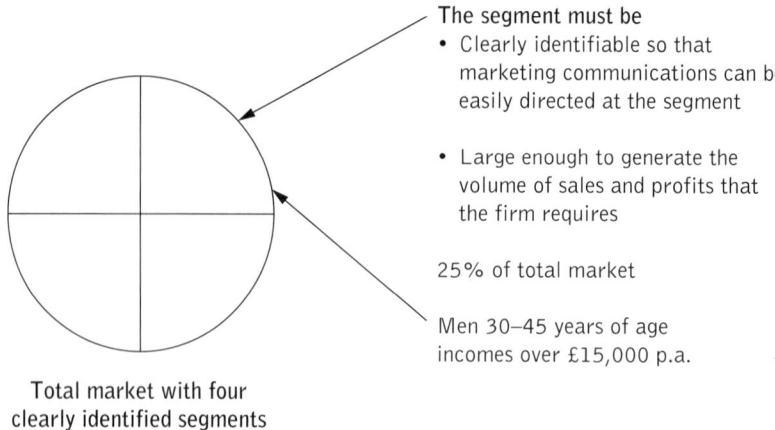

The segment must be
• Clearly identifiable so that marketing communications can be easily directed at the segment

• Large enough to generate the volume of sales and profits that the firm requires

25% of total market

Men 30–45 years of age incomes over £15,000 p.a.

Total market with four clearly identified segments

Figure 10.1   Requirements of a market segment

Identifying what each segment wants, what it can afford and whether it is loyal to a particular competitor and how it might respond to an offer is vital information for the marketer. Careful segmentation and accurate targeting keeps a firm close to the market, reduces waste, finds the best customers and helps to keep them satisfied.

One can segment consumer markets using many different variables including:

■ geographic
■ demographic
■ geodemographic
■ psychographic
■ behavioural

■ *Geographic* segments mean location and this can include: streets, towns, cities, regions, countries, continents, trading blocs like the European Union and NAFTA.
■ *Demographics*, or social statistics, includes: age, sex, family, life cycle, job type/socio-economic and group income level.
■ *Geodemographics* mixes geographic and demographic data to create categories of house types and locations, for example, people who live in detached houses in exclusive suburbs.
■ *Psychographics* attempts to segment according to psychological profiles of people in terms of their life-styles, attitudes and personalities, for example, active go getters.
■ *Behavioural* segments address behaviour patterns which include: usage (e.g. heavy or light users) and uses, the way a product or service is used, in other words, the benefit enjoyed.

Haley (1968) and Wind (1973) proposed the segmentation of markets on the basis of benefits sought by identifiable groups of consumers. For example, some people use toothpaste for healthy teeth, others to prevent bad breath, and some people buy it for both reasons.

More than one variable can be used when segmenting markets, and indeed, the more variables the better since it helps to focus on a tighter target market. Tighter targeting means less waste, more relevant offers to appropriate customers and higher customer satisfaction.

Industrial, organizational or business-to-business markets can also be broken into segments and the most appropriate ones selected as target markets. Different variables are used for these types of markets: customer type, size, location, how they operate or the corporate culture. Customer type categorizes the type of product or service which the customer organization produces. In the UK, industry type is defined by the SIC, Standard Industrial Classification code. The size of the customer in terms of sales, number of staff and usage may determine whether it is worth targeting or not. Size of customer is also influenced by whether they are heavy or light users of a particular product or service, and whether they are very loyal to a particular competitor.

CARTOGRAPHY AND GEOGRAPHIC SEGMENTATION

Computer technology has enabled the ready production of maps which display segmentation data effectively. Depending on the data source, the map(s) can be displayed in varying colours or shading patterns (with almost unlimited possibilities, according to category, such as proportion of potential or actual customers, per capita spending in a particular product or service group, or sales achievement versus potential). Such maps can be produced with the aid of a spreadsheet package. Most mapping sources can produce maps on paper, transparency film, or slides, and colour transparency overlays are almost always a possibility.

SEGMENTATION, TARGETING AND PRODUCT POSITIONING

Having introduced the nature of market segmentation, it is now appropriate to examine how it relates to targeting and product positioning. Marketing executives employ the following steps:

- segment the market
- target the users
- position the products.

In order to segment a market, characteristics have to be identified which distinguish among customers according to their buying preferences. Profiles of market segments which reflect different combinations of these characteristics then have to be constructed.

To target the users, the financial appeal of all segments should be assessed and segments which have the greatest appeal should be selected for targeting. The selection criteria should take account of the relative financial attractiveness of the segments and the organization's capability to exploit them.

In positioning a product, one should aim to match it with that segment of the market where it is most likely to succeed. This involves identifying possible positions for products within each target segment and then producing, adapting and marketing them towards the target market. The product or service should be positioned in such a manner that it stands apart from competing products. The positioning of a product or service indicates what the product represents, and how customers should evaluate it.

Positioning is accomplished through the use of the marketing mix variables, in particular product design and marketing communications. Positioning to achieve product differentiation applies equally to consumer and to industrial goods. Sometimes product positioning can be effected on the basis of tangible differences (e.g. product features). In many instances, however, customer perceptions about products can be utilized in order to differentiate and position products.

In attempting to meet the specific needs of an identified market segment, a firm can put itself in a better position to obtain a demonstrable competitive advantage for its product. Market segments must, of course, be:

- clearly identifiable, so that marketing communications can be easily directed at the segment.
- large enough to generate the volume of sales and profits that the firm requires.

Having introduced the nature of market segmentation and looked at how this relates to targeting and positioning, we will now consider strategic aspects of market segmentation.

SEGMENTATION STRATEGY

It has also been found (Abell, 1978) that market segmentation may lead to profit opportunities and strategic windows that allow new competitors to challenge established market leaders. The concept of a strategic window implies that there are only limited periods during which the 'fit' between the key requirements of a market and the particular competencies of an enterprise competing in that market are at an optimum. For example, Ever Ready dominated the small battery market until Duracell used lithium technology to replace conventional zinc cells The new batteries had operating lives two to three times those of Ever Ready, whose market share collapsed (Doyle, 1994).

The timing of investment and disinvestment in a product or service should coincide with periods during which the strategic window is respectively open and shut. Moreover, as a market develops, new segments become visible and older ones disappear. The marketing strategist is usually primarily interested in those segments which appear to offer the best growth and profit potentials. However, it may be possible to operate very profitably in declining segments as competition withdraws.

Expanding market segments intuitively may seem to be the most appealing. However, it should be borne in mind that such segments will also appeal to competitors. Gaining a good position in such segments will be difficult and it will be expensive in terms of application of resources to maintain a position in an expanding market segment. A successful strategy, however, could have a substantial pay-off.

Static or declining market segments seem less appealing. To a potential new entrant they will seem decidedly less attractive than ones which are expanding in size. Nevertheless, contracting market segments can cause some companies to pull out, thereby not only reducing competition in the market segment but also artificially enlarging the market for those firms remaining in it. Firms may sometimes operate very profitably in a declining market segment provided there is a close fit between the needs of the segment and the firm's own capabilities. Resources and objectives must be considered when selecting segments. The fit between the market needs and the company's capabilities is important.

Some firms place a product within a single market segment. Few resources or a lack of competitors in the segment may make this strategy attractive. In so doing a firm may be able to develop a strong market position through gaining an in-depth knowledge of the segment's needs over a long period of time. Operating economies may also be obtained through specialization. Such a strategy is of course risky since a downturn in the market or the sudden emergence of a strong competitor can have a drastic impact on profits. A more conservative strategy is to look for a match between capabilities and the demands of several different segments. This makes it possible to spread the risk so that if one segment starts to become unprofitable there are still others that can bring in cash for the firm.

Firms sometimes concentrate on producing one product or service which is supplied to several different customer groups. In pursuing this strategy a firm can build a good reputation in the area of the specific product. This also can be a risky strategy since it involves concentrating on a single product or service.

Concentrating on serving the needs of a particular group of customers represents yet another way of segmenting the market. This can involve making available many different products or services. Risk in this case is associated with a downturn in the fortunes of the particular group of customers selected.

SEGMENT SYNERGIES

Firms which decide to serve more than one segment need to pay close attention to synergies between segments with respect to cost, performance and technology. Two or more segments might provide just the opportunity for exploitation because they share common distribution channels, manufacturing facilities, etc. The joint effect of marketing to all segments creates synergy. That is, the overall effect of marketing to two or more segments is to produce greater sales and profits than if each segment had been exploited one at a time in complete isolation from the others.

In international markets it is sometimes a good strategy to use a segment to which one can gain access as a stepping stone to other segments which may be difficult to access unless one already has a base in the country concerned.

SEGMENT INVASION STRATEGY

Having selected segments to enter, the final strategic decision concerns the method of 'invading' the segments. The question is whether firms should invade all the segments at once or whether they should 'pick them off' one at a time? Much depends on the resources that firms have available. A firm is more likely to be successful if it concentrates its efforts on one strategic objective at a time. In so doing it ensures that resources are not too thinly spread. It is also more prudent to enter one segment at a time and to conceal the overall plan. It is also more productive to market goods to selective market segments where synergy can be achieved.

MARKET TARGETING AND POSITIONING

A target market is the market or market segment which form the focus of the firm's marketing efforts. Once segments have been identified, decisions about how many and which customer groups to target must be made. The options include the following.

- *Mass marketing strategy:* offering one product/service concept to most of the market, across many market segments. Although scale economies can be achieved, there is a risk that few customers will be adequately satisfied. The underlying assumption of this approach, referred to as undifferentiated marketing, is that all customers in the market have similar needs and wants. It is argued that they can therefore be satisfied with a single marketing mix – that is a standard product or service, similar price levels, one method of distribution and a promotional mix which is directed at everyone.

There are probably only two conditions under which a mass marketing approach is the most appropriate. The first reflects the demand side of the equation and is the position where there is little variation in the needs of consumers for a given product or service This is a situation which is becoming increasingly rare since in both consumer and industrial markets different individuals and organizations have widely varying characteristics, wants, needs and interests. The second condition reflects the supply side of the equation and refers to the ability of the enterprise to develop and sustain a single marketing mix that satisfies all. Where markets are large this capability requires the availability of substantial resources.

More prevalent strategies are those which take account of the wide variation in customer wants, needs, characteristics and interests. For example:

- *Single segment strategy:* concentrating on a single segment with a product/service concept. This is a relatively cheap option to use in terms of utilizing resources, but there is a risk of putting all the eggs in one basket – if the segment fails the company's financial strength will decline rapidly. Rolex, for example, targets relatively high-income consumers with its prestigious wristwatches. When world economies are buoyant sales will be good, but in times of economic recession even the better off can change their spending patterns.

There is also a problem with regard to flexibility in changing the product-market posture. High-quality image companies experience difficulty in terms of moving into product-market segments which have a lower-quality image. Rolex, for example, would find it impossible to manufacture and market cheap quartz watches in competition with firms such as Sekonda. Rolex does, however, move slightly 'down-market' by producing the Tudor range of watches which retail at prices considerably less than those for the Rolex brand range. But it can only do this by offering a product under a different brand name and ensuring that the product is not too far removed price-wise from the main brand of Rolex. On the other hand, a single segment strategy does permit a firm to specialize and the firm can concentrate all its energies on satisfying the wants of a particular market segment.

- *Multi-segment strategy:* targeting a different product or service concept at each of a number of segments and developing a marketing mix strategy for each of the selected segments. Although this approach can spread the risk of being over-committed in one area, it can be extremely resource demanding.

Which target segment strategy a company adopts will be dependent on a wide range of market, product and competitive factors. Each of these must be carefully considered before a decision is made about segments to be targeted.

FACTORS INFLUENCING CHOICE OF TARGETING STRATEGY

Having looked at some of the ways of targeting let us now consider the kind of factors which influence choice of strategy.

Stage of product-market maturity

Segmentation strategies are most critical during the maturity stage of the product market, because buyers' needs are different. At the introductory stage of the life cycle there are few, if any, product-type competitors; however, competition can occur among alternative product types. If product-type substitution exists, the new market entrant may benefit from targeting one or more segments in the existing product markets. Where there are no product-type substitutes, a broad or relatively undifferentiated targeting strategy may be appropriate at the introductory stage of the life cycle. This may amount to attempting to identify a broad segment of potential buyers. The nature and intensity of competition at each stage of the product life cycle are important in guiding market targeting decisions.

Extent of buyer differentiation

When buyer wants are similar throughout the product market, there is less opportunity for extensive segmentation than there is in markets with buyers with different wants. A product market made up of a relatively small number of end-users is more suitable for a broad or relatively undifferentiated targeting strategy, particularly if the value of purchases of individual buyers is small. In addition, the more complex that the product-market structure is with respect to competing firms, variety of product-market offerings, variations in user needs and wants, etc. the more likely it is that a useful method of segmentation can be found.

Market position

A firm's market share in an existing product market plays an important role in determining the target market strategy that it uses. Low market share firms have to compete in segments where their strengths are most highly valued and where large competitors are unlikely to compete. The strength may be in the type and range of products that are offered, the method by which the product is produced, the cost and speed of distribution or the credit and service arrangements. In these firms, management has to spend time identifying and exploiting unique segments rather than attempting to serve entire industries.

Structure and intensity of competition

When several firms are competing in an industry, selective targeting is often an appropriate strategy. Such selectivity is often essential for small firms in fragmented, transitional and global industries. Large firms may be able to reap the benefits of extensive targeting using a multiple-segmentation strategy.

197

Adequate resources

The possession of considerable resources can often place an organization in a position where it can consider various target market alternatives. Where resources are limited, however, a company may be forced to adopt a single-segment targeting strategy. The ability to analyse market capabilities is a decided asset, particularly where the task of market segmentation is a complex one. Thus possessing both resources and the capacity to undertake such complex analyses provides firms with flexibility in choosing market targets.

Production and marketing scale economies

Choice of target market strategy may be influenced by production and marketing scale economies. The production process, for example, may require large-scale output to achieve necessary cost advantages. The same may also apply to marketing and distribution programmes. In such cases an extensive market coverage strategy may be required in order to gain the sales volume necessary to support large-volume production and distribution.

Choice of segment(s)

Five factors govern the attractiveness of a segment (Doyle, 1994):

- segment size
- current and potential competition
- segment growth
- capabilities of the business.
- profitability of the segment.

Deciding whether or not to enter a particular segment depends essentially on the match between the companies' capabilities and the characteristics of the segment Although a large, expanding and lucrative market segment must be intuitively appealing, it will attract considerable competition so a firm must have the capabilities (resources) to compete effectively in such a market segment. Similarly, as segments contract, larger competitors may tend to withdraw making the segment less competitive and more attractive to firms with lesser capabilities.

Having looked at market targeting we will now move on to look at positioning.

POSITIONING

Positioning, it has been suggested, represents the most important decision and action that management has to take for the company and its marketing (Davis, 1977), and yet it remains one of the most nebulous and controversial areas of new product development (Marken, 1987). Targeting and positioning strategies are interrelated. The choice of one or more target markets is based, at least in part, on the feasibility of the organization designing and implementing an effective positioning strategy to meet the target's needs. Positioning strategies used to pursue target markets may vary considerably or they may have common features. For example, a firm may have a unique combination of the product offering, distribution approach, price, advertising and personal selling to serve each segment. Alternatively, some marketing mix components may be similar for different segments. An airline service, for example, can appeal to business and holiday makers although different advertising and sales efforts are aimed at each market niche and fare prices may vary across segments.

What is it that differentiates one product or service from another, even when they are almost identical? The answer seems to reflect the way in which the marketers of the product or service position them in the minds of users. Positioning refers to the decisions and activities intended to create and maintain a firm's product concept in customers' minds. Market positioning amounts to arranging for a product or service to occupy a clear, distinctive and desirable place – relative to competing products – in the minds of target customers (Exhibit 10.1).

What is being marketed must be perceived by the selected target customers to have a distinct image, relative to competitors, which meets with their own desires/expectations. The position of an offering is related to the attributes ascribed to it by consumers. These might be such attributes as its standing, its quality and type of people who use it, its strengths and weaknesses, and any other unusual and memorable characteristics it may possess, its price and the value it represents to users.

The whole of the marketing mix is important in developing effective positioning, as attributes of the offering must be closely in line with the targeted customers' expectations and needs, as must the associated price points and channels of distribution. However, promotional activity is one of the

EXHIBIT 10.1   GENERIC POSITIONING

Hooley and Saunders (1993) propose a generic positioning model. This provides the broad alternatives: *consolidation, latent position, deposition and membership position. Consolidation* might be used by market leaders or non-leaders with a strong reputation and where the characteristics of this reputation can be stressed – Land Rover's ruggedness, tradition and cross-country capability or Volvo's safety reputation. Where there is an unfulfilled need or want *latent positioning* can be used to establish a reputation – that is, positioning is based on the promise that need or want will be satisfied by the product or service – Sensodyne toothpaste promised comfort for people with sensitive teeth. *Depositioning* is directly competitive, although the competitor may not always be mentioned – e.g. 'our product offers *this and that*, which is more than can be said for other products we could mention'. *Membership positioning* is attractive for lower-order competitors within a market. Firms might do this by identifying themselves as one of the main providers of the products or services – Lloyds Bank identifies itself as 'one of the big four'.

Within each of the generic positions, the positioning strategy determines the means by which each of the product's positions are communicated. These include positioning by attribute (e.g. distinctiveness or similarity to other products are mentioned), competition (e.g. offers more than competitors), application (e.g. how the product will benefit the user), user portraits (e.g. people who use the product) and product class association (e.g. with a nostalgic, desirable group of products that have a vintage appeal) (see Aaker and Shanby, 1982).

fundamental elements of creating an effective positioning, as it is through promotion that the positioning is communicated to the target audience.

Positioning concepts

The positioning concept may be functional, symbolic or experiential. The *functional* concept is relevant to products designed to solve consumption-related problems for externally generated consumption needs. Toothpastes aiming to prevent cavities and banks offering convenient service fall into this category. The *symbolic* concept relates to the buyer's internally generated need for self-enhancement, role position, group membership or ego satisfaction. Cosmetics relating to life-style and clothes stressing image or appropriateness of occasion are examples of this. The *experiential* concept is used to position products that provide sensory pleasure, variety or cognitive stimulation. Documentary films and books are examples of this.

QUALITATIVE APPROACHES TO POSITIONING RESEARCH

Through the use of protective techniques during qualitative research, images can be uncovered that serve to show how the brand of a firm is positioned in the mind of the respondent. Some of the most popular techniques include:

- *The brand of the company as an animal or a person*. Under this approach, respondents are asked to name a person or an animal that embodies their view of the product or company under study.
- *Role play*. In role playing the respondent is asked to assume the role or behaviour of another person, or of an object under research. During discussion, group members are asked to role play the object under research and explain their feelings. This is followed by further probing and discussion to identify how the product is positioned in the mind of the customers.
- *The friendly Martian*. In this approach, the interviewer or group moderator assumes the role of an alien recently landed from space and asks members of the group to explain a particular product and how it is used. By acting the alien, the moderator can pose basic questions which the respondents would normally assume the moderator knew the answers to.

A number of stimuli can be used to prompt respondents and aid them in articulating the images they hold of objects. These include:

- *Association techniques*. Here the respondents are asked for associations with a particular stimulus.
- *Concept boards*. Boards with pictures of the brand or its logo are shown to respondents and their reactions sought through probing.
- *Animatics*. Drawings of key frames from a commercial with bubble speech. Respondents are then asked for their reactions and helped to describe the feelings they have towards the item being advertised.
- *Cartoon and story completion*. Cartoons of situations, such as the purchase of a specific brand, where the speech bubbles are left blank for the respondent to fill in.

- *Visual product mapping.* This is a qualitative form of the perceptual mapping approaches. Here respondents are given a large piece of paper – the size of a flip chart – with two dimensions drawn at right angles to one another. Respondents are then given a number of objects (such as brands or companies) on small cards. They are then asked to position the cards on the chart with similar brands close to each other but far apart from dissimilar brands. The dimensions which can be used to explain these differences are then discussed and written on to maps. Alternatively, the identity of the dimensions may have been elicited from earlier parts of the research (e.g. price and quality) and respondents are then asked to position the objects on the dimensions directly.

QUANTITATIVE APPROACHES TO POSITIONING RESEARCH

Although qualitative approaches to image research often focus on the core object (brand, product, company, etc.) in isolation, the more quantitative approaches typically consider positioning relative to the positioning of major competitors and relative to the desires, wants and needs of the target customer segments. As a starting point, therefore, it is necessary to define the competitive set that will be analysed along with the focal brand, product or company.

One of the simplest methods of collecting quantitative positioning data is through the use of attitude or attribute scaling. In this approach, the dimensions that the respondent uses to differentiate and choose between alternative offerings are included in a survey and presented as a semantic scale to enable respondents to express their views.

Semantic differential scale

The scaling technique was originated by Osgood *et al.* (1987). The originators of the technique discovered that the perceived meaning of a variety of words and concepts could be deconstructed in terms of three components: potency, activity and evaluation. In marketing research, the semantic differential is frequently used to measure attitudes towards the imagery surrounding products and services. In general, only the evaluative (e.g. good/bad) component is measured.

The scale consists of a number of bipolar adjective phrases and statements that could be used to describe the objectives being evaluated. In the original work of Osgood *et al.* only single-word bipolar adjectives, not phrases, were used. However, common practice in marketing research applications is to use adjective phrases as well. An example is shown in Exhibit 10.3. Each bipolar adjective rating scale consists of seven categories, with neither numerical labels nor category descriptions other than for the anchor categories. To remove any position bias, favourable and unfavourable adjective phrases are randomly distributed to the left hand and right hand anchor positions. The respondent is asked to mark one of the seven categories that best describes his or her views about the object along the continuum implied by the bipolar object pair. An overall attitude score is computed by summing the responses on each adjective pair. Before computing the overall score, the response categories must be coded. Usually the categories are assigned values from 1 to 7, where 1 is assigned to the unfavourable adjective phrase and 7 is assigned to the favourable adjective phrase. Thus, before assigning codes and summing the researcher must be careful to reverse the individual scale items where necessary so that each attitude continuum ranges from unfavourable to favourable or vice versa.

201

Ratings on each of the bipolar adjective pairs are frequently used to provide a profile or image of the objects being investigated. This is achieved by plotting the mean ratings on each of the bipolar adjective pairs for each of the objects. Exhibit 10.2 shows an example of such profiling. In order to facilitate interpretation of the profile, all of the favourable adjective phrases are positioned on the same side. From this kind of plot it is possible to obtain an overall impression of people's perceptions of the object.

In Exhibit 10.3, a comparison is made between two restaurants. Not only does the scale permit such comparisons to be taken in at a glance but it also allows one to see fairly readily where more in-depth research is required. The décor of 'our restaurant', for example, is perceived to be at or about

EXHIBIT 10.2 SEMANTIC DIFFERENTIAL

We would like you to let us know what you think about our restaurant. Below are a number of statements that could be used to describe what we have to offer. For each pair of adjective phrases we would like you to mark the category that best describes your feelings about us.

Old-fashioned	__:__:__:__:__:__	Modern
Expensive	__:__:__:__:__:__	Cheap
Friendly service	__:__:__:__:__:__	Unfriendly service
Helpful assistance	__:__:__:__:__:__	Unhelpful staff
Wide range of menus	__:__:__:__:__:__	Limited range of menus
Inviting atmosphere	__:__:__:__:__:__	Cold atmosphere
Slow service	__:__:__:__:__:__	Fast service
Attractive décor	__:__:__:__:__:__	Unattractive décor
Convenient opening hours	__:__:__:__:__:__	Inconvenient opening hours

EXHIBIT 10.3 SEMANTIC DIFFERENTIAL PROFILE

Old-fashioned	__: 2 __: __: __1 : __: __	Modern
Expensive	__:__: 1 __: __2 : __	Cheap
Friendly service	__:__: 1 : 2 __: __:__	Unfriendly service
Helpful assistance	__: 1 : 2 __:__:__:__	Unhelpful staff
Wide range of menus	__:__: 1 : 2 :__:__	Limited range of menus
Inviting atmosphere	__:__: 2 : 1 :__:__	Cold atmosphere
Slow service	__:__: 2 :__: 1 : __	Fast service
Attractive décor	__: 2 :__: 1 :__:__	Unattractive décor
Convenient opening hours	__: 12 :__:__:__:__	Inconvenient opening hours

Key 1: Our restaurant   2: Competitor's restaurant

the neutral point. Further research is warranted to uncover how it might be improved to the taste of the clientele.

MULTI-DIMENSIONAL SCALING AND PERCEPTUAL MAPPING

Product maps, sociograms, sociometric maps, psychometric maps, stimulus-response diagrams, relationship maps, concept maps, etc. are names which are sometimes given to perceptual maps. A perceptual map is assumed to be a map that involves object-to-object relationships that are not amenable to simple, physical measurement.

It is easier to understand relationships between facts, events or objects if we can visualize these relationships spatially. In marketing research there are a number of techniques which go under the heading of multi-dimensional scaling and perceptual mapping techniques which enable us to do exactly that. They allow us to see visually how products and services are perceived in relationship to one another by users. The appropriateness of the technique depends on the type of data collected.

Correspondence analysis

Consumers are classified into one of 10 categories according to their favourite soft drink. They are then asked to pick any of 8 product attributes describing their favourite soft drink. Exhibit 10.4 identifies the number of times each attribute was associated with each favourite drink category.

MDPREF

Another useful mapping device involves having people rate products against a list of attributes and then using the average scores obtained by products against each attribute as a basis for producing a map (see Exhibit 10.5).

EXHIBIT 10.4 CORRESPONDENCE ANALYSIS METHOD

Respondent category	1	2	3	4	5	6	7	8
Pepsi	4	5	5	20	1	21	2	1
Coke	2	5	7	13	1	16	4	2
Coke classic	9	9	8	12	2	17	5	3
Diet Pepsi	5	11	10	20	1	15	3	2
Diet Slice	25	25	19	19	20	11	11	8
Diet 7 Up	25	25	21	20	19	14	12	10
Dr Pepper	22	23	18	15	20	12	14	8
Slice	17	17	18	11	11	10	11	3
7 Up	7	11	8	4	3	7	3	2
TAB	12	13	13	9	11	8	12	9

Correspondence analysis provides a perceptual map showing the relationship between the various brands and attributes on which they were judged

```
J    8                                          B

     7

5                                             6
G                        C                       A

                                              4
  F
E          3
   1
  H
     2                              D

     I
```

		High score	
A	Pepsi	1 Fruitiness	non-fruity
B	Coke	2 Carbonation	high carbonation
C	Coke Classic	3 Calories	low calories
D	Diet Pepsi	4 Tartness	very sweet
E	Diet Slice	5 Quenching	not quenching
F	Diet 7 Up	6 Popularity	popular with others
G	Dr Pepper	7 After taste	no after taste
H	Slice	8 Pick me up	a pick me up
I	7 Up		
J	Tab		

Correspondence analysis can also be used in a different way to produce a perceptual map. In this case respondents indicate with a 1 or 0 whether they purchase the brand or not –

Brand (+ –)	Respondent
	1 2 3 4 5 ....
(purchased)	
Coke +	1 0 0 0 1
Diet Coke +	1 1 1 1 1
.	
.	
(not purchased)	
Coke –	0 1 1 1 0
Diet Coke –	0 0 0 0 0

Perceptual maps are produced by correspondence analysis which shows the clustering of the products in terms of similarity and also the clusterings of the people in terms of their similarities in tastes.

EXHIBIT 10.5 MDPREF METHOD

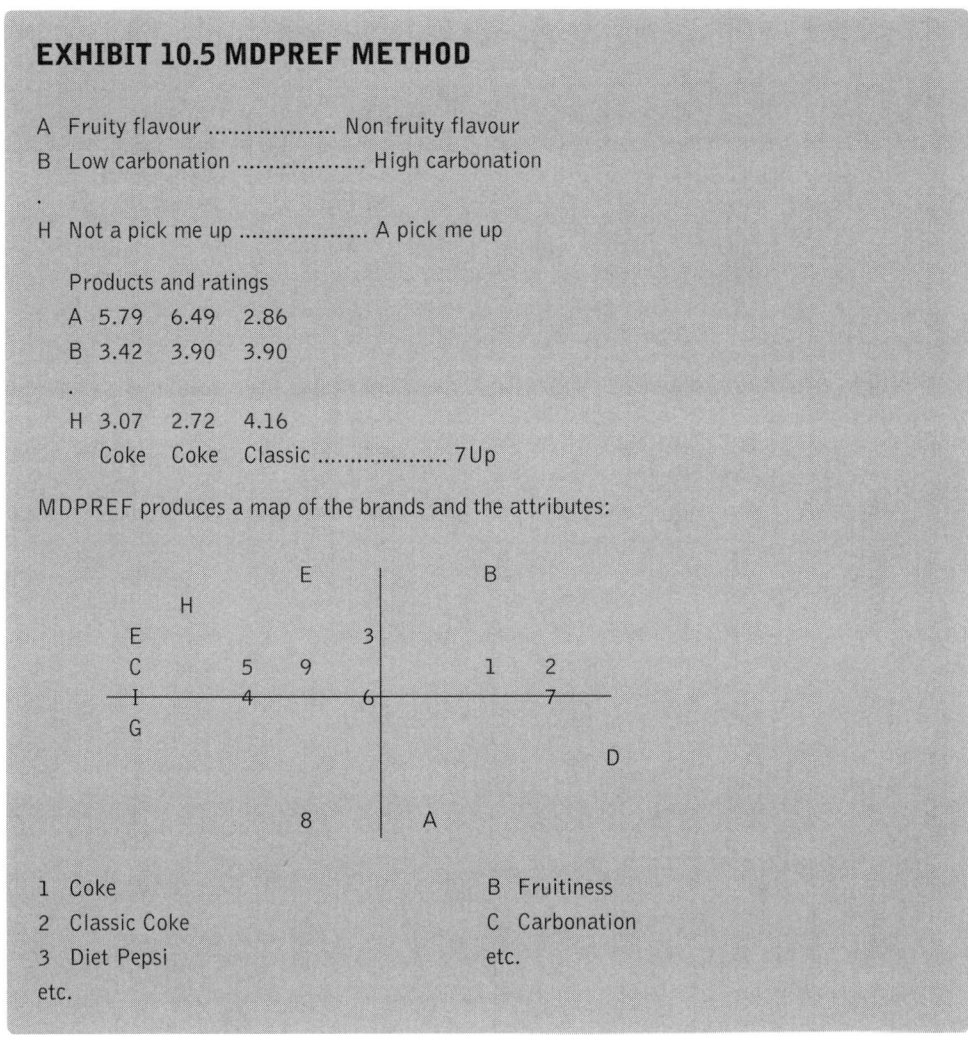

A Fruity flavour .... Non fruity flavour
B Low carbonation .... High carbonation
.
H Not a pick me up .... A pick me up

Products and ratings
A 5.79   6.49   2.86
B 3.42   3.90   3.90
.
H 3.07   2.72   4.16
   Coke   Coke   Classic 7Up

MDPREF produces a map of the brands and the attributes:

1 Coke   B Fruitiness
2 Classic Coke   C Carbonation
3 Diet Pepsi   etc.
etc.

KYST and associated techniques

KYST works with data which have been rank ordered (see Exhibit 10.6).

KYST and PREFMAP

Here we are interested in seeing how products are perceived with respect to 'ideal points'. First, a diagonal matrix averaged out and re-ranked is obtained for KYST (assuming several people are participating in the exercise). Next, respondents are asked to rank order the products in order of preference (see Exhibit 10.7).

EXHIBIT 10.6 RANK ORDERED DATA METHOD

Here is a list of 45 pairs of soft drinks. Please rank them in terms of similarity from the most similar to the least similar. Assign the number 1 to the pair that is the most similar, 2 to the next most similar pair, and so forth, until the value of 45 is assigned to the least similar pair.

	Rank
Coke – Coke Classic	____
Coke – Diet Pepsi	____
.	
.	
.	
Coke Classic – Diet Pepsi	____
.	
.	
Tab – 7 Up	____

Rank order of similarities between pairs of drinks

	P	C	CC	etc.
Pepsi	1			
Coke	3	2		
Coke Classic	7	9	8	
Diet Pepsi	27	28	32	
Diet Slice	41	42	43	
Diet 7 Up				
.				
Tab	12	11	10	

Dimension 1 = Cola flavour	Dimension 2 = Dietness

```
          Dimension 1 = Cola flavour      Dimension 2 = Dietness

               * Dr Pepper
                                                    * Slice
                  Coke

               * Coke Classic
   dim 2          Pepsi                                  * 7 UP

                                                     * Diet slice

               * Tab                                  * Diet 7 UP

                  * Diet Pepsi

                              dim 1
```

NB. Where more than one person makes a rating, which is usually the case, the diagonal matrix is redrawn to show average rankings. The lowest average ranking is then redesignated '1' and so on.

EXHIBIT 10.7 AVERAGE RANKINGS: PREFMAP METHOD

Here the average rankings were:

Pepsi 3.91, Coke 3.37, Coke Classic 5.00, etc.

The rankings along with the numerical output of the KYST program (two vectors defining the position of products on the grid) are then fed into the PREFMAP program. In this case a map is produced which shows the positioning of the products and the ideal points.

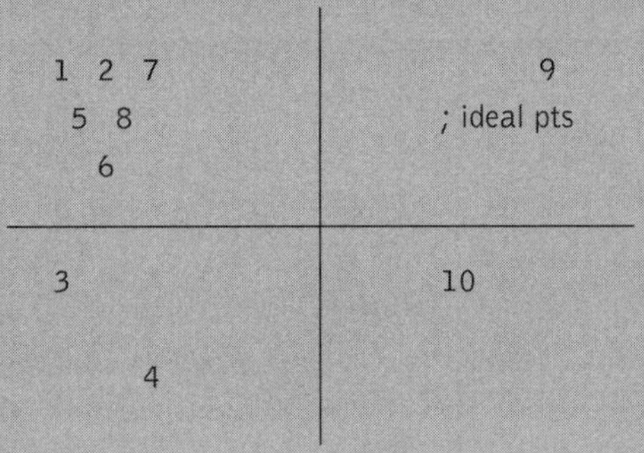

```
        1   2   7                        9
            5   8                    ; ideal pts
            6
    ────────────────────┼───────────────────────
        3                           10

            4
```

For the group of people 9, '7 Up' appears nearest the ideal points.

KYST with PROFIT

Instead of preference ordering, this time ratings for each of the attributes of the product are obtained in addition to the KYST output vectors. The average values for scores on the attributes are fed into PROFIT along with the vector scores from KYST (see Exhibit 10.8).

A simple approach to perceptual mapping

Nakanishi and Coop (2003) argue that marketing researchers commonly interpret joint-space solutions as if the distances between the points from different sets are meaningful and that this is despite appropriate warnings from the authors of joint-space methods that the origin (or metric) of the row objects is not the same as the origin (or metric). They develop a method of metric unfolding as an alternative method (Nakanishi and Coop, 2003). They also argue that marketing practitioners and academics have lost interest in multidimensional scaling (MDS) in general, and joint-space solutions in particular, in recent years because neither marketing academics nor psychometricians have developed straightforward answers for the most compelling questions.

Of course the point of perceptual mapping representation is that it appeals to our visual senses and as has been often quoted a picture is worth a thousand words. Indeed the whole idea of graphical representation of numbers is to make it easier for the viewer to comprehend the meaning of what he or she is examining.

EXHIBIT 10.8 ATTRIBUTE RATINGS: PROFIT METHOD

```
                                    6
            FD
        B                              9
                              58

    ────────────────┼──────────────────

        1                          A
                              H
        4
        #                    CG
        7        E
```

Products are number 1 to 9, except # = products 2 and 3 (i.e. the same point):
A = Appearance, B = Fruitiness, C = Carbonation, D = Calories, E = Tartness, F = Thirst quenching, G = Popularity, H = After taste, I = Pick me up

Bearing this in mind the following simple way of representing data collected from a survey has some value and could be construed to be a perceptual map of sorts. It assumes that we can identify the principal criteria upon which to make judgements – perhaps by means of a focus group study – and various other relatively unsophisticated approaches to statistical representation are also applied in the approach.

In Table 10.1 we assume that a sample of 36 people are asked to rate on an 11-point scale running from -5 to $+5$ their perception of various means of going on holiday to continental Europe from the UK. The two criterion variables assessed are convenience (convenient $= +5$, inconvenient $= -5$) and cost (expensive $= +5$, inexpensive $= -5$). The data is entered into sheet 1 of a spreadsheet as shown in Table 10.1 and the average value is calculated on each rating that has been taken.

We can then show the summary average along with estimated market shares of each travel methods diagrammatically as follows on the second sheet of the spreadsheet (Figure 10.2). Clearly such an approach does have limitations but on the other hand it does appeal to the need to have a visually comprehendible representation of data that can easily be collected and analysed.

Corporate positioning

A more recent development has been the recognition that positioning is not just a matter between the brand owner and customers, but between the brand owner and every one of its stakeholders. The task has become one of deciding what is to be positioned and among whom it is to be positioned. In general terms, the solutions fall in two categories. In the first, it is the traditional view where a product, a marketing mix and a brand has to be positioned among the targeted customers. In the second, it is the soul of the entire organization – all-inclusive of its partners up and down the value

Table 10.1 Perceptual mapping example

Responder	Air and car hire cost	Convenience	Air and public transport cost	Convenience	Rail and car hire cost	Convenience	Rail and public transport cost	Convenience	Ferry and own car cost	Convenience	Ferry and public transport cost	Convenience	Coach tour cost	Convenience
1	2	−4	2	−2	2	−3	1	−3	0	2	1	1	1	1
2	3	3	4	4	4	5	5	3	4	2	5	−1	5	−1
3	2	2	3	3	0	1	3	3	2	1	−1	−1	−1	−1
4	2	2	2	−1	3	3	3	−2	2	1	2	4	–	−1
5	2	−4	4	−4	4	3	3	3	−3	−2	2	−1	−4	−3
6	4	4	4	4	5	5	4	4	4	4	3	3	3	1
7	5	5	4	4	4	4	5	3	−3	−3	1	2	–	−3
8	2	3	3	3	3	3	5	3	0	1	3	4	1	2
9	4	3	−2	2	−3	0	3	3	−5	−4	−4	−4	1	−3
10	4	4	2	1	3	4	0	−3	1	−1	2	2	2	−1
11	4	4	4	4	4	3	3	4	3	3	3	2	2	2
12	4	4	−3	−3	3	3	3	5	−5	−6	2	2	−5	−2
13	4	4	3	3	3	3	4	3	−1	2	−1	0	−3	−5
14	3	2	4	4	3	3	3	3	2	1	2	3	2	2
15	1	1	−1	−1	3	3	1	1	−3	−3	2	2	−4	−4
16	5	4	5	4	5	4	5	4	5	−3	4	3	−3	−2
17	−5	−3	−5	−3	−5	−3	−5	−3	−5	−5	−5	−5	−5	−5

continued

Table 10.1 continued

18	4	4	3	2	4	5	4	4	3	-2	3	-2	3	4
19	4	-5	3	1	3	3	5	1	-3	-5	1	4	-2	-3
20	4	4	3	4	4	3	4	5	-5	-5	3	0	-5	-5
21	2	5	-1	3	1	-1	2	3	-1	-1	-1	3	-2	-5
22	4	2	-1	2	1	-2	1	3	-2	-2	-2	2	-3	-5
23	2	4	1	2	1	-1	2	3	-2	-2	-1	-1	-1	-3
24	3	3	2	2	-1	-1	2	2	-5	-5	1	-3	-2	-3
25	3	4	3	4	2	2	3	4	-2	-2	3	2	-4	-3
26	3	4	3	3	5	5	3	4	-1	-1	4	3	-5	-3
27	2	2	0	1	2	0	0	0	-2	-3	2	-1	-2	-2
28	3	3	0	3	4	4	2	3	1	-1	4	2	-1	-4
29	2	3	-1	3	1	-3	1	3	-3	-3	-2	3	-3	-5
30	1	2	1	2	-1	0	1	2	-5	-5	1	-1	-3	-3
31	3	3	2	4	3	5	2	3	-1	1	4	2	-2	-3
32	2	3	1	4	3	3	2	3	-5	-5	-1	3	-4	-5
33	4	3	5	3	5	4	5	5	5	-3	3	-1	-1	-5
34	3	4	4	4	5	4	4	4	1	-2	2	1	-1	-4
35	4	4	4	5	5	5	5	5	2	1	1	1	-1	-4
36	3	4	5	5	5	5	4	5	1	2	2	1	-4	-5
	2.777777778	2.5555556	1.944444	2.19444444	2.583333	2.25	2.722222	2.583333	-0.72222	-1.44444444	1.333333	0.944444	-1.55556	-2.47222222

Perceptual map of cost and Convenience of travel arrangements when spending a holiday

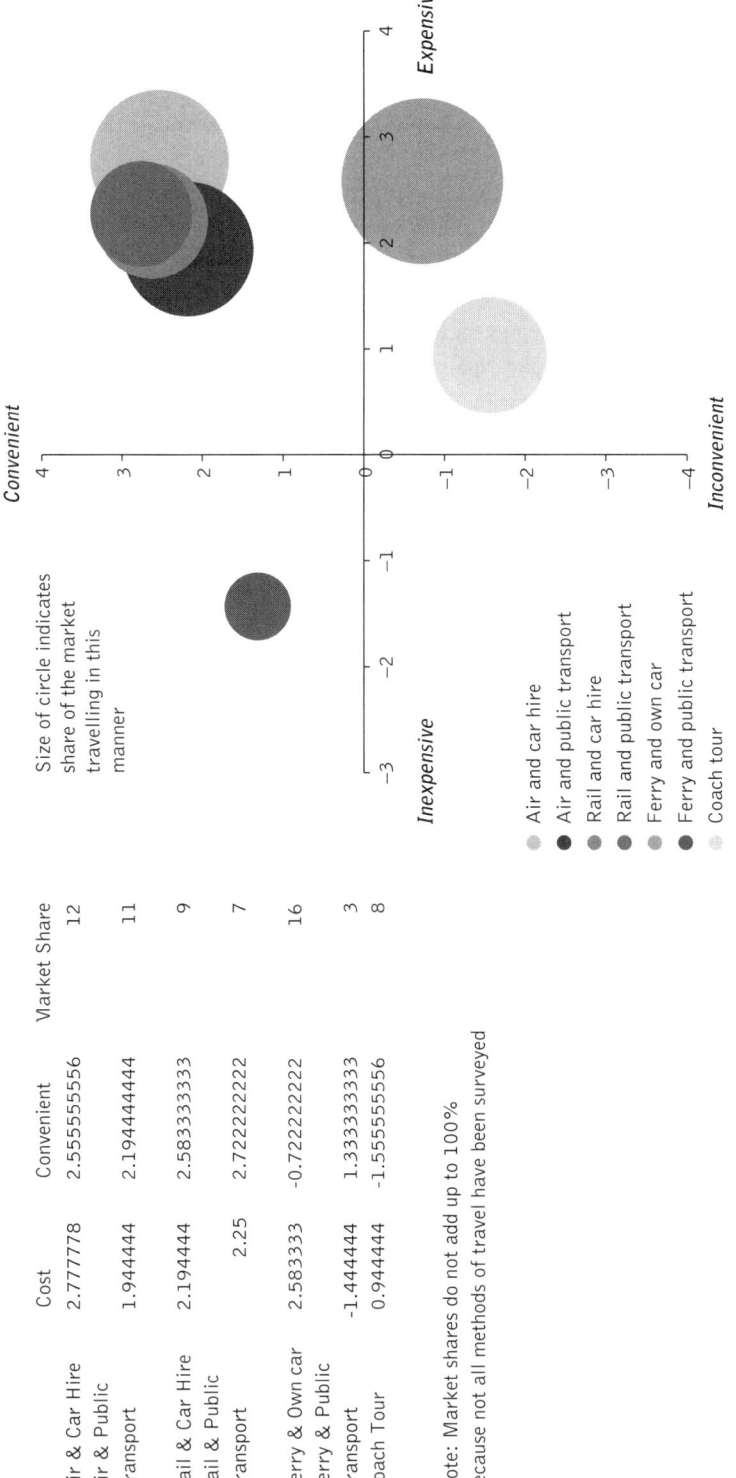

	Cost	Convenient	Market Share
Air & Car Hire	2.777778	2.555555556	12
Air & Public Transport	1.944444	2.194444444	11
Rail & Car Hire	2.194444	2.583333333	9
Rail & Public Transport	2.25	2.722222222	7
Ferry & Own car	2.583333	-0.722222222	16
Ferry & Public Transport	-1.444444	1.333333333	3
Coach Tour	0.944444	-1.555555556	8

Note: Market shares do not add up to 100%
because not all methods of travel have been surveyed

Size of circle indicates share of the market travelling in this manner

Legend:
- Air and car hire
- Air and public transport
- Rail and car hire
- Rail and public transport
- Ferry and own car
- Ferry and public transport
- Coach tour

Convenient — Expensive — Inconvenient — Inexpensive

Figure 10.2 Perceptual map of cost and convenience of travel arrangements when spending a holiday

chain – which has to be positioned among all the stakeholders of an organization. The second, more recent view, reflects that positioning is developing into an integrative construct which depends upon and affects every individual in the organization.

Kapferer (1992) argues that brand positioning is a process of emphasizing the brand's distinctive and motivating attributes in the light of competition. Positioning refers both to the product segment the brand belongs to and how it differs specifically from other brands in the segment.

Positioning is becoming the universal strategic preoccupation of entire organizations and the concern of top management. Eisenhardt and Brown (1999) note that in a business environment of continuous flux it is more important to build corporate level strategic processes that facilitate dynamic repositioning than it is to build any defensible position. In the pursuit of this, organizations engage in 'patching'. This is the strategic process by which the business is routinely re-mapped to changing market opportunities. A good example was been illustrated by Virgin (Branson, 1998). The Virgin brand was repositioned to represent service and value for the customer, supported by an organizational culture and approach to business that stressed employee satisfaction, creativity, irreverence and fun.

QUESTIONS

1. What benefits are to be gained from employing market segmentation as opposed to treating the market as a single entity? Why should some bases of segmentation be more suitable for some products than others?
2. What factors impact upon a firm's selection of market segments? What do you understand by 'segment strategies' and how do these influence a firm's approach to market segmentation?
3. What do you understand by a competitive positioning strategy? How is product or service positioning accomplished? Discuss the factors that influence choice of positioning strategy.
4. What is repositioning and why are products and services repositioned periodically?
5. How would you evaluate competitive advantage based on positioning analysis?

CASE STUDIES

Home Baker

Making cakes and other similar pastimes are a regular domestic occupation in many homes. However, home baking of bread was for many years considered a bit old fashioned and a time-consuming chore which did not make a great deal of sense given the amount of off-the-shelf bread that could be bought. Home baking of bread on a regular basis was dead many years before the arrival of convenience shopping – at least in western developed countries. However, everything has its revival in due course it seems. With the turn of the twenty-first century, an interest in home baking may once again be just around the corner.

Easy to use, even if you have never baked before, the Home Baker enables even the absolute novice to produce perfect loaves of bread. The producers of Home Baker claim that nothing could be more gratifying to people than adding basic ingredients to the stylish, attractive bread-making machine, walking away and returning later to a loaf of fragrant, just-baked bread.

The programmable Home Baker can be set up to 13 hours in advance and has 6 different bread settings for all types of loaf and even mixes dough for pizza and pitta bread. There are also a wealth of other features which include crust colour control, fruit and nut bread capability, easy removable basket and other important features. The Home Baker can make loaves up to 680g (1.51b) and includes a fitted mains plug and a bread-making recipe book.

The firm intends to introduce the product into the UK later in the year and has plans to move into west European markets early next spring. Key questions concern market segmentation, market targeting and strategic positioning of the product.

QUESTIONS

1 How should this product be marketed?
2 How should the firm segment the market – international and domestic?
3 What are likely to be the market targets of interest?
4 How should it position itself towards identified target markets?

The Observatory: segmentation strategy

One can just catch sight on a clear day of the radio telescope looming up as one approaches the area. The telescope has stood there for the past fifty years and while today there are more powerful telescopes it still remains as a potent reminder to scientific endeavour in scanning the heavens for information about the universe in which we live. Since being built it has played a major role in the discovery of exciting objects such as quasars and gravitational lenses. The University astronomers who work at the facility use the telescope and others around the world to observe many exciting events – the birth and death of stars, new planets outside our solar system, super massive black holes at the hearts of other galaxies and the origin of the universe in the Big Bang. Now it is used in a network of telescopes stretching across the world.

The Visitor Centre comprises an exhibition room, 3D theatre, large arboretum, café and shop. Visitors can learn about the work of the Observatory in the exhibition room. The theatre provides an experience of a journey to planets in the solar system in 3D. For others, various trails and natural habitats of the extensive arboretum with its 2,000 species of trees and shrubs

QUESTIONS

1 How might the organization segment the market for with respect to people who might be interested to make use of its facilities.
2 In what ways might the wants or needs of the different market segments differ?

Casa Resort

Casa Resort is located about 60 kilometres away from Kuala Lumpur, the capital city of Malaysia, in the resort town of Port Dickson. Port Dickson is one of the most frequented seaside resorts on the west coast of Malaysia due to its close vicinity to Kuala Lumpur and easy accessibility for visitors from Singapore. Port Dickson derived its name from Sir John Frederick Dickson, the British resident responsible for developing the area into a significant trading port in the eighteenth century. Now Port Dickson, or more popularly known as PD, has been a weekend retreat for city dwellers seeking a break from the hustle and bustle of city life.

The popularity of this resort town and its close vicinity to Kuala Lumpur, has attracted a number of property developers to focus their investment and property development here. The mid-1990s saw the booming of resort and hotel development in this area. However, the financial crisis of 1997 that hit a number of Southeast Asian countries including Malaysia, was bad news to the least stable developers and this led to a number of abandoned projects. That was the story of Casa Resort which was a site of an abandoned hotel development whose fate was sealed until the Urban Development Authority or UDA Holdings decided that this was an opportunity that could lead to a potentially lucrative business undertaking.

Established by the government on 12 November 1971, the Urban Development Authority (UDA) was given the responsibility to promote planned urban development but it has now expanded into the hospitality industry. Casa Resort in Port Dickson is one of several projects undertaken by UDA where abandoned projects are turned into attractive sites. Today, Casa has been transformed from three blocks of ugly abandoned buildings at the much frequented Telok Kemang or Kemang Bay beach in Port Dickson, into a resort that is always bustling with activities and always filled with the sounds of visitors.

When it first opened in May 2003, business at the beginning was slow but it later picked up its momentum when it introduced a totally new concept in resort marketing in Port Dickson, i.e. by targeting mainly to corporations who are keen to organize family days or corporate functions for staff and their families. Business picked up tremendously and Casa's weekend occupancy rate jumped to almost 90 per cent and at times 99 per cent on extremely busy weekends. The target market has become more defined and the resort is positioned as a family resort but it targets corporations and government agencies rather than individual families. This became its main strategic focus as Casa moves to operationalize its marketing strategies. Thus, marketing programmes that are aligned to corporation needs in the form of personalized selling and event marketing was put in full force. By the end of 2005, Casa was experiencing positive growth and this has continued until today.

Resort and hotel operators in Port Dickson are well aware that it has never been easy to attract a strong pool of customers because of the competitive pressure with too many operators targeting similar markets. Yet, Casa promises something different and its performance since its inception has proven that with the right positioning and marketing orientation, it is possible to attract and sustain loyal customers. Indeed, customer loyalty is something they value and they understand its significance. Satisfied customers constitute the resort's customer relationship capital and are likely to contribute to brand equity. Casa is banking on its loyal customers to sustain its existence and to ensure long term profitability. However, there is a need to constantly reassess its offerings and at times changing tactical steps to ensure that customer needs are met. This is a challenge that Casa currently faces when competitive pressure mounts as new hotel and resort operators who have forgotten the painful experience of 1997 and have decided to try their luck and open new outlets in Port Dickson.

QUESTIONS

1 In the face of aggressive competition, how should Casa reposition itself?
2 Should Casa focus on a new market segment with the entrance of new competitors in the market? Why?
3 What suggestions would you make to ensure that Casa could retain its loyal customers?

Contributed by Associate Professor Dr Rosmimah Mohd Roslin,
Universiti Teknologi MARA, Malaysia

COMUN International

Company overview

COMUN International, Inc. ('COMUN' or the 'Company') is a rapidly emerging communication services firm providing messaging and communication infrastructure services to the Latin American region, starting with Mexico. The Company designs, develops, sells, and supports complete messaging services for both individuals and corporations seeking to extend communications to the Internet.

The Company aims to become the leading provider of integrated email, messaging solutions, and communications services for enterprises and individuals across Latin America.

Core business

COMUN aims to become the leading provider of complete end-to-end Internet messaging and collaboration solutions across the Latin American region starting with Mexico. The Company's complete range of services has positioned it at the forefront of the messaging revolution in Latin America.

- *Outsourced Messaging Solutions ('OMS')*. COMUN's messaging platform is capable of providing services, both on a hosted and licensed basis, that enable clients to provide feature-rich email, messaging, collaboration, and directory services to their customers and employees. The Company's all-encompassing strategy provides flexibility to clients by giving them the option of: (1) using COMUN's hosted services; (2) licensing the software to run on their own hardware; or (3) selecting a combination of both. These solutions enable clients to improve messaging performance with customers and employees, reduce the cost of providing messaging services, and focus on other core aspects of their businesses.
- *Consumer Email Services ('CES')*. Offered through a variety of targeted affiliate websites, COMUN currently has about 200,000 consumer email users and is on track to exceed 1 million users. This service, offered mostly free to end users, is comprised of a basic webmail application and email redirection services using the Company's expansive registry of popular domain names.

■ *Domain Registry Services ('DRS').* To date, COMUN has registered approximately 2–3 per cent of all Mexican domain names through an alliance with the governing body for the Mexican Internet. Through another working relationship, the Company has acquired a valuable inventory of unique names (cities, sports teams, and affinity groups) that it uses to personalize and enhance its consumer email services as well as to provide competitive synergies for its affiliate websites and partnerships.

These three primary services, coupled with an experienced management team, have positioned the firm to capitalize on the growing market opportunity to serve Mexico's digital workplace. The Company's competitive edge lies in its ability to cater directly to the regional markets by offering services tailored to local cultures and needs. In the dominant business trend of globalization, the successful player will be one who offers a local approach to its products or services. COMUN has positioned itself to offer such localized messaging services to the Mexican market, one of the fastest growing Internet service markets in the world and a growing economy.

Global strategy

The Company plans to become the premier provider of messaging and communication infrastructure services in the Latin American region through the following key strategies:

■ *Strengthen technology platform for messaging application.* COMUN intends to continue developing and expanding its suite of services by improving the functionality of its technology architecture. The Company also plans to develop complementary applications that will extend the functionality of the messaging platform to wireless devices and collaboration platforms.
■ *Develop and leverage strategic relationships.* The Company aims to expand its existing relationships with other Internet infrastructure service providers, data centres, communications providers, and leading web portals to increase its customer base.
■ *Increase sales and marketing efforts.* COMUN will begin to build up a substantial account management and customer service team to support its growing corporate client base. In addition, the Company plans to hire experienced sales professionals to ensure this growth.
■ *Expand throughout Latin American region.* In addition to targeting the Mexican market, the Company anticipates an extensive rollout throughout the Latin American region.

Market opportunity

No Internet business is more ubiquitous than email. Jupiter Communications estimates that 93 per cent of Internet users worldwide regularly use email, making this activity the most popular use of the Internet (searching is second with 83 per cent, and downloading software is third).

With more than 500 million people and 7 per cent of the world's GDP, Latin America is a large market opportunity for the development of the Internet. According to Lehman Brothers estimates, the total number of unique web users in Latin America was projected to grow at a CAGR of 37 per cent from 15 million in 2000 to almost 75 million by 2005. Internet penetration was expected to increase from less than 3 per cent in 2000 to over 10 per cent by 2005.

A young population (one-third of the population is under 15 years old) makes the region an even more interesting target for technologically advanced services such as e-messaging and online collaboration. In fact, 90 per cent of the users expected to be online in 2005 were not yet connected.

Products and services

COMUN offers its messaging solution through both outsourced services, whereby COMUN hosts the software on its servers, and server software packages, whereby the customer licenses the software to run on the customer's own servers. Through either of these approaches, or a combination thereof, COMUN's messaging solutions can satisfy virtually all the messaging needs of corporate customers (Table 10.2).

This targeted messaging solution is packaged and customized to satisfy each customer's communications needs. In addition, the product interface is branded with the corresponding corporate logo and company identity. The free consumer email service, on the other hand, is defined by limited features and directed consumer advertising. Although the underlying technology platform is the similar, the visible product varies greatly between the OMS product and the CES product.

Target industries

COMUN currently offers unified messaging products and services to thousands of end users across its target markets. COMUN focuses on various types of consumers and companies that have either a focus on technology or that are small to medium-sized professional services firms that would benefit by providing employees and clients with remote access to corporate information and services. Some of the segments targeted by COMUN are:

- *Outsourced Messaging Solutions ('OMS')*. COMUN's corporate messaging platform is targeted at delivering a service to the following types of businesses: Internet Service Providers, Telecommunications Providers, Web Portals, Web Hosting Companies/Data Centers, Small/ Medium Sized Companies, Large Corporations.To these customers, COMUN aims to deliver complete, turnkey, private-label email and messaging solutions that in effect can help each business reduce operating costs and increase focus on core businesses.
- *Consumer Email Services ('CES')*. The mail service, offered primarily through email on the Internet, is targeted towards the following types of users: Regular Users, Affinity Users, Affiliate Users. To each of these types of users, COMUN offers directed opt-in mail distribution allowing each end user to receive special offers and information from premier content providers.
- *Domain Registry Services ('DRS')*. The Mexican portal, through its varied services, is positioned to serve almost any individual user or organization seeking to build a presence online: Individual Users, and Collective Organizations. Domain registration, as one of the first activities performed by any user seeking to begin using the Internet, complements the Company's suite of offerings and creates a point of access for both the Outsourced Messaging Solution or Consumer Email Service.

Table 10.2 COMUN's messaging solutions

Core service	Description	Defined benefits
Web-based email	Hosting service based on a web mail interface	■ Requires no software downloads ■ End-users simply point any browser to http://mail.userdomain.com and enter account name and password for full email access
POP3 hosting	Hosting service based on Post Office protocol	■ Allows users to connect to a shared mail server and download email to their desktop client which stores the message on the user's hard drive
Web-based administration	Customized multi-user management interface	■ Allows email administrators to add, delete, and modify accounts online
Spelling correction	Feature that verifies spelling in 13 languages	■ Allows for emails to be correctly written in English, Spanish, Portuguese and French, to name a few
Secure delivery	Secure delivery of documents	■ Reliably and securely delivers documents to only the intended recipient
Spam blocking	Utilizes comprehensive filtering system	■ Protects users from unsolicited bulk email ■ Identifies and eliminates 'spam' and 'junk' mail
Virus scan	Up-to-date anti-virus solution provides real-time virus detection	■ Real-time scanning and automatic cure for continual protection ■ Virus quarantine isolates the source of infection to prevent damage
Digital signature	Latest Pretty Good Privacy (PGP) key encryption standards	■ Allows for private and secure email delivery ■ Ensures authenticity of sent messages
Wireless redirection	Directs messages to paging services	■ Allows users to automatically redirect certain messages to any pager

Strategic alliances

The Company has been extremely successful in forging marketing and business development alliances with a wide range of companies in the region and significantly major international players looking for competent and well positioned local partners. These range from data centres to equipment suppliers. It is through these alliances that the Company has been able to reach such a high level of recognition and market presence in such a short amount of time. COMUN has formed strategic alliances with a leading supplier of hardware, software, and e-business services, a facilities-based Internet infrastructure and communications provider, and a major software producer.

Contributed by Ioanna C. Papasolomou

QUESTIONS

1   What benefits is COMUN trying to gain from employing market segmentation, as opposed to treating the market as a single entity?
2   What market opportunities and 'strategic windows' have resulted for COMUN from market segmentation?
3   Has COMUN adopted a mass-marketing strategy? Justify your answer.
4   How in your view COMUN may try to accomplish product or service positioning?

Chapter 11

Marketing mix strategy

INTRODUCTION

The organization has to communicate with the customer through the strategic window. This can be achieved in a variety of ways ranging from spoken and written communications (advertising, selling, etc.) to more symbolic forms of communication (the image conveyed in the quality of the product, its price and the type of distribution outlet chosen). This is the function of the marketing mix. The point is that the elements of the marketing mix should not be seen as individual entities, but as a set of interrelated entities which have to be set in conjunction with one another and in the context of the strategic window presented.

Positioning products in people's minds and making them attractive to market segments requires careful formulation of the marketing mix. Getting the right blend of the product, promotion price and distribution is essential to put the carefully carried out analysis into operation. The aim is to portray an image for the product or service that will match with how one wants the product to be visualized in people's minds, i.e. its positioning. Image is not only reflected in the promotional messages which are directed towards the market target but also in the pricing strategy, the mode of distribution and, of course, in the appearance of the product or service itself.

The chapter reviews the product as a complex entity, stressing the quality dimensions. Attention is also given to the strategic implications of product mix policy. Distribution is a critical element in the marketing of products and services and we examine the different types of decision that have to be made with regard to channel strategy. Pricing is not just a mechanistic process involving knowledge of costs and the addition of a profit margin. There are strategic pricing decisions to be made and pricing is inherently limited to product quality specification. Strategic considerations with respect to marketing communications are considered. This is a very complex area since there are several promotional methods and each requires detailed consideration of matters relating to qualitative marketing communications as well as, in the case of advertising, choice of media. Finally, people, processes and physical evidence are also considered as elements of the extended marketing mix.

THE PRODUCT AS A COMPLEX ENTITY

The products or services of an organization help to create the image of the organization in the mind of the customer. This image is reflected in the customers' perceptions and feelings about its products or services. It is important, since experience with only one of a firm's products or services can affect a person's attitude to the organization's other products or services. This can apply even if the customer has never used the other products. Products are more than tangible objects and services are more than a visible activity. People purchase products and services to satisfy needs or wants and obtain benefits as a result. Organizations have to understand the nature of the needs and wants in order to appreciate the kind of benefits people expect to obtain.

Among the different kinds of benefits that people can obtain from buying goods and services are:

- good value for money
- ease of use
- novelty
- safety
- availability
- economy in use
- good design.

Benefits enter into the equation when a customer decides to buy one product in preference to another. Similarly, when marketing a product or a service an organization should give attention to the benefits it creates for the user. It is the benefits which make a product or service attractive to a customer. Organizations have to communicate these benefits to the user, directly or indirectly, in order to persuade the latter to make a purchase. The capability of a product or service to produce the kinds of benefits desired by the user is exhibited in various characteristics of the product or service.

'Product decisions' have to be made with respect to these various attributes. When a producer of goods or services makes decisions about 'the product', he or she is making decisions about the following: quality, features, options, style, brand name, packaging, sizes, services, warranties, returns. One of the most important of these is quality.

Quality

Quality reflects differences among products or differences among services. As long as it is possible to create differences among products then it should be possible to create differences in quality. Even in cases where it is difficult to create differences, producers can still try to promote products through 'perceived' quality differences, i.e. the way in which they are perceived by the customer.

Quality is a relative value that people attribute to things. It reflects people's expectations concerning a product or service and how well it will provide the various benefits they require from using it. Fortunately, large groups of people have shared ideas about quality and it is possible to produce and market products and services that will meet with the perceptions of large groups of customers. Groups of customers sharing a common perception of a particular level of quality form market segments. A firm can direct its promotional messages to these groups of customers provided that it knows how to reach them.

Product quality contributes to business profitability. It has been found to be positively related to market share and return on investment over a wide range of products and in different market situations. Moreover, high quality is usually associated with premium prices. A business has to build sufficient quality into its goods and services to satisfy customer requirements. If quality levels are set too high or too low, under- or over-engineering as it is called, this can result in leaving customers disgruntled. (See also Chapter 3, for more on quality.)

PRODUCT MIX

Except in the case of very small firms, it is rare to find a firm offering a single product or service. It is much more common to find firms offering a mix of products or services. The product mix has:

- *width*: quantity of lines the firm carries, e.g. radios, TVs, video recorders, etc.
- *length*: quantity of items in the product mix, e.g. three kinds of radio and four kinds of TV
- *depth*: number of variants of each product offered in the line, e.g. clock radios, car radios, pocket radios, etc.
- *consistency*: how closely related the various product lines are in terms of the use to which they are put, e.g. all electrical leisure/entertainment goods.

The above provides a basis for defining the company's product strategy since the company can increase its business in four ways.

1 *New lines* can be added to widen the product mix, e.g. a manufacturer of radios could introduce a line of cassette players.
2 *The length of existing product lines can be increased* by introducing additional items, e.g. the radio manufacturer may introduce larger or smaller radios than are currently being offered.
3 *New product variants can be added* to deepen the product mix, e.g. the radio manufacturer can add new models which are the same size as existing items but which have different features.
4 *Product consistency can be made more or less* depending upon whether a firm wants to acquire a strong reputation in a few or many different areas.

Product-line decisions

The various items within a product line make different contributions to sales and profits. In cases where a couple of items make up the bulk of the contribution, this means that a product line is vulnerable in the event that competition increases since sales of these items could fall substantially. Where products are making very low contributions it would probably be better to drop them from the product line unless there are good reasons for doing otherwise.

Attention needs to be paid to what competitors are offering. Gaps in the product line may become apparent when product offerings are compared with those of competitors. If a product line is too short, a firm may be able to increase its profits by adding items to the line. On the other hand if it is too long, profitability may be improved by dropping products. There is a tendency for product lines to grow longer over time. This may result from excess production capacity at various times and the need to introduce new items to take up excess capacity and increase overall profitability. However, as items are introduced to the line, costs may rise. When a product line is reviewed for its profitability, it may become apparent that profits can be improved substantially by pruning less profitable or unprofitable products and shortening the line.

Three broad categories of action can be taken with respect to a product or service. It can be introduced to the market, it can be given a 'face lift' and it can be withdrawn, discontinued or eliminated. The first two of these are discussed in the next chapter in the context of new products. They relate to the introduction of entirely new product lines into the product mix, to the introduction of new items within a product line and to major changes to existing product items within a line. Here, we will briefly review the third option of discontinuance, elimination or withdrawal.

Product elimination

Recalling the discussions of the BCG matrix and other portfolio models it will be recognized that there can be benefits to a firm from discontinuing a product/service or line of products/services. It may, for example, free up resources which can be assigned to more viable or profitable products. The resources comprise money, staff and machine time.

There are three courses of action which can be taken with respect to the product elimination strategy:

1 *Harvesting*. This involves getting the most from the offering while it lasts. Efforts should be made to cut costs to help improve cash flow. Alternatively, prices may be increased without a simultaneous increase in costs. Harvesting produces a slow decline in sales and when the business no longer provides a positive cash flow, it should be dropped.
2 *Line simplification*. Here a line is trimmed by pruning the number and variety of products or services on offer. The aim is to keep the falling line stable and to restore the health of the line. It is a strategy which becomes especially relevant during times of rising costs and resource shortages.
3 *Total line divestment*. In this case the whole product line is discontinued.

DISTRIBUTION STRATEGY

Channel decisions

There are six basic channel decisions to make. These are:

1 Whether to distribute direct to the customer or indirectly through middlemen

The advantages of going direct are that it enables firms to exercise more control over marketing activities and it reduces the amount of time spent in the channel. The disadvantages are that it is difficult to obtain widespread distribution and more resources are required to maintain distribution. Going direct is the method widely used by industrial goods producers. In the case of consumer goods, examples of going direct to the customer are to be found in marketing cosmetics and encyclopaedias.

2 Whether to adopt single or multiple channels of distribution

The advantage of using a single channel is that it guarantees a minimum level of sales. Intermediaries can be asked to accept a minimum non-returnable order quantity. The exclusivity of using a single channel guarantees attention to the product. and the fact that a product is only available from very specific outlets suggests that it is difficult to obtain because it is exclusive. The harder it is to get, the more people will want to know about it – or so the argument goes. On the other hand, the disadvantage of using exclusivity is that it does limit sales.

In contrast, the use of multiple channels should lead to increased sales and a potential for wider distribution. It must be argued that the more establishments put the product on view, the more likely it is that sales will be substantial. Restricting the number of channels through which the product is sold, restricts the number of people who can come into contact with the product. On the other hand, there are disadvantages with using multiple channels. First, greater investment, more salespeople in the field, more marketing effort in general and more administration are required. Second, it can lead to detrimental competitive rivalry among channel members. Channel members who find themselves competing with one another to sell the same product may not behave in the best interests of the producer.

3 How long the channel of distribution should be

In determining the best channel length to adopt, the following factors have to be taken into account:

1 *The financial strength of the producer*: those in a strong position can carry out the functions provided by intermediaries.
2 *Size and completeness of the product line*: the costs of carrying out the distribution function can be spread across the various items in the product line. The more items, the more economical it might be to consider a shorter distribution channel.
3 *The average order size*: large orders may be distributed direct to customers.
4 *The geographical concentration of customers*: geographically dispersed customers merit a longer distribution channel since servicing them requires substantial investment of resources.
5 *The distance of the distributor from the market*: geographical distance makes it less attractive for the producer to want to supply direct.

The above are guidelines and of course exceptions may be encountered in practice.

4 The types of intermediaries to use

This effectively means choosing between different types of retailer in the case of consumer goods, e.g. supermarkets as opposed to cash and carry, and different types of distributor in the case of industrial goods, e.g. whether to use franchised dealerships or not.

5 The number of distributors to use at each level

In principle, more distributors are required if:

1 The unit value of the product is low and/or the physical quantity of stock held is likely to be high.
2 The product is purchased frequently.

3 There is a high degree of technological complexity in the product.
4 The service requirement is high.
5 The inventory investment is high.
6 Geographic concentration is low.
7 Total market potential is high.
8 The market share of the producer is high.
9 Competition is intense.

6 Which intermediaries to use

This is a qualitative decision and reflects whether the image of the particular outlet, the way in which it performs and the deals which can be struck with the distributor are satisfactory. It may mean choosing C&A rather than Marks & Spencer, or Tesco rather than ASDA.

Even when strategies have been selected they have to be implemented and this involves producers and intermediaries working together in the most effective manner. We will explore this topic in detail in the next section.

EVOLVING CHANNELS

Over time the nature of channels change. The change is brought about by changes in the marketing environment such as evolving customer needs and technical progress and innovation which creates new and better ways of delivering value to customers. The development of low-cost channels and the growth of vertical, horizontal and multi-channel systems are apparent at the present time.

Growth of low-cost channels

The growth of low-cost channels results from market evolution and the decline in the value added by a channel. At the early stages in market development, intermediaries provide high-level support in helping manufacturers to find customers and in offering help and service to customers. Later on, customers become more familiar with the product, prices decline and product reliability improves. A shift then takes place from specialist to higher-volume, low-added value channels. Eventually mass merchandising channels may be used and even mail order and discount shops may distribute the product.

This has been characteristic of the changing pattern in distributing personal computers. Initially, they were only available from specialist dealers who helped to educate the customer in how to use the machines. Although post-purchase technical service is still required by most users today, the market has evolved to a stage where customers are quite knowledgeable about the products available. This is helped to some extent by the availability of computer magazines which provide information on different models, their capabilities, etc. However, consumers today are much more informed about PCs and their operation and capabilities than they were ten years ago and many now buy through mail order.

The technical complexity of the product obviously plays an important role in determining the speed at which the growth of low-cost channels can develop. Given an educated consumer who has access to informative magazines and given also a not-too-complex product, the speed of development of low-cost channels can be quite rapid. This is evidenced by the camcorder and mobile telephone markets where low-cost channels feature fairly early in the life cycle.

Development of vertical marketing systems

The trend is towards vertical marketing systems in which channel activities are integrated and managed by one member of the channel – either a manufacturer, intermediary or retailer. Such systems reduce cost, minimize conflict among channel members, and build on the experience and expertise of channel members.

Corporate vertical marketing systems are found in vertically integrated companies which have their own manufacturing, wholesaling and retailing operations. The current trends, however, are to build administered vertical marketing systems and contractual vertical marketing systems. In the former case, channel members maintain their financial independence and legal autonomy, but are led by the most powerful member of the channel. In the latter case, channel members' rights and obligations are defined by legal agreements. These may take the form of collaborative or franchise agreements.

Development of horizontal marketing systems

Strategic alliances and networks facilitate the development of horizontal marketing systems. They reflect the readiness of two or more autonomous units, who may even be competitors, at the same level in a channel to co-operate. Co-operation reduces the risks for an individual firm. It facilitates access to other channels of distribution thereby accelerating market penetration. Moreoever, it provides access to new technologies and knowhow.

Development of multi-channel marketing systems

As a result of markets becoming highly fragmented with customers having different product and service needs as well as price sensitivities, different channels have emerged to meet customers' expectations. Although a multi-channel marketing system provides the opportunity for a firm to serve a range of segments, it is a potential source of channel conflict. A producer has therefore to guard against the problems that this can create by being seen to be as fair as possible in dealing with channel members.

PRICING DECISIONS

There are market conditions under which organizations can exert some control over the level at which price is set. If an organization cannot exert any control over the setting of pricing then it has to accept whatever the market determines will be the price.

Perfectly competitive markets specify that there is a homogeneous product, complete information among buyers, rational buyer behaviour and large numbers of producers. In a perfectly competitive market, a producer has almost no control over prices. They are determined by market forces brought about by competitive pressures and patterns of consumer expenditure. There are extremely few such markets in reality. Most markets are imperfect and some control over the setting of prices is possible.

Over time there have been various ideas expressed on how prices should be set. These range from theoretical ideas of economists through to ideas of modern-day practitioners who are concerned with earning revenues for their organizations. In the next section we will explore these various approaches from a strategic perspective. We have to distinguish between a cost-oriented approach – based solely on a knowledge of a firm's own costs – and those which also take into account the demands of the market place.

Pricing: the classical economics perspective

Economic theory argues that price balances supply and demand for goods and services in the market place and uses the 'law of demand' to explain this phenomenon. The law of demand purports that the quantity demanded per period of time is inversely related to price. With an increase in price, demand will fall, and as price falls then demand will increase.

In this context, price elasticity of demand is a key concept. This is defined as the ratio of the percentage change in demand to a percentage change in price. While, by definition, the ratio usually has a negative sign – this is because as price rises, demand usually falls – it is customary, in illustrating elasticities, to drop the sign. A price elasticity equal to one signifies that demand rises (falls) by the same percentage that price falls (rises). Knowing the price elasticity of demand for its products or services can help a firm to set its prices.

Estimating the price elasticity of demand can be more difficult. In essence one needs to monitor the effect of price changes on demand. One can do this by looking at price changes over a period of time but care must be taken to ensure that the prices examined are deflated in value. Price, of course, is only one element of the marketing mix and the other variables may well have an impact on demand. Other factors such as disposable income and competitive activity may also cloud the picture so while price elasticity is conceptually useful its practical usefulness as a tactical or strategic tool may be somewhat limited in value.

Marginal pricing

An important cost-oriented approach is that of marginal pricing. Suppose a firm manufactures widgets which carry a fixed overhead charge of £100,000 and variable costs of £0.50 per widget. The firm currently supplies 1,000,000 widgets to breweries in the UK at £0.75 each and has considerable spare capacity. An enquiry has come in from a company in the Far East which is interested in using the same widgets for a different purpose. The interesting question is: at what price should it offer to sell the widgets to the firm in the Far East, assuming that additional production capacity is not required?

Commonsense tells us that the firm will have already recovered the fixed overhead on the widgets it supplies to the brewery industry. One million widgets at £0.75 generate £750,000 of revenue; 1,000,0000 widgets at a unit cost of £0.50 per widget generate a variable cost of £500,000. This leaves £750,000–£500,000 = £250,000 to cover the fixed costs and the profit. With fixed costs at £100,000 this means that the firm is already making a profit of £250,000–£100,000 = £150,000.

The price to be charged to the company in the Far East need only take account of the variable costs and additional transportation and delivery costs. This may mean that, in theory, the price charged to the firm in the Far East can be lower than that charged to brewery firms at home and the firm will still be generating profit! This is what is known as marginal pricing.

The key point, however, is whether the two markets supplied know that a price differential exists and that essentially the products supplied are identical. If such information is available to both parties, then a marginal pricing strategy may be impossible to implement since the parties will argue for equal treatment. In addition, the application of a marginal pricing policy does require that no new fixed costs have to be incurred – which would seem to be satisfactory in the foregoing case.

Demand-oriented pricing

A demand-oriented approach to pricing takes account of the strength of demand. Firms ask a high price when or where demand is strong and a low price when or where demand is weak, even if there is no dissimilarity in costs in either case. Differences in the strength of demand in the market enable firms to charge different prices in different market segments. The ability to practice this kind of price discrimination requires:

- different levels of demand in market segments
- inability of buyers to resell at a higher price
- that competitors will *not* undersell the firm in the segment being charged the higher price
- cost of segmenting and policing the market not to exceed the extra revenue obtained
- that price discrimination is legally permissible
- that customers who pay more do not react negatively.

Such an approach is commonly referred to as charging what the market will bear.

Price discrimination helps suppliers to increase sales and profits, improve market share and contribute to the full capacity utilization of manufacturing plant. However, when it is exercised by a firm in a dominant position in an industry or market it is sometimes used to remove troublesome competition or as a means of exploiting buyers.

OTHER DIMENSIONS TO PRICING

Price squeeze

Discriminatory prices may sometimes be charged by a firm which is vertically integrated for the supply of inputs to non-integrated rivals in order to put the latter at a competitive disadvantage. This can occur when the integrated firm produces both the input and the finished product, while its customer produces only the finished product, and is dependent on the integrated firm for supplies of the materials, sub-assemblies or parts.

A 'squeeze' occurs where the integrated firm charges the non-integrated firm a high price for the input but sells its own finished product at a low price. This allows the non-integrated firm only minimal profits or even forces it to make a loss.

It is common for there to be many suppliers of partly finished goods in an industry so that the power of any one supplier to effect a price squeeze is limited. However, as a result of acquisitions, takeovers and mergers it is not beyond the bounds of possibility for a group of companies to come to dominate the supply side for certain materials and components and thence to exert a price squeeze on the industry. Such a practice may be regarded as anti-competitive and, in the UK, cases referred to the Monopolies and Mergers Commission are scrutinized for evidence that practices such as price squeezing may result from formal linkages among firms.

Penetration versus skimming pricing strategies

Penetration and skimming policies are most often encountered when dealing with new products but they are sometimes used in other situations.

Penetration strategy

When introducing a new product, the objective may be to achieve early market penetration. The strategy may amount to setting a comparatively low price to instigate market growth and capture a large share of it. The effect of the experience curve will cause long-run profitability to rise as a result of gaining a large market share or a growth in market share. A penetration strategy may be appropriate if the market seems to be highly price sensitive, or if a product is favoured by economies of scale in production or, where a low price discourages actual and potential competition.

Skimming strategy

A skimming strategy contrasts with a penetration strategy and is used to take advantage of the fact that some buyers are prepared to pay a much higher price because they want the product very much. Firms adopting this strategy may initially set a high price to gain a premium from such buyers and may only reduce it progressively to bring in the more price-elastic segments.

This strategy is appropriate where there exists a substantially large number of buyers whose demand is relatively inelastic. It may also be used where the unit production and distribution costs associated with producing a smaller volume are not so much higher that they cancel out the advantage of charging what some of the market will buy, or where little danger exists that a high price will stimulate the emergence of competition.

Competition-oriented pricing

In this case, a firm makes sure that the prices it sets are in keeping with those charged by competitors and it is often referred to as the going-rate price. This kind of pricing is used often in homogeneous product markets where the market structure ranges from pure competition to pure oligopoly. In a purely competitive market, the firm exercises little choice in setting its price. In the case of pure oligopoly it has more choice, firms can charge the same price as competitors. In view of the fact that there are only a few firms, each one of them knows the other's price, and buyers are also well abreast of prices.

Psychological dimensions to pricing

Goods may be priced at £2.99 or £4.99 rather than £3 or £5 reflecting the fact that research into consumer perceptions suggests that people tend to round down prices in their minds, so that the prices in fact are perceived to be £2 and £4 respectively.

Another interesting point is that putting up prices can actually increase sales and price is often seen as a surrogate for quality. In the absence of information to the contrary, people tend to assume goods or services are of better quality if they carry a higher price tag. This can lead to nonsenses whereby two products which have the same intrinsic value may fetch vastly different prices because the consumer considers one to be more 'special' than the other.

A good example is to be found in the purchase of jewellery. Rings, in particular, can be composed of exactly the same gems in terms of size and be of the same carat gold. However, because of the way the gems are cut and the ring is set, there can be large differences in the price which is asked.

Pricing points

Retailers like to sell goods in stores at specific pricing points. Pricing points may, for instance, always end in the number 9. That is 9p, 19p, 29p, etc. The retailer may argue that these are the prices which consumers prefer to pay. A producer and a retailer may agree on a point-of-sale shop price of say 89p. The retailer is obtaining a satisfactory margin on the product at this price and the producer is also happy with the price. Were the producer to require extra shelf space then it would probably have to offer the retailer more promotional discount so that the retailer can sell the product at 79p. The retailer will not agree to sell it at 80p or 85p because these prices do not correspond with pricing points. The producer then has to determine whether this would be worthwhile. One way round this problem, of course, is to produce products in different packet sizes to meet with retailers' specific pricing points.

Increasing prices without increasing prices

Sooner or later organizations have to adjust their prices. When it is in a downward direction this usually pleases the customer and the firm does not need to disguise its actions. However, when an upward adjustment in price is required, consumer resistance is often felt quite strongly.

Organizations can often disguise price rises, permanent or temporary, by making it appear that no price rise is in fact occurring. This can be achieved in any one of the following ways:

1   The discount structure can be altered so that the total profit to the company is increased but the list price to customers remains the same.
2   The minimum order size is increased so that small orders are eliminated and overall costs thereby reduced.
3   Delivery and special services are charged for.
4   Invoices are raised for repairs on purchased equipment.
5   There is a charge for engineering, installation and supervision.
6   Customers are made to pay for overtime required to get out rush orders.
7   Interest is collected on overdue accounts.

8   Lower margin models in the product line are eliminated and more profitable ones sold in their place.

9   Escalator clauses are built into bids for contracts.

10   The physical characteristics of the product are changed, e.g. it is made smaller.

PRICE LEADERSHIP STRATEGY

This is the position where a particular supplier is generally accepted by other suppliers as the 'lead' firm in introducing changes in market prices. There are two principal forms of price leadership.

The first form of price leadership occurs when the largest firm in terms of market share, and/or the lowest-cost producer, leads on price changes and where other firms are prepared to follow because the price change yields them adequate profits. The second form, sometimes referred to as barometric price leadership, is where a particular firm, often a smaller firm, is 'adopted' as the price leader, because it has demonstrated itself to be capable of spotting changes in market conditions.

In theory, a market leader enjoys all the advantages over competitors that are associated with higher-volume sales. The leader should be able to set the price structure for the market. In the event that the market leader decides to take a low unit profit margin, then because of the volume of sales achieved, profits generated should be substantial. This profitability will not be enjoyed by competitors who do not have the same high volume of sales. In fact, these competitors will have higher unit costs, higher distributor margins and probably lower selling prices to the trade.

A market leader which takes a higher unit profit margin gives the whole market a form of price umbrella. Since all firms can charge higher prices, then profitability all round can be increased. This allows competitors to introduce product improvements, funded by retained additional profits. Competitors can also invest in more aggressive marketing. The net result will probably be to weaken the market leader's position.

Price leadership is often viewed by suppliers as a way of co-ordinating pricing policies so as to limit price competition and avoid the problems of price wars.

The leader's strategy in relationship to the product life cycle stage

If the market is in the growth stage of the product life cycle then extra sales volume is available. The leader will want to take a major share of new business and so it will want to keep competitors' actions under control and persuade other firms not to enter the market. By keeping the unit margin of profitability low, the leader can make progress towards this end.

As volume sales of a market increase, the effects of the experience curve are felt and product unit costs should decline. The dilemma facing the market leader is whether to reduce prices and, if so, the speed with which this should be effected. The answer is to be found in the leader's designs with respect to the next stage in the product life cycle – the maturity stage. If it is the market leader's intention to lead in this phase then it will have to maintain its leadership through the transition phase. It must ensure that its prices move downwards as the volume moves ahead and unit costs decline. If it does not do this then there is always a chance that competitors will take advantage of the position and increase capacity and market share. It is usually advantageous for the leader to maintain its position since the additional volume of sales generated can mean that total margins will increase despite the lower selling prices.

Other firms will not enjoy the same cost advantages as the leader and as they are operating on tight profit margins, they are not in a position to achieve great improvements in differentiation. A potential entrant on seeing this situation may feel deterred from entering the market.

During the market maturity or the decline phases, the horizon for the market leader can be altogether different. There will be little chance of a new competitor entering the market and brand loyalty will have been established. In such circumstances, the leader should be able to take higher margins without taking excessive risks.

Firms with a lower level of market share should follow the leader when it comes to changes in prices. Marketers of low share brands do not want to engage the leader in direct price competition. Direct and indirect costs of production of these competitors are higher than the leader's and price to the trade is probably lower.

PRICE WARS

Price wars arise from time to time and involve general price cutting within a market. Haphazard price wars may materialize from gossip and slip-up. Others may be introduced intentionally. In neither case does the end result bring about an improvement for any of the parties involved. Once in a while a price war can work to the aggressor's advantage. It is clearly an advantage in a price war to have lower unit costs than competitors. In such a position the aggressor may fare well from the experience.

MARKETING COMMUNICATIONS

Communication objectives

In developing an effective communications programme the basic steps involve:

- identifying the target audience
- determining the communications objective
- designing the message
- selecting the communications channels
- allocating the total promotions budget
- deciding on the promotions mix
- measuring the results of the promotion.

We have already discussed targeting in Chapter 10 and will therefore start with communication objectives.

Marketing communications efforts can have different communications objectives. Some of these are listed below:

- to create awareness of a product or service
- to provide information about a product or service
- to generate enquiries
- to build recognition of a company name

- to reach those people who are beyond the reach of salespeople
- to evoke desire for a product or service
- to make the selling task easier
- overcome prejudices
- to remind people about a product's benefits
- to allay cognitive dissonance.

Designing the message

Effective communications have to appeal to the needs and wants of the recipients. They should give the recipient a motive or incentive to act. They also need to generate involvement with the message on the part of the recipient by asking questions which leave the message incomplete. In addition they should also spell out exactly what course of action it is expected that the recipient will follow.

Getting people to consider purchasing a product or service can be achieved through appeal to their cognitive processes. One needs to arouse desire, indicate a need or give a logical reason why a product or service offers the best means of satisfying a need. In so doing the message becomes implanted in the recipient's memory and can be triggered by future needs, motives and associations. However, one does have to bear in mind that the rational approach may not be so effective for less educated recipients or in situations where there is likely to be less involvement in the purchase, i.e. little search behaviour. In these cases emotional appeals may be used.

Promotion through mass media requires that the story be told in such a way that it will communicate to groups of sales prospects. This is an inflexibility that may cause the message to miss the mark with some individuals. The salesperson, by contrast, is free to vary the message to meet each situation; this is a powerful advantage of personal selling.

The appeal, theme, idea or unique selling proposition is what the communicator has to get over to the target audience in order to produce the desired response. Benefit, identification, motivation are all concepts that can be built into the message.

Messages can be built around rational, emotional or moral appeals, themes, ideas or unique selling propositions. Economy, value and performance are used in messages with a rational content. This type of message is often directed at industrial buyers and consumers making expensive purchase items such as cars, houses and substantial consumer durables.

Emotional appeals make use of both positive and negative themes. On the negative side this can involve fear, guilt and shame, whereas on the positive side it may comprise humour, love, pride and joy. Too much fear in a message may cause the audience to reject it. The use of humour may generate 'noise' and interfere with the message.

Moral appeals are attractive to people's sense of what is right and just. They can be used in 'green' advertising or in promoting social causes or even in things for children, e.g. books and safety prams.

The promotional mix

There are a number of promotional vehicles available to a firm:

- advertising
- sales promotion

- publicity
- personal selling.

The proportion of a firm's marketing communications budget that is spent on each of these activities varies somewhat across organizations and industries. There is a tendency, for example, in the case of industrial and business goods for more effort to be put into personal selling, whereas advertising features prominently in the case of fast-moving consumer goods. Despite these broad generalizations, considerable variation exists within product classes. In the case of advertising there is also the complicating factor that there are a number of advertising vehicles which can be used to communicate about the product: television, radio, newspapers, magazines, mobiles, posters, etc.

The most appropriate marketing mix for a product will be influenced by a number of factors:

1 *The available budget*. The amount of money available for expenditure on promotion is obviously a critical factor. Small firms have comparatively small budgets for promotional expenditure and hence have to select the most cost-effective means of communicating with the market. TV advertising for such firms, for example, may be prohibitively expensive.

2 *The promotional message*. The nature of the message, as influenced by the objectives which have been set for the communication, will exert considerable influence over the choice of mix. Where a product is to be demonstrated, either face-to-face selling or a visual medium such as television or cinema advertising will be most appropriate. In addition, if we take the hierarchy-of-effects communication model into consideration then it will be recalled that at the various stages of the step-by-step process, different messages are deemed appropriate.

3 *The complexity of the product or service*. In some cases, a large amount of service support is required and in this case the only appropriate communication method is personal selling. Where this kind of support is not required, as is the case in fast-moving consumer non-durables, then advertising is more appropriate.

4 *Market size and location*. Large dispersed markets tend to favour mass communication coverage, such as advertising. Local markets or small numbers of buyers may favour direct mail, specialist press or even personal selling.

5 *Distribution channels*. The key to successful marketing of a product often lies in obtaining suitable distribution for the product. Distributors therefore can exert considerable influence over the choice of promotional medium used to communicate with the ultimate customer.

6 *Life cycle*. In the same way that application of the hierarchy-of-effects models suggests that different messages may be appropriate, so too does the stage in the life cycle a product has reached. If the service or product is in the introductory stage of the life cycle, building awareness is the main aim. If it is in the growth stage, the requirement is to persuade customers to change their buying patterns and switch brand loyalty.

7 *Competition*. Matching or beating competition is obviously a key component in determining the strategy behind the formulation of the promotional mix. Where a firm does not have the financial resources to match competitors in terms of expensive promotional campaigns, for example, it must find some other mechanism.

ADVERTISING STRATEGY

For a product or a service to be successful in the market place it has to be noticed and it has to be trusted by the customer. This means that the advertising will have to stand out from the crowd. Advertising faces a major challenge in so far as much of the information provided to the customer is ignored. Advertising has therefore to catch the customer's attention and deliver the message in an original way that will enable the customer to remember and identify with the message and the brand.

In addition to its key function to inform, advertising is also expected to entertain. Following on from this, advertising has to rely more heavily on emotions and images to attract the customer's attention and interest. The emphasis is therefore on images. Images have the capacity to capture the essence of a thousand words. They can also be absorbed and remembered with much less effort by a viewer. Images also have much more power to satisfy viewers' needs for entertainment.

Advertising will need to become increasingly more emotional as it becomes increasingly more difficult to base a competitive advantage on the functional attributes of a brand. Differentiation will be achieved through emotional attributes of a brand.

All this means that advertising will have to become more creative.

MEDIA DECISIONS

In choosing media in which to advertise, organizations seek to discover the most cost-effective way to deliver the desired number of exposures to the target audience. This involves examining the reach, frequency and impact of advertisements that are placed in different media.

The media planner has to be familiar with the reach, frequency and impact of the major media types. Each type – newspapers, TV, direct mail, radios, magazines and outdoor posters – has advantages and limitations in terms of reach, frequency and impact. Media planners match limitations and advantages with the requirements of the message. For example, a message announcing that a sale is taking place today may be given over the radio. Obviously, the nature of the product, the nature of the message, the cost and the type of audience using the media are key factors in the process.

Assessing the cost effectiveness of media vehicles

The size and composition of the target market and the cost of reaching that audience are indicators of the effectiveness of the media and are studied carefully by planners. In addition, circulation and type of audience are important measures taken into account by the planners. They calculate the cost per thousand of the target reached by a particular vehicle. One should bear in mind that this is not the same thing as the cost per thousand reached with respect to users of the media. Many of these people may not be in the target group. Other things being equal, a planner prefers media vehicles that have the lowest cost per thousand reached of the target media group. Other considerations are the quality of the editorials and the extent to which people pay attention to the advertisements.

Media scheduling

A firm can vary its advertising expenditure to suit the seasonal pattern or it can advertise throughout the year. Most firms do the latter. Kuehn (1962) showed that the appropriate pattern of timing should reflect how much advertising carry-over effect exists and the degree of habit that exists in customers' choice of brand. Where both are low, it is appropriate to use a seasonal pattern and it is better to time the advertising so that it coincides with the seasonal pattern. Where carry-over effects and habit are high, it is better to time advertising to lead the sales curve. The higher the carry-over then the greater should be the lead time. Steady advertising expenditure should be used when habitual purchase patterns are greatest.

Having decided how to vary expenditure, a firm has then to look at advertising over a short period of time so as to obtain the maximum impact. More continuous advertising should be used when the rate at which new customers appear in the market is high. This should also be the case when the frequency with which people make purchases is high or the rate at which people 'forget the brand' is high.

Advertisers tend to use continuous advertising when the market is expanding. Concentrated advertising in a single period of time occurs when the product is sold in a single period. In the case of seasonal or infrequently purchased items or when limited funds exist, bursts of advertising are used. An alternative is to use continuous advertising at low weight levels reinforced periodically by waves of heavier activity.

SELLING

Selling involves:

- creating positive attitudes towards a product or service
- motivating people to want to purchase a product or service
- convincing people that they are acting wisely if they do buy
- clinching a sale
- reassuring people that they have acted wisely in making a purchase.

Selling can influence any or all of the various stages in the purchase decision-making process. Earlier, we saw that advertising creates awareness, interest and desire but only rarely produces action. Selling, too, can effect the first three stages but it is most frequently associated with the action stage. Salespeople are often paid, at least in part, by results and results inevitably means action in the form of purchase by the customer.

Selling is a face-to-face encounter with the customer. It is time consuming, puts considerable emotional strain on the salesperson and is a relatively slow way of influencing the purchase process. Where it is possible to achieve the same effect with other promotional tools, such as advertising, for example, selling will not be preferred since it will not be more cost-effective in terms of time and money. However, it is possible to use selling as a marketing communications tool in niche market situations where advertising would be wasteful. For example, there is a niche market which comprises people who like to shop at home for one reason or another. Direct selling is involved when salespeople call on people in their own homes to sell them products which they might normally purchase at retail outlets in towns and cities.

The amount of marketing effort that firms put into personal selling varies according to the types of goods and services that are on offer. The magnitude of the effort often reflects the nature of the target market which is being addressed, though as pointed out above, there are exceptions to the rule. Industrial goods manufacturers put a greater financial emphasis on selling in the marketing mix, whereas large consumer-goods producers tend to spend more on other forms of promotion.

The task of the salesperson

The selling task is influenced by the nature of what is being sold and to whom it is being sold, e.g. whether it is a consumer product, an industrial product or a service.

Consumer goods

Fast-moving consumer goods salespeople often must negotiate with professional buyers who have responsibility for a large number of sales outlets. In such a situation, the retailer's buyer expects that the account manager will be very familiar with the retailer's operations. Large retailers, such as multiples, expect to be consulted in advance about a manufacturer's new product plans, including pack and package design, and expect co-operation!

In addition to informing the buyer about new lines and persuading the buyer to stock quantities of the products, the salesperson has to persuade the retail management staff, with the aid of the buyer, to ensure that the product is stocked and displayed in an eye-catching manner at the point of sale.

Industrial goods

The selling task of an industrial goods salesperson is somewhat different. In this case, the first task is to identify the persons who are involved in the often complex process of purchase decision-making and then find ways of influencing them. Sometimes the decision-making may incorporate recommendations by outside consultants. Because of the technical and specialized nature of the selling situation, salespeople in such a situation need to have the skills and the knowledge to negotiate with these kinds of specialists.

Services

Selling can be important in marketing services either to industrial or consumer markets. On account of the intangible nature of services, some people take the view that it is more difficult to sell services. Products are tangible and the benefits can be readily demonstrated and this makes the selling task easier. This is not the case with services, however, and getting people to persuade themselves that they need or want a particular service can be a hard task. This is particularly the case with services which do not seem to offer any immediate benefits, such as life assurance policies.

If people do not attach a high personal priority to something they may well put off the decision to purchase even if they recognize that it is a service which they NEED. Moreover from the salesperson's point of view it may be difficult to relate long-term benefits to the cost of the service.

237

SALES PROMOTION

Sales promotion offers consumers the chance to get more than they expected and at the same time reduces the risk associated with buying. For example, product sampling affords the consumers the opportunity to try the product without actually buying it. Moreover, in terms of providing motivation to purchase, an extra discount or rebate means that the consumer is more likely to buy a product.

Many product managers find it difficult to differentiate their product in a real way from that of their competitors and sales promotion methods enable product managers to achieve this end. Every time we need to visit the petrol station to fill up our car's tank of petrol we are enticed to visit one or other station because of special promotions that are being offered – free air travel mileage, redeemable tokens which we can eventually exchange for goods, or even drinking glasses. We may in fact not perceive or be conscious of any differences between the brands of petrol at the different filling stations but we can differentiate in terms of the kinds of promotions that are being offered. One promotion may have more appeal than another and we may purchase the product from that source because of the promotion.

From management's point of view, sales promotions often provide exactly what it most requires: an immediate boost in sales. New life, albeit temporary, can be pumped into ailing brands by dropping coupons in the mail.

At a more general level, the use of sales promotion has been stimulated by factors that have adversely affected advertising, such as the high costs of mass media advertising. In addition, retailers, working on small profit margins and needing the increased sales volume generated through sales promotion, have encouraged the growth of sales promotion.

The severest criticism of sales promotion is that it diminishes the value of the brand. The move from brand-building advertising to trade promotions and couponing, critics argue, can lead to consumers who view all products as commodities. Other critics say that the management of sales promotion over a long period of time is fraught with difficulties. Many sales promotion tools are short-run, tactical devices. Coupons, premiums and contests, for example, set out to produce immediate responses.

Whereas advertising provides reasons why a customer should buy a product or service, sales promotion provides the incentive to buy. Sales promotion can take many forms (see Figure 11.1). Some of these apply to sales promotion to consumers and others to sales promotion to the trade.

The extra three Ps

While the four Ps are generally regarded as the traditional marketing mix variables one should not overlook the additional three Ps which were traditionally associated with a service organization but now have considerable relevance to all kinds of organizations.

People

An organization's 'people' are its most valuable resource in terms of creating a successful business. Staff need to be committed to raising performance standards and improving service encounters with customers and other stakeholders. In this context it is imperative that they should have a clear understanding of the business and its visions and values. Improving customer service and the customer

Figure 11.1 *Types of sales promotions*

experience can be achieved through having an organizational culture that is in line with the business vision and values. In addition the organization needs to provide motivation/incentive packages for new ideas that improve sales, customer service. Getting people to adopt a customer orientation is the key to making best uses of the organization's human resources. Staff can be encouraged by implementing clear communication channels, for example regular team briefings; weekly/monthly newsletters; email and intranet services. Ensuring that staff understand the business objectives and implementing a business development plan for the short/medium-term future is also important. Introducing a reward scheme to involve staff in thinking about and generating ideas for better ways of working and exceeding customer expectations may also produce good results. Even giving recognition to the work of individuals or teams gives a positive feedback to staff and signals that the organization is responding to staff accomplishments.

People are the organization – the receptionist, doorman, janitor, carpark attendant may be the first person a visitor or customer encounters when visiting an organization. It is imperative that these first point of contact staff are well trained in how to represent the organization.

Physical evidence

The *physical evidence* is the environment in which the service is delivered to the customer and where the organization and customer interact. The physical evidence is concerned with the physical building and infrastructure; the quality and availability of promotional material (prospectuses, information leaflets, newsletters, websites) which provide information about the services on offer. Décor and surroundings project the cultural image of the organization. They also provide another means of reinforcing customer satisfaction.

The organization's publications promoting products and services should contain information about the organization and its performance. The way this is presented will have an impact upon customer and other stakeholder perceptions of how the organization does business.

Processes

This is the way enquiries and purchases are handled and it is crucial to the competitive success of any company. The way in which an organization operates often revolves around its processes. The less cluttered these are then the better the opportunity to provide value for money to customers as well as give a good return to investors and shareholders. The organization should be looking to implement processes to ensure quality. Notice should be taken of feedback from customers and others regarding how the processes are viewed by them. This will show to customers that it is a listening organization, committed to continuous improvement and ensuring customers have an input and influence on its operation.

A process can be looked at from various perspectives depending on the kind of information required. Usually, this concerns what work is going to be done, who will do it and how is it going to be done, when will it be done, and who will take the decision. Hence, a process has functional, behavioural, organizational, informational, decisional and resource-based content. Example processes might be: a quality system for the answering of telephones, an open-door policy enabling prompt consultation with the public and staff, surveys and questionnaires and a complaints procedure.

A management information system should be in place to record, evaluate, monitor and review the information gathered.

MARKETING MIX STRATEGY FOR INTERNATIONAL MARKETS

Firms that operate in one or more foreign markets must decide how much to adapt their marketing mix to local conditions. They can either standardize the product, advertising, and distribution channels to produce the lowest costs because it involves no major changes to the domestic market or adjust the marketing-mix elements to each target market. In the case of using an adaptation-marketing strategy it will be necessary to consider the following adaptations.

Product adaptation

This involves altering or adjusting the product or service to meet local conditions or preferences. This may also mean adapting to local superstitions or beliefs, too.

Promotion adaptation

Firms can use the same promotion campaigns as in the domestic market but adapt them for each local market. However, the use of media will require international adaptation because media availability varies from country to country.

Price

Prices of products and services usually differ across countries. The increased costs of transport, supplies, taxes, tariffs and other expenses that are necessary to adjust a company's operations to international marketing can raise prices. However, firms do have to be competitive and match offerings from other foreign competitors and home producers.

Place

Across countries the nature of channels of distribution vary considerably. There are differences with regard to the number and types of intermediaries (e.g. product wholesalers, regional wholesalers; retailers) serving each foreign market. Another difference refers to the size and character of retail units abroad. Getting distribution for a product is a key to successful marketing operations and a thorough understanding of distribution channels and how they function is of paramount importance.

Developing an internationalization strategy

In order to operate beyond the bounds of its domestic market, an organization needs to internationalize its core business strategy. Choice of markets in which to operate is the first item on the agenda and initial matters include identifying the market attractiveness of different options, assessing potential competition and studying ways in which to adapt to local conditions. Account of how to adapt products and programmes to respond to foreign needs, preferences, culture, language, climate, etc., is essential. One has also to consider barriers to trade, such as import tariffs and quotas and foreign ownership rules, as well as differences from the home country in laws, language, tastes and behaviour.

Internationalization can bring with it disadvantages and in order to overcome the disadvantages it creates then companies need to adopt a globalization strategy that aids their search for a competitive advantage in world markets. Firms need to systematically analyse industry conditions and appreciate how they can best take advantage of the situations that exist. Market, cost, government and competitive drivers influence the industry conditions that affect competing with a global strategy. Market drivers relate to customer behaviour, the structure of distribution channels and the nature of marketing in the industry. Cost drivers relate to the economics of the business. Government drivers are set by the decisions laid down by national governments. Competitive drivers are produced by competitors strategies.

Employing a global marketing strategy implies that a consistent marketing approach is used across different countries, although a small amount of latitude is allowed in terms of varying the marketing mix. Whether a product or service can be globally marketed depends on the extent to which usage of the product or service is rooted in national traditions. For example, the marketing of household cleaning products is rooted in traditional concepts of the role of homemaking. As these roles often differ considerably from country to country, there is often little scope for transferability advertising that depends on such roles. On the other hand, products and services not influenced by national culture permit transferable advertising/marketing messages and themes. By and large this applies to most business to business products and services and also many newer consumer products and services, such as fast food and electronic entertainment goods.

Using a global positioning strategy and marketing mix

Using a common global positioning strategy can strengthen the effectiveness of a marketing programme since it has been tried and tested in many countries. Nevertheless, differences in the business's competitive position, purchase motivation and use/consumption patterns may strengthen the case for differing positioning strategies. However, firms that use a common positioning often find that they can make a large part of the marketing mix globally uniform

Global brand names facilitate building global recognition for the product or service. In addition, combining a globally standard umbrella name with a local product name can be advantageous. The appeal of a global brand name is partly related to the global acceptance or prestige of the home country of the brand name, how important it is to have a name that means something, and how easy the name is to pronounce. Brand names that mean something usually need to be translated in order to carry out the positioning job for which they were intended.

Having a global price is seldom possible because of international differences in market price levels and other factors influencing price. A useful strategy is to try to set the prices in relative to competitors in each market.

Global advertising can be varied in a number of ways:

- *Use the same copy*: here a product, service or brand is positioned in the same way making the same claims.
- *Use the same script*: the advertising employs the same script in different countries, but the actual execution is different. Being able to use a common script depends largely on the universality of the images chosen, and of the situations and characters to be used, and also the need for differentiation from local competitors
- *Use the identical advertisement*: in each country the same advertisement is used and only the voices or text or translated.

Some companies use two types of campaign for different purposes. First, a globally uniform campaign which sets out the main theme, and then local campaigns for tactical purposes.

Conditions where a global marketing approach may be most useful

A firm may benefit more from applying global marketing in larger countries. In this case cost reduction, improved programme effectiveness, enhanced customer preference, and increased competitive leverage can be more significant. However, larger markets can be more challenging from the point of view of local adaptation than smaller markets. Customers in smaller countries are more accustomed to products and programmes that are not specifically adapted for them and are usually subject to more cultural influence from larger neighbours.

Disadvantages of adopting a global strategy

Globalization has its disadvantages. For instance, it can lead to increased management costs through increased co-ordination, reporting requirements, and human resources. It can also decrease management effectiveness if over-centralization adversely affects local motivation and morale. Product standardization can produce a product or service that fully satisfies no one.

USING THE INTERNET

The 1990s saw the growth of the Internet or World Wide Web as a facilitator of mass communication. Businesses soon realized the potential of the Internet as a strategic marketing tool. However, despite the involvement of many large and small firms in the use of the net it is a medium which presents new kinds of problems both for firms and customers alike. At the turn of the twenty-first century, many possible customers remain nervous about the security of doing business over the net with credit cards. This is despite the fact that in reality it presents fewer problems than using credit cards over the telephone. In addition, while the Internet brings goods to the screens of very geographically distant customers, the same distance creates difficulties in returning unsatisfactory goods and in many cases even the payment for such goods. Although credit cards facilitate intercontinental transactions, people are reluctant to give out their credit card numbers over the Internet for reasons of security as mentioned above. The alternative ways of paying for goods are often too daunting for the uninitiated user of such mechanisms.

Firms doing business with customers in other countries have to be aware of the laws that apply when promoting their goods and services over the Internet. This is more of a problem for some goods and services than for others. The promotion of financial services is a case in point. In addition, in the online community there is a general feeling that unsolicited e-mail is unacceptable. Organizations need to be wary of considering such approaches in order to induce dialogue with consumers. Such approaches may even incur legal action. However, the Internet will be an important source of communication for marketers and customers alike in the future. It is unlikely to stay in its present form and the traditional marketing tools will no doubt have to change their nature when applied to Internet communications.

In order to get the best out of website marketing, organizations need to understand how the potential customers are making use of the web. Users of the web tend to surf or skim its contents so would-be marketers need to find something with immediate appeal to potential customers. The site would need to be updated regularly as well and information given as to the changes that have taken place. Advertisements on the Internet must be useful and/or entertaining if they are to appeal to viewers. At present, few advertisers can take advantage of the Internet technology.

MARKETING MIX AND THE INTERNET

The growth of the Internet and the World Wide Web presents opportunities for marketers to reach customers with new products. Successful online marketers exploit the interactive capabilities of the World Wide Web for the benefit of their customers. The web pages they create become communities where people swap information and buy regularly.

More and more companies are recognizing the value of the World Wide Web to provide 'infotainment' which can foster brand identity and loyalty and develop long-term relationships with customers. Marketers are also advertising their products on the websites of other organizations. This is found in the form of *banner ads*, which are small, static or animated rectangular ads that typically appear at the top of a web page. Users can click on the banners to visit the advertiser's site for more information. Finally, *sponsorship* or *co-branded ads* integrate companies' brands and products with the editorial content of certain websites. Their role is to link the advertiser with the website's mission in the user's mind.

Consumers can gain ready access to prices. This helps customers in comparative shopping and gives manufacturers that want to make price a key element in their marketing mix another opportunity to get pricing information to customers. Many organizations implement low-price policies through the Internet.

QUESTIONS

1 Discuss the importance of the price quality relationship in formulating marketing strategies.
2 What does the term strategy mean in the context of channel management?
3 How might the accuracy of communication be influenced by noise or distortion which enters into both the message and the channel?
4 Suggest some of the kinds of objectives that might be set for marketing communications. How might these objectives be pursued in practice?
5 Three important marketing communication tools are advertising, selling and sales promotion. To what extent are they:
   (a) complementary
   (b) mutually exclusive as promotional tools?
6 Discuss the value of the Internet as a vehicle for marketing goods and services.

CASE STUDIES

Eau de Nuit

Distributing and promoting soft drinks is largely achieved through fairly traditional methods. Promotion is often in magazines and directed towards selected target audiences (usually younger people) although billboard advertising close to schools and colleges is also used. Distribution follows the classical route of wholesaler to retailer with many soft drinks these days being sold direct to large supermarket chains which buy in bulk. The latter prefer on the whole to stock branded labels rather than have their own private label drinks. There are also vending machine operators who buy direct and distribute through thousands of vending machines strategically located in sports centres, colleges, universities and other sites which attract large numbers of young people.

Traditionally, Colette Soft Drinks has followed the methods outlined above. However, in recent times it has taken an innovative approach. Six months after launching a fizzy drink called Eau de Nuit, Colette Soft Drinks allowed shops and supermarkets to stock the product. Shop owners expressed surprise saying: 'It's really strange – the kids know all about Eau de Nuit, but we've never heard of it. Now it's flying off the shelves by ityself.' Colette's marketing strategy for Eau de Nuit might seem highly unusual. For the first six months it did no advertising and restricted distribution to a handful of popular clubs.

Getting the products stocked in these venues required a strategy all of its own. Colette recruited people off the street to be its salespeople. They tended to be scruffy, but knew the music, so the clubs took them seriously. Having convinced venues such as France's Ministry of Sound to stock Eau de Nuit, the idea was that its reputation would spread by word of mouth. Ten months after the launch, Eau de Nuit is now being advertised, and distribution includes supermarkets.

Colette effectively has two marketing budgets. One is the mass market, but to maintain credibility it has to nurture its original people. Credibility is the most important thing. It is important to gain this sort of credibility as a growing number of consumers are both wary of large companies and extremely sophisticated judges of marketing.

A senior market researcher working for a company specializing in youth markets commented that at one time firms used to just put an ad on television next to a particular programme or in a particular magazine. Now there are magazines for everything and no one can be sure that they have reached the audience. Because of all this there is a move to alternative ways of promotion and distribution and to alternative agencies.

QUESTION

Do you think that the marketing mix strategy employed here could be applied equally as well to other products? Why or why not?

Longevity bulbs

Light bulbs always seem to burn out with amazing alacrity. It often seems as if it were only yesterday that we put in a new bulb only to find that it has burned out yet again. Light bulbs are not eco-friendly and in an age when the emphasis is on protecting the environment and reducing waste in what we produce and consume, it is a product that needs some hard thinking about.

Ordinary electric light bulbs have a very short rated life of 1,000 hours. Longevity introduced its premium-priced, 10-year light bulbs to the market in Japan a couple of years ago. Although the product has taken off rather slowly, the company is hopeful of higher sales in the future when its newly appointed distributor, backed up by a substantial national advertising campaign, gets under way later this year.

The 10-year light bulbs offer a number of important benefits – they are designed to last in excess of 16,000 hours and are ideal for locations where the bulb is hazardous to reach for replacement or for bulbs in and around the home where a blown bulb could make the going dangerous. In independent tests in Japan, the bulbs recorded an average working life which actually reduced the need to replace them to once every ten years. Finally, unlike low-energy fluorescent bulbs, these bulbs can be dimmed to create more atmospheric lighting effects. Moreover, because they are exactly the same shape as conventional bulbs they fit all lampshades and fittings.

Each bulb is guaranteed to last a full 10 years and bulbs are available in screw or bayonet fitting and are supplied in a choice of 60 W or 100 W, opaque or clear glass.

Longevity is keen to introduce the product on to international markets. Since growth in home sales has been slow it feels that it could increase its output substantially if it could find international markets. This would lead to economies of scale in production and the benefits of lower prices could then be passed on to customers which in turn would stimulate sales growth.

Key questions relate to choice of markets, pricing and advertising strategy and distribution methods.

QUESTION

How should the firm set about determining its marketing mix strategy?

Chapter 12

Growth strategies

Product-market expansion

INTRODUCTION

Strategic windows are dynamic entities that change over time. They represent opportunities in which it is possible for the organization to increase sales both in volume and cash. A firm can have more than one strategic window open at a time and these may be related to the different types of growth strategy that an organization can pursue.

This chapter examines the strategic alternatives that are available. Essentially this involves the various strategies outlined in the well-known Ansoff matrix (market penetration, product-market expansion and diversification) along with vertical integration strategies (Figure 12.1). The chapter explores the rationale behind these strategies.

The importance of new product development is explored and causes for failure in exploiting new product opportunities are examined. Ways of screening out winners and losers in terms of new product opportunities are considered. Leading on from new product development, diversification is highlighted as an important strategy in the search for new strategic windows. An alternative strategy of vertical integration is also explored.

Ansoff's Product Market Expansion Grid

	Existing products	New products
Existing markets	Market penetration strategy	Product development strategy
New markets	Market development strategy	Diversification strategy

Figure 12.1 *Ansoff matrix*

Ansoff's product-market expansion grid provides a useful though not exhaustive framework for looking at possible strategies to cope with the problem of strategic windows and finding ways of creating overlapping strategic windows. All four of the strategies suggested by Ansoff are discussed below along with others (see e.g. Exhibit 12.1).

MARKET PENETRATION STRATEGY OF EXISTING MARKETS

Here the strategy amounts to increasing sales of existing products while at the same time trying to maintain current margins of profitability on sales. When the market is expanding this may be accomplished with nominal outlays of marketing expenditure by getting more first-time users to buy the product or to increase product usage of existing buyers or to increase the frequency of use. In a saturated market, extra sales may only be generated as a result of increased market share. Another possibility, however, is to promote new applications for existing product users. Such new uses can best be identified by market research aimed at determining exactly how customers use the brand.

Increasing market share puts heavy pressure on marketing resources and can impact negatively on short-run profitability. However, if economies of scale or the impact of the 'experience curve' are felt as a result of increased supply to the market then this may more than offset the impact on profitability of any additional marketing expenditure.

A share gain can be based on tactical actions such as advertising, trade allowances, promotions or price reductions. The problem is that such share gains can be difficult to sustain. A preferred option is to generate a more permanent share gain by winning a sustainable competitive advantage with enhanced customer value or by matching a competitor's sustainable competitive advantage. The aim is to create or enhance the assets and skills of the business and neutralize those of competitors.

Attempts to increase market share will very likely affect competitors directly and therefore precipitate competitor responses. The alternative of attempting to increase usage among current customers is usually less threatening to competitors. Heavy users are usually the most fruitful target. Light users, however, should not be ignored because there may be a way to unlock their potential. Increased product usage can in fact be stimulated in three different ways. First, the frequency can be increased. Second, the quantity used in each application can be increased. And finally, new applications can be promoted.

EXHIBIT 12.1   GENERIC STRATEGIES BASED ON ANSOFF MATRIX

Market penetration strategy	*Product development strategy*
Increase purchase use by existing customers	New features
Win customers from competition	Different quality levels
Convert non-users	New products
Market development strategy	*Diversification strategy*
New market segments	Through organic growth
New distribution channels	Through acquisition
New geographic markets	Through joint venture

In order to increase the frequency of use, reminder communications are necessary. In the case of getting people to use more of the product, this may simply involve repositioning the product from one which is used occasionally, to one that is used regularly and this can be achieved through a repositioning promotional campaign. Other increases of frequency of purchase may be sought through providing incentives – competitions and sales promotions.

Similar techniques can be used to increase the quantity used on each occasion, e.g. reminder communications and incentives.

MARKET DEVELOPMENT STRATEGY

Finding new markets does not guarantee long-term or short-term profitability but economies of scale in producing for the market or in supplying the market will contribute to profitability. However, there may well be barriers to entry to the market which means that neither short-run nor long-term contributions to overall profitability are attractive.

A logical avenue of growth is to develop new markets by duplicating the business operation, perhaps with minor adaptive changes. In the case of market expansion, the same expertise and technology and sometimes even the same plant and operations facility can be used. There is thus potential synergy and resulting reductions in investment and operating costs. Of course, market development is based upon the premise that the business is operating successfully.

Geographic expansion may involve changing from a regional operation to a national operation, moving into another region, or expanding to another country. A firm can also grow by reaching into new market segments. There is, of course, a variety of ways to define target segments and hence growth directions. A key to detecting new markets is to consider a wide variety of segmentation variables. Sometimes looking at a market from different perspectives will uncover useful segments:

- *usage*: the non-user can be an attractive target
- *distribution system*: new markets can be reached by opening up additional distribution channels
- *age*: pulling in additional age categories in the population (consumer goods).

A key to detecting new markets is to consider a wide variety of segmentation variables. It is especially useful to identify segments that are not being well served. In general, segments should be sought for which the brand can produce value.

GROWTH INTO INTERNATIONAL MARKETS

Many firms engage in international marketing activities. The reasons for this vary and we will explore these below. There are also several different ways in which firms can become involved in international marketing. These approaches can range from supplying goods to intermediaries in the home market who then arrange the shipping of the goods to various overseas markets to actually setting up in business in other countries to undertake production and/or marketing activities.

Reasons for engaging in international marketing

Some firms prefer to supply goods or services just to their domestic markets if these are large enough to produce the kinds of financial returns they desire. For such firms they would not then need to learn another country's language and laws, deal with volatile currencies, face political and legal uncertainties, or design their products to suit different customer needs and expectations. As a result, business negotiations would be much easier to conduct.

However, there are several reasons why a firm might decide to become involved in international marketing operations. In the first place, foreign competitors offering superior products or lower prices might attack the company's domestic market. The firm might want to counterattack these competitors in their home markets to tie up their resources. Another point is that the firm might discover that some foreign markets present higher profit opportunities than the domestic market. Under such circumstances even if there were risks and additional effort and resources required to secure business it might be deemed worthwhile. Many firms also seek to grow sales and recognize the benefits to be gained from economies of scale. In the pursuit of such an objective a firm might need a larger customer base to achieve economies of scale and see additional sales in international markets as a means of achieving this end. A further reason might be that while there is additional risk involved in operating internationally, a firm may wish to reduce its dependence on any one market so as to reduce risk arising from such over-reliance on a domestic market.

International market entry methods

Once a company decides to become involved in international marketing it has to decide upon an approach. There are five broad market-entry strategies: indirect exporting, direct exporting, licensing, joint ventures and direct investment.

Indirect export

Here, firms work through independent intermediaries to export their products. There are four types of intermediaries:

- *A domestic-based export merchant* who buys the manufacture's products and then sells them abroad.
- *A domestic-based export agent* who seeks and negotiates foreign purchases and is paid a commission.
- *A co-operative organization* which conducts exporting activities on behalf of several producers and is under their administrative control.
- *An export-management company* which agrees to manage a company's export activities for a fee.

Direct export

In this case, firms can decide to handle their own exports. The investment and risks are greater, but so is the potential return as a result of not paying an intermediary. There are several approaches and these can be made through the mechanism of:

- *A domestic-based export department or division* where there is an export sales manager and a team of salespeople who carry out the actual selling and draw on market assistance as needed.

249

- *An overseas sales branch or subsidiary* which allows the firm to achieve greater presence and programme control in a foreign market.
- *Travelling export sales representatives* where the firm can send home-based sales representatives abroad where they will operate in much the same way as they do in the domestic market.
- *Foreign-based distributors or agents* where the company hires foreign-based distributors or agents to sell its goods on its behalf.

Licensing

This is a simple and relatively low-risk way for a firm to become involved in international marketing. The licensor licenses a foreign company to use a manufacturing process, trademark, patent, trade secret, or other item of value for a fee or a loyalty. The licensor in this way achieves entry into the market at little risk; the licensee gains production expertise or a well-known product or name without having to start from scratch. This is an approach which may be preferred where there is high monetary inflation or political instability in a country.

Joint ventures

Foreign investors may join with local investors to create a joint venture in which they share ownership and control. Forming a joint venture might be necessary or desirable for economic or political reasons. The exporting firm may lack the financial, physical, and managerial resources to undertake the venture alone.

Direct Investment

One form of foreign investment is the direct ownership of a foreign-based assembly/manufacturing or service facility. The would-be international marketer can buy part or the whole of a local company or even build its own facilities. As a company becomes more experienced in exports, and if the foreign market is large enough, then foreign production/marketing or service provision facilities can offer significant advantages. For example, a firm can secure cost economies in the form of cheaper labour or raw materials. It can also gain a better image in the host country because it creates jobs.

The amount a company needs to invest varies with the degree of control it requires and the degree of risk it will encounter in entering a foreign market. It is often the case that the higher is the degree of investment, the higher the degree of risk. This is particularly the case if the company is attempting to enter the market alone.

Sometimes firms enter international markets with the co-operation of other firms already operating in the market. Developing strategic alliances and licensing agreements can allow entry to an international market which would otherwise have been expensive or very difficult to enter.

The most appropriate entry method to a new market is dependent upon various considerations. These include the extent of the company's existing international operations, the nature of competition in the market, the potential barriers to entry, the degree of control required by the company, the availability of financial resources and the company's objectives in wishing to enter the market

PRODUCT DEVELOPMENT STRATEGY

One of the avenues to gain a competitive advantage is through innovation (viz. Nieto and Quevedo, 2005; Olson *et al.*, 2005). Moreover, it has been specifically argued that one of the components for the success of industrial firms is the extent of their innovativeness (Hult *et al.*, 2004). Innovativeness has been described as 'possession of newness' (Roehrich, 2004), or the degree of newness of a product (Freel, 2005). However, although the introduction of new products can have a positive impact on sales growth, initially, profitability may not increase since there may be substantial research, development and launching costs associated with the venture which have to be recouped.

Longer-term rates of return on investment which are at least equal to the current rate of return on capital employed are required from new products. This may not be possible and firms may have to accept the possibility or even certainty of lower profitability, just to stay in business. Predicting demand for new products can be difficult and hence so is the estimation of profit potential.

A 'new product' can be defined in several different ways. A product can refer to a physical entity or a cluster of expected customer benefits, depending on whether the perspective adopted is that of the business or that of the market. From the point of view of a business, a product innovation may represent a change in, or addition to, the physical entities that make up its product line. From a market perspective, the term refers to a new or revised set of customer perceptions about a particular cluster of benefits. Thus, that which is considered a product innovation by a business enterprise may not be recognized as such by its customers. Here we will adopt a business perspective.

A new product is one that is new in any way for the company concerned (McCarthy and Perreault, 1993). Additions to existing product lines and improvements of an existing product may also be thought of as 'new products'. In practice only a few new products are actually new to the firm and new to the market (Exhibit 12.2).

Importance of new products

Theodore Levitt (1960) stressed the importance of innovation in the market place in the 1960s when he warned against the dangers facing firms which did not respond to new developments in the market place and which lurked in the shadow of product obsolescence. Two important trends in the market place have been of major importance in stimulating product innovation: the increasing instability of consumer preferences and the growing intensity and sophistication of competition.

EXHIBIT 12.2   WHAT IS A NEW PRODUCT?

- *New to the world products:* inventions – in-line skates, Polaroid camera, etc.
- *New category entries:* P&G's first shampoo, Ford's first Mini
- *Additions to product lines:* Tide liquid detergent
- *Product improvements:* current products made better
- *Repositionings:* Arm & Hammer's baking soda repositioned several times as drain deodorant, refrigerator deodorant, etc.

Changes in consumer and competitor behaviour are not the only external forces affecting product innovation. Technological advances have an equally significant impact, often leading to the radical changes in size and characteristics of established product markets. A good example is the impact of the microchip on the world market for wristwatches. This was initially dominated by Swiss manufacturers making use of mechanical movements but latterly manufacturers in the Far East have moved in using microchip technology. Moreover, improvements in product and process technology are often introduced to a wide range of product markets simultaneously.

New products can account for a substantial proportion of a firm's sales and profits over a relatively short time period. A good illustration is provided by Lever which, between 1968 and 1984, introduced 12 new brands of soaps and soap powders to UK national markets. Five of these introductions became brand market leaders and three others became sectional leaders (Hardy, 1987).

A business develops new products for one of two reasons:

1   to replace or supplement its existing offerings in their present markets; or
2   to serve new markets, defined in terms of customer benefits or geography.

It can develop new markets without new products by making appropriate adjustments in the pricing, promotion and/or distribution policies associated with an existing offering.

Although new products are essential to companies, much expense can be incurred and squandered in developing and launching unsuccessful ones. In the next section we look at why new products fail.

NEW PRODUCT FAILURES

Innovation may be thought of as the cornerstone of success in many industries, but not all innovations are successful. Indeed, the incidence of failure in introducing new products is extremely high. Of course what is a failure for one firm may well be a successful product for another firm. It all depends upon the expectations of the firm. Failures are never absolute entities in themselves.

The usual measure taken when evaluating the comparative success of a new product is the financial return on investment it generates. But of course what will satisfy one company will not necessarily satisfy another. A company accustomed to earning an overall after-tax rate of return on capital employed exceeding 30 per cent per annum will on average need to introduce new products which will generate at least this level of after-tax return on investment in order to maintain long-run profitability. Firms with different rates of return on capital may have different expectations, reflecting the nature of the industry in which they operate. In addition, firms of substantially different size, yet considering the same product-market opportunity, will also have different expectations.

Forecasting sales, profits and costs for new products is difficult and the estimates made can sometimes be widely inaccurate. Potential new product opportunities that are likely to incur heavy R&D costs need to be screened out at a very early stage to avoid unnecessary losses. In the early 1980s, spending in the early phases of new product development accounted for 10 per cent of the total cost of bringing out the product. By 1990 this figure had risen to 20 per cent. In the face of uncertainty and soaring costs, firms would definitely benefit from examining ways of screening new product opportunities.

During the early stages of the product life cycle of the tumble drier, the larger firms, such as Philips, were deterred from entering the market because they considered they would be unable to generate sufficient profits in order to earn the level of return on investment they required. It was only later when the market had increased in size that they felt the market was attractive (Proctor, 1989).

Large firms working on the frontiers of technology often come up with good ideas but because the initial market size or even long-term market size is small they may not choose to develop the product. Instead they may 'transfer the technology' to a smaller firm, for a royalty payment. The smaller firm is better able to exploit the opportunity. Of course the reverse can happen too when a small firm lacks the resources to exploit a new product idea it may call upon the help of a larger firm which has the resources required.

Reasons for failure

There are many different reasons for new products failing to meet up with the expectations of the firms which launched them. Some major reasons for new product failure are as follows:

- products lack useful/meaningful uniqueness
- planning is poor during the introduction phase
- the introduction is badly timed, e.g. before the market is ready for the product
- key important points are sometimes overlooked in the enthusiasm to go ahead
- poor marketing and failure after launch
- the top management in the organization does not provide adequate support for the product
- company politics intervene, e.g. between various brand managers
- unforeseen high product costs.

A firm's inability to use commonsense reasoning or inattention to the management task of marketing the product are often causal factors of new product failure (Proctor, 1993). It is also easier with hindsight to evaluate the success or failure of a new product – this too can sometimes be difficult.

In the next section we will look at how firms can try to avoid new product failures by adopting a systematic approach to finding, screening and evaluating new product ideas.

A methodical approach

Costs accumulate as firms progress through the six phases and the earlier potentially poor product ideas are screened out the better it is for the company (Figure 12.2).

Idea acquisition

It is suggested that particular attention should be given in the first place to an organization's resources and that the organization's major problems should be analysed. Attention should also be given to identifying external growth opportunities ready for exploitation – expanding markets, technological breakthrough or rising profit margins. This will help to determine the product fields that are of primary interest to the organization (Exhibit 12.3).

The dual drivers of innovation are technology and market demand (Exhibit 12.4). Although the impact of technology is primarily felt in the R&D environment, market drivers have to be ascertained primarily with the aid of market research. Essentially this involves generating new product concepts based upon the notion of problem-based ideation (Exhibit 12.5).

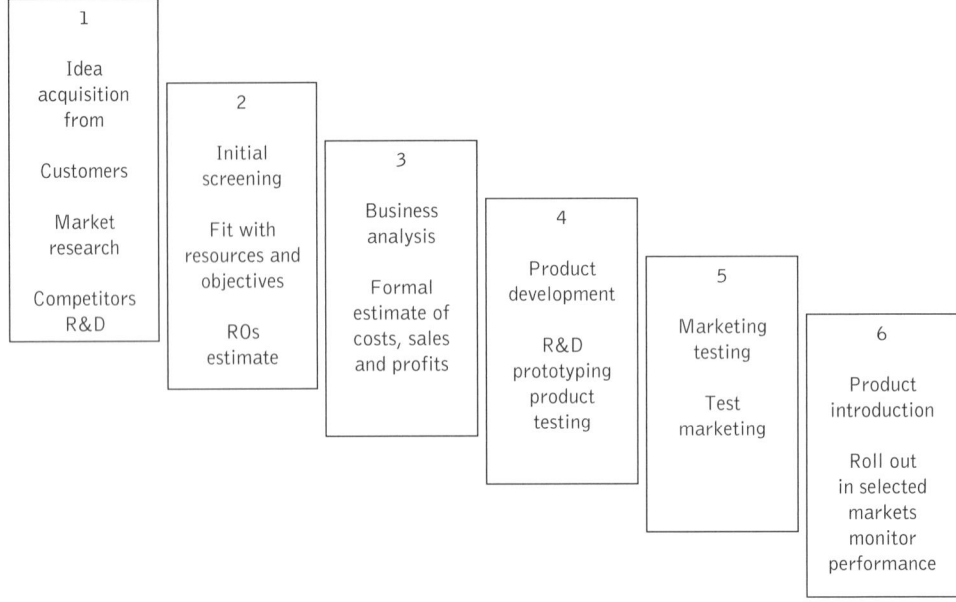

Figure 12.2 Six phases of the new product development programme

---

EXHIBIT 12.3   STRATEGIC PLANNING

■ *Opportunities for new products*: under-utilized resources – e.g. strong franchise with dealers
■ *New resources* – e.g. particular technical discoveries
■ *External mandate* – e.g. market driver
■ *Internal mandate* – e.g. derived from classical gap analysis

---

EXHIBIT 12.4   DUAL DRIVERS

■ *Technology*: laboratories, etc.
■ *Market*: customer group, end use

Example:
■ University Microfilms International was oriented to the technology of microfilming and the market activity of education.
■ Microfilm readers for libraries were just one new line.
■ Signode used plastic extrusion and food manufacturing to come up with plastic trays for packaging food that could be put in a microwave oven for warming.

There are a variety of ways of obtaining new product ideas. Monitoring competitors' new product development, feedback from customers, market research, contact with R&D establishments, a firm's own R&D. There is not one best method and firms should try all methods wherever possible.

The use of a creativity technique (Exhibit 12.6) such as morphological analysis can help executives to generate many new product ideas. The basic premise behind using the technique is the idea that a product is an entity that has different dimensions. It may come in different shapes and sizes, appeal to different target markets, be made of different materials, etc. It is the combination of attributes of these different dimensions that go into creating the product entity itself. A desk may be made of wood, be relatively large with respect to comparable products, be styled in the classical mould and appeal to the user at home. It is even possible to go beyond tangible dimensions.

Morphological analysis entails recognizing the most important dimensions of a product – usually two, three or four – and then generating a list of attributes relating to these dimensions. The next stage involves taking combinations of the attributes listed (one for each dimension) and deciding whether or not this kind of product is already marketed by the firm. For example, taking fast foods as an example, one combination might be as shown in Table 12.1.

The technique can be elaborated and 'computerized' by making use of a random word generator to suggest possible attributes. If the combination generated does not represent a current product

Table 12.1   *Morphological analysis example*

Type of dish	Target market
Curry	Late night supper callers
Pizzas	Evening meal
Fish and chips	Lunch-time shoppers

offering and it is felt that it could constitute an attractive product-market opportunity then it could be retained as a possible idea to be progressed to the next of the six phases – screening.

An organization needs to establish a programme for planned idea generation. This could involve identifying idea-generating groups and giving them a clear concept of the organization's interest fields. Conducting exploratory technical research can also be productive. Yet another fruitful approach is to use scenario analysis (see Chapters 5 and 6 for fuller accounts; see also Exhibit 12.7).

Figure 12.3 provides some ideas of sources of inspiration which may lead to new product ideas. The sources shown are not exhaustive and the readers may care to extend these sources for themselves. However, although some of these sources (e.g. responding to needs for convenience) have given rise to the proliferation and introduction of many new products and services (e.g. convenience shopping, vacuum cleaners, remote controlled televisions, etc.) many of the sources have still to be more fully exploited (e.g. the use of leisure in a work way). Conceptualizing new product development within the framework presented offers a creative and constructive way of searching for potentially profitable new products and services. For example, while 'responding to unconscious needs' has already resulted in the generation of new product ideas in the food and fashion industries (need not to be fat – dietary products; need to be appear thin – clothes that help one appear slim) or in the insurance and property protection industries (security for one's possessions) there are many other unconscious needs of people and businesses to which creative and innovative firms might respond in the form of new products and services.

EXHIBIT 12.7   SCENARIO ANALYSIS

Need to know future consumer problems:
1   paint future scenario
2   study it for problems and needs
3   evaluate those problems and try to solve the more important.

Scenario analysis example
Apartments 20 years from now might have lots of windows and sunlight streaming in. Furniture analysts might see two new problems:
1   upholstery needed which is more resistant to the sun
2   chairs needed that will permit normal activities – such as conversation and eating – but at the same time allow more exposure to the sunlight.

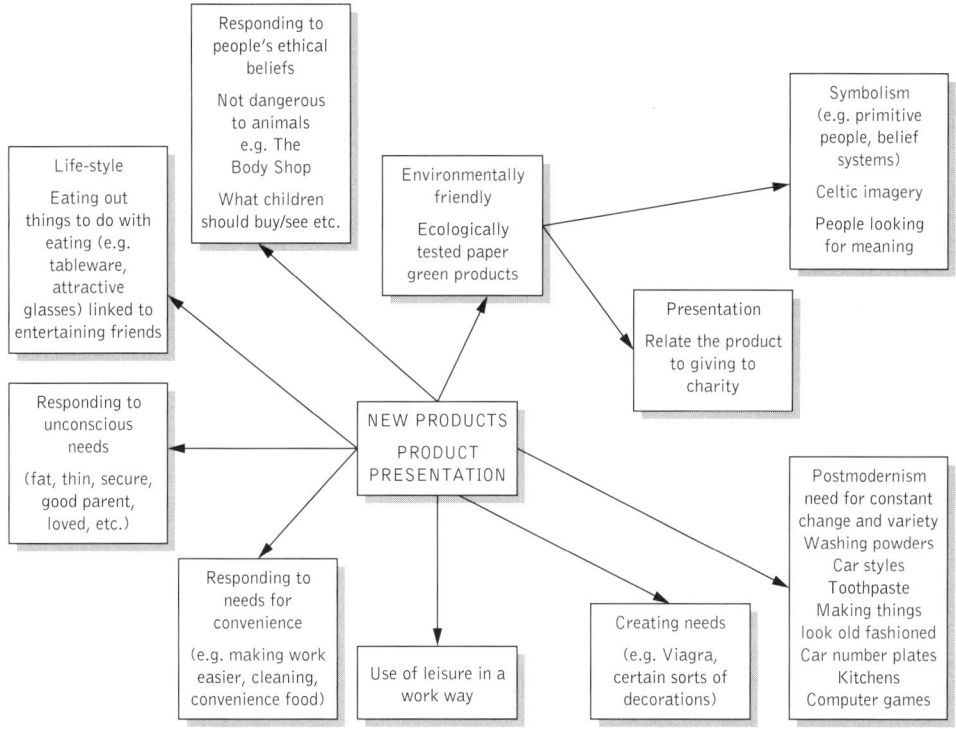

Figure 12.3 *Conceptualizing new product development*

Recently, the demand for environmentally friendly products has come into focus. As the twenty-first century unfolds, the need to respond to people's ethical beliefs or needs and to finding meaning through symbols may increase in importance. This will have a wide range of potential consequences for a vast array of consumer goods. The effects of 'postmodernism' have already been felt – the need for constant change and variety has been expressed and satisfied through changes in style and in the increased variety which has been made available in many products. Life-style also presents a powerful influence on the demands that people make for consumer goods and services. Although this has already had a significant impact, its influence is likely to increase as people become more affluent and adopt patterns of life-style which at the present time cannot even be imagined.

Screening

Usually, ideas for new products arise sequentially, one at a time, and cannot be compared and evaluated along with a large set of alternative ideas for new products – unless a technique such as morphological analysis is used. Benchmarking against important criteria is thus an important procedure to follow.

Clearly, the likely financial performance and implications of developing and/or adopting a new product idea are the key factors that need to be taken into account. However, without undertaking desk and/or field research it is difficult to quantify what we might expect to sell. Pooled estimates of subjective expert opinions, however, can sometimes provide remarkably close estimates. Members of the firm who might have some idea of the quantities of the various new product ideas that the firm might expect to sell should be consulted. With such estimates it should then be possible to make rough financial estimates of likely profits to be generated. These rough estimates are turned into more precise estimates at the third phase – business analysis – where a full quantitative analysis and evaluation is made.

The initial screening stage is characterized by a checklist of benchmarks which new products have to satisfy before they can be moved on to the next phase in the six-step process. For example:

- Is the product compatible with present distribution channels?
- Is the product complementary to current products?
- Can it be priced competitively alongside products of a similar quality?
- Will promotion of the product be easy?
- Will there always be uses for the product?
- Is there a wide variety of potential customers?
- Are existing resources sufficient to facilitate production and marketing of the product?
- Will the product fill an unsatisfied need in the market place?
- Is the market likely to grow in size?

Experience seems to indicate that successful products:

- fit well with the internal functional strengths of the business
- fit with the need of the market.

Such a checklist can of course be extended and modified. New product ideas can be rated against the items on the checklist and those satisfying key criteria moved on to the next phase – business analysis.

Business analysis

At the business analysis phase sales, costs and profit projections have to be made in order to determine whether the adoption of the new product into the product mix will satisfy company objectives. The phase involves predicting sales and cost behaviour so that profitability of the product can be estimated. This can be done in a variety of ways and it is always advisable to use as many different ways as is feasible. Approaches include:

- examining sales histories of similar products
- surveying market opinion
- using expert opinions
- statistical models (see chapter on marketing information and decision support systems).

Irrespective of the approach taken, minimum and maximum sales estimates need to be obtained to provide an idea of the amount of risk involved. The method of forecasting depends on whether the product is a one-time purchase, an infrequently purchased product or a frequently purchased product. In the case of infrequently purchased products, attention has to be given to predicting first-time sales and replacement sales. In the case of frequently purchased products, attention has to be given to first-time buyers and repeat purchases. In using any of the identified methods of forecasting it is essential to gain a separate estimate, as appropriate, of:

- first-time purchase
- replacement purchase
- repeat purchase.

Costs also have to be estimated and these may change over the time span of the sales forecast. This has to be taken into account when estimating profits and likely sales since costs do have uncertainties attached to them. Escalating prices of raw materials or bought-in parts can stifle the sales growth of a new product because of the need to continually adjust its price upwards.

Placing a value on the financial appeal of a new product is of course very important. However, it does have to be borne in mind that a large amount of uncertainty surrounds any estimates that are made. Moreover, there is always the danger that once numbers are put down on paper they will be treated as if they represent certainties. It is therefore a good idea to keep in mind the more qualitative aspects of evaluation as defined in the checklist of criteria used at the screening stage.

The financial evaluation of new product ideas should examine the following:

- estimated after-tax return on investment
- payback period
- variance in the estimates of return on investment and payback between the best scenario and the worst scenario – to indicate risk.

Surveys of market opinion can be particularly helpful at the business analysis phase since in addition to helping to quantify potential demand they can also help to provide other information as well. It may be possible that with some adjustment to the product or service it will sell better. It is important to get this right at the outset. The kind of qualitative questions to ask here relate to whether:

- the benefits of using the product are clear to the user
- the product solves a problem or fills a need
- other products already fill this need and give satisfaction
- the price is right in relationship to the perceived value.

One should, of course, pick an appropriate group of target customers. Where the new product is only a concept it can be presented symbolically. At this stage a word and/or a picture description will suffice. Products that satisfy the criteria set for this phase can then move on to the product development phase.

The A-T-R model and an example of its application in evaluating the financial potential of a new product is shown in Exhibit 12.8.

Product development

Development is the stage at which a new product proposal is developed into a physical entity and plans are put together for its production and introduction to the market place. Some products are obviously more complex than others. Product development can therefore be an extremely lengthy business or

EXHIBIT 12.8 A-T-R MODEL

Profit = Units sold × Profit per unit

Units sold = % who become aware of the product × % who opt to try the product if they can get it × % of intended triers who can get the product (if it is available to them) × % of triers who like the item enough to repeat purchase × the number of units that repeaters will buy in a year.

Profit per unit = Revenue per unit (unit list price less trade margins, promotion allowances, freight etc.) – cost per unit (usually cost of goods sold plus direct marketing costs)

Therefore: Profit = Buying units× % aware × % trial × % availability × % repeat × annual units bought × (revenue per unit – cost per unit)

(See Antil, 1988.)

A-T-R example: a new compound for polishing sports cars

- Number of owners of sports cars: 3 million
- % who become aware of the new polish: 40%
- % of those aware who will decide to try the new polish: 20%
- % of stores that will have stocked the product (assumes potential user will not seek beyond one store if they cannot find it there): 40%
- % of triers who like the product and try more: 50%
- Number of cans typical user buys in a year: 2
- Dollar revenue at the factory, per can, after trade margins and promotion discounts: $2
- Unit cost of can at the intended volume: $0.65
- Profit contribution forecast: 3 million × 0.40 × 0.20 × 0.40 × 0.50 × 2 × ($2–$0.65) = $129,600

it can be reasonably short. As a stage in the new product development process it is important for all products.

It is the stage where the product moves into R&D and engineering (in the case of a complex technological product) and it is here that the really heavy costs can start to mount up. Efforts are directed at trying to turn the idea into a technically and commercially feasible product. This involves what is known as prototyping. The objective is to develop a physical version of the product (a prototype) which:

- will meet with consumers' expectations
- will perform safely under normal use and conditions
- can be produced for the budgeted manufacturing costs.

Developing a prototype can take days, months or years according to the nature of the product. For example, commercial aircraft take several years to develop. When completed, the prototype is subjected to rigorous functional and consumer tests. These tests are carried out both on the bench and in the field to ensure that new products perform safely and effectively (Exhibit 12.9). There are a variety of approaches to consumer testing. These include bringing consumers into the laboratory to try out the product or allowing them samples or models to try out in their own homes.

Test marketing

Where launch costs are high it would seem commonsense to test market new products before embarking on commercialization on a national or international scale. However, not all products are test marketed. It is possible under certain circumstances that test marketing the product may provide important business knowledge to competitors. Nevertheless, test marketing, on the other hand, can avoid disasters and save firms millions of pounds.

The amount of test marketing to be given to a product reflects investment cost and risk on the one hand and pressure of time and cost of research on the other. Clearly the greater the amount of investment, the more need there is to proceed with thorough testing. The same is also true of high-risk new products.

A variety of test marketing methods exist and there are differences between test marketing industrial and consumer goods.

One of the most important factors these days is speed in new product development (Exhibit 12.10). New products have to be put into the market quickly in order to stay ahead of competition.

DIVERSIFICATION

Diversification involves moving simultaneously into new products and new markets. It is a risky strategy but with careful selection of the right kind of businesses, considerable improvements in profitability can be experienced. Diversification represents an opportunity for growth and revitalization. A diversification strategy can be implemented by an acquisition (or merger), new business venture or strategic alliance.

EXHIBIT 12.9   CONCEPT TESTING

- Uniqueness of the concept
- Believability of the concept
- Importance of the problem being addressed
- Extent to which the concept is interesting
- Extent to which it is realistic, practical, useful
- Extent to which it solves a problem or meets a need
- How much they like the concept
- How likely they would be to buy the product
- Their reactions to the proposed price
- What problems they see in using the product.

EXHIBIT 12.10   TECHNIQUES FOR ATTAINING SPEED IN NEW PRODUCT DEVELOPMENT

- Do the job right first time
- Find certain winners not those that 'also ran'
- Train everyone involved
- Communicate with everyone who needs to be 'in the know'
- Be flexible and include contingency arrangements
- Make speedy decisions and implement them quickly
- Cut things out but show caution and prudence
- Use venture teams, etc.
- Work in small groups to get round bureaucracy
- Empower a team and motivate it
- Break down organizational barriers
- Make sure supporting departments are ready when called on
- Use computer-aided design
- Use design-aided manufacture: reduce parts; set tolerances according to needs; etc.
- Use common components
- Make it easy to product/service test
- Incorporate qualities that make for fast trial
- Use rollouts not test markets
- Spend what it takes to get immediate market awareness
- Make trial purchasing as easy as possible
- Get customer service capability in place ahead of need, and test it out.

It is usual to differentiate between diversification that is 'related' from that which is 'unrelated'. A related diversification is one in which the new business has meaningful commonalities with the core business. These provide the potential to generate economies of scale or synergies based on exchange of skills and resources. Diversification can take place into related or unrelated products. A firm in microcomputer production might move into making personal telecommunications equipment. This might be seen as diversifying into related products since both products make use of micro-electronic technology and the experience gained in one field might be usefully employed in the other. The same firm diversifying into shoe manufacturing would be shifting into unrelated products.

Moving into areas where a firm does not have any prior experience is highly risky and firms may prefer to move into related markets. Moreover, there may be some synergy to be gained from moving into related markets. The synergy may be in marketing or even in production. In theory, as a result of diversification, the business should be able to improve its return on investment (ROI) because of increased revenues, decreased costs or reduced investment. Meaningful commonalties can involve similar

- distribution channels
- images and their impact on the market

- sales and advertising efforts
- facilities
- production processes
- R&D efforts
- operating systems
- staff needs.

It is important to determine whether there is any real area of commonality that will affect the ROI. Sometimes an unrelated diversification can be justified but it does require a different rationale.

Related diversification

Related diversification provides the potential to attain synergies by sharing assets or skills across businesses. When related diversification is achieved by internal expansion, the goal is to export assets or skills. When acquisition of or merger with another business takes place, the goal is to combine two sets of complementary assets and skills – brand names, marketing skills, sales and distribution capacity, and R&D capabilities. The aim is to find business areas where the assets and skills can be applied to generate an advantage. One approach is to examine each asset for excess capacity and ascertain whether it is under-utilized. Implementation problems have to be ascertained, too. Assets and skills may require adaptations when applied to different business and new capabilities may have to be found or developed. There are the cultural problems which can arise as two organizations may have to merge and, if not carefully handled, these may negate the benefits of diversification. The following also have to be taken into account.

Continuing to use the brand name

A strong brand name can provide name familiarity that will aid in the tasks of acquiring awareness, generating trial purchases and gaining distribution for new products. Most important is the brand association – what the brand means. Four types of association are commonly found:

- image of high or low perceived quality
- attribute associations with the brand or product class
- attribute associations that would be negative in a new context
- association with a product class.

Three factors influence what associations will carry over into a new context:

- the strength of the attribute or quality association in the existing context
- the fit of a brand into the new context
- whether it is plausible to consider the brand in the new context.

Developing brand extension options starts by finding out on what products a brand name would fit and what associations it would bring to the new product class. A brand extension can provide substantial support for a brand name by increasing its awareness level and by increasing its associations. However, brand extensions do have the potential to damage a core brand by creating undesirable attribute associations or weakening those that exist.

Making use of marketing skills or compensating for lack of them

A firm will either possess or lack strong marketing skills for a particular market. Thus a frequent motive for diversification is to export or import marketing skills.

Capacity in sales or distribution

A firm with a strong distribution capability may add products or services that could exploit that capability. A firm with capacity in its sales or service organization can look to diversify into products that can use that capacity.

Manufacturing skills

Manufacturing or processing ability can be the basis for an entry into a new business area.

R&D skills

Expertise in a certain technology can lead to a new business based on that technology. Creativity is often required to provide opportunities for basic technology and the R&D capability that supports it.

Achieving economies of scale

Related diversification can sometimes provide economies of scale. Sometimes a critical mass is required in order to be effective.

Risks of related diversification

There are three problem areas:

- Similarities and potential synergy simply do not exist.
- Potential synergy may exist but it is never realized because of implementation problems.
- An acquisition is over-valued.

Unrelated diversification

The objectives of unrelated diversification are mainly financial, to generate profit streams that are either larger, less uncertain or more stable than they would otherwise be.

Manage and allocate cash flow

Unrelated diversification can balance the cash flows of strategic business units. A firm which has many such units that merit investment might buy or merge with a cash cow to provide a source of cash. The acquisition of the cash cow may reduce the need to raise debt or equity over time. Conversely, a firm with a cash cow may enter new areas seeking growth opportunities or simply areas to generate future earnings.

Entering business areas with high ROI prospects

A basic diversification motive is to improve an ROI by moving into business areas with high growth and ROI prospects.

Obtaining a bargain price for a business

A way to improve ROI is to acquire a business at a bargain price so that the investment will be low and the associated ROI will therefore be high.

Reducing risk

The reduction of risk can be a motivation for unrelated diversification. Heavy reliance on a single product line can stimulate a diversification move. Risk can also be reduced by entering businesses that will counter or reduce the cyclical nature of existing earnings.

Risks of unrelated diversification

The very concept of unrelated diversification suggests risk and difficulties because there is no possibility of synergy. Among the major risks are:

- attention may be diverted from the core business
- managing the new business may be difficult
- the new business may be over-valued.

Unrelated diversification, if unsuccessful, may actually damage the core business by diverting attention and resources from it. The potential for difficulties in managing a diversification is magnified when an unrelated business is acquired. The new business may require assets, skills and an organizational culture that differ from those of the core business. Indeed, the skilled team in an acquired firm might well leave and be difficult to replace. A new business area might be incorrectly evaluated. Environmental threats may be overlooked or misjudged and if an acquisition is involved, its strategic liabilities, weaknesses and problems may be undiscovered or miscalculated.

Selecting the right entry strategy

The right entry strategy depends on the firm's familiarity with the product market to be entered. One may envisage familiarity being defined along two dimensions: market; and technology or service embodied in the product.

With respect to the market factors, three levels of familiarity are defined:

- *base*: existing products are sold within this market
- *new/familiar*: the firm is familiar with the market because of extensive research, experienced staff or links with the market as a customer
- *new/unfamiliar*: knowledge of and experience of the market are lacking.

There are also three levels of familiarity with the technologies or services embodied in the products:

- *base*: the technology or service is embodied within existing products
- *new/familiar*: the company is familiar with the technology because of work in related technologies, an established R&D effort in the technology, or extensive focused research in the technology
- *new/unfamiliar*: knowledge of and experience with the technology are lacking.

The basic suggestion is that as the level of familiarity on these two dimensions declines, the commitment level should be reduced (see Exhibit 12.11).

VERTICAL INTEGRATION

Vertical integration can take two forms. It can be forward integration, as when a producer takes over a distributor, or backward integration as is the case when a manufacturer takes over a supplier. Integrative strategies enable firms to gain greater control over the chain of production and distribution. For example, a manufacturer may have difficulty in gaining vital components from a supplier. It may be because the supplier is also selling the same component to other firms and cannot produce enough to satisfy everyone. Under such circumstances the manufacturer may be tempted to try to buy out the supplier (i.e. become the owner of the supplier's business) to ensure that it can always have supplies of the key component.

A good way to understand when vertical integration should be considered and how it should be evaluated is to look at the possible benefits and costs of a vertical integration strategy. These may be such things as:

- *Benefits*: operating economies, access to supply or demand, control of the product system, entry into a profitable business, enhanced technological innovation.

EXHIBIT 12.11 ENTRY STRATEGIES

Technology of service embodied in the product

		Base	New familiar	New unfamiliar
Market factors	New unfamiliar	joint ventures	venture capital or educational acquisitions	venture capital or educational acquisitions
	New familiar	internal market developments or acquisitions (or joint ventures)	internal ventures or acquisitions or licensing	venture capital or educational acquisitions
	Base	internal base developments (or acquisitions)	internal product developments or acquisitions or licensing	joint ventures

Combining operations can result in improved production and related economies. In some contexts, a key success factor is access to a supply of raw material, a part or another input factor – backward integration can reduce the risk. Similarly, forward integration could be motivated by concern about product outlets. Whenever only one buyer and one seller exist for highly specialized products and services, there will be an incentive to consider vertical integration. When such specialization occurs there is a real danger that one party may hold up the other by taking opportunistic advantage of a change in either its circumstance or the environment. It may be necessary to integrate vertically to gain sufficient control over a product or service to maintain the integrity of a differentiation strategy. Vertical integration may be the only way to ensure that quality is maintained. A vertical integration decision can be motivated by an attractive profit potential or an advantage in achieving technological innovation.

- *Costs*: operating costs, management of a different business, increase in risk, reduced flexibility, cost of inward focus.

Vertical integration often involves adding an operation that requires organizational assets and skills which differ markedly from those of a firm's other business areas. As a result, the firm may not be suited to run the integrated operation, effectively and competitively. The classic way to reduce risk is to avoid having too many eggs in one basket – to diversify. Vertical integration tends to increase the amount of commitment and investment that are tied to a certain market. If that market is healthy then integration may enhance profits. On the other hand if the market turns down, integration may cause profits to be more depressed. Integration also raises exit barriers. If the business becomes weak, the additional investment and commitment created by integration will inhibit consideration of an exit alternative. Furthermore, if one operation becomes dependent on the other, it may be awkward to try to exit from one.

Vertical integration usually means that a firm is committed to an in-house supplier or customer. The flexibility of changing suppliers may be limited because of commitment made to an integration partner. There is often a trade-off between flexibility and commitment. Increased commitment provides the potential of higher profits but is associated with a reduction in the ability to adapt to changing circumstances.

The process of actively dealing with suppliers or customers in the market place and of anticipating a supplier's technological developments and new customer applications can be extremely healthy. The integrated firm with captive supplier–customer units has a reduced need for that process (Exhibit 12.12). Furthermore, there is the reduced pressure on cost control.

EXHIBIT 12.12   INTEGRATIVE GROWTH STRATEGIES

	Current products	New products
Current markets	Backward integration	Horizontal integration
New markets	Forward integration	Unrelated acquisition

FURTHER DEVELOPMENTS OF THE ANSOFF MATRIX

Egan (1998) has extended the Ansoff matrix to incorporate other contemporary issues such as product augmentation, acquisition and internationalization but still stays within Ansoff's two by two format (Exhibit 12.13). The new matrix differentiates between organic and acquisitive market penetration. The former indicates reaching more of the target users through growth in the core, existing product offering. Acquisition, it is argued, if not a new product is an extended offering. It is only if a product is truly of a generic unbranded nature that it can be regarded as offering the same product. Egan places the concept of vertical integration in the area of diversification. Aaker (1995) views this fundamentally differently. He places vertical integration as a third dimension to Ansoff's matrix. Vertical integration, he implies, can occur alongside penetration, product or market development.

Aaker uses the example of the forward integration of Nike into opening retail outlets and backward integration of Safeway into in-store bakeries. These, he suggests, constitute a new dimension to market penetration strategy. Egan's argument concludes that this is really diversification since the new product is in fact the retail experience rather than the item purchased.

Vertical integration may be performed for reasons of increasing economic power (i.e. reducing costs, supplier or distributor power) or improving competitive intensity. However, Stein *et al.* (1996) suggest that vertical integration is not necessarily the best answer since the same outcome can be achieved more cost effectively through improved supply chain arrangements.

GRAND STRATEGY MATRIX (GSM)

Another useful tool is 'The Grand Strategy Matrix' (GSM: see Figure 12.4). The matrix considers two parameters, namely

EXHIBIT 12.13   EGAN'S EXTENSION OF THE ANSOFF MATRIX

	Current products	*New products*
Current markets	Penetration – organic – acquisition	Product augmentation
	Market expansion – increase usage rejuvenate PLC	Product development – related – unrelated
New markets	Market development – new uses – new users	Diversification – related – conglomerate
		Vertical integration Internationalization

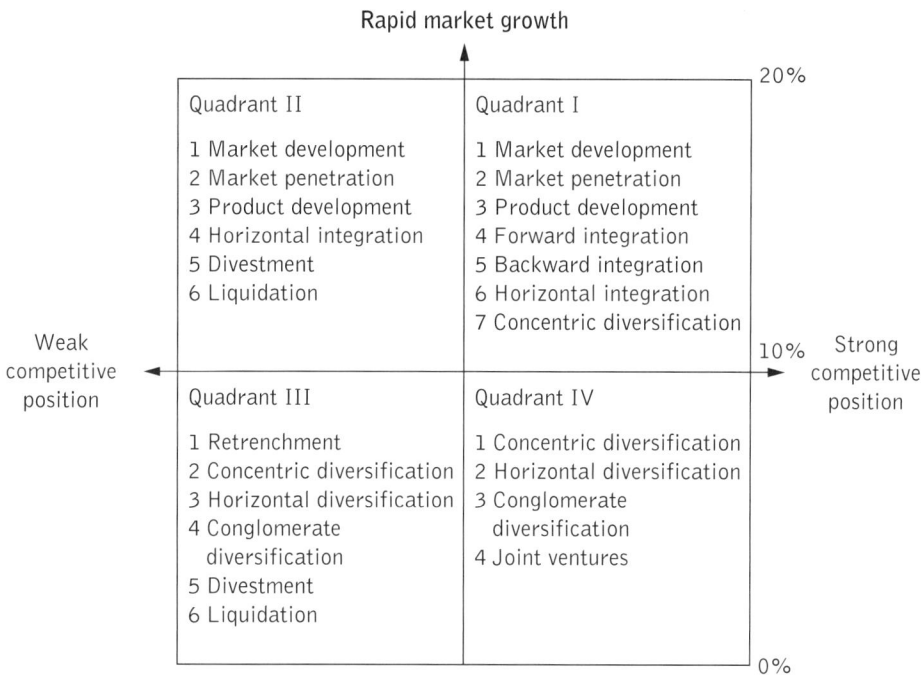

Figure 12.4   *The Grand Strategy Matrix*

Source: David, Fred R. *Strategic Management: Concepts and Cases*, 9th Edition, © 2003, p. 215, by permission of Pearson Education, Inc., Upper Saddle River, NJ.

■ competitive position
■ market growth

(See the Boston Consultancy Grid and Directional Policy matrices in Chapter 2.)

Competitive position could be measured by a Directional Policy Matrix. The GSM matrix indicates 'appropriate' strategies for the organisation or business unit in order of attractiveness.

Quadrant 1 (SO)

Here a firm is in a strong strategic and competitive position in a high growth market. An organization in this position should concentrate on its current markets and products, e.g. *market development*, *market penetration*, *product development*. Of course an organization or business unit may wish to change its position for a number of reasons. For example, it may wish to apply excess resources (physical, financial, human) to a more profitable activities. A narrow product portfolio may indicate the need for *concentric diversification* to safeguard its future prosperity.

Quadrant 2 (WO)

In this situation while there may be opportunities for expansion an organization may be relatively weak in terms of its resources at its disposal, the strength of its products or services or its management capabilities. In such a situation an intensive strategy may be advisable but there may be other possible options including horizontal integration possibly in collaboration or alliance with another organization that can make up for these weaknesses. If the organization cannot find a competitive advantage to exploit the market growth then divestment and even liquidation may even be the only other options.

Quadrant 3 (WT)

An organization in this quadrant has a weak competitive position and is competing in slow growth industries. The options are divestment or liquidation though retrenchment and even diversification may be possible if exit costs are too high.

Quadrant 4 (ST)

Here an organization has competitive strength but operates in low growth industries. The best move would be into a more attractive industry by concentric, horizontal or possibly conglomerate diversification.

EVALUATING GROWTH STRATEGIES

While the A-T-R model described above is a useful tool there are also other financial approaches to evaluating growth development alternatives. In essence the central aim is to identify costs and benefits associated with the available alternatives and, taking account of the differences among the various alternatives, to decide upon the course of action that is most appropriate for the organization.

Effect on cash flow is a major concern when examining alternative courses of action. One needs to treat each alternative as a project and estimate the nature of anticipated cash flows over the period of time that the project is likely to be alive. Initial and end of project flows have to be taken into account as well as inflows and outflows of cash during the time the project is up and running. Initial investment and one time set up costs may be needed at the beginning while there may be disposal costs and shut down costs at the end of the project and even inflows of cash resulting from selling equipment at scrap or residual values.

There are a number of methods that can be used to appraise projects. These include the *payback period method*, the *average rate of return* method and the *discounted cash flow method*. The *payback period* method is simple to use but ignores profitability so that its use in the context we wish to consider is only really useful for non-profit making organizations. The *average rate of return* method does take account of profitability but does not take into account the timing of benefits. *Discounted cash flow* methods make up for the limitations in the other two approaches. We will illustrate each method in turn.

Payback period method

Suppose a Council runs a sports centre and wants to expand its existing facilities but has a limited budget to spend in order to do so. Imagine that there are two possible projects that can be considered – expansion to the range of non-aquatic sports facilities available and expansion of the swimming facilities. The life of the project is put at 10 years in each case and account has to be taken of different charging and running costs. The projected net cash flows for the two projects are shown in Table 12.2.

Initial investments are shown as an outflow in year – £50,000 in the case of non-aquatic sports facilities and £60,000 in the case of the swimming facilities. The surplus in cash flow is shown in each of the next 10 years for both projects. It will be observed that in the case of the non-aquatic sports facilities then the initial investment of £50,000 will not be recovered until the end of year 5 (as indicated by the bold figure in the table) and that in the case of the swimming facilities it will be some time during year 6 when the initial investment (£60,000) will be recovered since in this last case only £55,000 will have been recovered by the end of year 5.

The analysis provides interesting information since both projects will generate the same surplus of £50,000 by the end of their lives. The decision taken with regard to the projects will be affected by many other factors, of course, and the criterion of payback time will be only one such factor.

Average rate of return method

This approach enables one to evaluate alternative strategies by comparing the return on the original sum invested in each and every instance. Using the example above again then we have the data shown in Table 12.3. This would indicate that expanding the sports facilities offers the better returns in financial terms. But of course there may be other considerations, too, particularly since in this case profitability may not necessarily be an important criterion. However, in the case of a privately run sports centre it would certainly be relevant.

Table 12.2 *Projected net cash flows for two projects (payback period)*

Year	Non-aquatic: sports facility improvement	Swimming facilities improvement
	£000	£000
0	−50	−60
1	10	11
2	10	11
3	10	11
4	10	11
5	**10**	11
6	10	**11**
7	10	11
8	10	11
9	10	11
10	10	11
Total 1–10	100	110

Table 12.3 *Average rate of return method*

	Non-aquatic sports facility improvement	Swimming facilities improvement
Period	*£000*	*£000*
Initial investment	−50	−60
Cash flow over the life of the project (years 1–10)	100	110
Net inflow	100	100
Average annual inflow Net Inflow/10	10	10
Average rate of return (Average inflow/initial investment) as a %	10/50 = 20%	10/60 = 16.7%

Discounted cash flow

Money we receive today is worth more than the same amount of money we receive in the future. This principle reflects the fact that any money can be invested and earn interest for the period it is invested so it must be more valuable than the same amount received at a later date. The discounted cash flow principle takes into account this factor.

In applying this method one can either use the *net present value approach* or the more sophisticated *yield method*. In the case of the *net present value approach* the present values for future cash flows are calculated assuming a given rate of discount. This is usually the minimum rate that the organization considers acceptable. One calculates the *net present value* of the cash flows each period and sums these over the period of the project. As long as the summed amount remains positive then it will have met with or exceeded the rate of return criterion as reflected in the discount rate used. Applying the *yield method* involves uncovering the discount rate at which the sum of all the discounted values is zero and this reflects *the internal rate of return of the project*. Using the above example again and using a discount factor of 15 per cent as the minimum acceptable discount factor produces the results shown in Table 12.4.

Using the net present value approach shows that both projects failed to exceed the 10 per cent minimum rate of return set down by the organization but that the non-aquatic sports facilities improvements seems to offer the better return on investment since the value of −4.3 for this option in the table is greater than that of −9.71 for the swimming pool facilities improvements.

The actual *yield* of the two projects individually can be determined experimentally with the aid of a spreadsheet by increasing the discount rate until the total net present value of the project equates to zero. Since this will be less than the minimum requirement of a 10 per cent return in both cases then on purely financial terms both projects might reasonably be rejected. However, there may be reasons other than financial ones for giving the go ahead for one or other of the two projects.

Table 12.4 Minimum acceptable discount factor

Year		Non-aquatic sports facilities improvements	Non-aquatic sports facilities improvements	Swimming facilities improvments	Swimming facilities improvments
(£000)	Discount factor (10%)	Cash flow	Present value	Cash flow	Present value
0	1	−50	−50	−60	−60
1	0.909	10	9.09	11	10
2	0.756	10	7.56	11	8.33
3	0.631	10	6.31	11	6.94
4	0.526	10	5.26	11	5.78
5	0.438	10	4.38	11	4.82
6	0.365	10	3.65	11	4.02
7	0.304	10	3.04	11	3.35
8	0.254	10	2.54	11	2.79
9	0.211	10	2.11	11	2.32
10	0.176	10	1.76	11	1.94
Total net present value			−50 + 45.7 = −4.3		−60 + 50.29 = −9.71

COST BENEFIT ANALYSIS

Cost benefit analysis usually involves trying to evaluate opportunities using measures that are not directly comparable with one another. If everything could be measured, say, in simple financial terms then comparisons would be relatively easy to make. However, since this is not always possible, an alternative is to make use of subjective judgements using ratings and weightings for the different criteria. In the example shown (Figure 12.5) below, a 10-point scale is used to evaluate the options and the scores are then weighted to obtain an overall value for benefits and costs.

The data supports the view that as far as the firm is concerned Poland, Romania, Austria and Greece are not attractive propositions. None of the other countries seem anything like as attractive as the home market (in this instance the United Kingdom). However, Germany and the Scandanavian countries may be worth further consideration.

QUESTIONS

1 How might the Ansoff matrix be usefully employed when looking for new marketing strategies?

2 In what order should an organization consider the various strategic approaches which make up the Ansoff matrix along with integrative strategies. In particular when is each one most appropriate?

3 What is a new product? What is a new product success? How can risk of failure in introducing products to the market be minimized?

Cost benefit analysis – international sales

Country	Costs — Learn Language	Laws	Volatile Currency	Political/Legal Uncertainties	Design products to suit market customers	Benefits — Deter Competition	High Profits	Grow Sales	Reduce Dependency	Costs (10 = high)	Total Costs	Total benefits	Benefits /costs ratio
Weighting	1.1	1.2	1.5	1.6	1.4	0.8	1.6	1.4	1.4	1.7			
France	5	6	1	1	2	1	4	5	5	5	18.6	22.7	1.22043011
Germany	6	6	1	1	2	6	5	5	5	5	19.7	28.3	1.43654822
Spain	5	5	1	2	3	2	5	5	5	5	20.4	25.1	1.23039216
Italy	6	6	1	2	3	2	6	5	5	5	22.7	26.7	1.17621145
Belgium	5	5	1	2	2	0	6	5	5	5	19	25.1	1.32105263
United Kingdom	0	5	1	0	0	4	5	5	5	5	7.5	26.7	3.56
Holland	5	6	2	1	1	0	3	5	5	5	17.2	20.3	1.18023256
Denmark	3	6	2	1	1	0	4	5	5	5	16.5	21.9	1.32727273
Sweden	3	5	2	1	1	0	4	5	5	5	15.3	21.9	1.43137255
Norway	3	6	2	1	1	0	5	5	5	5	16.5	23.5	1.42424242
Finland	3	5	1	1	1	0	3	5	5	5	15.3	20.3	1.32679739
Greece	6	7	1	2	3	0	4	5	5	5	23.9	21.9	0.91631799
Portugal	6	6	2	2	3	4	3	5	5	5	22.7	23.5	1.03524229
Poland	7	7	3	3	3	4	3	5	5	5	28.1	23.5	0.83629893
Roumania	7	7	1	4	3	0	2	5	5	5	31.2	18.7	0.59935897
Austria	5	7	1	2	2	0	2	5	5	5	21.4	18.7	0.87383178
Switzerland	2	5	1	1	1	0	2	5	5	5	12.7	18.7	1.47244094
Cyprus	1	7	2	1	1	0	3	5	5	5	15.5	20.3	1.30967742

0 = low   10 = high

Costs:
1 Need to learn another country's language
2 Understand laws
3 Deal with volatile currencies
4 Face political and legal uncertainties
5 Design their products to suit different customer needs and expectations

Benefits:
1 Prevent foreign competitors offering superior products or lower prices might attack the company's domestic market
2 Some foreign markets present higher profit opportunities than the domestic market
3 Grow sales and recognize the benefits to be gained from economies of scale
4 Reduce its dependence on any one market so as to reduce risk arising from such over reliance on a domestic market

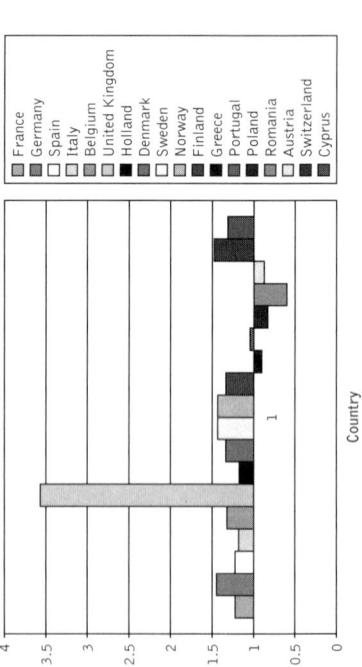

Cost benefit analysis

Legend: France, Germany, Spain, Italy, Belgium, United Kingdom, Holland, Denmark, Sweden, Norway, Finland, Greece, Portugal, Poland, Romania, Austria, Switzerland, Cyprus

Benefit/cost ratio — Country

Figure 12.5 Cost benefit analysis

4   Diversification is simply a form of horizontal integration. To what extent would you agree with this point of view?

5   What are the benefits and disadvantages of vertical integration? How might the advantages best be sought in the twenty-first century?

6   Using the yield method calculate the internal rate of return of the two projects illustrated in the text above. What other factors might govern whether or not one or other of the projects might be implemented?

CASE STUDIES

Remote Applications

People are getting lazier – or is it that they need more time to relax? Or is it simply that manufacturers think that people are getting lazier? Or think that people need more time to relax? It may just simply be part of the convenience culture that has grown up over the past forty years. First, there was remote controlled television – switching the TV receiver controls on/off/over from a distance. Next the same principle was applied to video recorders. Cameras, too, began to appear which could be operated from a distance. No longer was there any need to ask a passer-by to photograph one when travelling alone or needing to be photographed with another person. The new device enabled one to set up the camera so that it would point at the spot where you were going to take your picture, then on returning to the spot, at the flick of a button, one could then photograph oneself. No longer was there any need to rush back to the spot for a timer on the camera to perform the same function. Remote control devices have taken different forms and operated in different ways. Sensors on outdoor lights can pick up the presence of people nearby and automatically switch themselves on to illuminate possible intruders to the premises. Garage doors can be made to open automatically in response to flashes from car headlights – and so on.

Founded in 1993, Remote Applications defines its business as that of improving convenience in the home. Essentially an electronics-based company, it has invented a device which enables the user to convert any appliance to remote control. The device itself consists of two parts – an adaptor that one plugs into any mains power socket or light fitting and a remote control device that fits into the palm of the hand. Activating the latter enables one to switch an appliance on or off at a distance of up to 25 metres.

The equipment enables one to turn appliances on or off from the comfort of one's armchair or to boil a kettle before one gets up. It enables one to switch on the greenhouse heater from the comfort of one's kitchen in the winter and a myriad of other similar actions it is preferable to do from a distance. Indeed the applications are virtually endless.

The handheld controllers use powerful radio signals that transmit their power even through walls and ceilings. Each one is pre-programmed with security codes so that it will not interfere with other remote controlled appliances or devices. The controllers are also pre-fitted with a 12 V battery for immediate usage. Two types of adaptor are supplied – one for mains plug sockets and the other for bayonet bulb light fittings. The adaptors are controlled in a choice of three ways, either by the remote handset, by an instant-fit surface mounted on/off switch or via a wall-mounted dimmer switch.

The producer, based in Taiwan, is looking for a marketing strategy to introduce the devices into European markets. Key decisions relate to pricing, promotion and distribution.

QUESTIONS

1 How should the company set about marketing its products?
2 What steps do you think the firm should take prior to launching such a product?
3 Do you think that there really is a world-wide market for this product? Why or why not?
4 What would you see as being the major application for such a product?

Surplus Garden Furniture

The Gardening Experience owns a chain of gardening superstores selling a wide range of gardening equipment, furniture and plants and shrubs across the whole of the UK. Founded originally as a small garden centre in Sussex the firm has grown now to a multi-million pound enterprise.

In recent times the firm has developed the gardening furniture side of the business. Its main competitors on this side of the business are DIY superstores most of whom market somewhat inferior quality garden furniture which typically lasts only for two to three years of usage by customers. The Gardening Experience chain's furniture is much more durable and known to last for much longer periods of time even with heavy usage by customers.

Forecasting demand for garden furniture is a bit of a hit and miss business since demand depends largely on sudden surges in fine weather. Businesses buy in furniture from foreign suppliers and hold stocks in anticipation of estimated average demand during the spring and summer months. In a poor year this means that at the end of the summer many businesses are left with surplus stock which is disposed of at prices at or even below cost to make way for new designs in furniture in the following spring.

The Gardening Experience is keen to expand its customer base and is considering entering international markets as a means of achieving this end. Such a strategy it feels would enable it to reduce the seasonal effect on demand and lessen the need to sell of items at ultra-low prices at the end of the summer since stocks could be transferred from one international market to another with comparative ease.

QUESTION

How would you advise the firm in matters relating to international marketing?

NEW PRODUCT EVALUATION

A firm is considering three proposals for new products to add to its range. The average of the worst and best estimate of net cash flows for each of the products is shown in Table 12.5.

Table 12.5 *New product evaluation*

Period	Product A cashflow	Product B cashflow	Product C cashflow
0	−100	−110	−125
1	20	25	20
2	25	30	30
3	25	30	35
4	25	30	35
5	25	30	35
6	25	30	35
7	25	30	35
8	25	30	35
9	25	30	35
10	25	30	35
Total	145	185	205

QUESTIONS

1   Which product appears to offer the best return on investment?

2   Assuming that the firm does not want to go ahead with products that offer less than a 20 per cent return on investment as measured in the answer to question 1, how would this influence its evaluation of the new products under consideration?

3   The figures in Table 12.5 show the estimate of cash flows associated with each of the products – that is the average of the worst and best scenarios. If the worst scenario would show a reduction of 10 per cent in the positive cash flows in all cases how would this influence the firm's assessment of the situation, assuming it wanted to use the worst scenario criterion as the basis on which to make a judgement.

Profit contribution forecast for pet food

A firm is introducing a new food for pet hamsters. It is estimated that the number of families owning hamsters is 4,500,000. Previous research indicates that 80 per cent of families are likely to become aware of the new food and of these 15 per cent will try it. The firm estimates that it can get 40 per cent of pet shops to stock the food. Of those families who try the food it estimated that 30 per cent will like the product and try more and that the number of packets of the food that a typical user buys in a year is 25. The revenue the company will receive at the factory per packet is put at 50p per packet and the unit cost at the intended volume is 15p.

QUESTION

Estimate the profit contribution of the hamster food.

Vertical integration

A firm is considering the costs and benefits of vertical integration as a means of gaining more control over the management of its products and achieving cost economies. Preliminary analysis of the situation provides the data shown in Table 12.6.

QUESTION

What might the preliminary analysis suggest?

Electric cars

Electric cars have been proposed for years but now they are more than a possibility. Some manufacturers have moved to the intermediate technology stage of combining electricity as a power source with traditional fuels but others have gone the whole way and begun to produce cars dependent solely on electricity.

The performance of electric cars in the past has always been the main problem when trying to assess their viability a product that will appeal to the user. The traditional image of an electric vehicle is that of the milk float meandering its way slowly around housing estates helping the milk delivery person perform his job. Fork lift truck in factories also come to mind. The whole image is one of bulkiness, slowness of operation and small distances that the vehicles can cover once their batteries have been fully charged.

All this is about to change! Battery power alone can now enable a two-seater sports car to reach 60 mph in 4 seconds, attain a top speed of 140 mph and travel up to 220 miles when fully charged. Of course these vehicles need many thousands of battery cells to achieve this kind of performance and the battery itself can weigh up to a third of the weight of the car. Cars also need to be made of very light materials. Nevertheless, so much progress has been made that a manufacturer now has started up a production line to produce these vehicles and plans are in hand to produce a four-seat family saloon.

From the consumer's point of view cars using only battery power will have some attractions and not least of these is the estimated running cost in terms of fuel and maintenance. Fuel cost are put at 1/20th of the average price of petrol in Europe and the 'engine' does not require oil and has less than a dozen moving parts. This is very appealing!

There are downsides to these new electric cars that depend on batteries alone, however. A range of 220 miles is relatively small. One might just about manage to drive from Liverpool to Birmingham and back when the battery has been fully charged, but what happens if one does get a flat battery on the return motorway journey? In addition continuous driving for distances of over 210 miles (roughly 3 hours motorway driving in the UK) are not possible and would require a long stop to recharge the batteries before the journey could be completed. So one does have to consider how such vehicles might be used. Daily commuting over short distance does not constitute a problem.

So what price tag should be attached to such vehicles? The manufacturer of the sports car set the price at roughly £45,000 for such a vehicle and quickly got advanced orders for the first year's production.

Table 12.6 Cost benefit analysis: vertical integration

	Costs					Benefits				
	Operating	Managing different business	Risk	Reduced flexibility	Inward focus	Operating economies	Access supply/ demand	Control product system	Profitable business	Enhance technology innovation
Weighting	1.5	1	1.1	0.7	1	1.5	1.9	1.3	1.7	1.4
Forward	2	2	2	2	3	2	4	7	4	5
Backward	4	6	3	2	3	5	5	5	3	3

Note: 0 = low

QUESTIONS

1   Is the solely electric car a viable proposition at the present time? Why or why not?
2   To which market segments is the car likely to appeal?
3   Does a car that uses the dual technology offered by electricity and traditional oil-based fuels have a better short-term future? Why or why not?

Chapter 13

Facilitating the implementation of strategies

INTRODUCTION

In this chapter we introduce the notion that strategic windows offer possibilities for opportunities to be shared with other organizations where it is of mutual interest to co-operate. Even the traditional idea of competition may be sacrificed in favour of collaboration and co-operation if the circumstances are right and it is mutually beneficial to all concerned.

In the last decade of the twentieth century, changes in the environment put a greater emphasis on collaboration and partnership between organizations as a means of enabling all to benefit from the independent strategies which they were pursuing. Marketing partnerships, strategic alliances and networks became fashionable ways of achieving this end. Such inter-organizational arrangements have fostered the need for *relationship marketing*. The emergence of networks of collaborating organizations linked by various forms of alliance has become a dominant form of strategic development in many different industries. The international airline business, for example, is dominated by a small number of groupings of airlines operating as competing alliances throughout the world.

One of the most significant trends in marketing thinking and practice during the 1990s has been the shift in focus from achieving single transactions to establishing longer-term relations with customers. Whereas transactional marketing is concerned with making a single sale, *relationship marketing* is more concerned with establishing a rapport with the customer that will result in repeat business and opportunities for further business development.

Service quality and internal marketing have both come to the fore in terms of importance as a result of the focus on *relationship marketing*. In particular, ways and means of assessing level of service quality have been developed and a whole new emphasis on internal marketing of the customer focus ideology has sprung into being. In order to get staff to implement the company focus strategy, management itself is now seen as needing to treat its employees as internal customers to whom messages and other forms of two-way communication have to be directed and received. The chapter introduces some of the current thinking both on service quality measurement and on internal marketing.

In essence, this chapter is looking in a broader perspective at how an organization can seek to keep the strategic window open by ensuring how its human assets – other organizations and its own staff – can best be applied to the opportunity presented by the strategic window. Through strategic collaboration the organization can gain access to markets and even products and services that it would otherwise find difficult to acquire. Internal development of such products and services might not be feasible alternatives given the organization's capabilities alone. However, it is often on the delivery of product and services and the use of the seven ps of the marketing mix that strategic collaboration can be beneficial. The organization's own resources alone for this purpose may be inadequate and the implementation of strategy is thus aided by collaboration with other organizations which are able to offer suitable expertise. However, collaboration alone is not sufficient. It is through good customer relationship management and an internal marketing philosophy and approach that the alliance or network heightens the probability of successfully implementing strategic marketing decisions. Good customer relationship management ensures a receptive audience for new product and service ideas. Good internal marketing helps to ensure that the entire network or alliance will be customer orientated which in turn will help to guarantee the best chance of implementing strategy successfully.

STRATEGIC COLLABORATION

Rapidly changing markets, new technologies and a shortage of skills and resources have made firms think in terms of building relationships with other companies so that together they can present a more powerful front. This has led to a shift from an emphasis on competition, to an emphasis on strategic collaboration. The latter varies, ranging from vertical channel relationships and supplier/ manufacturer collaboration, to horizontal relationships in the form of strategic alliances and joint ventures.

The new organizational forms resulting from collaborative relationships with customers, suppliers, distributors and even competitors are referred to as networks. In these kinds of organizational structures, marketing and other business functions are carried out by different independent organizations and individuals. Many networks have been created in the service sector and networks spanning complexes of supply chains have also begun to develop. Networks can be complex in nature and are often controlled and directed by management information and decision support systems which perform many of the command and global functions of the traditional organization. As a result, networks tend to be flexible and adaptable to change. The relationships among the firms in a network can include simple transactional contracts of the conventional buyer–seller type; supplier–producer collaborative agreements; strategic alliances or partnerships; consortia; franchising; and joint ventures.

REASONS BEHIND COLLABORATIVE STRATEGIES

Risk is part and parcel of business life and risk sharing with other organizations is one way of dealing with problems that risk brings. Risk arises in different ways. For example, the disappearance of market boundaries in the information industry illustrates this. Telecommunications, consumer electronics, entertainment media, publishing and office equipment industries have all come together so that the industry is an amalgam of other industries. Individual firms trying to compete for the attention of customers encounter problems where there is a widening of the range of customer requirements and technologies available to satisfy customer requirements. Products required often exceed the design, manufacturing and marketing capabilities of a single company. It is often not cost effective for an individual firm to develop internally the full range of skills and capabilities required to compete effectively. Indeed, such skills and resources are more cheaply available through alliances with other firms which can contribute their own core competencies.

Firms are also motivated to co-operate by the notion of *efficient consumer response* where emphasis is on category management instead of the traditional product and brand approach. Under this approach, the emphasis is on the elimination of weak brands, more efficient promotion by substituting value pricing for special offers; continuous replenishment systems to reduce and possibly eliminate stocks in the channel; electronic data interchange for automated ordering and information flow.

ALLIANCES AND PARTNERSHIPS

One can visualize collaborative business relationships in terms of a spectrum running from transactional relationships to complete vertical integration. At one end of the spectrum, a firm buys in goods and services from outside as an alternative to producing them internally. It might go outside for services such as advertising, marketing research and direct marketing. At the other end is the fully vertically integrated firm which does very little or no outsourcing at all. In between there are a number of different kinds of collaborative arrangements.

- *Partnerships* are alliances between organizations some of which may have a short-term focus and involve limited co-ordination, whereas others have a longer-term focus and move beyond co-ordination to integration of activities. Yet another type of partnership may be an arrangement viewed as permanent where each party views the other as an extension of its own firm.
- *Joint ventures* are alliances where the ownership of a project or operation is shared between the parties concerned. Some joint ventures focus on partners from different industries sharing innovative design abilities, technological expertise and marketing capabilities to innovate.
- *Vertical integration* is where an activity is fully owned by the core organization although the relationship may still be seen as a strategic alliance.

TYPES OF NETWORK

There are different types of networks, some of which are very important from a marketing perspective:

- *Vertical market networks* or marketing channel networks reflect traditional vertical channel relationships along with the focal firm that co-ordinates upstream supplier firms and down-stream distributor firms. The integrating firm often specializes in marketing functions and uses specialists for manufacture and distribution.
- *Inter-market or concentric networks* are encountered often in Japan and Korea. They represent alliances among firms operating in a variety of unrelated industries. They comprise institutionalized affiliations among firms operating in different industries along with firms linked in vertical exchange relationships with them. They are characterized by dense interconnections in resource-sharing, strategic decision-making and culture and identity. The centre may be a trading company – possibly functioning as the marketing arm of the network – associated with manufacturing affiliates, which in turn have large vertical clusters of subcontractors, distributors and satellite companies, and are often involved in technology alliances with competitors.

283

■ *Opportunity networks* comprise a set of firms specializing in various products, technologies or services that form temporary relationships around specific projects or problems. At the centre of the network is a marketing organization specializing in collecting and disseminating market information, negotiating, co-ordinating projects for customers and suppliers and regulating the network.

STRATEGIC ALLIANCES AS A COMPETITIVE FORCE

In developing marketing strategies in some markets one has to take into account that competition may be based on the relationship between alliances and the networks that they create and not between individual companies. Any analysis of competition should take this into account. Strategic alliances can go badly wrong and the strength and permanence of strategic alliances should be viewed with caution.

Other important factors limit the effectiveness of collaborative strategies. *The power relationships* within a network are important. If the locus of power does not suit all the parties concerned it could have a negative influence on the viability of a project or a strategy that is implemented. *Commitment and interdependence* reflect whether people in the organizations are really supporting the alliance and whether the mechanisms are in place for ensuring that there is commitment and proper liaison between the parties concerned. If this is not the case then the alliance may be very ineffective. *Trust* is required on behalf of all the alliance members. The network organization requires that each partner relinquishes some degree of influence or control over important issues. This is a key aspect of relationship management in a network. Network organizations should also be viewed in terms of behavioural issues like solidarity – unity of action among network members; mutuality – network members acting for the common good and receiving a pay-off in terms of benefits from the collaboration; flexibility, and so on.

STRATEGIC ALLIANCES: MANAGEMENT ISSUES

Collaboration and partnerships permit each organization to focus on its own core competencies and to benefit from the specialization of other organizations in their own area of expertise. Clarity in defining core competencies is essential and this can sometimes be difficult to do. Failure to accomplish this can undermine the purpose of the alliance. Choice of partners is critical and one has to take account of whether an environment of trust, commitment and co-operation between the members of the alliance is likely to occur (Exhibit 13.1).

An important issue for the marketing strategist is the impact of networked operations on the market orientation of the new type of organization and its ability to deliver the required levels of customer service and customer value. Where the primary motivation for collaboration is technological or supply chain efficiency, this may be a particularly significant concern. There is often a lack of clarity about how marketing is located and operated in a network organization and applying relationship marketing skills to managing the links between partners in the network is important.

EXHIBIT 13.1 CONDITIONS WHICH FACILITATE PARTNERSHIP

Success is most likely where there is:

- corporate compatibility – cultures and objectives mesh
- compatibility of managerial philosophy and techniques – in terms of organizational structures, attitudes towards employees and methods of working
- benefits for all partners
- similarity between the companies which facilitates inter-firm communication
- willingness to shut out others who are not part of the network
- shared competitors
- prior experience of successful collaboration
- shared end-users.

CUSTOMER SERVICE AND RELATIONSHIP MARKETING

Fewer new customers are to be found in many markets which are now mature or growing very slowly. Moreover, competition may be strong and the costs of getting new customers high. Customers that have been with a company for some length of time tend, on average, to spend more on each transaction, offer more opportunities for selling them other products and services and give better recommendations to their friends and colleagues than other customers. Customer loyalty is considered to be an important driver of success and increased profitability. However, customer loyalty and customer retention need to be distinguished from one another. Customer retention reflects only repeat purchase behaviour. Customer loyalty, however, is more to do with how customers feel about the firm – whether they trust the firm, whether they actively want to do business with the firm and whether they will recommend the firm to others. Customer loyalty is closely related to customer satisfaction. While retention can be obtained through discounts for repeat purchase and so on, getting high customer loyalty requires greater long-term investment. It involves emphasis on achieving excellence in the service activities that augment the basic product offering. Some of the reasons for customer defection are shown in Figure 13.1. To achieve customer loyalty firms must, among other things, prevent defection.

THE GOODS AND SERVICES SPECTRUM

Most offerings in the market place are some combination of tangible and intangible elements. Tangible elements can be seen, touched, smelled, heard or tasted. They constitute the physical aspects of the offer, such as the product itself and the surroundings in which it is bought or consumed. The intangible elements are often more elusive. They comprise the level of service offered in support of the tangible and the image or beliefs that surround the product.

At one end of the spectrum are offers to customers that are primarily tangible. These include packaged goods such as canned peas and light bulbs and consumer durables such as CD players and

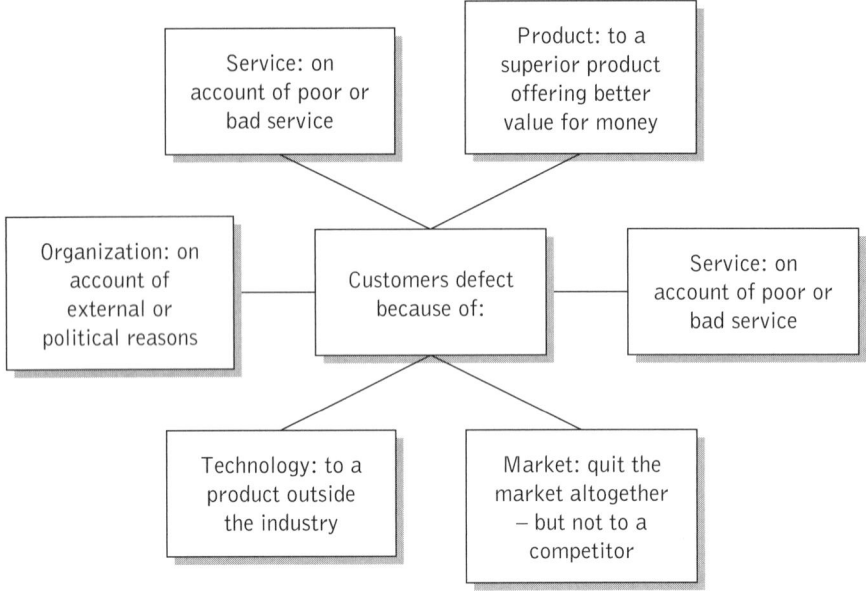

Figure 13.1   *Reasons for customer defection*

personal computers. However, from the perspective of the customer the benefits from the purchase of such items may well be less tangible – canned peas overcome hunger, light bulbs turn darkness into light, CD players provide entertainment and personal computers greater efficiency both at home and at work. The distinguishing factor is that these benefits are primarily delivered by the physical features and characteristics of the product. There are, of course, less tangible elements to such purchases. Tangible products are sold through retail outlets where sales staff may provide advice and demonstrations. Individual brands, through their media advertising and other promotional activities, will have established images and reputations in the minds of customers that may enhance value to them.

At the other end of the spectrum, intangibles are much more important. In legal services, the essence of the offer is intangible. It is concerned with the service provided to the customer and the way in which the legal executive interacts with the customer and third parties. There are some tangible, physical elements involved, such as legal documents and the physical surroundings. The essence of legal services, however, is the intangible process that takes place in dealing with the customer's affairs. Between these two extremes lie offers which combine tangible and intangible elements in more equal proportions.

More and more firms which are marketing essentially tangible products are looking to enhance differentiation through focus on the intangible elements of the offer. This includes branding the offer and the delivery of service to augment the physical product offer. Essentially, service providers, on the other hand, are recognizing that the type and quality of the service is the major means of differentiation. The line between tangible and intangible elements is becoming blurred so that the intangible elements are becoming increasingly more important across the whole spectrum.

RELATIONSHIP MARKETING

Relationship marketing brings long-term financial benefits to an organization. It is a means to an end and is based upon two economic arguments. First, it is more expensive to win a new customer than it is to keep an existing customer. Second, the longer the association between the company and the customer, then the more profitable the relationship for the firm should be.

Relationship marketing evolves ties between the organization and its customers to improve feedback and develop customer loyalty. Customers are open to the pressures of competitive promotions and may readily switch brands or store so a firm needs to establish a stronger relationship with customers. Relationship marketing tries to get customers to actively support the firm and its products and to encourage others to do the same. The aim of relationship marketing is to find ways of enhancing the mutual benefits derived from the relationship. Successful relationship marketing involves the targeting of customers of sufficient value to justify the investment in creating a relationship with them. Relationship-building resources can be directed to those customer groups where this is mutually advantageous. The strongest relationships are based on the establishment of mutual trust and respect between organizations concerned.

Getting employee commitment to the relationship-building and maintaining process is important since its success is in the hands of those who implement it. Everyone needs to understand their role in the relationship building, be committed to it and be motivated to ensure that it succeeds. This is the function of internal marketing which will be discussed later in the chapter.

BUILDING RELATIONSHIPS WITH CUSTOMERS

The moving of customers from the situation where they are simply prospects to the position where they are brand loyal customers requires an active and creative approach. Firms should stress to the customers the benefits which are to be derived from loyalty to the supplier. Benefits include discounts for bulk or repeat purchase or some other form of reward. Practical examples include store loyalty cards where shoppers can amass credits towards free purchases. Financial benefits, of course, are not the only mechanism that can be employed. Preferential treatment in terms of access to updated models or preferential treatment when purchasing or taking advantage of special offers illustrate the kind of benefits that can be offered.

Structural ties with customers which make it difficult or costly for customers to switch brands are useful. In the case of business to business relationships, some firms offer to rectify costly repairs to plant, machinery and vehicles at relatively low cost. In some industries the structural ties may be based on legal agreements and commitments, particularly where the use of protected patents is concerned. The sharing of knowledge and expertise that the client would otherwise not have access to also creates bonds between the parties concerned. Offering groups of interrelated products at favourable terms, for example, may deter brand switchers who might otherwise defect on a single product item. The essence of the whole approach is to create barriers to discourage customers from defecting and switching brands.

Getting people to realize that they are benefiting more from a relationship than they had initially anticipated can also discourage defectors. Customers need to be more than just satisfied with a product to remain brand loyal. To improve the probability of customer retention and develop loyalty one has

287

to deliver greater value to customers than they had expected. This demands a high priority to be given to customer service both in the strategies the organization designs and the action it takes in the market.

CHARACTERISTICS OF A MARKETING RELATIONSHIP

Relationship marketing is about healthy associations which are typified by concern, trust, commitment and service. Relationship marketers are concerned for the welfare of their customers and want to meet, or preferably exceed, customers' expectations, producing satisfaction or delight. It is vital therefore for firms to understand the expectations of customers.

Trust and commitment encourage organizations to work at preserving relationships. Organizations do this by co-operating with exchange partners, resisting attractive short-term alternatives in favour of the long-term expected benefits of staying with existing partners. Commitment is a lasting desire to maintain a relationship, and trust is the confidence that one partner has in the other's reliability and integrity. Relationship marketing requires an organization-wide commitment to provide high-quality service which is reliable, empathic and responsive. The framework incorporates the sequence shown in Figure 13.2.

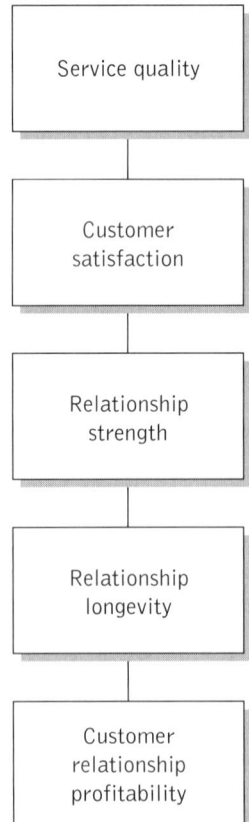

Figure 13.2   The ladder leading to customer relationship profitability

REQUIREMENTS FOR SUCCESSFUL RELATIONSHIP MARKETING

A supportive organizational culture is necessary for relationship marketing to flourish since the latter represents a paradigm shift from older, transactional ways of doing business. Paradigm shifts inevitably pose threats to and demand changes of existing corporate culture. Relationship marketing is characterized by mutual co-operation and interdependence between customers and suppliers. Under a transactional régime the relationship is better characterized as manipulation of customers.

Internal marketing is a second prerequisite. The aim of internal marketing is to convert employees to the new ideology of relationship marketing, to promote the development of the new culture, to persuade them that it is a reasonable approach to business, and to motivate them to develop and implement relationship marketing strategies. The internal market's expectations and needs have to be met. If the organization is unable to meet its employees' needs, it is likely that they will defect to other jobs before being able to build long-lasting relationships with customers.

The third point is that the firm needs to understand the customers' expectations. This means that there must be a continuous flow of information into the business regarding customers' expectations since these change over time.

Fourth, a sophisticated customer database is required which provides information in actionable format for the development and monitoring of relationship marketing strategy and tactics. Firms can use databases to track retention rates, conduct root-cause investigations of defections, segment their markets and establish retention objectives.

Lastly, new organizational structures and compensation or reward schemes may be required. The traditional marketing and sales function is organized around products or geographic markets. Under the influence of relationship marketing, organization around customers is more appropriate. Customer or account managers are better placed to build long-term relationships with clients, more deeply understand their expectations and build financial, social and structural links to the firm.

THE SEARCH FOR CONSUMER FOCUS

Within the retail sector, firms are moving into database marketing with their so-called loyalty cards. Supermarkets, in particular, have long been criticized for a low level of service and have been attempting to increase the service element in their stores and stress this in their communications. Initiatives such as Tesco's Clubcard enable the retailer to communicate with the customer on almost a one-to-one level and develop an offer which can be heavily focused towards individual consumers according to their purchasing patterns.

In two years from launch, British Airways' worldwide executive club grew from 100,000 to 1.3 million members. Starting as a lounge at Heathrow airport, the club is now based on card ownership and the provision of multiple benefits. The cards are linked to BA's customer database which tells the airline which seat is preferred by the customer, whether the customer is a smoker and the customer's flying history.

Renault's relationship marketing programme is mediated by the car firm's dealership network. Notes thanking owners for buying Renault, service reminders and special offers are printed on dealers' headed note paper and personalized.

The above represents the efforts of three organizations in their search for an improved customer focus.

CUSTOMER SERVICE: STRATEGY, SYSTEMS AND STAFF

A clear service strategy is needed which is communicated throughout the organization so that everyone knows their role in providing service to customers and clients. The strategy should demonstrate the organization's commitment to service and its role in overall corporate strategy. Often customers are using customer satisfaction measures alongside financial and other criteria for measuring overall performance, signalling the higher priority that they now give to customer satisfaction. Indeed, some of these companies now promote and reward staff on the basis of customer satisfaction ratings achieved.

Firms need to be committed not just to superior service in their strategies but they also need to put in place systems to enable their staff to deliver service to their clients. This may entail computer systems to share information rapidly and easily throughout the firm, or even simply queuing practices. The use of new technologies in improving customer service is a characteristic of modern-day enterprises.

Staff must also recognize the importance of customer service and must be committed to providing it. This demands recruiting, training and empowering employees to provide levels of service that will give satisfaction to customers. Rewards for staff are important but so also is the provision of information made available to staff – information on what customers require and how well the organization is providing that service.

PROVIDING SUPERIOR SERVICE

Research into customer satisfaction measurement suggests that customers measure their experiences against a benchmark of the service that they expect to receive. The quality of a service provision and subsequently the level of satisfaction of the customer is directly related to the gap between experiences and expectations.

Expectations may be used as comparison standards in two ways (Parasuraman *et al.*, 1991). First, there are expectations of what customers believe will occur in a service encounter. These are called predictive expectations. Second are what customers want from the service encounter, their desires. These constitute adequate and desired levels of service and between these two extremes is a zone of tolerance. A performance level above the zone of tolerance is likely to delight the customer and strengthen loyalty, whereas performance below the zone of tolerance will create customer dissatisfaction, frustration and ultimately may lead to decreasing customer loyalty.

A number of factors influence expectations. These range from the personal needs of the customer, through the alternative services considered, to the specific promises made by service providers in their bid to win business in the first place. Word of mouth communications with influencers and the customer's past experiences also affect the level of service expectations. In addition, expectations tend to rise with time.

The promises the firm itself makes prior to the customer using the product or service are relevant. Promising too little can result in failing to attract customers, whereas promising more than can be delivered may result in dissatisfied customers.

Exceeding customers' expectations

Customer expectations have to be exceeded in order to produce delight. This can be achieved by either providing an excellent service or product or by managing customer expectations' downwards so that the expectations can easily be exceeded. There are a number of ways of doing this. The first is to ensure that promises are kept or even exceeded. Closely associated with this is placing a premium on reliability – that is doing what you say you will do when you say you will do it. Another important factor is keeping in touch with customers to understand their expectations and to explain the limits of service possibilities. Communication can encourage tolerance, demonstrate concern for the customer and even serve to widen the tolerance zone (Exhibit 13.2).

EVALUATIONS

Parasuraman *et al.* (1988) suggest that customers evaluate a service provided against five major criteria: reliability, assurance, tangibles, empathy and responsiveness. Reliability is the ability of the provider to perform the promised service dependably and accurately – conformance to specifications. Assurance relates to the knowledge and courtesy of employees and their ability to convey trust and confidence in their technical abilities. Tangibles relate to the physical features of the firms providing the service. They include such things as: equipment, personnel, reports, communication mechanisms and so on. Empathy is the provision of caring, individualized attention to customers. Responsiveness is the ability of the organization to react positively and in time to customer requests and requirements.

EXHIBIT 13.2 BUILDING RELATIONSHIPS WITH THE CUSTOMER IN THE NHS

Ormsby district hospital has a notice pinned on the wall in every waiting area. It reads:

'This hospital is keen to ensure that customers receive the very best attention when waiting to be seen by consultants and other medical staff. Every waiting area has a board which shows the average waiting time that you will have to spend on the day of your visit before the person you have come to see will be able to attend to you. Unfortunately delays are often inevitable since emergencies do often occur and staff have to interrupt their pre-planned schedules in order to attend to the pressing needs of emergencies.

The nurse on duty will keep you informed of any delays that are impending and explain to you what is happening if the delay time you are experiencing is excessive. Please feel free at any time to speak to the receptionist in this area if you have any queries regarding delays or any other queries for that matter.'

MEASURING AND MONITORING CUSTOMER SATISFACTION

Complaint and suggestion schemes are one way of getting started on this task. Of course it may be too late to do anything about some things by the time a complaint has been lodged. There is thus a need for a more systematic procedure which may be able to pre-empt the majority of complaints from occurring. Some car repairers, for example, make a telephone call to everyone who has had work carried out on his or her car within ten days of the work being carried out. They check to see if the customer is satisfied with the work and if there are any problems.

Another method is the use of regular customer satisfaction surveys. The usual approach involves identifying factors that are important to the customer, assessing the relative importance of the factors identified and measuring customer satisfaction on those factors and finally assessing performance of the service provider on the factors important to the client. In this case it can be useful to assess performance relative to expectations directly.

SATISFACTION GAP ANALYSIS

Such analysis as illustrated in Exhibit 13.3 shows the ways in which a satisfaction gap can arise. By working systematically through the framework, the root causes of the dissatisfaction can be identified and remedied. A good starting point is to establish whether the provider really understood the expectations and needs of the client in the first instance. This could be brought about through inadequate research on customer wants and needs or through arrogance on the part of the supplier in assuming knowledge of the customer. It could also be brought about through poor internal communications, such that customer requirements are not passed on from the marketing researchers through to those responsible for designing the service that will be provided.

Where customer expectations are understood, they may still not be adequately catered to in the service specification. The design gap is the difference between what the supplier believes the customers expect and the service specification. This might be caused by resource constraints where a provider is too stretched to provide the level of service he or she knows the customer expects. Rather than admit the deficiency, the provider tries to get as close as possible to customer expectations.

The production gap is the difference between the service specification and the service that is actually delivered to the customer. There are a number of reasons that give rise to this. First, the service may be so complex that accurate delivery is not possible. Service promises may be unrealistic given the resources put into them. In addition, staff may not have the skills or system backup to deliver the service as it is specified. Poor employee training, poor provision of technological aids or even poor internal communications can result in frustrated employees unable to deliver a service as specified to the customer. Variability in terms of the ability of different employees, or even the same employee, to deliver a consistent quality of service is also a potential problem. Quality control is a difficult concept to implement as far as providing a service is concerned.

The perceptual gap relates to the customer's reluctance to believe that his or her expectations have been met when this is, in fact, the case. Poor tangible cues are often causes of this. It requires the service provider to demonstrate to the customer that the service really has been delivered and that expectations have been fulfilled.

EXHIBIT 13.3 ORMSBY MOTORS

Ormsby Motors' records indicate that less than 40% of its new car buyers remain loyal service customers after the first free service and the dealer is keen to increase the percentage to at least 50%. Some 14 different attributes have been identified as affecting patronage of a service facility and a small survey has been conducted among new car purchasers who have bought cars during the past two years. Respondents were asked two questions about each of the identified attributes:

1   How important is the attribute?
2   How well did Ormsby Motors perform in terms of this attribute?

Mean importance and performance rating from some 311 of 682 contacted previous purchasers are shown in the following table.

No. attribute		Mean importance rating	Mean performance rating
1	Job done first time	3.79	2.68
2	Complaints dealt with speedily	3.61	2.78
3	Warranty work attended to promptly	3.57	3.11
4	Can do any job required	3.59	2.96
5	Service available when required	3.42	3.02
6	Friendly/courteous service	3.36	3.28
7	Car ready when promised	3.33	3.00
8	Only necessary work performed	3.42	3.06
9	Low service prices	3.26	1.95
10	Clean up after service done	3.22	2.97
11	Convenient for home	2.46	2.21
12	Convenient for work	2.39	2.47
13	Courtesy cars available	2.32	2.33
14	Maintenance reminders posted	1.99	3.38

A five-point rating scale was used in both cases. In terms of importance the scale ran from extremely important (5) to not important (0). In the case of performance the scale ran from excellent (5) to poor (0).

From such analyses the firm is able to assess what action it needs to take to improve customer service. The items on the scale are regularly updated and added to an importance rating checked systematically from time to time.

SERVICE QUALITY MEASUREMENT

SERVQUAL has proved to be a popular instrument for measuring service quality. It aims to measure perceptions of service across five service quality dimensions identified by Parasuraman *et al.* (1988):

- tangibles
- assurance
- reliability
- empathy.
- responsiveness.

The instrument consists of two sets of 22 statements: the first set aims to determine a customer's expectations of a service firm: for example, 'they should have up-to-date equipment'; and the second set seeks to ascertain the customer's perceptions of the firm's performance: for example, 'XYZ has up-to-date equipment'. The respondent is asked to rate his/her expectations and perceptions of performance on a 7-point Likert scale ranging from 1 (strongly disagree) to 7 (strongly agree). The results of the survey are then used to identify positive and negative gaps in the firm's performance on the five service quality dimensions. The gap between expectations and performance perceptions (perceived service quality) is measured by the difference between the two scores (performance minus expectations).

A more recent version of the instrument (Parasuraman *et al.*, 1991) includes a third section that measures the relative importance of the five dimensions to the customer. These scores are then used to weight the perceived service quality measure for each dimension, the main purpose being to give a more accurate overall perceived service quality score.

Despite its popularity, a number of criticisms are levelled at the SERVQUAL instrument, aimed at both the conceptual and the operational level. Cronin and Taylor (1992) and Teas (1993) are particularly vociferous in their critiques, both developing their own measurement instruments. Based on a review of the service quality and customer satisfaction literature, Cronin and Taylor (1992) conclude that current performance best reflects a customer's perception of service quality and that expectations are not part of this concept.

INTERNAL MARKETING

For a firm to be truly customer oriented, it has to be employee oriented. Internal marketing is a management approach which enables and motivates all members of the organization to examine their own role and communication competence and to adopt a customer consciousness and service orientation. Customer orientation and internal marketing are complementary. Internal marketing appears to be a philosophy of emphasizing the importance of employees in the organization's efforts to satisfy its external customers. If the external customers experience high-quality service because of the organization's internal marketing efforts, they will repeat their purchase.

Internal marketing (IM) has the potential to provide management with valuable information in relation to organizational policies and procedures, and to their own behaviour towards employees (Parasuraman, 1987). It encourages people to find out about the needs of co-workers in the organization and helps people assess how they can satisfy those needs. It is suggested that IM means that firms must train and motivate staff to work as a team to provide customer satisfaction.

Parasuraman (1987) advocates establishing and maintaining an internal environment which motivates employees to respond favourably to management's decisions and demands.

Positive employee outcomes, e.g. feelings of satisfaction, are encouraged by management's support and by the extent to which the organization, through its practices and procedures, demonstrates a 'climate for service'. Indeed, it is suggested that effective service firms depend substantially on climate and cultural mechanisms such as shared service norms and values, in developing and maintaining service quality (Heskett, 1987; Shetty and Ross, 1985). It is the needs of employees that IM aims to fulfil. Research findings published by Bateson (1995) suggest that it is important for the provision of service quality that managers create two related but different climates: a climate for service and a climate for employee well-being. The climate for employee well-being serves as a foundation for a climate for service. In other words, employees need to be assured that their needs have been met before they can show interest and concern for meeting the needs of customers. IM is thought to act as a prerequisite for external marketing. Satisfied employees are motivated to deliver high service value, which then creates satisfied customers.

IM is concerned with what people as individuals want and expect from their work experience and what the business needs and wants to achieve, in terms of corporate goals. It is about aligning corporate and personal needs and interests, i.e. an exchange which is negotiated. The essence of IM is the process of negotiation to get employees to see themselves as part of the organization and then to make sure that the organization is consistent with what people can do and want to do.

The link between internal service quality and external service quality and hence customer satisfaction, customer loyalty and the profitability of the organization was proposed by Heskett *et al.* (1994). They proposed that high-quality internal services lead to increased employee satisfaction which in turn leads to increased service value, leading to increased external customer satisfaction. This is supported by Brooks and Smith (1993), Brooks (1993, 1995). Magidson and Polcha (1992) also discuss the problem of the inferior quality of many internally produced products and services having a direct relationship with the ability of companies to adjust to changing customer needs and meet competitive challenges. Equally, Azzolini and Shillaber (1993) propose that quality service to internal customers converts to quality service to external customers.

Some authors such as Rafiq and Ahmed (1993) and French and Bell (1995) suggest that IM has a wider scope than the motivation of employees towards customer consciousness. In particular, IM can be used to motivate non-contact employees to engage in behaviour which is aimed in serving the end customer in a better way. IM has the potential to be applied as a means for overcoming organizational resistance to change as well as aligning motivating and integrating employees towards the effective implementation of corporate and functional strategies (Rafiq and Ahmed, 1993).

In Exhibit 13.4, an illustration is given of some of the methods of implementing internal marketing within an organization.

EXHIBIT 13.4   INTERNAL MARKETING IN PRACTICE: AN OVERVIEW OF SOME OF THE METHODS THAT CAN BE ADOPTED

1   Informing the internal market about the organization's mission and its role within it.

2   Ensuring that the internal information and communication channels work effectively in order to sell ideas and services internally.

3   Implementing special motivation programmes directed at front line service providers that recognize that front-line personnel form a critical means of meeting competition.

4   Applying mechanisms that measure the gap between internal customer expectations and perceptions.

5   Recognizing a greater desire on the part of employees to play an active role in all aspects of work life that affects them.

6   Auditing employer–employee interactions: training, communication.

7   Developing internal audits to critically assess organizational performance with respect to the internal service and determine where performance gaps occur.

8   Using marketing tools and concepts (e.g. segmentation) internally with employees.

9   Getting managers to accept the need for understanding employee capabilities – their attitudes, knowhow and skills – and to participate in an IM strategy.

10   Continually striving to create an internal environment which enhances employee–customer interaction.

11   Establishing an open information climate in order to improve interpersonal, interactive communication channels and to apply an IM programme.

12   Using mass communication techniques – e.g. newsletters, videotapes – about new marketing strategies, etc. to provide employees with helpful information.

13   Initiating a programme to educate employees on important industry issues.

14   Viewing the development of knowledge and skills in employees as an investment rather than a cost.

15   Teaching employees 'why they should do things' and not simply 'how they should do things'.

16   Motivating employees through reward incentives to provide excellent service.

17   Demonstrating how the work of every employee fits the broader scheme of business operations and how their work contributes to the firm.

18   Continually practising internal market research.

19   Continually keeping employees informed of new developments within the organization.

20   Continually trying to define to employees, management's perceptions and expectations of them.

21   Encouraging employees to innovate without fear.

22   Encouraging the participation of employees in the use of quality management techniques across the organization.

23   Establishing a network service which answers employees' questions, fields their complaints, remedies situations, and alerts top-level management to potential trouble spots in employee concerns.

24 Using staff manuals, bulletin boards and meetings to disseminate knowledge about firm policies, plans and actions.
25 Seeking employee suggestions as to changes and improvements that would be beneficial in improving the level of customer service.
26 Taking actions based on what is learned from the internal survey.
27 Ensuring that there are sufficient objective indicators of IM results to be able to judge its overall usefulness.

QUESTIONS

1 What are the advantages of strategic alliances and networks over previously used methods of gaining access to new products, new markets and more diversified activities?
2 What do you regard as the key issues that need to be assessed when considering strategic alliances?
3 Is relationship marketing really any different to any other form of marketing? Why do you think it has come into fashion at the present time?
4 Customer service has become more and more important in recent times. Would you agree or disagree with this statement? Explain.
5 Discuss ways of measuring customer satisfaction with the level of service that is provided by an organization.

CASES STUDIES

Manufacturer ACI

ACI is a Malaysian manufacturer of a popular brand of spices, soup mixes, and flour-based products. Incorporated in 1984, ACI's annual sales in 2004 were RM87 million. At present, it has a total workforce of more than two hundred people. An entrepreneur who was a school teacher, initiated this business, and now he has succeeded in making the product a household name. Today, it has become more aggressive in its marketing strategies and is constantly developing new food products and food ingredients.

Its distribution channel is characterized by a total of thirteen subsidiaries responsible to distribute its products throughout the country. These subsidiaries distribute to wholesalers who will then move the products to the retailers. ACI has always relied on the wholesalers to provide intensive distribution for its products but now with more and more high-traffic outlets emerging. ACI sees the need to have one manager who is responsible in overseeing the supply and distribution of the products to these outlets through the wholesalers. Thus, they have created one subsidiary that is solely concentrating on the high traffic outlets. This direct distribution channel appears to work well in the present channel environment where personalized relationship is sought by the big retailers or the high traffic outlets.

The only contention that ACI has is how best to deal with the wholesalers who at times are demanding and only want to concentrate on the more popular lines of ACI products. ACI is currently aggressively pursuing product development where new products are being developed by its R&D division at a rate of two new products every three months. Although product failures are common, ACI is still pursuing this strategy in the hope that a new bestseller will finally be conceptualized to replace its current bestseller, the soup mixes. The sales of the soup mixes have somewhat stagnated and ACI is now looking for a new product that can be as popular if not more popular than this current bestseller.

ACI has no specific policy that requires wholesalers to market and distribute their whole product range. The wholesaler may be distributing more than one manufacturer's brands and there is no loyalty amongst the wholesalers to solely concentrate on ACI brands. However, ACI is optimistic that when new products are well accepted by consumers, the wholesalers are more inclined to accept a wider range of ACI products. This appears to be the best way of ensuring the support of the wholesalers.

Contributed by Rosmimah Mohd Roslin

QUESTIONS

1   Suggest various courses of action for ACI. Which course of action would you recommend and why?
2   What role is there for relationship marketing in the firm's operations?

Wan Mart

'*No hypermarkets in smaller towns*', reads the headline of the business section of the *New Straits Times* newspaper dated 17 February 2004 when the government imposed a ban on hypermarkets in towns with less than 350,000 people in a move to protect small retailers. Indeed, the emergence of multinational retailers, especially in grocery retailing, has changed the retail scenario in Malaysia over the last decade. If in the past, grocery retail formats such as supermarkets, mini markets and night markets dominate the Malaysian retail scene, consumers are now given the choice of shopping in large retail outlets in the form of hypermarkets and superstores. The small retail outlets are experiencing a decline in customers because of the many retail choices that consumers have. This is the dilemma faced by Wan Mart, a mini market that is still operating but with major changes in their retail offerings.

Wan Mart is a typical mini market situated in the heart of Shah Alam, a campus town located about thirty kilometres away from Kuala Lumpur. It is operated by a young couple who started the business in 1990. When they first started they were the agent for Ramly burgers, the manufacturer of frozen burger meat. They were not in the mini market business but rented a part of the mini market for their cold storage area from the previous owner who sold the business to them in 1990. They were then left operating both the mini market and the cold storage section.

Reflecting on their initial venture, the couple acknowledged that business was good when they first started. They were serving the people in the housing areas around the campus town and business was brisk and profitable. However, when GIANT, a well-known supermarket chain entered the area in 1991 their business was badly affected. Their customers were drawn to the relatively lower prices and the wider assortment of merchandise offered by the supermarket. Their business did stabilize after some time but the emergence of new, bigger and aggressive retail competitors has forced them to divert their retail operations.

They have now concentrated fully on their burger distribution as they find this venture to be more stable. Although still retaining their mini market, they are no longer dependent wholly on the mini market. Their relationship with Ramly, the burger manufacturer has been well established and Wan Mart has become the authorized agent for the supply of Ramly's products to the burger stalls and restaurants around the area. Wan Mart values the trust given by Ramly and sincerely feels that the firm relationship with Ramly is a reflection of their relational bond which indirectly dictates the path of their relationships, very much like the concept of *guanxi* – the Chinese philosophy of special relationships. The term (*guanxi*) refers to special relationships two persons have with each other. It can be translated as friendships with implications of a continual exchange of favours and this understanding has transcended into business relationships. Although, still retaining their relationship with key suppliers of their grocery products, the bond that they have with Ramly is special, one which they feel, they will preserve for a long time. Despite the problem with the bigger competitors in their retail business, they feel that the established business with Ramly will ensure their continued existence in the distribution business.

Contributed by Rosmimah Mohd Roslin

QUESTIONS

1 How are Chinese business philosophy and relationship marketing similar in their business outlook?
2 How might relationship marketing concepts help Wan Mart to maintain its successful business operations in the future?

Chapter 14

Marketing planning and implementing marketing strategy

INTRODUCTION

Research indicates that firms performing well have a greater ability to adapt to changes (viz Annunzio, 2004; Light, 2005) and to react quickly to the changes and possess a long-term orientation (viz. Light, 2005). Such organizations demonstrate that the strategy, structure, processes and people are aligned throughout the organization (O'Reilly and Pfeffer, 2000) and that they focus continually on improving and reinventing core capabilities (viz. Sirota *et al.*, 2005). In the case of small and medium sized enterprises recent research has shown that there is a significant association between a SME's approach to strategic planning and its business performance (Perry, 2001) and those who engage in a 'strategic' approach to performance management are likely to be more profitable (Roper, 1997) with a greater capacity to grow, innovate and develop new products (Joyce *et al.*, 1996). However, Webster, Malter, *et al.* (2003), observe that marketing has greatest influence and stature in firms where there are clear measures of marketing's contribution. The importance of having planning and control procedures to show the effectiveness of a systematic approach to marketing strategy implementation is thus underlined.

In order to get the best out of opportunities presented by strategic windows it requires a systematic approach to planning and implementing marketing strategies. What we have looked at so far represents the necessary background for the development of sound marketing plans and marketing planning procedures.

In this chapter we examine the putting together of the marketing plan based upon our analysis of the marketing environment and the strategic options that are available. The plan is the culmination of our analysis of the requirements of the strategic window and is related to the overall corporate plan of the organization.

Plans and strategies do not implement themselves and there are often problems in implementing strategies. There is often resistance to change and new ideas. First, we consider the various sources of resistance to implementing strategies. Next, we look at the role of communication in overcoming this resistance. This is followed by an examination of how strategies might be put into action.

Finding out what resistance and difficulties there will be is a precursor to introducing strategies. Getting people to accept the need for new strategies through good communication is a key element in the process of effecting change. The chapter looks at various communication models and methods which are relevant.

CORPORATE STRATEGY AND THE CORPORATE PLAN

The corporate strategy of an organization reflects its objectives and goals, and produces the principal policies and plans for achieving those goals. The corporate strategy normally defines the nature of the business the organization is to pursue which in turn has a great bearing on the kind of economic and human organization it needs to possess. Goals and objectives are usually set within a time framework.

Strategy entails matching the company's activities to its resource capability. There is little point in trying to take advantage of some new opportunity if the resources needed are not available or cannot be made available. An organization must formulate strategy within the boundaries of the resources that are likely to be made available. This is a fundamental consideration that must be addressed when formulating corporate strategy.

Strategy is also to do with the matching of the activities of a company to the environment in which it operates. Since the environment is continually changing, strategic decisions necessarily involve coping with change. The extent and speed of environmental change will vary and the pace at which strategy must change will necessarily vary too.

The corporate plan

The corporate plan is the plan for the company as a whole. It defines the business in which the company operates, indicates financial objectives that have to be accomplished, specifies how revenues are to be generated through various marketing programmes and assesses the various costs that will be incurred in achieving these objectives (Exhibit 14.1).

The corporate plan answers the questions:

- Where are we now?
- Where do we want to go?
- How do we organize resources to get there?

Defining the nature of the business in which the firm operates is crucial. For example, if Cunard had not seen its business as being that of transportation, it is less likely that it would have moved into containerization from its position as a provider of a passenger liner service.

EXHIBIT 14.1   HIERARCHY OF PLANNING OBJECTIVES

- *Auditing* – where are we now?
- *Objectives* – where do we want to be?
- *Strategy* – which way is best?
- *Tactics* – how do we get there? Implementation – getting there
- *Control* – ensuring arrival.

Goal setting

Goals must be realistic and an organization has to be aware of where it stands in relation to the competition and the various markets it serves. It also has to be reasonable in terms of specifying what it wants to achieve. For example, it may not be realistic for a small electronics firm to expect to grow to the size of a multinational company within five years. Nevertheless, in the Far East there are now some giant international corporations competing successfully, which did not exist in the early 1980s.

The first phase of corporate planning entails setting long-term goals in terms of sales turnover, profit before tax and return on capital invested.

Auditing

The next stage involves a management audit. All of the functional areas of management are audited: marketing, production, finance and personnel. We will restrict ourselves to examining the marketing audit here. A marketing audit amounts to an evaluation and assessment of all factors which affect the firm's marketing performance. The factors can be internal to the firm or can be part of the external environment.

The internal marketing audit

The internal audit comprises a detailed analysis by product/service of the market share and profitability of the various lines. Strategies relating to marketing mix elements are reviewed and studied together with the use made of marketing research data. An examination is also made of marketing budgets and how they were drawn up and related to previously set agreed objectives.

The external marketing audit

The external audit commences with a review of the general economy and makes an assessment of the prospects for the firm's markets. It estimates what should be the appropriate action taking into account economic and market indicators. Many factors have to be considered. Economic, fiscal, social, business, legal and technological developments all have a substantial impact on the business. In addition, market segments, channels, products, end uses, needs, tastes, attitudes, stocks and profits also have to be taken into account. Attention also has to be paid to the activities of competitors and potential competitors.

Gap analysis

Forecasting what is likely to happen in each business sector in the immediate and longer-term future is necessary. The organization must make predictions that take into account factors which are external to the firm such as market trends, economic trends, competitive trends, socio-cultural trends and technological trends. The implications of these trends are then compared with the likely performance of the company based on internal factors such as product strengths, material costs, technical ability, productivity prospects and financial capacity.

The next step is to project earnings from existing business over the time-scale of the forecasts and to make comparisons with the required objectives. For example, a manufacturer of wristwatch batteries would recognize that technology and the market demand for cells with longer life are likely to have an impact on future product requirements. The next step is for the firm to examine its current position. It would see that if it carried on producing the current capacity of battery, using existing technology, it would start losing sales some time in the foreseeable future as competitors introduce larger capacity cells or an alternative technology. It has to predict when the changes are likely to occur and what impacts these will have on its sales and profitability.

Predicted changes in technology often indicate the presence of a potential profit gap arising. That is a gap between what the firm wants to achieve in terms of profit and what it is likely to achieve on the basis of its existing portfolio of activities (Figure 14.1). Usually this will mean that there is a need to find ways of filling the profit gap by generating products and projects which will generate the required profit.

A firm has to relate the expected profit from any new ventures to the amount of resources employed to achieve that profit. The measure it needs to consider is the return on investment generated by new actions it may take. Return on investment for individual products can be linked to the overall rate of return on capital employed earned by the business. Performance of the firm in the latter respect is reflected in the general confidence of other firms and financial institutions in dealing with the firm in the market place and in the firm's ability to attract and retain shareholders' investments.

As a rule, firms strive to maintain their existing rate of return on invested capital. In pursuit of such an objective they should only accept new projects which promise a return on investment potential which is at least equal to the current rate of return on capital employed. Of course, even then, as its more profitable offerings start to decline, firms may not be able to maintain the existing rate of return on invested capital. In practice, of course, firms have to accept the best available projects. These may generate below the required rate of return with an inevitable negative impact on medium/longer-term profitability (Exhibit 14.2).

THE MARKETING PLAN

The final step involves developing the marketing plan so that objectives which have been identified and decided upon can be systematically pursued. The plan will vary from organization to organization

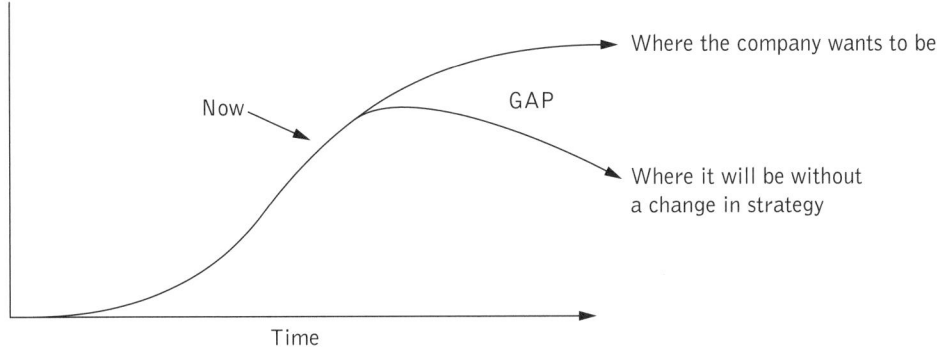

Figure 14.1 *Classical gap analysis*

Note: Figure shows the gap between expected and required profits

EXHIBIT 14.2   MARKETING AND CORPORATE STRATEGIES

Marketing objectives and strategies are subordinate to corporate ones. Some typical objectives are:

Corporate	ROI	Marketing	Market share
	Industry leadership		Sales level
	Share price		Awareness

and strategies of:

Corporate	Acquisitions	Marketing	Intensive distribution
	Investment in R&D		Market entry
	Global presence		Price leadership

and situation to situation. However, the composition of the overall marketing plan is such that it is built up from separate sub-plans. Sub-plans comprise:

- *A product mix plan.* This indicates product deletions, product modifications and product additions, when they are to occur, and the volume, turnover and profit objectives, broken down by product groups and even product items. Products may be grouped together and each grouping should have its own set of objectives.
- *A sales plan.* The sales plan specifies desired servicing levels for existing accounts together with targets relating to the obtaining of new accounts. Targets are broken down by area and by individual sales representative.
- *An advertising plan.* Where advertising is deemed important there should be an advertising plan. This plan should specify the timing, nature and amount of advertising to use by media. It should also include information appertaining to communications objectives, such as increasing the level of interest in a brand or achieving penetration of new users for each main brand.
- *The sales promotion plan.* This is assembled in a similar fashion to the advertising plan.

Other sub-plans could include physical distribution, market research and research and development, pricing and even regional plans.

Formulating the plans

With the exception of advertising and certain expense items, goals need to be established by region, district and salesperson's territory. Territory goals should be undertaken jointly by the salesperson and his or her manager. Sales goals are then broken down by weeks, taking into account seasonal variations. These then become budgeted figures against which subsequent performance is measured.

At the next stage, strategy and tactics feature predominantly. Strategy selection involves working out the best way to attain specific objectives. Tactics appertain to the specific action that must be taken, by whom it should be taken, when and within what constraints. Taken together they specify how the plan is to be put into effect.

Control procedures are incorporated into a plan and are concerned with specifying those measures in the organization which have to be monitored to assess how well a plan is succeeding. Control establishes the standards, measures the activities and results, compares the measurements with the standards, and reports variances between the measurements and the standards. This enables a plan to be kept on course and facilitates the kind of decisions that need to be made with regard to modifying the original plan if need arises.

Contingency planning is undertaken to specify what action will be taken if key objectives cannot be accomplished subsequent to implementing the plan. One must also be on the look-out for cases where achievements greatly exceed planned expectations.

THE NATURE AND CONTENTS OF A MARKETING PLAN

The marketing planning process tends to have the following stages and these are reflected in the plan:

1   corporate objectives
2   marketing audit
3   SWOT analysis
4   assumptions
5   marketing objectives
6   strategic options
7   appraisal of strategic options
8   recommendation of strategy
9   contingency plans
10   implementation
11   feedback/control.

Although there is no absolute prescription for the format of a marketing plan, the following provides an indication of a suitable layout.

The executive summary

The plan should commence with a summary of the main objectives and recommendations. Such a summary allows the reader to get to grips with the major thrust of the plan. Following the executive summary there should be a table of contents for the planning document.

The executive summary might point to:

1   The anticipated level of sales and profits in the planning period as compared with the same figures for the previous period.
2   The planned changes in the marketing mix which are intended to facilitate the achievement of the planned levels of sales and profits.
3   The level of the marketing budget, compared with that for the previous period, which will be required to achieve the planned levels of sales and profits.

305

The current marketing situation

This might comprise five sections:

1 *The market situation*. In this case data may be made available concerning the target market. It may consist of the size and growth of the market and trends that are taking place. Data might be shown for several years and certainly for all the different market segments – geographic and otherwise. Data might also be presented on identified customer needs and buying behaviour.

2 *The product situation*. In this case a breakdown of sales, prices, contribution margins and net profits for each of the major product lines over the past few years is required. Actual data might show such things as industry sales, company market share, average price per unit, variable cost per unit, gross contribution per unit, sales volume, sales revenue, gross contribution margin, overhead, net contribution margin, advertising and promotion expenditure, sales force and distribution expenditure, marketing research expenditure and net operating profit (Table 14.1).

3 *The competitive situation*. The purpose of this section is identify the major competitors, their size, goals, market share, product quality, marketing strategies and any other characteristics that are needed to understand their intentions and behaviour.

4 *The distribution situation*. Data indicating the size and importance of any new channels of distribution should be shown in this section, along with any developments or trends in distribution methods.

5 *The macro-environment situation*. This section should provide data on relevant broad macro-environment trends that have a direct bearing on each product line's prospects for the future. The trends might include demographic, economic, technological, political and socio-cultural factors.

Table 14.1 *Product line widgets*

Industry sales	2,000,000
Company market share	0.03
Average price per unit	£200
Variable cost per unit	£120
Gross contribution per unit	£80
Sales volume	60,000
Sales revenue	£12,000,000
Gross contribution margin	£4,800,000
Overhead	£2,000,000
Net contribution margin	£2,800,000
Advertising and promotion expenditure	£800,000
Sales force and distribution expenditure	£700,000
Marketing research expenditure	£100,000
Net operating profit	£1,200,000

Opportunity and issue analysis

Here the main opportunities and threats in the environment, strengths and weaknesses of the organization and issues facing product lines might be identified.

1 *Opportunities and threats analysis*. This is the part of the SWOT or TOWS analysis which identifies opportunities and threats facing the organization with respect to the product lines.
2 *Strengths and weaknesses analysis*. This is the part of the SWOT or TOWS analysis which looks at the strengths and weaknesses of the product lines.
3 *Issues analysis*. Here the organization has to review the findings of the analysis so far in order to come up with key questions or issues that must be addressed in the marketing plan. Issues might relate to questions such as whether the organization should stay in its current business; whether it can compete effectively; and whether it should maintain its existing marketing mix policies.

Objectives

The next part of the planning document might relate to the financial and marketing objectives that the organization wants each of its business units to achieve.

1 *Financial objectives*. In this case, return on investment aspirations, net profits and cash flow figures need to be provided for each of the product lines.
2 *Marketing objectives*. Financial objectives have to be expressed in terms of marketing objectives. This is illustrated in Table 14.2.

In order to increase the market share from 9 to 10 per cent the firm will have to set certain goals for increasing consumer awareness, distribution and so on. Market research data should be able to provide this kind of information and past experience will indicate what is required in the way of marketing expenditure in order to move the firm towards its sales and profit targets.

Thus in the case of the Table 14.2 example, the objective might read:

■ To increase market share from 9 to 10 per cent by selling 100,000 units, increasing the number of distribution outlets by x per cent and realizing an average price per unit sold of £200.

Table 14.2 Marketing objectives

Profit target	£2,000,000
Target profit margin	10% on sales
Sales revenue target	£20,000,000
Average price per unit	£200
Sales requirement in units	100,000
Expected industry sales	1,000,000 units
Target market share	10%
Current market share	9%

Marketing strategy

The marketing plan might be structured along the following or similar lines:

1 Specify the target market.
2 Indicate how the product is to be positioned in the minds of the customers.
3 Indicate how the product line is to be changed by the addition/deletion of product offerings.
4 Indicate the pricing strategy or strategies to be adopted.
5 Indicate how effort is to be expended to improve or change levels of distribution.
6 Show how the sales force is to be motivated, compensated or altered in strength in order to sustain the new selling effort.
7 Show how service levels are to be maintained, improved or curtailed in order to facilitate the achievement of the plan's objectives.
8 Indicate the nature of the advertising campaign that is going to help achieve the increase in level of consumer awareness, etc. that will eventually lead to increased market share achievement.
9 Indicate how the sales promotion is to be changed in order to stimulate consumer purchases at the point of sale.
10 Indicate how the R&D budget is to be altered to enable the market share to be sustained in the long term through the introduction of new products and new models.
11 Indicate what is to be spent on marketing research to improve knowledge of consumer wants and needs and to monitor competitor moves.

Plan of action

The points outlined in the previous section represent the broad strategic plan that is necessary to achieve the company's objectives. In this next stage, each marketing strategy element has now to be elaborated to show:

- what will be done
- when it will be done
- who will do it
- how much it will cost.

Projections of profits and losses

The action plan will enable the marketing manager to develop a budget requirement. On the revenue side it will show predicted sales volume in units and the average realized price. On the expense side, it will show production costs, physical distribution costs and other marketing costs broken down into fine detail. It will also show the projected profit based on these figures.

Controls

The final section of the planning document should outline the nature of the controls to be employed in monitoring the progress of the plan when it is put into operation. This section of the plan might also contain contingency plans. Such plans would outline what action would be required as a response to specific adverse developments which might have a profound effect on the achievement of what has been set out in the budget.

An alternative approach is set out in Exhibit 14.3.

PLANS ARE NOT READILY IMPLEMENTED

Getting new strategies off the ground can meet considerable opposition and it is important to recognize this. Resistance to the introduction of new strategies has many sources – fear of the

EXHIBIT 14.3   MARKETING PLAN OUTLINE: AN ALTERNATIVE

1   *Overview.* A brief description of the assumptions of the plan, its goals and the major actions to be taken. This should be short and to the point. Its purpose is to give the reader a quick snapshot of the plan, whether they are reading it for the first time or rereading it to assess progress. Anyone must be able to understand the plan from reading the overview.

2   *Background or situation analysis.* Those points of information that are the foundation for any action recommended. They might include: corporate goals, consumer or customer information, demographics, psychographics, economic factors and trends, product facts, company capabilities and limitations, competitive assessments, projections, personnel issues, research findings, etc. Any of these (and others) may be included but only those that are actionable or affect the plan should be in the situation analysis.

3   *Objectives.* What it is hoped to accomplish in measurable, quantifiable and actionable terms. They will be related to corporate objectives and financial issues that have been established independent of the development of the plan.

4   *Positioning.* This is the key to any plan. It identifies in concise terms what is being marketed, who the competition is, who the target is, and why a customer should purchase the product or service.

5   *Strategies and tactics.* Setting objectives and developing a positioning establishes what needs to be done. Strategies and tactics define how it will get done. Therefore, one must look at the situation analysis and define where action must be taken, then look at the positioning to see what that action might be. Strategies and Tactics are the actual defining of those actions. There should be at least one for each area one will take action in i.e: advertising, promotion, merchandising, publicity, packaging, research, etc. Each of these must have clear linkages back to the situation analysis, objectives and positioning. If the linkages aren't clear, the plan won't work. There must be budgets and timetables for every strategy and tactic and all must be quantifiable, measurable and actionable.

6   *Budget.* This should be a summary of the individual tactic/programme budgets you have already put together. It needs to be linked to the corporate financial objectives, showing how the contribution will be made to the overall financial goal of the organization.

7   *Evaluation plan.* Each strategy and tactic must be measurable and measured. In this way, one will be able to see what worked and what didn't. Evaluation must be done based upon pre-set, agreed upon goals.

unknown, lack of information, threats to status, fear of failure and lack of perceived benefits are examples of such sources. People like to feel that they are in control of what affects them and the more that change is imposed from the outside by others, the more they will see it as something to feel threatened about and the more they will resist it. People resort to using their last remaining power base – their will to co-operate.

Blocks to implementing strategies reflect such things as a lack of adequate resources to implement strategies, a lack of commitment and motivation in those required to implement strategies, resistance to change, procedural obstacles, perceived risk associated with implementing strategies, political undercurrents, lack of co-operation in the organization and so on. The important thing is to uncover what resistance is likely to arise and what the reasons for the resistance are likely to be. With this information one can look for ways of implementing plans so that the resistance encountered can be reduced.

ROLE OF COMMUNICATION IN GETTING PLANS ADOPTED

The key to effecting plans is to involve people in the process early, to consult with them and get them to take ownership of the new strategies that are to be introduced for themselves (see for example Coch and French, 1948). It is essential to understand the culture of the organization. New strategies that run counter to the traditional values of an organization are the ones that are most difficult to introduce. Organizational culture is the pattern of shared values and norms that distinguishes it from all others (Higgins, 1994; Kotter, 1997). One needs to think of the organization as an internal market for change initiatives where strategies have to be marketed. This means that opinions and attitudes have to be assessed and potential sources of resistance have to be identified. Commitment to new strategies can be instigated by helping people to develop a shared diagnosis of what is wrong in an organization and what can and must be improved (see Kotter, 1997).

Communication is the spearhead of ensuring that successful strategies can be implemented. It helps to overcome ambiguity and uncertainty and provides information and power to those who are involved. It enables them to have control over their destiny, to understand why the strategies are necessary and provides the suppressant to fear. Through open communication channels people can express their doubts about the effectiveness of proposed strategies and can understand the necessity for new strategies. Relying on an attempt to implement strategies only from the top is likely to meet with difficulties. Grassroots adoption is the only way to ensure that the process becomes firmly embedded. It is natural for people to resist change and by anticipating, identifying and welcoming resistance we convert resistance into a perceived need for the strategies.

PUTTING STRATEGIES INTO PRACTICE

Strategies may have to be sold to people who can authorize their implementation. This may make it easier to arouse subsequent motivation to implement strategies among those who have to do the job and make the chance of a successful implementation more likely. Putting strategies into practice usually requires:

1 An ability to get people to accept ideas.
2 An ability to cope with difficult obstacles.
3 An ability to plan and manage time in an effective manner.
4 An ability to create the enthusiasm and motivation to follow through strategies.

Persuading people to view new strategies in a favourable light when they are not readily disposed to do so essentially involves influencing and changing attitudes. To do this it is first necessary to convince people that they need to be dissatisfied with the *status quo*. It is important to note that people may not readily recognize that they are dissatisfied with the current situation. One cannot assume that people will readily accept that a problem exists, even when it is blatantly obvious to an outside person. It may be necessary to:

1 Create an awareness of problems that exist and make people recognize that there is a need for the new strategy and a need to adopt the idea that is being put forward.
2 Point out to people the potential hazards and pitfalls of not accepting the need for change.
3 Stress the benefits of change to the individuals involved since they will only be motivated to accept and to adopt new strategies when they perceive and acknowledge that it is in their own best interest to do so.

Effective communications need to appeal to the needs and wants of the recipients. They should give the recipients a motive or incentive to act. They also need to generate involvement with the message on the part of the recipients by asking questions which leave the message incomplete. In addition, they should also explain exactly what course of action it is expected that the recipients will follow.

Getting people to consider adopting new strategies can be achieved through appealing to their cognitive processes (see Burnett, 1993). One needs to arouse desire, indicate a need, or offer a logical reason why they should co-operate. In so doing the message becomes implanted in the recipient's memory and can be triggered by future needs, motives and associations. However, one does have to remember that the rational approach may not be so effective for some recipients or in situations where there is likely to be less involvement in the action required. In these cases emotional appeals may be used.

Post-implementation

One has to make sure that what has been implemented actually works for more than just a couple of days and does not fall down because of some oversight. That is not to say that there will not be complaints about what has been implemented. It is quite likely that the implementers will be inundated with messages from both people who supported the plan and people who were not too favourably disposed to the plan. Feedback messages about new strategies that have been implemented may take the form of:

- *Grousing*: this usually does not require action.
- *Errors of detail*: aspects of detail may have been overlooked. When the detail is not critical it is usually possible to remedy the situation fairly easily. Elements that are critical to the functioning of the whole, however, are more problematic and may require thorough analysis

and reflection. In some cases they may even temporarily hold up matters until they can be resolved.

■ *Apparently major errors*: these can be either real or supposed. In the latter case it is simply a case of reassuring all concerned that it is only supposition. Where the problem is real then the implementation of the whole plan may be at risk.

Strategies must be workable and reliable. Thinking through and testing out strategies before they are finally implemented is highlighted as a critical stage of the process.

QUESTIONS

1 A small firm marketing computer software is keen to introduce a system of marketing planning into its management process. What steps would you advise it to take in order to achieve this?
2 Examine the relationship between marketing planning and marketing control.
3 Getting good strategies adopted by management can often pose problems. Indicate the nature of the problems and outline the mechanisms that can be applied to overcome the difficulties presented by the problems.

CASE STUDIES

Folix: industry transition from 'growth' to 'maturity'

Folix operates in an industry that is experiencing a transition to maturity and there are fundamental changes taking place in the competitive environment. Unfortunately, many executives in the firm do not perceive the need for change, while others perceive them very clearly but are reluctant to make the substantial changes in strategy that are required. This is perhaps because they feel it has implications for organizational structure and leadership and that it is not in their own personal best interests.

The slow down in growth rates of the industry implies that the firm cannot maintain its own growth rate in the industry simply by maintaining market share. To maintain growth rate in sales, market share has to be increased at the expense of competition. This sudden change in strategy may be interpreted by Folix's competitors, who have so far coexisted amicably, as aggressive and irrational and may lead to substantial retaliation. Warfare in terms of price cutting, uncharacteristic promotional activity and novel additional services may manifest itself and this is not in anyone's interest. Another problem has been that as customers have become used to using the product they have also become more critical in their appraisal of the offerings and more brand aware. Customers' attention has moved from deciding whether to purchase the product at all to making choices among brands. The slower growth rate and more knowledgeable customers has caused competition to be based more upon level of service and keeping down costs.

During the time of growth and expansion, capacity additions to the industry were continual and regular. The situation has now been reached where over-capacity has occurred. Scaling down operations or at least careful monitoring of any further demands for increasing capacity have to be carefully examined. Over-capacity can lead to over-production and thence to price warfare to take up the production capacity.

The ability to find new products and applications has diminished and where they can be found they tend to be more risky and costly. A reorientation in terms of approach to R&D is required. There are also international competitors which possess different cost structures and these represent a powerful threat as potential new entrants to the industry.

There has been some general reduction in profit levels. The fall in profits has reduced cash flow and decreased the value of shares in the firm.

QUESTION

In trying to introduce a new way of strategic thinking into the organization there are obviously going to be many organizational problems that need to be met. Indicate the nature of these problems and suggest a programme for implementing the new way of strategic thinking which will also get to grips with the organizational issues that may raise obstacles to implementation.

Maturity to decline

One is apt to think that declining markets are ones from which firms are anxious to depart; in fact, they represent good opportunities for firms that tailor their strategies successfully to the demands of the situation. This is because declining markets are not as attractive as growing markets to many competitors and sooner or later scale economies may cause the larger firms to seriously consider withdrawal, thereby leaving an often relatively large market without major forces within it.

Kirkby Engineering Company (KEC) has been in business for the past 40 years. Originally founded by William Stacey the company is now run jointly by his two sons Samuel and John. The firm is based in Merseyside and serves a predominantly local market. The business of the firm is to machine parts for any kind of mechanical purpose. By and large its customers are to be found within a 50-mile radius of the firm's factory in Kirkby. Customers usually experience a breakdown of some kind with one of their machines and need a spare part to be produced. It is either very expensive to get spares from the original manufacturers of the machines or else spares are just not available. Not infrequently, the producers of the machines have gone out of business many years previously. This is not unusual as much of the machinery in British firms, and elsewhere for that matter, is quite old and spares are often hard to come by or not available at all.

The company recognizes that local markets and UK markets, for that matter, are declining ones. For many years the UK manufacturing base has been shrinking with more and more people going to work in services and other industries. This has particularly been the case on Merseyside and within the region defined by a 50-mile radius of the KEC factory. Another peculiarity is that the company feels that the type of business in which it operates is such that it is there to meet a relatively local demand. John Stacey argues that customers often want parts at very short notice and that they prefer to deal with someone who is not too far away. 'That is why we have remained local in our outlook,' he explains.

'Export markets don't mean anything to a firm like ours, because they are too far away and customers would not want to make use of our services.'

The size of orders taken by the firm varies from £30 to several thousand pounds. 'We prefer larger orders of course,' says Sam, 'but at the end of the day, a great deal of our business is these very small orders. We are in a situation akin to that of the traditional clockwork watch repair specialist these days. We like the kind of business we are in but much of the work we undertake is barely economical. In addition, we feel we have a duty to employ our staff to the end of their working lives. Some of the people we employ have been with the firm for close on 30 years.'

This kind of business attracts many firms and the firm still has several competitors even in Kirkby itself. There is no one dominant competitor, however. Although the firm does have a number of fairly strong established relationships with profitable customers, it does not have the advantage of a strong brand name, and is experiencing some difficulty in operating profitably with its currently under-utilized assets. There is very little room to cut costs as the business shrinks. However, it does have some flexibility in applying assets and resources.

QUESTIONS

1 What do you recommend is the best strategy for the firm?
2 Draw up an outline marketing plan for the company for the next three years.
3 What kind of problems would you envisage in implementing the plan and how would you try to overcome such problems?

Succesful SMEs

Arguably, success is a relative concept reflecting the expectations of those involved in a venture. What to some may be a success may not be a success to others. Success is something toward which all organizations usually aspire and hence strategies need to be geared to ensuring the achievement of such an aim.

The TOWS matrix (reflecting Threats, Opportunities, Weaknesses and Strengths) helps identify conditions under which firm have a good chance of being successful in the pursuit of their marketing objectives if they devise appropriate strategies. Less successful firms are often plagued with shortcomings in areas identified with the TOWS matrix and often with other managerial problems too.

The following are examples of firms that have claims to be successful.

Company A

The firm made its way by being innovative in terms of technological developments and venturing into international markets. By producing computer software for monitoring medical conditions, the firm achieved rapid growth and now obtains more than 50 per cent of its sales turnover comes from international marketing operations. The firm first concentrated on the UK market before venturing onto the European scene. The software it produces facilitates the monitoring of heart conditions and rapid diagnosis of different kinds of cardiac problems. This software has helped heart specialists in many different healthcare institutions both in initial diagnosis and post treatment recovery,

The firm wants to explore how improvements in software and related hardware in the field of cardiac diagnosis and monitoring can benefit customers further. The enterprise's plans for growth centre around developing this activity. It also aspires to build relationships with key partners in healthcare provision. Other plans involve expanding geographically and in this connection it has already built up a network of contacts in the US, Australasia and Far Eastern territories as well as in Europe.

Company B

The firm offers consultancy help with a range of management and technical problems. It operates throughout the UK though, initially, it concentrated on one region and offered its services to one single industry. In that industry, it identified those market sectors forecast to have a solid future in the UK. Now, it offers a wide range of high-value services to a limited number of clients in growth markets in different industries. Its strategy is very much one of finding profitable market niches.

The firm argues that a lot of its success can be put down to developing close working relationship, with clients, allowing it to appreciate their business goals and helping to develop services which provide innovative, cost-effective solutions for customers of these clients. Such an approach has allowed it to differentiate its offerings from competition, develop new markets, and fortify its existing partnerships. It has been particularly successful in establishing an expanding client base and high level of retained business.

QUESTION

Using the TOWS matrix can you identify how the firms have achieved their success in strategic marketing terms?

The Wildlife Centre

The Wildlife Centre covers an area of some 12 square miles and is situated in the eastern counties. Over the last three years it has implemented a marketing plan which was developed by the organization in conjunction with a business consultant who charged £12,000 for services rendered. Putting the plan into action over the intervening period has worked out at £41,000 a year. The plan involved promoting a new corporate image and accompanying logo. In addition there has been much in the way of printed information, leaflets, publicity and advertisements in local newspapers and on radio stations. During the period of implementing the plan a review of current service provision, training for staff, regular internal and external newsletters was also undertaken. The consultant considers that the marketing plan has been a success and has achieved its objectives which were:

1 To raise the profile of the centre in the eyes of users and the general public
2 To promote new revenue producing activities

3   To educate users of the centre regarding the wildlife found in the centre

4   To increase customer satisfaction with the facilities at the centre.

The Chief Executive of the centre has just received a report arguing that the investment in marketing has been warranted. A summary of the main points of the report are as follows:

Over the three-year period, the consultant charged £12,000 for setting out the marketing plant and a further £8,000 for conducting reviews of progress. The cost of implementing the marketing programme amounted to £123,000 and cost £72,000 in terms of staff time to implement. Administration costs amounted to £20,000 and management time was costed at £12,000. In addition there were postage and stationery costs amounting to £28,000.

Set against these costs distinct benefits were noted as follows:

Three years previously it had been felt that the centre was not well regarded by occasional users and members of the public generally. The organization was assumed to have low-quality services and inefficient staff. Now, it was felt that the organization had a positive image amongst all concerned. Over the last three years, there had also been a lowering of staff turnover, saving £15,000 in recruitment costs. Moreover, three years ago a customer survey had indicated 46 per cent were satisfied with the provisions of the centre while in a more recent survey it had risen to 75 per cent. Before the marketing programme had been instigated revenue-producing services netted a total income after costs of £60,000 per annum. Over the last three years net income had risen to £120,000. Prior to the programme, a great deal of staff time had been spent explaining about the centre and its facilities to visitors. Over the past three years there had been a reduction in enquiries of this nature by 30 per cent due to the availability of comprehensive leaflet. Reduction in enquiries represented a saving in staff time which had manifested itself in the saving of salaries amounting to £42,000. It was argued that the marketing effort had been very successful and had produced results which showed that there had been gains in monetary terms which totalled £177,000 as well as increased satisfaction among customers.

QUESTION

Comment on the report.

Bibliography

Aaker, D. (1995), *Strategic Marketing Management*, 4th edn, Chichester: John Wiley.

Aaker, D. and Shanby, J. (1982), 'Positioning your product', *Business Horizons*, 25: 56–62.

Abell, D.F. (1978), 'Strategic windows', *Journal of Marketing*, 42(2): 21–6.

Achrol, R.S. (1991), 'Evolution of the marketing organisation: new forms for turbulent environments', *Journal of Marketing*, 55: 77–93.

Ackoff, R.L. and Vegara, E. (1988), 'Creativity in problem solving and planning', in R.L. Kuhn (ed.), *Handbook for Creative and Innovative Managers*, New York: McGraw-Hill.

Adams, J.L. (1974), *Conceptual Blockbusting*, New York: W.H. Freeman.

Annunzio, S.L. (2004), *Contagious Success: Spreading High Performance throughout Your Organization*, London: Portfolio Penguin Books.

Ansoff, H.I. (1987), *Corporate Strategy*, revised edn, Harmondsworth: Penguin.

Antil, J.H. (1988), 'New product or service adoption: when does it happen', *Journal of Consumer Marketing*, 9: 5–16.

Arnold, J.E. (1962), 'Education for innovation', in S.J. Parnes and H.F. Harding (eds), *A Source Book for Creative Thinking*, New York: Scribner.

Assael, H. (1987), *Consumer Behaviour and Marketing*, Boston: Kent Publishing.

Azzolini, M. and Shillaber, J. (1993), 'Internal service quality: winning from the inside out', *Quality Progress*, November: 75–8.

Barksdale, H.C. and Harris, C.E. (1982), 'Portfolio analysis and the product life cycle', *Journal of Long Range Planning*, 15(6): 35–64.

Bass, F. (1969), 'A new product growth model for consumer durables', *Management Science*, 15, January: 215–27.

Bateson, J.E.G. (1995), *Marketing Services: Marketing Text and Readings*, Orlando, FL: Dryden Press.

Bennis, W. and Nanus, B. (1985), *Leaders: The Strategies for Taking Charge*, New York: Harper & Row.

Boston Consulting Group (1979), *Specialization*, Boston: BCG.

Boston Consulting Group (2006) *Innovation*, Boston: BCG.

Branson, R. (1998), Addressing an audience at the Harvard Business School in the autumn as reported in the *Harvard Business School Bulletin*, February 1999.

Brooks, R.F. (1993), 'Internal service quality: a manufacturing perspective', *Proceedings of the Marketing Education Group*, Loughborough, pp. 93–4.

Brooks, R.F. (1995), 'Internal service quality: a theoretical development', *Proceedings of the Marketing Education Group*, Bradford, pp. 80–90.

Brooks, R.F. and Smith J.V. (1993), 'Service from within', *TQM Journal*, October: 41–5.

Brown, S. (1994), 'Marketing as multiplex: screening postmodernism', *European Journal of Marketing*, 28(9–9): 27–51.

Brown, S. (1999), 'Postmodernism: the end of marketing', in D. Brownlie, M. Saren, R. Wensley and R. Whittington (eds), *Rethinking Marketing*, London: Sage, pp. 27–57.

Brown, T.J. and Dacin, P.A. (1997), 'The company and the product: corporate associations and consumer product responses', *Journal of Marketing*, 61, January: 68–84.

Burnett, J. (1993), *Promotion Management*, Boston: Houghton Miflin.

Camp, R.C. (1989), *Benchmarking: The Search for Industry Best Practices that Lead to Superior Performance*, Milwaukee, WI: ASQC Quality Press.

Carroll A.S. (1993) *Business and Society*, 2nd edn, South Western Publishing Company, Ohio.

Clifford, D.K. and Cavanagh, R.E. (1985), *The Winning Performance: How America's High Growth Midsize Companies Succeed*, London: Sidgwick and Jackson.

Coch, L. and French, J.R.P. (1948), 'Overcoming resistance to change', *Human Relations*, 1: 512–32.

Cronin, J.J. and Taylor, S.A. (1992), 'Measuring service quality: a re-examination and extension', *Journal of Marketing*, 56: 55–68.

Davis, L. (1977) 'Grasp behavior before picking target markets', *Marketing News*, Chicago: American Marketing Association.

David, F.R. (2003), *Strategic Management: Concepts and Cases*, Upper Saddle River, NJ: Prentice Hall, 9th edn.

Day, G.S. (1990), *Market Driven Strategy, Processes for Creating Value*, New York: Free Press.

Day, G.S. (1993), *The Capabilities of Market-driven Organizations*, Cambridge, MA: Marketing Science Institute.

Day, G.S. (1994), 'The capability of market driven organisations', *Journal of Marketing*, 58(3): 37–52.

Day, G.S. and Wensley, R. (1988), 'Assessing advantage: a framework for diagnosing competitive superiority', *Journal of Marketing*, 58: 37–51.

Doyle, P. (1994), *Marketing Management and Strategy*, Hemel Hempstead: Prentice Hall.

Doyle, P. (2000) *Value-based Marketing: Marketing Strategies for Corporate Growth and Shareholder Value*, Chichester: John Wiley.

Dreyer, B. and K. Gronhaug, (2004). 'Uncertainty, flexibility, and sustained competitive advantage', *Journal of Business Research*, 57: 484–94.

Drucker, P.F. (1964), *Managing for Results*, New York: Harper & Row.

Duncker, K. (1945), 'On problem solving', trans. L.S. Lees, *Psychological Monographs*, 58(5), whole no. 270.

Egan, C. (1998), 'Market dynamics and marketing strategies', in C. Egan, and M.J. Thomas (eds), *The CIM Book of Strategic Marketing*, Oxford: Butterworth Heinemann.

Eisenhardt, K.M. and Brown, S.L. (1999), 'Patching: re-stitching business portfolios in dynamic markets', *Harvard Business Review*, May–June.

Ekvall, G. (1988), 'Change centred leaders: empirical evidence of a third dimension of leadership', *Creativity and Innovation Year-book*, 1: 36–46.

Engel, J.F., Blackwell, R.D. and Miniard, P.W. (1986), *Consumer Behaviour*, 5th edn, New York: Holt, Rinehart & Winston.

Evans, M. and Moutinho, L. (1999), *Contemporary Issues in Marketing*, Basingstoke: Macmillan.

Firat, A.F. and Venkatesh, A. (1995), 'Liberatory postmodernism and the reenchantment of consumption', *Journal of Consumer Research*, 22: 239–67.

Fisher, R.J., Maltz, E. and Jaworski, B.J. (1997), 'Enhancing communication between marketing and engineering: the moderating role of relative functional identification', *Journal of Marketing*, 61: 54–70.

Freel, M.S. (2005), 'Patterns of innovation and skills in small firms', *Technovation*, 25(2): 123.

French, W.L. and Bell, C.H. (1995), *Organisation Development*, Englewood Cliffs, NJ: Prentice Hall International Editions.

Ghemawat, P. (2002), 'Competition and business strategy in historical perspective', *Business History Review*, 76, spring: 37–74.

Gilbert, X. and Strebel, P. (1988), 'Developing competitive advantage' in J.B. Quinn, H. Mintzberg and R.M. James (eds), *The Strategic Process*, Englewood Cliffs: Prentice Hall.

Grant, R.M. (1991), 'The resource-based theory of competitive advantage: implications for strategy formulation', *California Management Review*, 33(3): 114–35.

Grant, R.M. (1996), 'Prospering in dynamically-competitive environments: organizational capability as knowledge integration', *Organisational Science*, 7: 375– 87.

Haley, R.I. (1968), 'Benefit segmentation: a decision-oriented research tool', *Journal of Marketing*, 32: 30–5.

Haliburton, C. and Hunerberg, R. (1993) 'Marketing in a European Environment', in C. Haliburton and R. Hunerberg (eds), *European Marketing: Readings and Cases*, Cambridge: Addison Wesley.

Handelman, J.M. and Arnold, S.J. (1999), 'The role of marketing actions with a social dimension: appeals to the institutional environment', *Journal of Marketing*, 63: 33–48.

Hardy, L. (1987), *Successful Business Strategy*, London: Kogan Page.

Heady, R.B. and Lucas, J.L. (1997). 'PERMAP: an interactive program for making perceptual maps', *Behavior Research Methods, Instruments, & Computers*, 29(3): 450–55.

Henderson, B.D. (1970), 'The product portfolio', *The Boston Consulting Group Perspectives*, No. 66, Boston, MA.

Heskett, J.L. (1987), 'Lessons in the services sector', *Harvard Business Review*, 87(2): 118–26.

Heskett, J.L., Jones, T.O., Loveman, G.W., Sasser, W.E. and Schlesinger, L.A. (1994), 'Putting the service profit chain to work', *Harvard Business Review*, March–April, pp. 164–74.

Higgins, J.M. (1994), *The Management Challenge*, 2nd edn, New York: Macmillan.

Hooley, G. and Saunders, J. (1993), *Competitive Positioning: The Key to Market Success*, Hemel Hempstead: Prentice Hall.

Hult, G.T., Hurley, R. and Knight, G.A. (2004), 'Innovativeness: its antecedents and impact on business performance', *Industrial Marketing Management*, 33: 429–38.

Hunt, S. and Morgan, R.M. (1995), 'The comparative advantage theory of competition', *Journal of Marketing*, 59: 1–15.

Jaworski, B.J. and Kohli, A.K. (1993), 'Market orientation: antecedents and consequences', *Journal of Marketing*, 57: 53–70.

Jensen M.C. (2001), 'Value Maximisation, Stakeholder Theory and the Corporate Objective Function', *European Financial Management*, September, 7(3): 297–317.

Johnson, G. and Scholes, K. (1988), *Exploring Corporate Strategy*, 2nd and 3rd edns, Hemel Hempstead: Prentice Hall.

Jones, L. (1987), 'The development and testing of a psychological instrument to measure barriers to effective problem solving', Unpublished MBSc. dissertation, Manchester Business School.

Joyce, P., Seaman, C. and Woods, A. (1996), 'The strategic management styles of small businesses', in R. Blackburn and P. Jennings (eds), *Small Firms: Contributions to Economic Regeneration*, London: Institute for Small Business Affairs.

Kapferer, J.N. (1992), *Strategic Brand Management*, London: Kogan Page.

Kaplan, R.S. and Norton, D.P. (1996), Using the Balanced Scorecard as a Strategic Management System. *Harvard Business Review*, January–February: 75–85.

Kay, J. (1993), *Foundations of Corporate Success: How Business Strategies Add Value*, Oxford: Oxford University Press.

Kohli, A.K. and Jaworski, B.J. (1990), 'Market orientation: the construct, research propositions and managerial implications', *Journal of Marketing*, 54: 1–18.

Kontes, P.W. and Mankins, M.C. (1992), 'Is global market leadership worth it?', *Across the Board*, 29(10): 13–15.

Kotler, P. (1988), *Marketing Management: Analysis, Planning and Control*, Englewood Cliffs, NJ: Prentice Hall.

Kotler, P. and Lilien, G. (1983), *Marketing Decision Making: A Model Building Approach*, New York: Harper and Row.

Kotter, J. (1997), 'Rethinking leadership', in R. Gibson (ed.), *Rethinking the Future*, London: Nicholas Brealey, pp. 166–7.

319

Kuehn, A.A. (1962), 'How advertising performance depends on other factors', *Journal of Advertising Research*, March: 2–10.

Large, M. (1992), 'Eco-mapping: how to avoid boiled frogs', *Management Education and Development*, 23(4): 317–25.

Levitt, T. (1960), 'Marketing myopia', *Harvard Business Review*, July–August: 45–56.

Light P.C. (2005), *The Four Pillars of High Performance: How Robust Organizations Achieve Extraordinary Performance*, New York: McGraw-Hill

Low, J. (2000) 'The value creation index', *Journal of Intellectual Capital*, 1(3): 252–62.

Magidson, D. and Polcha, A.E. (1992), 'Creating market economies within organisations: a conference on internal markets', *Planning Review*, January–February: 37–40.

Majaro, S. (1991), *The Creative Marketer*, Oxford: Butterworth Heinemann.

March, J.G. (1988), *Decisions and Organizations*, Oxford: Blackwell.

Marken, A. (1987), 'Positioning key element for effective marketing', *Marketing News*, 21(4): 7.

Marketing Science Institute (2005) '2004–2006 research priorities – research priorities for the customer management community", *Marketing Science Institute*, Cambridge, MA (available, http://www.msi.org/msi/rp0406.cfm#RPCMC).

McCarthy, E.J. and Perreault, W.D. (1993), *Basic Marketing*, 11th edn, Chicago, IL.

McDonald, M.H.B. (1989), *Marketing Plans*, 2nd edn, Oxford: Heinemann.

McDonald, M. and Dunbar, I. (2004), *Market Segmentation: How to Do It. How to Profit from It*, Oxford: Elsevier Butterworth-Heinemann.

McKee, D.O., Varadarajan, P.R. and Pride, W.M. (1989), 'Strategic adaptability and firm performance: a market contingent perspective', *Journal of Marketing*, 53: 21–35.

Mills, R.W. (1994), *Finance, Strategy and Strategic Value Analysis*, Slough: Mars Business Associates, UK.

Mintzberg, H. and Quinn, J.B. (1991), *The Strategy Process*, Englewood Cliffs, NJ: Prentice Hall.

Mitchell, A. (1995), 'Holidays: what lies behind the big discounts', *The Times*, 4 January, p. 19.

Morgan, G. (1989), *Riding the Waves of Change: Developing Managerial Competencies for a Turbulent World*, San Francisco, CA: Jossey-Bass.

Moullin, M. (2002), *Delivering Excellence in Health and Social Care*, Buckingham: Open University Press.

Nakanishi, M. and Coop, L.G. (2003), *Metric Unfolding Revisited: Straight Answers to Basic Questions*, Department of Statistics, UCLA, Department of Statistics Papers, University of California, Los Angeles, Paper 2003010112.

Narver, J.C. and Slater, S.F. (1990), 'The effect of a market orientation on profitability', *Journal of Marketing*, 54(4): 20–35.

Nieto, M. and Quevedo, P. (2005), 'Absorptive capacity, technological opportunity, knowledge spillovers, and innovative effort'. *Technovation*, 25: 1141–57.

Nohria, N., Joyce, W. and Roberson, B. (2003), 'What really works', *Harvard Business Review*, July: 43–53

Normann, R. and Ramirez, R. (1993), 'From value chain to value constellation: designing interactive strategy', *Harvard Business Review*, July–August.

Oldman, G.R. and Cummings, A. (1996), 'Employee creativity: personal and contextual factors at work', *Academy of Management Journal*, 39, June.

Olson, E.M., Slater, S.F. and Hult, G.T. (2005), 'The performance implications of fit among business strategy, marketing organization structure, and strategic behavior', *Journal of Marketing*, 69(7): 49–65.

O'Regan, N. and Ghobadian, A. (2002), 'Formal strategic planning: the key to executive business process management', *Business Process Management*, 8(5): 416–29.

O'Reilly, C.A. and Pfeffer, J. (2000), *Hidden Value: How Great Companies Achieve Extraordinary Results with Ordinary People*, Boston: Harvard Business School Press.

Osgood, C., Suci, G. and Tannenbaum, P. (1987), *The Measurement of Meaning* Urbana, IL: University of Illinois Press.

Ouchi, W.G. and Bolton, M. (1988), 'The logic of joint research and development', *California Management Review*, 3, spring.

Parasuraman, A. (1987), 'Customer oriented organisational culture: a key to successful services marketing', *Journal of Services Marketing*, 1(1): 73–6.

Parasuraman, A., Berry, L.L. and Zeithaml, V.A. (1991), 'Understanding customer expectations of service', *Sloan Management Review*, 32(3): 39–48.

Parasuraman, A., Zeithaml, V.A. and Berry, L.L. (1988), 'SERVQUAL: a multiple-item scale for measuring consumer perceptions of service quality', *Journal of Retailing*, 64(1): 12–40.

Patel, P. and Younger, M. (1978), 'A frame of reference for strategy development', *Journal of Long Range Planning*, 11: 6–12.

Perry, S. C. (2001), The Relationship between written business plans and the failure of small business in the US', *Journal of Small Business Management*, 39(3): 201–9.

Pfeffer, J. and Salancik, G.R. (1978), *The External Control of Organisations: A Resource Dependent Perspective*, New York: Harper & Row.

Porter, M.E. (1980a), *Competitive Strategy*, New York: Free Press.

Porter, M.E. (1980b), 'How competition forces shape strategy', *Harvard Business Review*, September–October: 137–45.

Porter, M.E. (1985), *Competitive Advantage*, New York: Free Press.

Porter, M.E. (1987), 'Michael Porter on competitive strategy reflections and round table discussions', *European Management Journal*, 6(1): 2–9.

Porter, M.E. (1988), Video film and pamphlet: *Michael Porter on Competitive Strategy*, Harvard Business School Video Series.

Prahalad, C.K. and Hamel, G. (1990), 'The core competence of the corporation', *Harvard Business Review*, May–June: 79–91.

Proctor, R.A. (Tony) (1989), 'Innovations in new product screening and evaluation', *Technology Analysis and Strategic Management*, 1(3): 313–23.

Proctor, R.A. and Kitchen, P.J. (1990), 'Strategic planning: an overview of product portfolio models', *Marketing Intelligence and Planning*, 8(7): 4–10.

Proctor, T. (1993), 'Product innovation: the pitfalls of entrapment', *Creativity and Innovation Management*, 2(4): 260–5.

Proctor, T. (2000), *Essentials of Marketing Research*, London: Financial Times, Prentice Hall.

Przybylowicz, E.P. and Faulkner T.W. (1993), 'Kodak applies strategic intent to the management of technology', *Research-Technology Management*, 36(1): 31–8.

Quinn, J.B., Doorley, T.L. and Paquette, P.C. (1990), 'Beyond products: services-based strategy', *Harvard Business Review*, March–April, pp. 58–68.

Rafiq, M. and Ahmed, P.K. (1993), 'The scope of internal marketing: defining the boundary between marketing and human resource management', *Journal of Marketing Management*, 9: 219–32.

Rappaport, A. (1986), *Creating Shareholder Value*, New York: Free Press.

Rickards, T. (1985), *Stimulating Innovation: A Systems Approach*, Aldershot: Frances Pinter.

Rickards, T. (1990), *Creativity and Problem Solving at Work*, Farnborough: Gower.

Ringland, G. (1998), *Scenario Planning, Managing for the Future*, Chichester: John Wiley.

Robinson, P.J., Faris, C.W. and Wind, Y. (1967), *Industrial Marketing and Creative Buying*, Boston: Allyn and Bacon.

Robinson, S.J.Q., Hichens, R.E. and Wade, D.P. (1978), 'The directional policy matrix: tool for strategic planning', *Journal of Long Range Planning*, 11(3): 8–15.

Roehrich, G. (2004), 'Consumer Innovativeness: Concepts and Measurements', *Journal of Business Research*, 52: 621–77.

Rogers, B. (1996), *Creating Product Strategies*, London: International Thompson.

Roper, S. (1997), 'Strategic initiatives and small business performance: an exploratory analysis of Irish companies', *Entrepreneurship and Regional* Development, 9: 353–6.

Rowe, A.J., Mason, R.D., Dickel, K.E. and Synder, N.H. (1989), *Strategic Management: A Methodological Approach*, 3rd edn, Wokingham: Prentice Hall.

321

Selznick, P. (1957), *Leadership and Administration*, New York: Harper & Row.

Sherrington, M. (1995), 'Branding and brand management', in M.J. Baker (ed.), *Companion Encyclopaedia of Marketing*, London: Routledge.

Shetty, Y.K. and Ross, J.E. (1985), 'Quality and its management in service businesses', *Industrial Management*, 27: 7–12.

Sirota, D., Mischkind, L.A. and Meltzer, M.I. (2005), *The Enthusiastic Employee: How Companies Profit by Giving Workers What They Want*. Upper Saddle River: Wharton School Publishing.

Speed, R.J. (1989), 'Oh Mr Porter! A re-appraisal of competitive strategy', *MIP*, 7: 8–11.

Sprenger, C. and Have, S. (1996), 'Kennismanagement als moter van de lerende organisatie', *Holland Management Review*, September–October: 73–89.

Stein, L.W., El-Ansary, A.I. and Coughlan, A.T. (1996), *Marketing Channels*, 5th edn, Englewood Cliffs, NJ: Prentice Hall.

Taylor, B. (1984), 'Strategic planning: which style do you need?', *Journal of Long Range Planning*, 17: 51–62.

Teas, R.K. (1993), 'Expectations, performance evaluation, and consumers perceptions of quality', *Journal of Marketing*, 57(4): 18–34.

Van Der Heijden, K. (1996), *Scenarios: The Art of Strategic Conversation*, Chichester: John Wiley.

Van Gundy, A.B. (1981, 1988), *Techniques of Structured Problem Solving*, New York: Van Nostrand Reinhold Co.

Vensim, Ventana Systems, Inc., 60 Jacob Gates Road Harvard, MA 1451, email: vensim@vensim.com, URL: www.vensim.com

Verdin, P. and Williamson, P.J. (1993), *Core Competence, Competitive Advantage and Market Analysis: Forging the Links*, Paris: INSEAD.

Wack, P. (1985), 'Scenarios: shooting the rapids', *Harvard Business Review*, November–December: pp. 139–50.

Webster, F.E., Malter, A.J. *et al.* (2003) 'Can marketing regain its seat at the table?' *Marketing Science Institute Working Paper Series*, 3: 29–47.

Webster, F.E. and Wind, Y. (1972), *Organisational Buying Behaviour*, Englewood Cliffs, NJ: Prentice Hall.

Weihrich, H. (1982), 'The TOWS matrix: a tool for situational analysis', *Journal of Long Range Planning*, 15(2): 54–66.

Weizenbaum, J. (1984), *Computer Power and Human Reason*, Harmondsworth: Penguin.

Wind, Y. (1973), 'A new procedure for concept evaluation', *Journal of Marketing*, 37: 2–11.

Wind, Y. (1978), 'Issues and advances in segmentation research', *Journal of Marketing Research*, 15: 317–37.

Further reading

CHAPTER 1: MARKETING STRATEGY: INTRODUCTION AND OVERVIEW

Abell, D.F. (1978), 'Strategic windows', *Journal of Marketing*, July: 21–6.

Bowman, C. and Ambrosini, V. (2000), 'Value creation versus value capture: towards a coherent definition of value in strategy', *British Journal of Management*, 11(1): 1–15.

Bryson, J.M. (2004), 'What to do when stakeholders matter: stakeholder identification and analysis techniques', *Public Management Review*, 6(1): 21–53.

Christopher, M., Payne, A. and Ballantyne, D. (2002), *Relationship Marketing: Creating Stakeholder Value*, London: Butterworth Heinemann.

Donaldson T. and Preston L.E. (1995), 'The stakeholder theory of the corporation: concepts, evidence and implications', *Academy of Management Review*, 20(1): 65–91.

Evan, W. and Freeman, R. (1988), 'A stakeholder theory of the modern corporation: Kantian capitalism', in T. Beauchamp and N. Bowie (eds), *Ethical Theory and Business*, 3rd edn, Vol. 97, Englewood Cliffs, NJ: Prentice Hall, pp. 101–5.

Jensen M.C. (2001), 'Value maximisation, stakeholder theory and the corporate objective function', *European Financial Management*, 7(3): 297–317.

Keefe L. (2004), 'What is the meaning of "marketing"?', *Marketing News*, 15 September, American Marketing Association, pp. 17–18.

Large, M. (1992), 'Eco-mapping: how to avoid boiled frogs', *Management Education and Development*, 23(4): 317–25.

Lehman D.R. (2004), 'Linking marketing to financial performance and firm value', *Journal of Marketing*, 68, October: 73–5.

Levitt, T. (1960), 'Marketing myopia', *Harvard Business Review*, July–August: 45–56.

Phillips, R. (2004), 'Some key questions about stakeholder theory', *Ivey Business Journal*, March–April: 1–4.

Porter, M.E. (1987) 'From competitive advantage to corporate strategy', *Harvard Business Review*, May–June: 43–59.

Porter, M.E. (1996) 'What is Strategy?', *Harvard Business Review*, November–December: 61–78.

Pitelis, C.N. and Wahl, M. (1998) 'Edith Penrose: pioneer of stakeholder theory', *Long Range Planning*, 31(2): 252–61.

Proctor, T. (1997), 'Establishing a strategic direction: a review', *Management Decision*, 35(2): 143–54.

Tournois L. (2004), 'Creating customer value: bridging theory and practice', *Marketing Management Journal*, 14(2) 13–23.

CHAPTER 2: PORTFOLIO ANALYSIS

Day, G.S. (1986), *Analysis for Strategic Market Decisions*, St Paul, MN: West Publishing Company.

Eng, T.Y. (2004) 'Does customer portfolio analysis relate to customer performance? An empirical analysis of alternative strategic perspective', *Journal of Business & Industrial Marketing*, 19(1): 49–67.

Ghemawat, P (2002), 'Competition and business strategy in historical perspective', *Business History Review*, 76, spring: 37–74.

Hambuck, D.C. and Macmillan, I.C. (1982), 'The product portfolio and man's best friend', *California Management Review*, 25, fall: 84–95.

Johnson, G. and Scholes, K. (1999), *Exploring Corporate Strategy*, 5th edn, Hemel Hempstead: Prentice Hall.

Levitt, T. (1965), 'Exploit the product life cycle', *Harvard Business Review*, October–November: 81–94.

Onkvisit, S. and Shaw, J.J. (1989), *Product Life Cycles and Product Management*, New York, NY: Quorom Books.

Pearson, G.J. and Proctor, R.A. (1994), 'The modern framework for marketing planning', *Marketing Intelligence*, 12(4): 22–6.

CHAPTER 3: ANALYSIS OF THE BUSINESS ENTERPRISE

Amabile, T.M., Conti, R., Coon, H., Lazenby, J. and Herron, M. (1996), 'Assessing the work environment for creativity', *Academy of Management Journal*, 39: 5.

Mintzberg, H. (1976), 'Planning on the left side and managing on the right', *Harvard Business Review*, July–August: 49–58.

Prathra, C.W. and Gundry, L. (1996), *Blueprints for innovation*, USA: American Management Association.

Radnor, Z. and Lovell, B. (2003), 'Success factors for implementation of the balanced scorecard in a NHS multi-agency setting', *International Journal of Health Care Quality Assurance*, 16(2): 99–108.

Simon, H.A. (1985), 'What we know about the creative process', in R.L. Kuhn (ed.), *Frontiers in Creative and Innovative Management*, New York: Ballinger.

Van Gundy, A.B. (1987), 'Organisational creativity and innovation', in S.G. Isaksen (ed.), *Frontiers of Creative Research: Beyond the Basics*, Buffalo: Bearly Ltd, pp. 358–79.

Walters D. and Lancaster, G. (2000), Implementing value strategy through the value chain', *Management Decision*, 38(3): 160–78.

CHAPTER 4: INDUSTRY ANALYSIS

Bengtsson M. and Marell, A. (2006), 'Structural conditions for static and dynamic competition after deregulation', *Competitiveness Review*, 16(1): 20–31.

Pelham, A.M. and Wilson, D.T. (1996), 'A longitudinal study of the impact of market structure, firm structure and market orientation culture on dimensions of small-firm perfomance', *Journal of the Academy of Marketing Science*, 2, winter.

Proctor T (2001), 'Corporate Restructuring: the pitfalls of changing industry structure', *Management Decision*, 39(3): 197–204.

Scherer, F.M. (1996), *Industry Structure, Strategy and Public Policy*, London: Longman.

Scherer, F.M. and Ross, D.R. (1990), *Industrial Market Structure and Economic Performance*, 3rd edn, Boston: HoughtonMifflin.

Sutton, J. (1998), *Technology and Market Structure: Theory and History*, Cambridge, MA: MIT Press.

Whisler, T. (1999), *The British Motor Industry, 1945–94*, Oxford: Oxford University Press.

Whittington, R. and Mayer, M. (2002), *The European Corporation: Strategy, Structure and Social Science*, Oxford: Oxford University Press.

CHAPTER 5: MARKET ANALYSIS

Abraham, B. and Ledolter, J. (1988), *Statistical Methods for Forecasting*, Wiley Series in Probability and Statistics, Chichester: John Wiley & Sons.

Carlberg, C. (2005), *Excel Sales Forecasting for Dummies*, Hobekin, NJ: Hungry Minds Inc.

Chakrapani, C. (2004), *Statistics in Market Research*, London: Arnold.

Grant R.M. (2003), 'Strategic planning in a turbulent environment', *Strategic Management Journal*, 24(6): 491–518.

Kahn, K.B. (2002) 'An exploratory investigation of new product forecasting practices', *Journal of Product Innovation Management*, 19: 133–43.

Levenbach, H., Tashman, L.-J., and Cleary, J.P. (2005), *Modern Forecasting: Practice and Process for Demand Management*, Belmont, CA: Brooks Cole.

Makridakis, S., Wheelwright, S.C. and Hyndman, R.J., (1998), *Forecasting Methods and Applications*, Chichester: John Wiley & Sons.

Moon, M. (2006), *Sales Forecasting Management: A Demand Management Approach*, 2nd edn, Academic Internet Publishers Incorporated.

Roberts, J.H. (1998) 'Editorial: marketing approaches to forecasting problems', *Journal of Forecasting*, 17: 169–74.

Rowe, Gene and George Wright (1999) 'The Delphi technique as a forecasting tool: issues and analysis', *International Journal of Forecasting* 15: 353–75.

Sall, J., Lehman, A. and Creighton, L. (2001), *JMP (R) Start Statistics: A Guide to Statistics and Data Analysis*. Duxbury/Thomson Learning. CA: Pacific Grove (Facilitates multiple regression for forecasting and includes suitable statistical computer software.)

CHAPTER 6: ANALYSING COMPETITION

Cravens, D.W. and Shannon H.S. (1991), 'Market-driven strategies for competitive advantage', *Business Horizons*, January–February: 53–61.

Dess, A. and Davies, G.G. (1993), 'Assessing Porter's (1980) model in terms of its generalizability, accuracy and simplicity', *Journal of Management Studies*, 30(4): 553–85.

Haverty, J.L. and Myroslow, J.K. (1991), 'What happens when new competitors enter an industry', *Industrial Marketing Management*, 20(2): 73–80.

Hunt, S.D. and Morgan, R.M. (1995), 'The comparative advantage theory of competition', *Journal of Marketing*, 59(2): 1–15.

Karakaya, F. and Stahl, M.J. (1989), 'Barriers to entry and market entry decisions in consumer and industrial goods', *Journal of Marketing*, April: 80–91.

Kim, W.C. and Mauborne, R. (2005), *Blue Ocean Strategy: How to Create Uncontested Market Space and Make the Competition Irrelevant,* Boston: Harvard Business School Publishing.

Langerak, F. and Commandeur, H.R. (1998), 'The influence of market orientation on competitive superiority and performance of industrial business', *Proceedings of the 27th EMAC Conference*, May, Stockholm, Vol. 3, pp. 91–105.

Leeflang, P.H., Dick, S. and Wittink, R. (2001), 'Explaining competitive reaction effects', *Internat. J. Res. Marketing*, 18(1–2): 119–37.

Polito, T., Watson, K., and Vokurka, R.J. (2006), 'Using the theory of constraints to improve competitiveness: an airline case study', *Competitiveness Review*, 16(1): 44–50.

Porter, M.E. (1985), *Competitive Advantage*, New York: The Free Press.

Porter, M.E. (1998, 1980), *Competitive Strategy: Techniques for Analyzing Industries and Competitors*, New York: Free Press.

Rothschild, W.E. (1984), *How to Gain and Maintain the Competitive Advantage*, New York: McGraw-Hill.

Wright, S., Pickton, D.W. and Callow, E.J. (2002), 'Competitive intelligence in UK firms: a typology', *Marketing Intelligence & Planning*, 20(6): 349–60.

CHAPTER 7: ANALYSING THE BUSINESS ENVIRONMENT

Alderman, G. (1984), *Pressure Groups and Government in Great Britain*, London: Longman.

Brooks, I. and Weatherston, J. (2000), *The Business Environment*, 2nd edn, Harlow: Financial Times, Prentice Hall.

Donaldson, P. (1984) *Economics of the Real World*, 3rd edn, Harmondsworth: Penguin.

Ela, J.D. and Manley, R.I. (1983), 'Technology changes market boundaries', *Industrial Marketing Management*, July: 153–6.

Mason, R.B. (2007), 'The external environment's effect on management and strategy: a complexity theory approach', *Management Decision*, 45(1): 10–28.

Morrison, A. (1991), 'The role of litigation in consumer protection', *Journal of Consumer Affairs*, winter: 209–20.

Palmer, A. and Worthington, I. (1992), *The Business and Marketing Environment*, London: McGraw-Hill.

Sundaram, A. K. and Black, J.S. (1995) *The International Business Environment: Text and Cases*, Englewood Cliffs, NJ: Prentice-Hall.

CHAPTER 8: ANALYSING THE CUSTOMER IN THE MARKET PLACE

Assael, H. (1987), *Consumer Behaviour and Marketing Action*, Boston, MA: Kent Publishing.

Blackwell, Roger D., Miniard, Paul W., Engel, James F. (2001), *Consumer Behavior*, 9th edn, Fort Worth, Harcourt: College Publishers.

Brown, S. and Turley, D. (eds) (1997), *Consumer Research*, London: Routledge.

Chisnall, P.M. (1985), *Marketing: A Behavioural Analysis*, 3rd edn, London: McGraw-Hill.

Enis, B. and Cox, K.K. (1991), *Marketing Classics*, 7th edn, Needham Heights, MA: Allyn and Bacon.

Hansen, F. and Hansen, M.M. (2005), 'Children as innovators and opinion leaders,' *Young Consumers*, quarter 1: 44–59.

Holbrook, M. (ed.) (1999), *Consumer Value*, London: Routledge.

Louder, D. and Dell Biota, A.J. (1988), *Consumer Behaviour: Concepts and Application*, 3rd edn, London: McGraw-Hill.

Ratneschwar, S. and Mick, D.G., and Huffman, C. (2000), *The Why of Consumption*, London: Routledge.

Schroeder, J.E. (2002), *Visual Consumption*, London: Routledge.

CHAPTER 9: SUSTAINABLE COMPETITIVE ADVANTAGE AND GENERIC STRATEGIES

Barney, J. (1997), *Gaining and Sustaining Competitive Advantage*, Reading, MA: Addison-Wesley.

Barney, J. (2001), 'Resource-based theories of competitive advantage: a ten-year retrospective on the resource-based view', *Journal of Management*, 27: 643–650.

Bharadwaj, S.G., Varadarajan, P.R. and Fahy, J. (1993), 'Sustainable competitive advantage in service industries: a conceptual model and research propositions', *Journal of Marketing*, 57, October: 83–99.

Brooksbank, R. and Taylor, D. (2007), 'Strategic marketing in action: a comparison of higher and lower performing manufacturing firms in the UK', *Marketing Intelligence and Planning*, 25(1): 31–44.

Campbell-Hunt, C. (2000) 'What have we learned about generic competitive strategy? A meta-analysis', *Strategic Management Journal*, 21: 127–54.

Cronshaw, M., Davis, E. and Kay, J. (1994), 'On being stuck in the middle or good food costs less at Sainsbury's', *British Journal of Management*, 5: 19–32.

Day, G.S. (1984), *Strategic Market Planning: The Pursuit of Competitive Advantage*, St Paul, MN: West Publishing Company.

Gronroos, C. (1987), *Developing the Service Offering: A Source of Competitive Advantage*, September, Helsinki, Finland: Swedish School of Economics and Business Administration.

Gronroos, C. (1988), 'Service quality; the six criteria of good perceived service quality', *Review of Business*, 9(3): 10–3.

Hamel, G. and Prahalad, C.K. (1989), 'Strategic intent', *Harvard Business Review*, 67: 63–76.

Mathur, S.S. (1992), 'Talking straight about competitive strategy', *Journal of Marketing Management*, 8: 199–217.

Mayfield, M., Mayfield, J. and Stephens, D. (2007), 'The relationship of generic strategy typing and organizational, longevity: a preliminary analysis in the comic book industry using the Miles and Snow typology', *Competitiveness Review*, 17(1): 94–108.

Parasuraman, A., Berry, L.L. and Zeithaml, V.A. (1991), 'Understanding customer expectations of service', *Sloan Management Review*, 32(3): 39–48.

Parasuraman, A., Zeithaml, V.A. and Berry, L.L. (1985), 'A conceptual model of service quality and its implications for future research', *Journal of Marketing*, 49: 41–50.

Parasuraman, A., Zeithaml, V.A. and Berry, L.L. (1988), 'SERVQUAL: a multiple item scale for measuring consumer perceptions of service quality', *Journal of Retailing*, 64(1): 12–40.

Peteraf, M.A. (1993), 'The cornerstones of competitive advantage: a resource-based view', *Strategic Management Journal*, 14: 179–91.

Quinn, J.B. (1992), *Intelligent Enterprise*, New York: Free Press.

Quinn, J.B., Doorley, T.L. and Paquette, P.C. (1990), 'Beyond products: services-based strategy', *Harvard Business Review*, March–April: 58–68.

Srivastava, R.K. and Fahey, L. and Christensen, H.K (2001), 'The resource-based view and marketing: The role of market based assets in gaining competitive advantage', *Journal of Management*, 27: 777–802

Van de Ven, A. and Ferry, D. (1980), *Measuring and Assessing Organisations*, New York: John Wiley & Sons, Inc.

CHAPTER 10: SEGMENTATION, TARGETING AND POSITIONING

Aaker, D.A. and Shanby, J.G. (1982), 'Positioning your product', *Business Horizons*, May–June, pp. 56–62.

Abell, D.F. (1978), 'Strategic Windows', *Journal of Marketing*, 42(2): 21–6.

Dibb, S. and Simkin, L. (2001), 'Market segmentation: diagnosing and treating the barriers', *Industrial Marketing Management*, 30(8): 609–25.

Dibb, S., Stern, P. and Wensley, R. (2002) 'Marketing knowledge and the value of segmentation', *Marketing Intelligence & Planning*, 20(2): 113–19.

Doyle, P. (1991), 'Managing the marketing mix', in M.J. Baker (ed.), *The Marketing Book*, 2nd edn, London: Butterworth Heinemann.

Doyle, P. (1994), *Marketing Management and Strategy*, Hemel Hempstead: Prentice Hall.

Haley, R.I. (1968), 'Benefit segmentation: a decision oriented research tool', *Journal of Marketing*, 32: 30–5.

Haley, R.I. (1991), 'Benefit segmentation: a decision-oriented research tool', in B.M. Enis and K.K. Cox (eds), *Marketing Classics*, 7th edn, Needham Heights: Allyn and Bacon.

Morgan, R. E., Strong, C.A. and McGuinness, T. (2003), 'Product-market positioning and prospector strategy: an analysis of strategic patterns from the resource-based perspective', *European Journal of Marketing*, 37(10): 1409–39.

Murphy, P.E. and Staples, W.A. (1991), 'A modernised family life cycle', in B.M. Enis and K.K. Cox (eds), *Marketing Classics*, 7th edn, Needham, Heights: Allyn and Bacon.

Ries, A. and Trout, J. (1981), *Positioning: The Battle for Your Mind*, New York: McGraw-Hill.

Sausen K., Tomczak, T. and Herrmann, A. (2005), 'Development of a taxonomy of strategic market segmentation: a framework for bridging the implementation gap between normative segmentation and business practice', *Journal of Strategic Marketing*, 13(3): 151–73.

Wedel, M. and Kamakura, W.A. (2002), *Market Segmentation: Conceptual and Methodological Foundations*, 2nd edn, Boston, MA: Kluwer.

Weinstein, A. (2006), 'A strategic framework for defining and segmenting markets', *Journal of Strategic Marketing*, 14(2): 115–27.

Woo, K. (1998), 'Using quality perceptions to segment customers in services', *Marketing Intelligence & Planning*, 16: 418–24.

Wright, M. (1996), 'The dubious assumptions of segmentation and targeting', *Management Decision*, 34: 18–24.

CHAPTER 11: MARKETING MIX STRATEGY

Burnett, J. (1993), *Promotion Management*, Boston, MA: Houghton Miflin.

Christopher, M. (1986), *The Strategy of Distribution Management*, London: Heinemann.

Cooper, J., Browne, M. and Peter, M. (1991), *European Logistics*, Oxford: Blackwell.

Coulson Thomas, C.J. (1983), *Marketing Communications*, London: Heinemann.

de Chernatony, L. and McDonald, M.H.B. (1992), *Creating Powerful Brands*, Oxford: Butterworth Heinemann.

Fernie, J. (ed.) (1990), *Retail Distribution Management: Strategic Guide to Developments and Trends*, London: Kogan Page.

Hartley, R.F. (1992), *Marketing Mistakes*, 5th edn, New York: Wiley.

Hendon, D.W. (1992), *Classic Failures in Product Marketing*, Chicago: NTC Business Books.

McBurnie, T. and Clutterbuck, D. (1988), *The Marketing Edge*, Harmondsworth: Penguin.

Schwartz, D.G. (2000), 'Concurrent marketing analysis: a multi-agent model for product, price, place and promotion', *Marketing Intelligence & Planning*, 18(1): 24–9.

CHAPTER 12: GROWTH STRATEGIES: PRODUCT – MARKET EXPANSION

Crawford, Merle and Di Benedetto, Anthony (2003), *New Products Management*, New York: McGraw-Hill.

Daneels, E. (2002), 'The dynamics of product innovation and firm competences', *Strategic Management Journal*, 23(12): 1095–1121.

Doole, I. and Lowe, R. (2004), *International Marketing Strategy*, London: Thomson Learning.

Hult, G.T., Hurley, R. and Knight, G. (2004), 'Innovativeness: its antecedents and impact on business performance', *Industrial Marketing Management*, 33: 429–38.

Majaro, S. (1991), *The Creative Process*, London: Allen and Unwin.

Stone, M.A. and McCall, J.B. (2004), *International Strategic Marketing*, London: Routledge.

Ulwick, A.W. (2002), 'Turn customer input into innovation', *Harvard Business Review*, 80(1): 91–7.

Urban, G. and Hauser, J. (199), *Marketing of New Products*, Englewood Cliffs, NJ: Prentice Hall.

Von Hippel, E. (1988), *The Sources of Innovation*, New York: Oxford University Press.

Von Hippel, Eric (2001), 'User toolkits for innovation', *Journal of Product Innovation Management*, 18: 247–57.

CHAPTER 13: FACILITATING THE IMPLEMENTATION OF STRATEGIES

Anslinger, P. and Jenk, J. (2004), 'Creating successful alliances', *Journal of Business Strategy*, 25(2): 18–22.

Buchel, B. (2002), 'Joint venture development: driving forces towards equilibrium', *Journal of World Business*, 37(3): 199–207.

Buttle, F. (ed.) (1996), *Relationship Marketing*, London: Paul Chapman.

Collins, B. and Payne, A. (1991), 'Internal marketing: a new perspective for HRM', *European Management Journal*, 9: 261–9.

Day, G.S. (2003), 'Creating a superior customer-relating capability', *MIT Sloan Management Review*, 44(3), 77–82.

Donovan, J., Tully R. and Wortman, B. (1998), *The Value Enterprise: Strategies for Building a Value-based Organization*, Toronto: McGraw-Hill/Ryerson.

Duncan, Tom and Moriarty, Sandra E. (1998), 'A communication-based marketing model for managing relationships', *Journal of Marketing*, 62, April: 1–13.

Greene, W.E., Walls, G.D. and Schrest, L.J. (1994), 'Internal marketing: key to external marketing success', *Journal of Services Marketing*, 8(4): 5–13.

Harrigan, K.R. (2003), *Joint Ventures, Alliances, and Corporate Strategy*. Washington, DC: Beard Books.

Rosenau, P. (1999), 'Building successful social partnerships', *Sloan Management Review*, 40(3): 17 23.

Sargeant, A. and Asif, S. (1998), 'The strategic application of internal marketing: an investigation of UK banking', *International Journal of Bank Marketing*, 16(2): 66–79.

Stone, R.N. and Mason, J.B. (1997), 'Relationship management: strategic marketing's next source of competitive advantage', *Journal of Marketing Theory and Practice*, spring: 8–19.

Varey, J.R. and Lewis, B.R. (eds) (2000), *Internal Marketing: Directions for Management*, London: Routledge

CHAPTER 14: MARKETING PLANNING AND IMPLEMENTING MARKETING STRATEGY

Adobar, H. (2006), 'Inter-firm collaboration: configuration and dynamics', *Competitiveness Review*, 16(2): 122–34.

Ashill, N.J., Frederickson, M. and Davies, J. (2003), Strategic marketing planning: a grounded Investigation', *European Journal of Marketing*, 37(3/4): 430–60.

Greenley, G., Hooley, G. and Saunders, J. (2004), 'Management processes in marketing planning', *European Journal of Marketing* 38(8): 933–56.

Hatton, A. (2000), *The Definitive Guide to Market Planning*, Glasgow: Financial Times. Prentice Hall.

Larsen, P., Tonge, R. and Lewis, A. (2007), 'Strategic planning and design in the service sector', *Management Decision*, 45(2): 180–95.

Lawrence, P.R. and Greiner L.R. (1970), 'How to deal with resistance to change', in G.W. Dalton, P.R. Lawrence and L.R. Greiner (eds), *Organisational Change and Development*, Homewood, IL: Irwin.

McDonald, M.H.B. (1989), *Marketing Plans*, 2nd edn, Oxford: Heinemann.

Noble, C.H. and Mokva, M.P. (1999), 'Implementing marketing strategies developing and testing a managerial theory', *Journal of Marketing*, 63(4): 57–74.

General further reading

Contemporary Strategy Analysis by Robert Grant (2007), Oxford: Blackwell, 5th edn.

Exploring Corporate Strategy by G. Johnson, K. Scholes and R. Whittingham (2005), Harlow: Prentice Hall

Getting Partnering Right: How Market Leaders Are Creating Long-term Competitive Advantage by Neil Rackham, Lawrence Friedman, and Richard Ruff, (2007), Maidenhead: McGraw-Hill Publishing Co.

Green to Gold: How Smart Companies Use Environmental Strategy to Innovate, Create Value, and Build a Competitive Advantage by Daniel C. Esty and Andrew S. Winston (2007), New Haven: Yale University Press.

Key Performance Indicators (KPI): Developing, Implementing, and Using Winning KPIs by David Parmenter (2007), Chichester: John Wiley & Sons.

Making Innovation Work: How to Manage It, Measure It, and Profit from It by Marc J. Epstein, Robert Shelton and Tony Davila (2005), Philadelphia: Wharton School Publishing.

Managing Customer Relationships: A Strategic Framework by Don Peppers and Martha Rogers (2004), Chichester: John Wiley & Sons Inc.

Strategic Market Management by D. Aaker (2004), 7th revd edn, Chichester: John Wiley & Sons Inc.

Strategic Marketing by D. Cravens and Nigel F. Piercy (2005), 8th edn, Maidenhead: McGraw-Hill Higher Education.

Strategic Marketing Decisions by Robin Lowe and Isobel Doole (2004), London: Thomson Learning.

Strategic Thinking (Essential Managers) by Andy Bruce and Ken Langdon (2000), London: Dorling Kindersley Publishers Ltd.

Strategy as Practice: An Activity Based Approach (SAGE Strategy) by Paula Jarzabkowski (2005), London: Sage Publications Ltd.

Strategy Bites Back by Henry Mintzberg, Bruce W. Ahlstrand, and Joseph B. Lampel (2004), Harlow: Financial Times, Prentice Hall.

Strategy Safari: A Guided Tour through the Wilds of Strategic Management by Henry Mintzberg, Bruce W. Ahlstrand, and Joseph Lampel (2005), Harlow: Financial Times, Prentice Hall.

The Best-laid Business Plans: How to Write Them, How to Pitch Them (Virgin Business Guides) by Sir Richard Branson and Paul Barrow (2005), London: Virgin Books.

Rise and Fall of Strategic Planning, by H. Mintzberg (1994), New York: Free Press.

The Boston Consulting Group on Strategy: Classic Concepts and New Perspectives by Carl W. Stern and Michael S. Deimler (2006), 2nd edn, Chichester: John Wiley & Sons.

The Committed Enterprise: Making Vision, Values and Branding Work by Hugh Davidson (2004), 2nd revd edn, Oxford: Butterworth-Heinemann Ltd.

The Pirate Inside: Building a Challenger Brand Culture Within Yourself and Your Organizations by Adam Morgan (2004), Chichester: John Wiley and Sons Ltd.

Value Based Marketing, by Peter Doyle, Chichester: John Wiley and Sons.

330

Index

Fundamentals of Marketing

Marilyn A. Stone, Heriot-Watt University, Edinburgh, UK and
John Desmond, St Andrews University, UK

Fundamentals of Marketing provides a sound appreciation of the fundamentals of the theory and practice of marketing. Using case studies drawn from a cross section of sectors, in particular the banking, hospitality, retail and public service sectors this textbook critically evaluates the effectiveness of different marketing strategies and approaches. Exploring the principles of marketing this volume engages the reader, not only in theory but also in practice, using a broad range of real-life case studies such as Coca Cola, Apple, FCUK, Virgin, Amazon.com, Barnes and Noble, Dyno Rod and New Zealand wool.

Featuring a support website that provides student and lecturer resources, *Fundamentals of Marketing* conveys the main principles of marketing in a challenging yet accessible manner and provides the reader with insights into the workings of marketing today.

Contents: 1.Marketing: Development and Scope of the Subject 2. Strategic Marketing and the Planning Process 3. Consumer Buyer Behaviour 4. Industrial Buyer Behaviour 5. Marketing Research 6. Segmentation, Targeting and Positioning 7. Branding 8. Product 9. Pricing 10. Promotion 11. Place 12. Virtual Marketing 10. Planning and Implementation

2006:246x189: 480pp
Hb: 978-0-415-37096-7: **£90.00 $180.00**
Pb: 978-0-415-37097-4: **£29.99 $59.95**

Routledge books are available from all good bookshops, or may be ordered by calling Taylor and Francis Direct Sales on +44(0)1235 400524 (credit card orders) For more information please contact Gemma Anderson on +44 (0) 207 017 6192 or email gemma.anderson@tandf.co.uk

International Marketing
Fifth Edition

Sak Onkvisit, San Jose State University, USA and
John Shaw, Providence College, USA

The fifth edition of *International Marketing* has been written to enable managers and scholars to meet the international challenges they face everyday. It provides the solid foundation required to understand the complexities of marketing on a global scale.

Fully updated, this book includes topical case studies, examples of contemporary marketing campaigns, the most relevant discussion topics and up-to-date theories, references and research findings. It is this combination of theory and practice that makes this textbook truly unique, presenting a fully rounded view of the topic rather than soley an anecodotal or descriptive. A companion website provides additional material for lecturers and students alike.

Contents: Nature of International Marketing: Challenges and Opportunities 2. Trade Theories and Economic Cooperation 3. Trade Distortions and Marketing Barriers 4. Political Environment 5. Legal Environment 6. Culture 7. Consumer Behavior in the International Context: Psychological and Social Dimensions 8. Marketing Research and Information System 9. Foreign Market Entry Strategies 10. Product Strategies: Basic Decisions and Product Planning 11. Product Strategies: Branding and Packaging Decisions 12. Channels of Distribution 13. Physical Distribution and Documentation 14. Promotion Strategies: Personal Selling, Publicity, and Sales Promotion 15. Promotion Strategies: Advertising 16. Pricing Strategies: Basic Decisions 17. Pricing Strategies: Countertrade and Terms of Sale/Payment 18. Financial Strategies: Financing and Currencies

August 2008: 246x189: 560pp
Hb: 978-0-415-77261-7: **£90.00 $180.00**
Pb: 978-0-415-77262-4: **£31.99 $63.95**

Routledge books are available from all good bookshops, or may be ordered by calling Taylor and Francis Direct Sales on +44(0)1235 400524 (credit card orders) For more information please contact Gemma Anderson on +44 (0) 207 017 6192 or email gemma.anderson@tandf.co.uk

Marketing: The Basics

Karl Moore, McGill University, Quebec, Canada and
Niketh Pareek, McGill University, Quebec, Canada

Marketing: The Basics is a clear, concise resource for students or practitioners looking to improve their understanding of marketing fundamentals in a global context.

Covering the basic functions of marketing, its role in corporate decision-making and the importance of competitive strategies, this accessible text provides international perspectives on the areas discussed through examples of practice from North America, Asia, Europe and the Middle East.

A user-friendly, easy-to-follow guide, *Marketing: The Basics* is perfect for sixth-form, first-year undergraduate and MBA students, plus those professionals who require an understanding of this important subject in their day-to-day working lives.

Contents: Introduction 1. What Is Marketing Management? 2. Marketing as a Corporate Function 3. Product and Placement 4. Price 5. Promotion 6. People 7. Segmentation, Targeting and Positioning 8. Market Research - Seeking Deep Insight into the Customer's World and Mind 9. Global Marketing. Glossary. Index

2006: 198x129: 232pp
Hb: 978-0-415-38080-5: **£55.00 $100.00**
Pb: 978-0-415-38079-9: **£9.99 $17.95**

Routledge books are available from all good bookshops, or may be ordered by calling Taylor and Francis Direct Sales on +44(0)1235 400524 (credit card orders) For more information please contact Gemma Anderson on +44 (0) 207 017 6192 or email gemma.anderson@tandf.co.uk